RURAL REVOLT

In Defence of Coromandel's Wild Kingdom

RURAL REVOLT

In Defence of Coromandel's Wild Kingdom

First They Came for the Goats
Don't Fence Us In
Save Our Wild Pigs
Voices of the Coromandel

Reihana Robinson

First They Came for the Goats, Don't Fence Us In, Save Our Wild Pigs, and *Voices of the Coromandel* comprise Volume I of *Rural Revolt in Defence of Coromandel's Wild Kingdom.* Volume II is *The Killing Nation New Zealand's State-Sponsored Addiction to Poison 1080*

  1/ *First They Came for the Goats*
  2/ *Don't Fence Us In*
  3/ *Save Our Wild Pigs*
  4/ *Voices of the Coromandel*

An Off the Common Book, Amherst, Massachusetts

Printed in the United States of America

ISBN 978-1-945473-97-5

Contents

Dedication

To the wild animal kingdom of the Upper Coromandel—feathered and furred and finned, large and small, living in harmony to conjure our sensate natural world.

And to all those who dwell around Moehau, who love mother nature, Papatūānuku, who work to raise traditional healthy food for others, and who could be described, in the words of the Scottish Information Commissioner Kevin Dunion's *Troublemakers,* as "seen by authorities to be obsessive, unreasonable and untrusting—just what is required in an environmental campaign to get the job done."[1]

Thanks

Arohanui and heart felt thanks to Geoffrey Ahuwhenua Robinson.

To all the signatories of the 2006 petition (including all the Ward family, Roland Gift, Louise Meldrum, Pat and Quinn Whiting O'Keefe, the Novis family) that halted construction of a well-intentioned but unfeasible and socially destructive wild animal barrier that would have stretched from coast to coast effectively cutting off the top of the Coromandel Peninsula and incarcerating farms, holiday homes and camping grounds in an unnatural and poisonous outdoor regime. Full thanks to Theodora Ward for her insights and editing, her friendship and her knowledge of feral goats around Moehau. And to Faith Seddon for her relentless publishing talents.

And to those supporters who have subsequently left this world: Anne Ward, our hard-working local hero, sorely missed. John Goudie, whom regional council referred to in 2001 as "one of the pivotal people to stop the (second) fence." Bill Axbey, whose bush craft was unsurpassed and whose efforts to end the poisoning of New Zealand remained creative to the very end. We like to think that we continue in the spirit of rabble-rouser John Henderson, advocate of deerstalkers and tireless opponent of 1080 toxin. And of wildlife advocate Betty Rowe, who passionately defended the Arapawa goats. We delight in our short time with Mike Meads who drove madly all the way to Port Charles from Pukerua Bay pleased to discover fellow scientists on his wavelength. Our gratitude to pig hunter and Coromandel youth mentor Bill Lightfoot, whose energy and commitment to the struggle to end 1080 continued to his dying day. And to Phillip Ward, the first member of the longtime farming Ward family to sign on in opposition to the pest-proof fence folly in its third incarnation. Their legacies live on in the hearts and minds of our farming community and beyond.

Coromandel Peninsula
Fletcher Bay
Stony Bay
Sandy Bay
Port Jackson
Port Charles
Moehau
Mercury Islands
Waikawau
Colville
Kennedy Bay
Coromandel
Whitianga
Whenuakite
Thames
Whangamata

Introduction

"In nature nothing exists alone."
Rachel Carson, *Silent Spring*

In early 2004 families living around the Moehau range at the top of the Coromandel Peninsula on New Zealand's east coast were shocked to learn of a government programme designed to wipe out the small tribes of wild goats that roamed the region's rocky coasts and mountain flanks for over a century. The 'Wall of Death' action however was just a first strike in stepped-up official efforts to rearrange the healthy and peaceful balance of nature up in the hills—plans that would also threaten the very fabric of rural life.

The Department of Conservation (DOC) in collaboration with the regional council government body, then known as Environment Waikato (EW), deemed it necessary to massacre each and every goat on public land as well as on sacred Maori land encompassing the summit and upper reaches of Mt Moehau and on any private land within the Northern Peninsula. Thus began our rural revolt. In hindsight, farmers could have united in opposition. However the Upper Coromandel Landcare Association (UCLA), a group dedicated to supporting healthy conservation, safe and humane wild animal control, and the freedom to live without steel barriers across the landscape, was yet to be formed. The only goats permitted to remain on private farmed property are in one or two pockets where landowners can prove goats are secured behind a conventional seven-wire fence or a similarly wired electric fence, at least one kilometre away from shared boundaries with public land. Feral goat happens to be the most widely consumed meat in the world. Thanks to DOC, local eco-entrepreneurs and regional government, all the Moehau goats were hunted down and destroyed. Another unique breed lost forever.

Don't Fence Us In chronicles efforts in 2006 by local eco-entrepreneurs and government bureaucrats to construct a steel barrier across the entire Peninsula and the concomitant struggle by locals to live free of such a barrier. No one takes original credit for the idea of cutting off the northern tip of the Peninsula with a steel barrier. Was it business backing government, or central government colluding with regional government? Was it government using a local eco- entrepreneurial group as a front? This was not the first time such a proposal was mooted. In its first incarnation a barrier would have put all residents of the whole of the Peninsula behind a fence erected south of Thames along the Wentworth Valley. As adjudged by the lack of any such barrier, that plan met its sensible demise.

A handful of years later DOC revived its plan—this time intending to construct an electric fence to cut across the Peninsula north of Coromandel town close to the small settlement of Colville. Rusting bales of fencing materials can still be found. Local sources, with knowledge of the energy industry, talk of a long-term government proposal to build a nuclear facility at the Peninsula's tip. Either way, those who lived and worked in the area were opposed to the plan, and it did not progress. Well-intentioned, misguided newcomers kick-start a third coast-to-coast, fence plan in 2006.

This time, a new steel barrier would cut off all the farming communities, tiny settlements and camping grounds, resulting in a socially disruptive colossal "gated community". Ostensibly the idea was proposed to facilitate the costly eradication of mammalian pests on Moehau. Where a community's social capital has not been dissipated and reflects a spirit of collectiveness, outside interference can be effectively challenged. On the upper Coromandel, that spirit and social capital arose in response to the plan to fence in and forever change the community. Initiators of the third barrier had miscalculated their equation by forgetting the factor that mattered most—the people who farmed and worked and fished and holidayed and retired on the Upper Coromandel and who would have been sealed in behind the fence. The Upper Coromandel Landcare Association (UCLA) was formed to protect the northern Coromandel wildlife and way of life. In its first mission, the group successfully put a halt to the latest multimillion-dollar fence fiasco.

Save Our Wild Pigs follows on from the fence campaign. UCLA initiated a Coromandel and wider Waikato challenge to a planned regional government policy change that would have taken wild pigs permanently off the menu throughout the region. Eventually an Environment Court case brought by the Tokoroa Pig Hunters

Club against the regional council joined by UCLA and others, resolved pigs would remain off the Waikato regional government's eradication pest list. Had regional council heeded the hundreds of written submissions, newspaper articles, letters, and resolutions of a public meeting attended by many hundreds of pig hunters and conservationists in Hamilton, an appeal to the Environment Court could well have been avoided. However bureaucrats chose to employ lawyers to defend a doomed stance that failed to reflect and respect the community voice.

The final part of this volume—*Voices of the Coromandel* tells some of the stories by those who have fought long and hard for humane wild animal control. This is an ongoing struggle reflecting a troublesome divide between city and rural folk pitting Coromandel communities against entrenched government bureaucracy and well meaning but misguided eco-entrepreneurs. The fight for humane wild animal control in the face of poison-obsessed officialdom continues to this day. Yet scientists who regularly work for DOC or Landcare Research agree cyanide is the only humane toxin for controlling unwanted wildlife.[2]

Learning to live in harmony with Mother Nature is a conflicted challenge in our contemporary world with debates raging as to what is natural or pristine, what is exotic, what is an invasive or pest, what is to live, what is to die; and the challenge for ordinary citizens is often flexed as a battle against the symbiotic relationship of government and big business. The ideal way of relating to our earth is one of kaitiakitanga, a concept that bestows the role of guardian or steward to each and every one. Those who live and work around Moehau know this is the goal. The Coromandel is a perfect location to begin to remove pesticides and herbicides such as glyphosate and chlorpyrifos from Aotearoa and to leave future generations a cleaner, healthier environment. However, the anti-invasive mania impacts policy aggressively while the agrichemical industry will only seek a sustainable clean future when incentives are given to chemical farmers to move toward more traditional, healthy farming. Organic, biodynamic and permaculture gardens are slowly gaining wider traction in spite of few government incentives. Humans are, as the eminent Australian mammalogist and environmentalist Tim Flannery put it, "future eaters". Humans are not good at conserving a healthy planet for the coming generations. Poisoning our way to the future is no future at all.[3]

Part One:

First They Came for the Wild Goats

photo credit: Theodora Ward

The Coromandel – Te Tara-o-te-Ika

Before the first humans paddled ashore the wilderness of the mountainous Moehau region at the top of the Coromandel Peninsula on New Zealand's east coast remained untamed. For the first hunter-gatherers Moehau (892m) offered up bountiful food — ngā manu/birds and kai moana/freshwater and inter-tidal fish and shellfish. We imagine it to be a garden for those who first lived here in peace. Evidence of kumara cultivation, moa hunting, seal consumption and tool making, as well as dwelling and defense sites, dates back more than 700 years.

Buried at the top of Moehau is the captain of the Arawa canoe, Tama te Kapua, hence the mountain's traditional full name, Te Moehau O Tama te Kapua. The final resting place of the Arawa canoe after its voyage across the Pacific lies further south in the eastern Bay of Plenty at Maketu. To some local tribes Moehau represents the stern of a great canoe or waka with its prow further down the Coromandel ranges at Te Aroha. To this day a continuing belief in the existence of fairies or Patupaiarehe on Moehau contributes to the sacred aura of the maunga/mountain.[4]

Ngāti Hako are said to be the oldest surviving tribe descended from the Polynesian voyager Toi.[5] Prolonged struggles for the area took place during the 1700s with Tainui tribes forming the Marutūahu federation fighting Ngāti Huarere and Ngāti Hei for mana whenua/ territorial rights. Invasion by the northern North Island Ngāpuhi tribe further dispersed populations. Disputes among iwi continue to this day, albeit no longer with hand weapons.[6] Those who declare Maori affiliation to Moehau include Ngāti Hei, Te Uringahu o Ngāti Maru, Ngāti Huarere, Ngāti Maru, Ngāti Pāoa, Ngāti Tamaterā, Ngāti Whanaunga, Ngāti Rongoū and Arawa.[7]

Te Tara-o-te-Ika translated as the jagged barb of Māui's fish and Te Paeroa-a-Toi or Toi's long mountain range, were two early names given to what is known today as the Coromandel Peninsula. The name Coromandel originated in southeast India where the Cholos dynasty ruled 900 years ago on the Tamilnadu coast of Cholamandalam. The New Zealand peninsula was named after HMS Coromandel that visited circa 1820. Its crew came to fell the mighty kauri for spars as the previously harvested kahikatea turned out to yield a soft timber ill-suited for the job. Kahikatea would later be used to make butter boxes.

Decades before, in 1769, Captain James Cook named Cape Colville and during his brief visit brought ashore goats, pigs, ship rats and various vegetables. Writing in his journal on the day before he left New Zealand (March 31, 1770) Cook noted, "The country is certainly destitute of all sorts of beasts either wild or tame except Dogs and Ratts, the former are tame and live with people who breed and bring them up for no other purpose than to eat and ratts are so scarce that not only I but many others in the ship never saw one."[8]

Whether the goats Cook left behind survived to create a feral population or whether earlier visitors (sealers and whalers) seeded the population remains a matter of debate.

Newcomers from Europe arriving and settling in the mid and late 1800s sought timber, gold and granite on the upper Coromandel. Hardy folk endured the strenuous harvest of kauri trees, gold mining and gum digging. Others cleared coastal blocks for dry stock farming with some of their descendants still working the land today. Traditional pursuits for many locals have included hunting of feral goats and the venerable wild pig. More recent harvests include seaweed and fur, skins and meat of the Australian brushtail possum.

West coast waters host a growing aquaculture industry (green-lipped mussels and oysters) and commercial crayfishing occurs down the east coast. Plans to establish a cage-farm kingfish industry further exploiting fragile inshore Hauraki Gulf ecosystems appear to have fallen over (as of 2019) due to well-researched opposition revealing numerous environmental risks posed by the industrial scale aquaculture scheme.[9] Environmental and conservation issues have always been a top priority for Coromandel dwellers and plans to restart mining exploration on the peninsula have drawn large-scale protests since 2013 carrying on from the 1970s anti-mining movement.

By the end of the last century hundreds of holiday homes sprouted in various nooks and crannies up the coasts and to the tip of the Peninsula. Summer now brings thousands of regular visitors and tourists to relax on quiet beaches, fish coastal waters and explore Moehau on tracks cut by government workers.

In spite of its history of extractive exploitation, forest burn-offs and natural disasters, vast tracts of native bush remain available to walkers and explorers up and down the peninsula. The sprawling Coromandel Forest Park (73,000ha), formally established in 1971 comprises nearly 40 percent of the peninsula's land area and thousands of those lush, mountain hectares make up the iconic forested and farmed slopes of that majestic mountain at the top of the Peninsula.

Te Moehau is often shrouded in mists and low cloud providing perfect growing conditions for beautiful ferns, beech trees, fuschia, exquisite orchids and all manner of swamp life. The Moehau stag beetle and Archey's frog are endemic to the region. Starting at the foot of the mountain near Sandy Bay, grassland at the skirts gives way to the under-storey of ponga, rangiora, nikau, hangehange and kawakawa with tawa dominating the flanks of broadleaf forest canopy and lesser numbers of mahoe, kohekohe and rewarewa. The walk that takes trampers nearly to the top is a challenge and somewhat mysterious.[10] Grassland reappears as the montane forest gives way to sub-alpine plants.

Day-trippers can walk the coastal trail around Moehau from Stony Bay or Fletcher Bay. Thousands of campers each year make one of New Zealand's most spectacular drives up the west coast to Department of Conservation managed campground reserves at Fletcher Bay or Fantail Bay. Campers who turn right just beyond Colville (the last stop for food and petrol at the classic Colville Store) journey to beautiful east coast reserves at Stony Bay or Waikawau Bay. For both longtime residents and first-time visitors, the mixture of exceptionally high ecological values amidst and beside a productive working community is what is remarkable. This unique blend of both nature and human activity is what motivates so many to protect and preserve.

From Stewardship to Management

"There are two spiritual dangers in not owning a farm. One is the danger of supposing that breakfast comes from the grocery, and the other that heat comes from the furnace."
Aldo Leopold, *A Sand County Almanac*

Against a background of stunning natural beauty and rich natural resources a conservation conundrum developed on the Coromandel as well as across New Zealand. Some say it all began back in 1987 with the amalgamation of the New Zealand Forest Service and the Lands and Survey Department with the resulting advent of the Department of Conservation (DOC). Just two years later the re-organisation of local government resulted in the formation of a new layer of regional bureaucracy with a broad environmental oversight mandate and an unchecked power to tax locally.

To the average, environmentally concerned urban dweller who both values our country's natural heritage and supports efforts to protect and enhance that beauty, the increasing animosity engendered by the freshly minted DOC and regional councils in rural New Zealand is puzzling. From a distance, heated controversy in the provinces over official conservation policy and operations seems unwarranted. But the perspective of those who live on the land is quite different, informed by years of observation and direct experience of wildlife and weather, water and soil, actions and consequences. They alone come face to face with the consequences of official desk-born policy.

Retired bushman Bill Axbey, who worked for both the New Zealand Forest Service and DOC, experienced the changes first-hand and did not mince words. "Created as a political ploy to place unwanted Forestry and Lands civil servants after the corporate shuffle the Conservation Department quickly became a haven for eco fundamentalists, Forest and Bird and sundry nature lovers whose greatest qualifications were they owned a canary and were just thrilled to be involved in such a high profile occupation as conservation. Training and knowledge of the subject was not as important as the state services system of grading.

"Suddenly the 190 highly trained wildlife staff were replaced by a couple of thousand comparatively untrained staff all keen to assert their authority and consolidate their positions and make a name in this new and exciting field. And boy did they ever? Senior positions were allocated by the state service system that had nothing to do with suitability for what were positions that required specialized knowledge. Knowledge in the wildlife field was not essential but a love of the bureaucratic system was; hence the selection of a member of the diplomatic core as its first leader surrounded by more eager bureaucrats than the entire staff of the old Wildlife Service.

"These highly trained wildlife staff were relegated to positions where their superior knowledge would not be an embarrassment to their new masters or mistresses. In this climate with regular shifts and restructuring and faced with bungling inefficiency, wildlife officers with years of hard earned training and experience simply got out."[11]

Fast forward to the year 2000 with the burgeoning growth industry of environmental management—an industry whose objectives shifted along with budget opportunities, and whose disengagement from affected residents increased along with bureaucratic entrenchment. Rural folk question DOC's heavy reliance on the chemical industry, in particular DOC's use of cruel poisons without adequate research into long-term results and subsequent damage to native species.

Conservation values on the Coromandel had been steadily improving over the years, in large part due to the unpaid, hands-on efforts of long-time residents and the increasing involvement of impassioned new arrivals and visitors. But conflict with local communities arose repeatedly as official missions crept and expanded and as new policy was shaped in the absence of real collaborative consultation with the public. Time and again operative plans were developed at the desks of managers in Hamilton and Wellington that flew in the face of the common sense solutions and real-life observations of residents who had been caring for the land for years. For long-time stewards of the land, the challenge seemed to be less about protecting flora and fauna from so-called pests and predators than it was about protecting natural New Zealand from the costly whims and destructive errors of distant "environmental managers".

The Letter

"I am perfectly aware there are real dedicated wildlife conservationists scattered through what has grown into a giant and arrogant bureaucracy and the failures and waste must be an enigma to those people."

Bill Axbey

Surveys of flora and fauna on Te Moehau were carried out in 2000 by locals and by government departments.[12] Native flora was found to be flourishing despite nearby human habitation, roads, commerce, tourism, adventure sports, farming, hunting, and an array of introduced mammals including dogs and cats and rats and stoats, wild pigs, possums and weasels. Thriving native birds, according to the surveys, included kaka, grey warbler, korimako/bellbird, kererū/wood pigeon, the flightless and endangered kiwi, kākāriki, tūī silvereye, yellowhammer, piwakawaka, ruru/morepork, shining cuckoo, long-tailed cuckoo, kārearea/NZ falcon, as well as other exotic transplants such as parakeet, harrier hawk, kingfisher, magpie and mynah.

By July 2006 DOC could report kiwi chick survival averaging 77 percent since the year 2000. Achieved without using poison indiscriminately dropped from helicopters. Kiwi bird populations were reported to be increasing at a rate of 14.8 percent. This statistic stands in stark contrast with the North Island annual rate of 6 percent.[13] At this time Te Moehau was said to be home to more than 450 kiwi with at least 100 birds encumbered with radio transmitters. Transmitters contribute to credible science but they can also cause deaths as kiwi become tangled in mangemange, a wiry fern commonly referred to as bushman's mattress. Unable to escape, kiwi birds die of starvation or predation by hawks. Despite deaths from such entanglements, dog attacks, road kill and natural causes the local kiwi population is thriving.

In the far north of the Coromandel Peninsula farmers are farming, fisherfolk are fishing, retirees are enjoying the simple life, and gardeners are planting. In other words, the small communities are living and caring for the land and each other. Then out of the blue (the year is 2004) comes a new goat-killing programme, casually referred to as "The Wall of Death." A military cry to be sure. But who is the enemy? What farmers and kaitiaki have sent out for troops? Whose land is suffering an invasion of feral goats? Who is not successfully controlling feral species on their land, as required by law?

It turns out that no farmer has sent out an SOS. Instead, this is an eradication scheme conjured up in faraway Hamilton and Thames by office dwellers keen to spend hundreds of thousands of ratepayer dollars on a wild animal no one around Moehau has a problem controlling. War plans had been developing over a few years behind closed doors. Then more recently, the eradication idea was floated at a couple of local meetings organized by newcomers to the area.

Then came the first public revelation of impending doom for the wild goats of the Moehau range. It arrived in the form of an official letter co-signed by DOC and regional council Environment Waikato (EW). In both substance and style, the letter turned out to be a watershed event defining battle lines between those who live, love and work the land and those for whom "conservation" is just a lucrative job.

6 September 2004
Dear Occupier
Moehau Goat Control

This letter is to inform you about a collective goat control plan to remove feral goats from all lands north of the road from Big Bay (Colville) to Waikawau Bay. Special for its rare plants and animal species, Moehau is the Department of Conservation's highest priority site for conservation in the Waikato and ranks as the sixth highest priority mainland site in New Zealand. The Environment Waikato 'Key Ecological Sites' (KES) programme has also identified private land around Moehau as its highest priority site for protection on the Coromandel.

Late last year, Moehau Environment Group convened a public meeting to gauge support for its vision of a pest free zone north of Colville. Feral goats were identified as a pest that could be eradicated from land where they were not wanted. It was also pointed out at this meeting that for those who wished to retain goats that they should be fenced in and clearly identified. There was significant support to these ideas from the community. (sic)

The Department of Conservation and its predecessor, the NZ Forest Service, have had goat control teams on Moehau every year since 1979 at a cost of nearly $1,000,000. Maintenance of the current low levels of goats costs the taxpayer on average $75,000 a year. This will be on-going unless we can stop reinvasion of goats back on to Moehau from neighbouring properties.

Many landowners in the Moehau area have taken a proactive approach to removing goats themselves or allowing the Department of Conservation hunters to remove them off their properties. It is estimated that for an outlay of $200,000 to $300,000 (or 3 years of current control effort) goats could be completely removed from all lands where they are not wanted, dramatically reducing this ongoing cost. Investing the savings into other pest control work would significantly advance the ongoing recovery of the Moehau.

Environment Waikato has identified feral goats as a Containment Pest in their Regional Pest Management Strategy (RPMS). Feral goats are also seen as a serious pest and one to be controlled in the EW Peninsula Project. The RPMS defines a feral goat as "those animals without identification or branding and are un-contained". The objective of the strategy is to "contain, and where practicable, reduce feral goat populations in and adjacent to high priority conservation areas."

In order to achieve this objective strategy rule 6.3.2 reads: "The landowner shall, on direction from an Authorised Person, destroy feral goats...being those goats unmarked and uncontained, on land that he or she occupies, adjacent to regionally significant conservation areas administered by the Department of Conservation, where goat control operations are ongoing." A breach of this rule is an offence under section 154(r) of the Biosecurity Act and carries a significant fine."

Whilst Environment Waikato does have the ability to enforce this rule we prefer to work in partnership with the occupier to assist them in meeting their obligations through education, consultation, and providing encouragement.

Environment Waikato, Department of Conservation and Moehau Environment Group are working together to address the feral goat issue in the Moehau area. We seek the support and cooperation of property owners in achieving goat eradication from lands of all tenure where goat free status has been determined.

Over the next month or so, staff from EW and DOC will be visiting all landowners to determine what is needed to remove goats off their land, obtain a secure commitment to do so, and offer assistance where required.

For those wishing to retain goats as an integral part of their land management activities, their commitment to secure fencing and identification of their goats is the obvious option.

Please contact us by 1 October 2004 if you have any feedback on this information or the Moehau Goat Control Programme.

Signed by DOC and EW employees.

Playing fast and loose with facts and figures to support operational plans contributes to rural distrust of DOC and regional council.

In this instance the $75,000 annual goat-control figure is repeated in all subsequent official documents and reports to justify a massive budget increase. But according to the detailed April 2004 publication, *"An Analysis of the Costs of Pest Control Options in the Northern Coromandel"*, by Sandra Barns and commissioned for the Moehau Environment Group (MEG), the actual annual cost of goat control on Moehau is only $25,000.[14]

As for any substantial community support, there were no consultations with local landowners as to how best achieve the new goal. The goat letter declaims "significant support" for the eradication of goats came from a Colville meeting. Reading both the Barns report and a subsequent MEG newsletter of December 2004, it is clear there is no consensus, let alone unanimity, regarding eradication of goats. Stoats, possums and ferrets head the list of worrisome animals, whereas goats receive the same level of concern as weasels, rats and feral cats. Rather than provide scientific data warranting the sudden goat slaughter, the letter relies on incorrect assumptions and is economical with the truth. No experimental or empirical data is offered.

And in the rush to spend private citizens hard-earned wages and salaries, the letter writers fail to note their own well-researched forest monitoring by Coromandel DOC ecologist Pim de Monchy. In his *Field Report Moehau Forest Condition Waikato Conservancy Monitoring Report 2000*, de Monchy clearly observes, "Goat preferred species such as kanono and hangehange have increased markedly in abundance and height, and goat impacts over most of the forest are negligible." These "negligible" impacts require only "sustained goat control every two years and [an] attempt to reduce the reinvasion of goats into western catchments". But suddenly we are confronted with a costly "Wall of Death" goat massacre.

DOC will cough-up $300,000 with EW matching. The only losers are taxpayers, ratepayers and the local feral goat tribe of the upper Coromandel. Had DOC invited hunters who value goat meat to do the job instead of contract marksmen with no carcass recovery plan, the work could have been undertaken at no cost to citizens of the Waikato — assuming locals had been supportive of the project in the first place.

The Barns report notes a lack of knowledge regarding the actual extent of habitat damage caused by exotic animals or any data concerning the population and range of any endangered species — information Barns states is necessary "to allow effective management of the area." Ideally, reinvasion of pests should be zero. But on Moehau it is just not practical, according to Barns. She goes on to note that, "even in the presence of exotic invaders, ecosystems maintain a delicate balance. A consequence of the intense control or eradication of species can result in harm to species that the intervention was designed to protect."

As Massey doctoral candidate Kim Suzanne McBreen wrote "Until the largely anecdotal, or descriptive, body of information is backed up with empirical and experimental evidence, predictions on the effect of either canopy health or ungulates cannot be made with confidence."[15]

From Arapawa to Moehau: DOC's 'Wall of Death '

*"Go now to the flock, and fetch me from thence two good
kids of the goats; and I will make them savoury meat for thy
father, such as he liveth"*

Genesis 27:9

Goats are playful, agile climbers known for their curiosity and
their intelligence. Social groups are built around the nannies. They
are daytime foragers. Today's feral goats are domestic relatives
from the true wild goat—the Middle Eastern *Capra aegagrus*. On
the upper Coromandel we are fortunate to have goats with a Boer
heritage, originally bred in South Africa.

Goats have played a significant role in farming throughout
New Zealand. On the hilly sheep and cattle farms of the northern
Coromandel, their main function has been to control pasture
weeds. They are also valued for superior carcass characteristics
and carry considerable commercial value in both export and local
trade meat markets. It is understood that the breed resident for
over 100 years around the mountain was unique because of the
remoteness of the area. As truly long-term residents goats have
inhabited the area since the 1870s (Moore and Cranwell 1934).

Farmers in the district have always farmed goats. Goats have
also roamed the forested government land surrounding Moehau
from whence they were regularly culled. Government hunters
first controlled these goats in 1956, with sustained work at regular
intervals occurring from 1981 onward. The local feral goats have
a preference for the open sunny areas that are scarce in the high
altitude, dense forest and the upper subalpine slopes of the
mountain itself.

Well-managed goats are of great value to the pastoral farmer,
and their potential as a revenue-earner for New Zealand is sizeable.
"On the positive side, feral goats can, under proper management,
control woody weeds such as blackberry and gorse," according to
a report commissioned by the Waikato Regional Council.[16]

In more recent decades an anti-invasive phenomenon has been
embraced at the national level that posits wild animals as aliens

to be exterminated by whatever means works cheaply, whether humane or not. There is a hungry promotion by conservation fundamentalists to return land in the countryside to a particular pristine, pre-human manifestation by destroying all rats and mice, all deer and pigs, all possums, stoats, weasels, magpies, and goats, along with a vast array of exotic flora.

It is fair to say that prevailing conservation policies embrace the simplistic mantra *exotic bad, native good*. Among the most vociferous adherents of this dogma are the bureaucrats, chemical companies, toxin promoters, contractors, and other private and industry groups that benefit directly from the flow of public money and donations to the extermination business.

Goat massacres were not invented on Moehau. Arapawa Island, off the top of the South Island, was home to a rare and endangered breed of feral goats. It was also home to the intrepid Betty Rowe who held out against extermination of the Arapawa goats in a battle of 40 years against DOC and the NZ Forest Service who employed shooters to slaughter the animals. Arapawa Island is partially farmed and its bush-clad regions were populated with wild goats, sheep, pigs and a few red deer.

The Arapawa goats had been living on the island for more than 200 years and were genetically unique. It is believed the British Captain James Cook released goats on a visit to Arapawa Island in 1773 at East Bay, and on a later visit in 1777 gifted several more to a Maori chief in nearby Ship Cove. According to the NZ Arapawa Goat Association (arapawagoats.org.nz) a group dedicated to the welfare and survival of the breed, "A few decades later in 1839 a visitor to the whaling settlement on Arapawa Island said it 'swarmed' with goats."

Betty Rowe, herself a rare breed, coming as she did from overseas to champion the Arapawa goat, was posthumously awarded the New Zealand Companion Animal Conference Assisi Award 2009. She had lived among these animals for 35 years and dedicated her life to their protection. Rowe was horrified by the perilous situation facing all introduced species as she observed the losing battle on the part of Arapawa pigs and goats…

"Within the forest there dwelled some beautiful goats, sheep and pigs all of ancient lineage and all condemned to extermination. The edict had been sounded that they were to be shot, but somehow I could not just let this happen. The goats held an immediate attraction for me because of their beauty and intelligence, and I had come to know the family groups as I walked the paths carved into the hillside over the years by the trekkings of the wildlife."

After her death, conservationist Tony Orman wrote, ""The recent passing of Arapawa Island resident Betty Rowe was a great loss, both as a person and as a wildlife advocate. This diminutive lady had a great heart, a ton of principles and a passion for what she believed in. She fought publicly funded wild animal policies pushed by cold-hearted bureaucrats that had little or no foundation in fact or science.

"The current intention of DOC to kill more goats later this year is no different from the Forest Service bureaucrats who, under the Marlborough Sounds Maritime Park Board, some 40 years ago, attacked the goats with policy dogma. It mattered not that taxpayer's money was being wasted and it seems not to matter today. But they launched their propaganda-based extermination based on an 'anti-introduced' paranoid phobic hatred of wild animals, with arrogance, aggressiveness and at times personal abuse to Betty. She was even threatened with action by the SIS and told she, an American migrant, was not wanted here. "Betty stood staunch and amassed evidence that the goats were genetically unique and almost certainly liberated long before Europeans colonized New Zealand. Betty has left us a legacy to fight for sensible wild animal policies instead of the 'anti-introduced' policy that still has its remnants today in the publicly funded DOC. She remains an inspiration despite her sad passing."[17]

Goats were originally brought to New Zealand shores as a food source. Later they were recognised as a godsend for weed control. When their numbers grew, conservation policy changed to sustained control in the 1920s. At the time of the planned Moehau goat massacre, the price for feral goat meat was over $5kg moving to $7.11kg only a few years later in 2010, with over 500 animals sold into the Auckland ethnic market annually.[18]

But unlike a regular goat cull where animals are butchered and the meat eaten or sold and sent off to the works, the Moehau operation was to result in utter destruction and complete waste. Goats slaughtered would be tailed for tally and left as carcasses to rot in the sun after they were shot on coastal slopes, forest margins, and hillsides. Goats mortally wounded but not chased down died slow gruesome deaths.

In spite of the massive spend, the 2006 DOC/EW Moehau extermination attempt would prove futile. As John Parkes, a Landcare Research scientist who had studied goats since 1975 when he joined the Forest Research Institute, observed in *Forest and Bird* magazine, "As long as we have domestic goats, we'll have feral goats. That's the ultimate message."[19]

Not a Good Barometer

On the upper Coromandel, farmers have heeded their legal obligations under both the Wild Animal Control Act and regional pest strategy. Farmers have actively monitored for passing goats, killing opportunistically for food for the table or the dogs. It was the rare hunter or farmer who would leave dead goats to rot in the wilderness.

So the original 2004 letter to landowners came as a bombshell to those who kaitiaki large areas of land, in some cases for generations. When the letter arrives, a few concerned calls are made.

A subsequent communication from DOC on December 2, 2004 references both the Wild Animal Control Act 1977 and the Biosecurity Act 1993 and offers what amounts to a thinly-veiled warning to landowners to get with the programme. The plan apparently would require a team of three to five hunters, each with two dogs and a rifle, keeping in touch by two-way radios as they sweep the land. This will happen no less than three times.

Many farmers found the message hostile, if not overtly threatening. DOC stated the hunters "would be able to give some notice of their expected arrival to enable you to either be off your property for those days or remaining around your house.

"Where we can amicably negotiate an agreement to remove (or contain) the goats off private land with the owner, the DOC and EW will bear the costs of the work. If we are forced (after reasonable efforts at negotiating a workable solution) to take legal action to remove the goats off a property we will be seeking costs both for the legal action and the goat removal."

To underscore the message, a follow-up letter (September 6, 2004) signed by DOC's Finn Buchanan and EW's Dave Hodges reads, "A breach of this rule is an offence under section 154 of the Biosecurity Act..."and carries a significant fine." The intimidating approach by DOC alienated farmers who were already following the law. An email sent on December 10, 2004 from Buchanan reminds farmers once again of the choices—to leave the property for up to three days or remain in or around the house while hunters with their dogs search out goats.

But the nail in the coffin disturbing farmers around Moehau was the complete flouting of the *Waikato Regional Pest Management Strategy, Operative 2002-2007 (RPMS)*. This official regional plan defined goats as a "Control Species" whereby landowners are required to keep wild goats under control by removing any that cross their land. Goats are not an eradication species. Northern Coromandel farmers were obeying the law. Out of the blue there is a new rule and feral goats are to be totally eradicated via the Wall of Death programme.

The foreword to the *RPMS* proudly declares, "Preparation of the Strategy would not have been possible if we had not listened to the views of the Regional community. Through detailed consultation with key stakeholders and submissions on the *Proposed Regional Pest Management Strategy*, a good understanding of pest management issues has been achieved. I would like to thank all those who have taken the time to be involved in the process."

For Coromandel farmers and hunters, the decision to ignore previous consultation as well as the region's official regulatory policy document presented more than a major issue. After all individuals hunt not only to follow the law but to provide sustenance to extended family, to friends and to farm dogs. Skins are tanned. Little, if anything, goes to waste.

In late January 2005, ministers of the Crown and other parliamentarians including Green Party leaders Rod Donald, Jeanette Fitzsimons and local National Party MP Sandra Goudie, received letters informing them of the draconian threats to landowners.

With little information forthcoming from EW, several farming families contacted council staff. What, they asked, was the basis for new requirements if landowners were already carrying out feral goat control on their properties in accordance with the *RPMS*?

EW replied on the same day. The regional council's February 3, 2005 response confirmed: "Our goal is eradication...If they [land occupiers] think they are complying with this rule then we would want to independently verify that using unarmed monitoring persons on the block at or before each of the three planned sweeps of the area takes place."

EW offered three options: 1/ That the contract hunters go onto the land and undertake the necessary work at no cost to landowners; 2/ If they don't want that, then we can serve a legal notice on them (under s.122 of the Biosecurity Act) giving a stipulated time to do the control work. If not complied with we could then do the work (s.128 of the Biosecurity Act) and recover costs from them (s.129 of the Biosecurity Act) and there are additional costs associated with this legal action under our *RPMS*, or; 3/ If they want to keep goats then they need to be adequately fenced and identified as being the goats."

But the regional council still refused to provide any justification for the expensive operation it proposed – a programme that ran contrary to its own animal pest control policy.

On April 19, 2005 farmers contacted the EW Northern Zone Bio-Security Advisory Subcommittee with an invitation for them to visit coastal properties where contract hunters intend to kill goats. The letter points out that coastal goats have never been documented crossing the road to threaten Moehau bush and that the animals are adequately controlled so as to not disturb farming or biodiversity on private land. The subcommittee was reminded of the current "containment" policy delineated in the publicly agreed upon *RPMS*. Would this subcommittee support the *RPMS* or would it kowtow to EW staff? [20]

By 30 May 2005 DOC area manager John Gaukrodger declaims, "Goat eradication is only intended to be undertaken on these properties where owners seek this option. Those landowners seeking to retain goats can do so as is their right. By law, this option does require the landowner to have the animals marked and contained behind secure fences to ensure infestation of adjoining properties does not occur. As mentioned on the phone, we are prepared to provide a level of support to costs associated with the construction of secure fences for holding goats on private property. This is an option you may wish to consider for the future."

But neither DOC nor EW could explain why, other than agency whim, this change of policy on goats is suddenly required. DOC's published report *Moehau Kiwi Sanctuary: The First Five Years 2000-2005* notes both forest canopy and under-storey are in very good condition when "last quantitatively assessed." In an unpublished DOC file note, Pim de Monchy comments, "Moehau is the highest ranked forested habitat in the Waikato Conservancy for biodiversity by the DOC". This would imply feral goat modification of the conservation area is minimal.

The DOC ecologist goes on to quote the International Union for the Conservation of Nature (IUCN) Invasive Species Specialist Group (ISSG). The panel's publication *Management of Feral Goat (Capra hircus)* articulates the need for monitoring native flora and fauna before and after goat control with surveys designed and published for the benefit of the public, scientists and conservation employees and that are carried out at least twice a year appropriate to climate conditions. These investigations would have the benefit of showing if and how removal of herbivores can impact the ecosystem. The section on ethical considerations states animals must be killed humanely and expertly.[21] Farmers on the Coromandel would have no beef with such an approach to goat control on public land.

While farmers were questioning the need for any change of policy, the next black and white newsletter arrives in letterboxes. (The communiqués had yet to blossom into glossy brochures.) "In September 2004 a project scoping meeting was held to determine the possibilities, strategies and requirements for a potential Moehau Goat Eradication Project. It was determined that although removal of goats from Moehau will be an expensive operation, there will be great cost savings (as well as ecological benefits) in the future. At the current costs of the ongoing control, eradication will have paid for itself in about eight years. The unanimous call by representatives of DOC, EW and MEG at the meeting was to go for it." As time would tell, projected savings fail to materialize and rates never decrease.

According to DOC, a culling firm Prohunt NZ Ltd is to be contracted. DOC, it seems, no longer has staff able to handle a rifle. However Prohunt did not in fact carry out the Goat Eradication during 2005/6. Jerry Newman, Anne Peart and their team were the preferred contractors. During the first sweep, 10 so-called "Judas goats" were to be "saved" then fitted with transmitters and released. Being naturally gregarious any surviving goats will form mobs around them. So the Judas goats will be exploited to help wipe out any strays not destroyed by the Wall of Death mass destruction approach. It is hoped the Judas goats may actually survive the second-round firing squad and go on to trap more of their whanau/family.[22]

All of this information is republished in the first glossy A4 brochure of January 2005 — *Moehau Goat Control Update Newsletter*. The title may have been a nod to EW's official policy on goats—a "control" not "eradication" species. Complete with a goat picture and caption "Goats can damage the understory of native bush" the brochure states there will be good value for money even though "eradication" costs are "high".

As time goes by, stapled colour brochures arrive but the title has evolved to *Moehau Feral Goat Eradication Update Newsletter*. The area to be hunted now stretches from the northern tip of the Peninsula to Colville including Port Charles and Waikawau Bay. Eradication is considered an impossible goal according to DOC's own Tongariro-Taupo Conservancy.

The logo of a local entrepreneurial eco-group now appears on the posted newsletters alongside those of DOC and EW. Questioned as to what exactly this logo indicates DOC's Pim de Monchy admits "MEG's role as a supporter was just that, a supporter...The group did not do any goat control or contribute any funds. MEG did not do anything in relation to the goat eradication. The group's objectives include the eradication of feral goats, and the committee therefore felt comfortable with supporting the operation. In reality, DOC and EW carried out all the work."

So the prominent inclusion of MEG's logo on the publicly funded brochures along with those of the two government agencies that exclusively funded and carried out all the work represented no more than free promotional advertising for the eco-entrepreneurs.

One local resident complained to DOC "MEG did nothing... providing neither money nor work product. DOC provided the free advertising at ratepayer expense in order to strengthen their local surrogate in the public eye. In the goat case, MEG is able to claim major credit for an expensive $600,000 project toward which it contributed absolutely nothing. This serves to bolster the group in the public eye when it presents its grant applications. In turn, the costly goat eradication plan provided an instant justification for the controversial MEG "pest-proof" fence plan."

It turns out that DOC's project manager for the goat eradication programme (de Monchy) is a voting committee member of the very group (MEG) getting the free adverts—suggesting a banal conflict of interest. "When the next goat brochure reaches letterboxes throughout the Coromandel," the complaint went on, "residents will be anxious to see whose logos are displayed...If they see DOC and EW promoting their proxy again, de Monchy's words will echo about the Waikato along with the derision and growing resentment of those stuck with the tab."[23] Subsequent newsletters posted to residents do not bear the MEG logo. The conflict of interest issue is raised with the Waikato Conservancy board, which indicates it would investigate.

But the question is why? In this land management struggle, farmers face a central government department (DOC), a local government body (EW), and a private eco-entrepreneurial group collaborating against landowner wishes. Why, and why now? Eventually it comes as little surprise to learn that eradication of goats is a prerequisite for regional council funding of an ambitious multimillion-dollar "pest-proof fence" scheme across the northern Coromandel promoted publicly that would be administered for a smart 20 percent fee, by none other than – MEG.

In an April 20, 2006 report to the North Zone Biosecurity Advisory Subcommittee, two senior EW managers write, "The ongoing success of this project (goat eradication) will in part rely on the aspirations of Moehau Environment Group in erecting a pest excluding fence." Surrogate group MEG, they go on to say, is to be "advocate for the project and act as a barometer of public opinion in the area." However, the council's private "barometer" proved faulty on a number of occasions, and the eradication of the goats could be seen as the first of many missteps resulting in a lack of community cohesion on wild animal policy.

Later in the year, acknowledgement of that failure is documented in a report to EW's Combined North and South Zone Biosecurity Advisory Subcommittees, (November 10) wherein MEG coordinator Wayne Todd comments, "The Goat Eradication Project has provoked a highly effective, extremely negative, but ill-informed protest against MEG and the pest-proof fence project after several landowners were forced/pressured to toe the line on goat eradication and didn't like it. "Their backlash has produced a campaign breeding and inciting fear and mistrust both in the due process MEG has had to respect from all landowners, especially some of whom are a part of this protest."(sic) Todd refers to the next big barometer failure, that of the pest-proof fence. But for now, let's say that EW and DOC were simply relying on the wrong barometer.

Moving Targets – The Mission Expands

You Liberals think that goats are just sheep from broken homes.

Malcolm Bradbury

Coromandel residents were originally told by DOC and regional council that the massive spend on goat eradication was just intended to protect biodiversity values at the "high value" ecological site of Moehau. However when the Wall of Death story reaches local newspapers on February 25, 2005 in the form of an EW press release, the revised story is that destruction of 1,000 goats will not only the benefit Coromandel forests, but will "help prevent flooding" as "part of the Peninsula Project, an extensive flood protection scheme with the focus on the Thames coast. The aim is to rid the forest of its pests so it can act as a natural sponge and stop rain flooding the streams."

The public is expected to believe this—in spite of the fact that Moehau goats live nowhere near the Thames coast and funding for the Peninsula Project is supposed to be limited to the southwest coast of the Coromandel where massive flooding hit hard in 2002 causing loss of life and land devastation. The subsequent devastating damage caused by debris roiling down western Moehau in June 2014 resulting in massive flooding on the West coast made a mockery of their claims.

The idea that browsing by possums and goats contributes to flooding is promoted heavily by the regional council. But that connection is widely disputed by laypersons and professionals alike. Wairarapa conservationist and author Bill Benfield, in his dramatic expose of New Zealand's commitment to poisoning wildlife, refers to work carried out in the Ruahine Ranges by hydrologist Patrick Grant. It showed how patterns of weather events cause erosion.[24]

"Grant writes of his earlier views, influenced by the official position of the time that animals caused erosion: 'The same philosophy appeared on official brochures of the Forest Service and Soil Conservation and Rivers Council, which proclaimed "these forests prevent floods". This was simple, intuitive and "scientifically seductive", but hydrological studies have since proven it to be demonstrably false.'"[25]

Nevertheless, the browsing-flooding theory has proven to be an effective tool in attracting additional budget dollars for pest control managers. As part of their combined Thames Coast Flood Protection Project EW and DOC reported increased funding for DOC "to carry out annual pest control along the Thames coast. The Government announced on 22 September 2004 that it would contribute a multimillion-dollar package to an integrated flood management plan which included funding for animal pest control."

Had Thames Coast residents affected by the June 19, 2002 "weather bomb" been asked, they may well have preferred to allocate all available funding for real flood protection works. There is no hydrologic study, or research to support the theory that animal pest control is an effective use of flood control monies. Yet the party line from EW is that killing possums and goats will contribute to flood control.

In the only authoritative published study of the weather disaster, Auckland University ecologist and town planning senior lecturer Marjorie van Roon described the heartbreaking effects of the flooding and went on to outline the root causes.[26] Van Roon listed recommended actions beginning with upstream activities and establishing rain gardens and storm water retention basins to help manage and minimise peak storm flows. Completely absent from her list was any mention of the effects of animal browsing or any benefit to be had from control of possums or goats.[27] Nevertheless flood control money is made available to continue goat eradication down the Coromandel coast.

Meanwhile, back at the top of the Peninsula, an August 2005 letter titled "Moehau Goat Project" announced a "single sweep reconnaissance" is to be carried out in Port Charles. And this is where things start to get even messier. The project has now grown to include a goat team using dogs and firearms and a possum team using poisons.

The newly appointed Biodiversity Threats (Peninsula Project) programme manager at EW declares an expanded war. "The forests have taken a hiding for over a century from kauri logging, mining, farming and fires. As if that wasn't enough the forests have had possums and goats released into them. The forest has begun its healing from the man-made devastation but we've got to stop this devastation from possums and goats." He had not read Pim de Monchy's detailed DOC field report revealing Moehau's healthy biodiversity in spite the presence of introduced wild animals.

There are also some thorny issues cropping up between the project's two main sponsors. The programme manager expresses confidence in the Wall of Death programme and confirms that DOC, while responsible for work on its own conservation estate, will also be employed as a contractor for EW's work on private land. Over half the project's area lies in private hands.

But DOC Hauraki manager John Gaukrodger shares his personal concern at the arrangement on August 30, 2005. Writing to the CEO of EW, he notes how the deal "effectively shifts responsibility and accountability for all activity on private land onto the Department of Conservation and specifically me personally... This is a high risk factor for the Department that has not been provided for in the overall undertaking with respect to resourcing... This issue is significant, and personal to me, as it presents me with the responsibility of overall and sole accountability for all aspects of the operation, including the efficient and effective management of EW's investment." There is no public record of how the issue was resolved.

Port Charles "Day of the Dead" ... and the Results...

Ideas are easy. It is the execution of ideas that really separates the sheep from the goats.

Sue Grafton

As 2005 drew to a close, so did the days of roaming wild goats on the Coromandel Peninsula. The local *Bay Beacon* newspaper published a DOC press release on November 24, confirming that goat hunting had begun the previous week with 172 goats culled in the first three days. It stated "five contractors and three DOC workers will be hunting for six months solid in a 13,000 hectare area of the Moehau range, west of Port Charles Road." Pim de Monchy says he does not expect "all 1,000 goats will be wiped out by 2007, but the plan is to keep going until there are none left." It mentioned MEG "has been helping DOC and EW by consulting local landowners and negotiating access across their land for the hunters."

A few landowner agreements were reached to allow herding of goats on private land for eventual sale, but this only accounted for a small number. Landowners who did not want unknown contractors on their land opted to keep watch and shoot if any fleeing goats were present on their land on the appointed slaughter days. The goats were wiped out in the original project area, and way ahead of schedule. But rather than packing away the guns and achieving some budget savings, the contract hunters were deployed further and further south.

During the first day's shooting, one farmer noted his relief that no goats had traversed his property. "But I have to say that as I sat up on one of our peaks, watching you all with binoculars and listening to the play-by-play slaughter of that mob of goats for hours, I was really sickened. I watched the goats from early this morning. Eating away in the kikuyu, watched them stalked, watched them scatter, heard the shots, heard about the wounded ones dragging away screaming to be put out of their misery, heard all the high-fiving and bravado of the contract hunters, and ended the day feeling completely nauseated."

As for the costs, Bill Axbey observed, "Surely the report on the goat eradication on Mt Moehau, in the November 24 *Bay Beacon* contains a major typing error? The estimate that $600,000 will be needed, to get rid of 1000 goats makes one wonder just who the goats really are. To ask the taxpayer to shell out $600 per goat has to be fairly typical of the present system of DOC overkill on such projects, when a bounty of even $100 a goat would make life dangerous for even those goats living in areas with so called difficult access. The $600,000 will certainly not be the last expenditure and one has to ask, if 172 goats were culled in the first three days leaving 828 to go, what on earth was the $75,000 a year being spent on? Certainly not on goat eradication. Once again we see huge sums of money allocated for a limited result under the guise that conservation is the catchword to obtain endless finance without question or justification. Six hundred dollars a goat? They have to be kidding."[28] From 1951 to 1957 a government bounty scheme for goats occurred. By 1988 about 40,000 hunters were estimated to "hunt feral goats, for an estimated harvest of 68,500 animals. (Nugent 1992)

In April 2006, regional council employees sign off on the Moehau Goat Eradication Project and identify four Key Ecological Sites with a total area of 4,300ha within the original 17.000ha goat eradication area.[29]

DOC and EW sign a memorandum of understanding. In his letter, DOC's John Gaukrodger notes that, "Forest browsing by feral goats modifies or removes the habitat that our existing native animals rely on for survival. The damage caused by goats is significant and in some cases can result in permanent changes to the composition of the forest." Ignored in this simple conservation equation is how moa browsed the under-storey for thousands of years prior to human habitation, and to a greater height than goats. By the time European settlers arrived, moa had all been eaten and the original Gondwanaland landscape was changing dramatically.

But there was another side to the goat cost-benefit ledger. While goats of great value to pastoral farmers they also are adept at keeping weeds out of public conservation lands.

This is a role attributed to feral goats by DOC researchers. Susan Timmins and Julie Geritzlehner who observe wild goats maintain effective control of "old man's beard, Japanese honeysuckle, pampas grass, woolly nightshade, wandering jew, mistflower, purple guava, African olive and Mysore thorn in areas that were damaged forest and forest margins."[30]

Goats do cause some damage in the bush, but Timmins' and Geritzlehner's research shows there are both positive and negative outcomes from control. They found weed species that increased in abundance after goat control on open land included gorse, old man's beard, buddleia, pampas grass, Mexican daisy, and kikuyu grass. On tussockland gorse, Himalayan honeysuckle, broom, blackberry, Chinese privet, buffalo grass flourished. An examination of the international literature, including a review of the topic by Zavaleta et al. (2001), also revealed several striking examples of weeds increasing after pest animal control".[31]

Back on the Coromandel, exotic weeds have indeed increased on the western side of Moehau since the Wall of Death goat massacre, with adverse impacts on both farming and conservation land. Species now thriving include blackberry, ragwort, Mexican devil weed, mistflower, tutu, foxglove, thistles of various species, apple of Sodom, woolly nightshade, privet, pampas and gorse.

In July 2006, the Thames DOC office publishes its irregular *Around the Traps* newsletter now touting its collaboration with Thames Coromandel District Council (TCDC) and Hauraki Maori Trust Board (HMTB) to "improve the health of the environment and better protect communities on the Coromandel from flooding" and updating the figures on goat eradication. So far, the tally is 1,330 dead goats, an estimated 15 remaining, and four radio-tagged goats being tracked. The dubious connection between goat culls and flood protection continues.

Somewhat questionable is the nature of DOC's ongoing relationship with iwi with regard to animal pest control spending. According to a Thames Coast flood control report back in 2005, many meetings were held and fenced Māori land was being used for the project's dog training sessions. All good, so far. But it also notes, "the informing of, and consultation with, tangata whenua has been somewhat hampered by iwi being embroiled in Treaty issues, giving them little time to meet or consider the operations within our required timeframes."

The report gives a shout-out to the Hauraki Māori Trust Board as project partner, and in particular its Animal Pest Control project team representative, Liane Ngamane. Ngamane, it says, "has given excellent guidance for our discussions with tangata whenua and considerations regarding tikanga māori." Whether HMTB's "excellent guide" was actually consulted on the decision to eradicate wild goats and, if so, whether she communicated the plan comprehensively with local iwi is far from clear.

DOC's peninsula-wide campaign to eradicate goats would not only be an assault on the animals themselves, but a serious affront to Māori cultural values and resources as well. In its submission to the proposed Waikato Regional Pest Management Strategy (2007-12), Ngāti Maru Runanga states categorically that feral goat is a prized, hunted food animal.

"If the three prized feral food animals are removed from their habitat," the submission notes, "then the potential for some families already struggling becomes worse and hunting as a means of choice becomes unavailable, effectively removing the ability of choice from every one of us. Our families and our communities, both Māori and non-Māori, believe they should retain the ability to choose to hunt...let's prioritise, plan and deal with the other 90 or so pests before we deal with the three prized food pests.

"This proposal, if granted, will adversely affect the relationship that we as Ngāti Maru and tangata whenua have with our culture, traditions, our ancestral lands, sites, wāhi tapu and other taonga, and also contravenes and undermines our kaitiakitanga status, which in the Act is a matter of national importance. Our rights and interests as guaranteed under the Treaty of Waitangi are also adversely affected." The submission ends with a respectful plea to the hearing committee that they decline the regional pest management strategy.[32]

The Waikato Raupatu Trustee Company Ltd submission also lists animals of value to their hapu and marae. " These animals and plants are also part of the Regional Pest Management Strategy in which Waikato-Tainui would like special recognition as being of some importance to Māori. They include, but are not limited to all deer, goats, pigs, and brown bull-headed catfish. The purpose for noting these animals is that they play a role in our traditions. Regardless of these species being introduced to our lands, they became a food source to our people."

These submissions from Maori to EW's revised pest strategy came too late for the Moehau goats and those on down the Peninsula. It is clear that DOC's consultation relationship with iwi is designed more to advance the agency's operative goals than to protect Māori interests. Pleas for goats to be recognised as "being of some importance to Māori" and to be managed accordingly, are completely ignored.

"Believe It or Not!"

"These are the beasts which ye shall eat: the ox, the sheep, and the goat."

Deuteronomy 14:4-5

With the Moehau goat slaughter in the rear-view mirror and a fresh regional pest plan coming hot off the press, the issue of wild goat control takes a turn to the weird. DOC national headquarters releases a press statement published in Hamilton and Wellington dailies titled, "Burping gets on DOC's goat".[33] Hard to believe, but killing goats is DOC's answer to global warming. And not just goats, but deer too! A DOC policy discussion report explains how the animals burp methane and eat "vast volumes of forest plants which would otherwise help absorb carbon dioxide." The report claims "sustained control of goats and deer on any 4,500 sq km forest block would offset the same volume of carbon emissions currently produced by all gas and coal- fired power stations in New Zealand." The article states that the killing of 2,000 goats from Taranaki's National Park over the past 10 years had "prevented emissions equivalent to a 1.4 litre car driving 17 million kilometers." It appears that goat extermination rather than improved public transportation or increased petrol taxes, is the answer to climate change.

Truth and Consequences

"The more clearly we can focus our attention on the wonders and realities of the universe about us, the less taste we shall have for destruction."

Rachel Carson

In June 2007, the *Moehau Messenger* newspaper reports, "More than 2,000 Feral Goats Culled Thanks to Teamwork". Contract killers leave goat carcasses to rot on public land. "EW biosecurity officer Dave Hodges says $630,000 was invested in the programme."

A letter from local farmer Ross Gardner offers some other insights. "John Gaukrodger from DOC claimed that a benefit of goat culling on the northern Coromandel Peninsula is enhancement of habitat for Archey's frog and kiwi. Are goats such a problem for these species? Archey's frog lives in pastureland, and kiwi live in other parts of the country such as Raetahi and Whangamomona where goats and wild pigs abound. The cost to the taxpayer of $300 per goat for the cull was rather large considering the count included goats shot in fenced farm paddocks in Colville and elsewhere and tails taken from goats killed by other private hunters.

"Farmers may be regretting giving access to hunters as goats are now worth more than prime lambs. Farm use of herbicide will rise dramatically as small blackberry plants appear everywhere from seed sources on DOC land. This has occurred on retired land at Fantail Bay, and parts of the Waioeka Gorge have turned into a giant blackberry bush. They are not covered in regenerating native vegetation as DOC predicted. What is the point of culling all the goats for claimed improvements in habitat if noxious weeds take over?[34]

As for kiwi, it's fairly obvious feral goats have very little or nothing to do with breeding success or survival. When goats roamed freely on Moehau, the kiwi actually thrived, with increases of around 14.8 percent annually as of 2006. Surprisingly, with the wild goats all shot, kiwi survival actually declined. While the April 2009 *Coromandel Town Chronicle* recorded a survival rate for kiwi chicks of 66 percent. A DOC report in 2005 had noted a 71.77

percent success rate. Further bad news arrives from the Moehau Kiwi Sanctuary in the *Panui* newsletter—chick survival is only 57 percent and of 23 hatched: nine were killed by predators (dogs, cats and stoats), and one by starvation. Transmitters stuck on the leg of a kiwi chick can get caught up in mangemange *(lygodium articulatum)*. That goat control and kiwi success might be somehow related reflects no science... just fantasy for the gullible.

Nevertheless, DOC gets on with the goat slaughter business. A November 25, 2008 advert in the *Hauraki Herald* reports the "goat team completed their first round in the Kauaeranga Valley prior to the aerial 1080 drop and are now working in the central operation area from Waiomu north. In the last six months over 200 goats have been culled..."

That very same week, an advert in *The New Zealand Farmer's Weekly* is looking for goats anywhere—"Feral Goats a Problem? We muster goats on a 50/50 share deal. Sale and trucking arranged". Yet another farming paper reports there is huge potential for goat meat and for fibre and milk confirmed by the three-year national goat-monitoring project established in July 2004.[35] "The project aimed to show that goats were complimentary to other farming systems and enterprises; and to show goats were effective for weed control, especially as the world becomes more aware of the overuse of chemicals."[36] Major markets in 2007 for New Zealand goat meat were the USA, Reunion Island, Martinique, Trinidad and Tobago, Guadeloupe, Fiji and the UK. And the domestic market is growing.[37]

Another farming paper reports: "Demand for Goat Meat Increasing". Apparently demand outstrips supply, and while the industry may be small, goat is the most widely eaten meat in the world. Boer goats are recognised as the best -- lean, low in calories, cholesterol and saturated fat, but high in iron and protein. "Young Boer goat meat, when cooked correctly is flavoursome, succulent, tender and tasty."[38]

Across the ditch, *Australian Geographic* says, "Feral Goats are Saving Some Drought-Hit Farmers". The magazine reports, "Long an unwelcome blot on this landscape— a feral pest shot on sight—the goat is now forging a reputation as one of the region's more valuable commodities and the saviour of drought-ravaged farming families...farmers have changed the goat's tag from 'feral' to 'rangeland'. The qualities that make goats such a pest – their resilience and adaptability – are exactly what make them desirable livestock." Valued as "controllers of invasive native scrub," the article continues, "goats may do less harm to the environment than sheep. They don't tend to follow the same pads as sheep do, reducing the likelihood of erosion and they have a far broader diet, so are less likely to eradicate plant species."[39]

The price in 2008 was $6.50 per kg, and for farmers the payoff is not just the price. When farmed in mixed stock, goats provide added benefits of improved flock and pasture health. The Boer Breeders Association is working to further improve goat traits. But up on the Coromandel wild Boer goats are left by DOC shooters to rot in the sun.[40] So much for "conservation". As for ethics, don't even go there.

The Wall of Death goat eradication programme on the Coromandel Peninsula promised, among other things, conservation budget savings, flood control, salvation for species from frogs to kiwi, and positive outcomes for tangata whenua. It delivered none of the above while flouting established regional policy and trading away the benefits of effective traditional management by the people who know the land best.

For many, the most regrettable outcome concerned people. By running roughshod over the rural community— a community deeply committed to environmental protection and deeply respectful of flora and fauna, large and small— government office workers with agendas and money to burn set back their own long-term effectiveness and objectives.

What Did We Learn?

"We need another and a wiser and perhaps a more mystical concept of animals...They are not brethren, they are not underlings; they are other nations caught with ourselves in the net of life and time, fellow prisoners of the splendour and travail of the earth."

Henry Beston, *The Outermost House*

A local Coromandel historian comments, "Exterminating the goats came at a huge cost to the country. The aim being to have the forest regenerate, which in places it has, although much of the temperate broadleaf forest canopy is so dense it does not allow enough sunlight to filter through to aid the growth of any small plants that may attempt to grow beneath. There are vast areas that are so dense, dark and cold, goats never ventured into. Where there had been tracks cut to give access for use in pest control work, maintenance has to be carried out physically by humans at an ever escalating cost. Formerly goats had aided in keeping these access tracks open. Where control work in the past had provided a good healthy life for many physically fit people, the current tendency is to turn away because of poorly maintained walking access and conditions. Since the goats have been removed there are many species of plant weeds in large quantities on the government land. These weeds are infesting neighbouring properties. In many areas there has been no attempt made to try to control plant pests on government land in the Moehau area.

"From the perspective of loss of available finance to the hill country farm and subsequently its export revenue earning ability, the loss of the use of goats for weed control is vast. Landowners, now, spend thousands of dollars controlling weeds with the use of chemicals, helicopters, tractors and many long hours of physical work. There are no options but to use chemicals. Many property managers do not like extensive use of toxic chemicals."

Geoffrey Robinson penned a summation of the eradication programme critiquing the process: "The recent undertaking by DOC and EW with the support of MEG is an example of an ad hoc pest control initiative undertaken technically within the law, from what can be gathered, but undertaken in a manner that should not be repeated. As the Committee is aware, feral goats were designated a "control" pest species, as opposed to an "eradication" species in the EW Regional Pest Control Strategy Operational 2002-2007.

"For certain reasons, DOC and EW undertook to alter policy in 2005 while the Strategy was still operational and eradicate feral goats in the northern part of the Coromandel. The programme was announced before any formal consultation with affected landowners, and landowners were required to cooperate in their eradication scheme. After ministerial involvement, DOC embarked upon an effort to meet with affected landowners individually to hear their concerns. On an informal basis, work such as fencing was individually negotiated at public expense and access to certain properties was secured by agreement with the landowners.

"Consultation with landowners was non-existent in the first instance and informal in the second instance. The financial expense of the eradication effort for coastal goats was of dubious value from an immediate environmental perspective. The coastal population kept to the coast. Its population had been controlled by area landowners and had been in steep decline for years.

"Culled goats had been used on the east coast as a food resource for the table and, in other cases, as food for working farm animals. Had full and proper consultation with affected resident landowners been undertaken, prior to DOC and EW publicly committing to and embarking on their programme of eradication by contract hunters, alternative and possibly better decisions could have been made to achieve conservation goals at reduced public expense."

Part Two:

Don't Fence Us In

Don't Fence Us In

"A perfect re-creation of a prehuman ecosystem is impossible and New Zealand conservation has to accept that the crucial issue of the next few years is to maintain what we now have."
R. Paul Scofield, Ross Cullen and Maggie Wang[1]

The year is 2006. When farming families around the Moehau Range north of Colville were served with a plan to physically fence them into a sprawling new 18,000 hectare eco-management zone, their response was swift, well informed and steadfast. These long-time residents knew a fair bit about the idea of a "pest-proof fence" and a so-called "pest-free zone" that would isolate the coastal flats and great mountain hillsides they called home. This plan for a coast-to-coast steel barrier at an upper-peninsula pinch point was nothing new. Similar schemes by the Department of Conservation (DOC) had come and gone back in 1982 and 1993—abandoned for a variety of reasons.

Knowing the land and knowing the wildlife as they did, these stewards of the northern Coromandel landscape saw the latest dream of a "pest-free zone" as just that—a dream. It made no sense. Where pest eradication is the goal, pest reinvasion is a certainty. To battle that certainty, a never-ending campaign of toxin applications and a raft of restrictions and regulations are a must. And to fund that battle, ongoing costs are high and usually borne by those caught in the crossfire.

More than 10 years after construction of a 47 km steel "pest-proof fence" and tonnes of toxin application, the 34 square kilometer showcase Maungatautari Ecological Island in Cambridge is still home to pest mammals, including stoats. Kingsley Field writes in *Country News* (October 2011) of a third drop of poison baits over the 3400 ha Maungatautari mainland island and this comes after the disastrous drop in May where hundreds of sheep and cattle were poisoned after eating broadifacoum, a second generation anti-coagulant. Earlier in 2007 more than 500 livestock were cruelly killed "including hundreds of sheep and 95 steers from three farms bordering the reserve. Maungatautari Trust has admitted the mistake and chief executive Jim Mylchreest has offered to replace livestock and compensate farmers." And in stark contrast to the northern Coromandel, Maungatautari includes no farms, no homes, no pets, no residents, no vehicles, no boats, no baches, no campgrounds, and no restaurants. Imagine the likelihood of a "pest-free Moehau", which is home to all of the above – and more.

New Zealand's other headline "pest-proof" tourist attraction, the re-branded Zealandia wildlife sanctuary in Karori, Wellington comprises just 225 hectares – about one percent of the proposed Moehau region and like Maungatautari, is home to not one farming family.

To those who gave the latest Moehau fence plan an hour of serious thought, the proposal was as ludicrous as it would be costly. Even the plan's public promoters had "inconvenient truths" safely tucked away as they continued to pump the project in public.

*

Summer holidays bring thousands of visitors to the upper Coromandel each year, filling baches and seasonal homes, a motel, a camper van park, a bush resort, and hundreds of sites at some of New Zealand's most popular campgrounds. Meanwhile, year-round resident families run farms, aquaculture and fishing businesses, organic gardens, and tourist operations. Others work the trades, teach, write, make art, heal, study, or simply live out their days

Pastoral farming covers approximately 10,500 hectares around Moehau and families abutting the 5,945 DOC mountain estate have always been keen environmentalists. They hunt and trap possums, wild pigs, stoats and rats on their own land, in their own time, and at their own expense. Their conservation work is done under the radar and without grant money handouts. And it is rarely acknowledged, either by government or the media.

Conservation is a way of life on the Coromandel – just part of the job. These families do not issue press releases or otherwise attract attention. They simply work with aroha for Mother Nature and with a sense of belonging to the land they only temporarily occupy. Their efforts are rewarded many times over by the kiwi calls, the swooping kereru, the haunting ruru, and the many other native and non-native species they know so well as neighbours and fellow creatures.

So imagine, for a moment, living in peace at the top of the peninsula only to be told that your home or farm is soon to be enclosed by a two-metre high, steel predator barrier to demarcate an official "pest-free zone". Imagine working and living inside that fence, with the routine toxins and restrictions and rules and bills to pay for it all, quick to follow. Those pet cats and traditional wild pork suppers? Forget about it. Farming practices as usual? Not a chance in a million. Camping and fishing as always? Maybe somewhere else. Toxin-strewn hillsides? Count on it. And that's just the beginning.

*

Back in the 1970s, before the creation of the Department of Conservation, the NZ Wildlife Service carried out surveys that classified Moehau an outstanding site of special wildlife interest. Farmers around the mountain would have been the first to agree.

Those families farming thousands of hectares had respect for the employees of both the Wildlife Service and the NZ Forest Service, who they knew put in the hard yards and could read the land. At one time, employees of the Wildlife Service completed a full four-year training before heading out to work in the wilderness. Some of those Forest Service workers lived out in the bush in harsh conditions, hunting possums, goats and pigs. But that was then.

In 1987, as part of New Zealand's neo-liberal lurch toward free markets, privatisation, and public sector "reforms", the Wildlife Service, Forest Service and Department of Lands and Survey were merged to form the Department of Conservation. DOC comprised a network of regional Conservation Boards, and all Crown land, including thousands of hectares at the top of the Coromandel, came under its management.

As one commentator put it, the regional boards "virtually control the organisation, a sort of giant quango system that ensured decisions were subject to little outside interference or input…a bureaucratic heaven. This resulted in the department acquiring more and more of the public domain unto itself as 'DOC land'."[2]

Present-day DOC is made up of an advisory Conservation Authority and a network of six so-called "Conservation

Partnership" regions. The Coromandel finds itself managed in conjunction with Northland and parts of the Waikato.

Those with a long history around Moehau confirm that back in the day, DOC field staff included some serious bush workers, with the skills and experience to know of what they spoke. But relations soured quickly.

Within a few years of its formation DOC unveiled a plan to fence off the northern Coromandel and relations between meddling department officers and locals became more fraught. West coast farmer John Goudie, held onto letters and newspaper clippings documenting landowner meetings like the one held under an old pohutukawa on his farm. The meeting was forced out under that tree because John's wife Peggy would not agree to have DOC people inside her house. It was little wonder that families around Moehau were upset. An earlier proposal to fence off the peninsula had been mooted and ultimately dismissed. Now it was back.

A July 1993 newspaper feature titled *Moehau Marsupial Myopia* explained why some locals were getting frustrated. "Although it may seem to some that the possum fence would reduce manpower, that is an illusion shared by every builder of so called vermin proof fences the world over…If it ever gets the chance to go ahead to certain failure, just how much of the taxpayer's money would be sucked up before any of the protagonists would admit the whole thing was created to justify DOC's presence on the peninsula? Bet you a possum subsidy you couldn't find a single official that would take the responsibility for it then. In so-called 'valid research projects' failure is just as interesting to researchers as any other result, particularly if those involved can walk away without accountability."[3]

Forest Service veteran and former DOC Southland Conservator of Wildlife, Bill Axbey had been equally blunt in a letter to the newspaper a year earlier. Axbey wrote of "close to a million bucks frittered away on a hair-brained idea. It's time someone stopped this Moehau stupidity…If the whole thing wasn't shaping up to be an endless financial drain, it could be the joke of the decade; unfortunately on us who will pay for the erection, operation and endless maintenance of this edifice to the fact that, in some cases, people do have less brains than a possum. Wanna bet?"[4] DOC purchased miles of wire intended for an electric fence outrigger system, but the materials were not up to the job. So the wire lay rusting, according to local farmers whose memories of this fantastic scheme still conjure wry grins.

Notwithstanding the two failed attempts to fence off the Moehau Range from the browsing Australian brush-tailed possum, DOC got good control results with a concerted fixed bait and trapping scheme through the 1990s on its steep, but accessible and well tracked, mountain estate.

By the year 2000 DOC ecologist Pim De Monchy was able to note in a detailed field study *Moehau Forest Condition Waikato Conservancy Monitoring Report 2000* "The forest canopy at Moehau, including the species most vulnerable to and preferred by possums, is in excellent condition. Indicator species such as northern rata and kohekohe are in similar condition to the same species on possum-free offshore islands, and are flowering and fruiting regularly. Possum control objectives are currently being achieved, demonstrating the success of the control programme that has been in place since 1989…In general, understorey regeneration of all species is occurring."

As for the hard data, de Monchy stated on page 18, "Possum densities have been low since control began, calculated as possum captures per 100 corrected trap nights (see Warburton 1997). Typical catch rates since 1994 have been less than 6 percent prior to control, and less than 2 percent afterwards." Even by regional council possum control standards, the documented results being achieved on the unfenced northern Coromandel were close to spectacular.

de Monchy also reported an estimated Moehau kiwi chick survival at close to 70 percent so DOC designated the entire Moehau area including all surrounding private land, the Moehau Kiwi Sanctuary (MKS). Despite failing to consult with affected landowners, DOC encountered no opposition. A sanctuary, after all, provides safety, protection, and shelter. It implies something almost sacred. Who would oppose that?

As it turns out residents would eventually realize the DOC-imposed "sanctuary" status of their land has unintended consequences. With the new MKS status comes new responsibilities as conjured up by regional council. Views on the kiwi zone would soon change as a result of regional council's soon to be announced wild pig control regulations.

So with possums well under control on the Moehau DOC estate, the mountain's bush species a success story and kiwi chicks making newspaper headlines, local residents could be excused for sloughing off the increasing chatter and informal meetings mentioning potential benefits of (yet another) "pest-proof" possum fence. Although abandoned twice before amidst serious opposition, the idea had never been officially declared dead. Just like the proverbial rust, pest-fence dreamers on the Coromandel had never slept and were about to re-awaken.

In retrospect, DOC's unexpected and expensive rush in 2005 to exterminate wild goats on the upper peninsula should have provided a telltale clue as to what was to come.

*

The announcement of firm plans to build a high-tech "pest-proof" fence across the peninsula hit the community like a bolt of lightning. A small article in a local weekly paper of 13 April 2006 carried the provocative headline, *Pest-Proof Fence Will Protect 20,000 Hectares of Land North of Colville.*[5]

The story outlined a well-advanced plan to erect eight kilometers of stainless steel fence designed to stop pigs, cats, possums, goats, ferrets, stoats, weasels, and even rats. Reportedly, a majority of landowners over whose land the fence would be erected were supportive. "The translocation of other species is dependant *(sic)* on the fence being in place to provide the necessary protection for the endangered animals and birds", according to main fence sponsor Moehau Environment Group (MEG). As two main roads cross the proposed fence route, a solution on "how to protect the security of the fence" was still being sought.[6]

Most readers of that matter-of-fact April announcement could safely assume that after 20 years of trying this third attempt to build a coast-to-coast possum fence across the Coromandel was finally a done deal. All that was left were a few minor details. What the article failed to note was that farmers and other residents, retirees and other landowners who live north of the proposed barrier —the people who mattered most—had not been directly consulted.

Entrepreneurial MEG had been doing some good work but did not have their collective ears to the ground. The group was by no means representative of the general public and certainly not of large-block landowners around Moehau. Most MEG members did not reside in the northern Coromandel, let alone the area that would have been fenced off.

Had the reporter laid eyes on the commissioned cost-benefit study: *An Analysis of the Costs of Pest Control Options in the Northern Coromandel,* she would have spotted the problem. As the study advises, "The importance of agriculture in the Moehau area obliges the MEG to pay particular attention to the concerns of pastoral farmers."[7] MEG's own report is crystal clear with regard to first steps: "Approaching and obtaining agreement from these landowners as to a way forward with this project is essential, and the first step in deciding where to from here."[8]

Concerned residents reacted quickly to news that the Colville-to-Waikawau fence was going ahead. Within days, a new group, the Upper Coromandel Landcare Association (UCLA), was organised to speak with a unified voice on behalf of residents and to express strong opposition to the destructive environmental and social ramifications of the imminent fence plan. UCLA came together in kanohi to kanohi/face-to-face meetings from Colville to Port Jackson on the west and to Port Charles on the east.

This meeting of the minds came easily because farmers were well up to speed. Over the years, many had attended informal meetings that touched on the subject. They had read articles supportive of the idea and updates by fence promoters. Several had visited predator fences elsewhere and most had at one time or another had chats with DOC or EW staffers about the fence pros and cons. Most had never considered that the "pest-proof fence" plan would actually come to fruition.

Within days, a UCLA petition and Statement of Opposition to the Moehau "pest-proof fence" gained more than 50 signatures of local residents, including those representing an overwhelming 85 percent of the privately owned land to be partitioned off.[9]

Petitioners cited a list of potential concerns including the certainty of blanket applications of toxin 1080 over the entire area; the necessity of restrictions and regulations affecting farmers, bach owners, and visitors alike; high costs of fence construction and operation; likely rules on pets, working dogs, and wild pigs; and, as MEG's own cost-benefit study confirmed, the likelihood of reinvasions and ultimate project failure. They objected to a plan that would change their lives for the worse and fail to achieve its stated conservation goals.

In the weeks that followed, locals who questioned the project were at first brushed off. Fence promoters suggested to the press that opposition was limited to a couple of people. However, on May 30 when top officials at DOC, EW, and Thames-Coromandel District Council were presented the UCLA residents' petition, the writing was clearly and indelibly on the wall. Despite claims to the contrary by frantic fence boosters, it was now clear that the people most affected were the people most opposed.

Residents put pen to paper. Critically important was a letter from the long-time and highly respected Port Jackson farming family of Philip, Clare and Alexander Ward titled, *Objection to the Pest Proof Fence*.[10] "As members of the Upper Coromandel Landcare Association, we support Reihana Robinson's leadership in our objection to the proposed 8 km pest proof fence. We oppose the use of 1080 poison near or on our properties. We feel the proposed fence will create an exclusive zone, which could be [easily used] to legalise greater restrictions on local people who live and work in the area full time. MEG has never consulted us directly or in surveys." Other writers followed.

Former DOC conservator Axbey applauded the UCLA effort and attacked the fence plan on the basis of cost and feasibility. His letter titled *The Moehau Myth* saw more strategic motives. "I am sure not even MEG, EW or TCDC are misled into believing that they are other than fronts for DOC hell bent on establishing control of a huge area to justify their presence in the Land Corp property they took over."[11] In the coming months Axbey's words were proven close to the mark.

Faced with certain meltdown of the "predator-proof fence", MEG barrier boosters reacted emotionally. In the pitched public battle that followed, the group's desperate charges of UCLA "misinformation" and "scare-mongering" failed to address the fundamental, undeniable reasons for widespread community opposition to their plan.

Pilloried in the press, MEG claimed they had been taken unaware, that they had not heard of residents' concerns. That much MEG had right. They had not "heard", however… because they had not been "listening."

The 2006 Coromandel Fence Fiasco:
How It All Began
Visions 1999-2001

"The only fence against the world is a thorough knowledge of it."

John Locke

While Moehau Range old-timers may have been surprised by the April 2006 definitive announcement of a third plan to erect a pest proof barrier, the story originates in the year 1999. That is the year when easy money begins to flow from regional council.

First on the payroll are Kevin Christie of EcoFX Pest Solutions Ltd together with Gerry Kessels and Associates who are contracted, in 1999 by Environment Waikato regional council (EW), to undertake a Key Ecological Site (KES) survey covering all private sites of ecological significance on the Coromandel Peninsula. They are paid \$49,000 for the job.[12]

The agreed upon fee amount is no accident, landing conveniently just below the \$50,000 threshold requiring full Council approval. The duo—one ex-employee of the regional council biosecurity department and one ex-DOC employee, produce a report that just happens to coincidentally gather information about a possible fencing off of the upper Coromandel.

While Christie and Kessels interview landowners around Colville, they note some "spontaneous" interest in revisiting the Possum-Proof Fence. Whether this is an actual survey question or a topic raised by locals themselves is not clear. Either way, the consultants do some historical tidying and make a recommendation for a predator-proof fence.

The *Key Ecological Site Report* debrief is held in the DOC Kauaeranga Field Centre near Thames on 22 August 2000 and a hot topic is the fence recommendation. "The study team considers that there is potential to explore the possibilities of a possum proof fence, originally suggested by DOC ten or so years ago. The reason being that key landowners spoken to were receptive to the idea, and the Department and several private landowners have spent considerable amounts of labour and money to eradicate possums from Moehau in recent years. This work will be wasted unless sustained control is carried out, which would be made much easier if a fence was constructed.

"The fence should not be constructed along the route originally suggested by DOC however, but at a point further south. The exact location of the line needs to be discussed with the local community at the beginning of the investigation process. Given that there appears to be a distrust of so-called 'Local Government Bureaucrats' and DOC personnel it was suggested that independent contractors with no political interest make initial contact with landowners within the Coromandel area. On that basis Roger Smith and Kevin Christie were quasi-nominated for the task of approaching the local community. There was also some validity in this decision because in the first instance Roger Smith is well known to most locals and both have an in-depth knowledge of pest control techniques and fully understand the new technology associated with the Ag-Research pest proof fence."[13]

Meetings are subsequently held with locals near Moehau on the 4th and 5th of October, 2000. Notes of purported conversations with landowners Terry Whitehouse, Marcus Ward, John Goudie, Trevor Tiller, Karl Johnston on behalf of his mother Mrs Merle Johnston, Les Ward, Henry Dobbs, David Small, and Wayne Todd on behalf of the Karuna Falls community are recorded.

"One overriding opinion was that there had to be sufficient funds available from the various stakeholders to undertake control on the whole peninsula north of the fence. If this did not occur in their (and the authors) opinion the erection of the fence would be a waste of tax and ratepayer money, i.e. it would become a bloody great white elephant."[14] This is the first revelation of the commitment of ratepayer and taxpayer funding of the proposed fence.

In February 2001, a DOC report titled *The Fence*, obtained as Official Information by UCLA, zeroes in on the problem. "Approximately ten years ago a proposal was made by the DOC to the local community that a fence be erected over the peninsula to prevent north-south migration of possums. This was to be erected at the narrowest point of the upper Peninsula located roughly between Colville and Waikawau Bay-Port Charles. The fence design at that time was limited to an electric fence, outrigger concept. It appears that poor consultation compounded by some fundamental flaws in the fence design lead to the community rejecting the fence proposal at that time. Given that the fence line would have crossed private land for nearly all of its distance the local landowners ultimately had and still have complete power of veto."[15]

Visions 2002

*"The wide world is all about you: you can fence yourselves
in, but you cannot forever fence it out."*

J.R.R. Tolkien

Fast-forward a year and a half. The wheels have been turning. A meeting takes place at DOC Hauraki headquarters in Thames on 29 July 2002. Invited attendees are MEG members Diane Prince, Kathi Parr, Andrea, Letticia Williams, Wayne Todd and Peter Buddle; DOC employees Josh Kemp, Fin Buchanan and Jason Roxbourgh; EW pest contractor Roger Smith; Kevin Christie of EcoFX; and EW employees Peter Russell and Kirsten Crawford. Not invited at this crucial juncture are local iwi nor any farming families whose land would be incarcerated behind the steel barrier.

It is clear from meeting minutes that the Colville possum fence is proceeding with full steam ahead. All parties who wish to promote the project are present and fully represented. "EW and DOC are willing to give support on the ground", the minutes show. In fact, DOC states the fence "is a number one priority, demonstrated by the amount of work gone into the area so far. The DOC can't guarantee long-term commitment because of the nature of the organisation. However *the money is there now* [emphasis added]. It was suggested that it is not likely to be a problem getting support higher up in the DOC because the costs will decrease over the long term." EW says it cannot guarantee long-term funding either, "however we are committed to what the group is trying to achieve and to funding further pest control this financial year."

Most intriguing in the official meeting minutes is the notation that "MEG are happy to be a 'face' for the project, including administration and consultation". MEG could not have asked for anything more as a hefty 20 percent of any budget disappears into "administration". With any MEG funding applications, administration fees are never overlooked. This project will easily top the $5 million mark, and administration fees to the "volunteer community group" could amount to a seven-figure jackpot. Despite the glossy brochures invariably stressing "volunteer" work, a number of MEG financial reports show over $200,000 cash in the bank.[16]

The minutes also state Tim Day and John McClennan (this could be a typo as Day has collaborated with an M. MacGibbon) "have done a cost benefit analysis" which could be compared with Coca Cola researching the impact of soft drinks on the health of young children. Tim Day is a founder and principal of the Xcluder Pest Proof Fencing Ltd—the very same business tipped to build the Colville-Waikawau barrier.

Call it manipulative, call it cunning, or just call it business as usual. Among strategies discussed for convincing the community to climb on board is to "demonstrate there are possibilities of increasing the value of property because their area is part of a 'sanctuary', that we 'don't take from but give to", as there is a "need to be able to appeal to economically driven landowners."

The need for a "vision for the project" highlights the vexed question of how to create excitement for the project. Suggestions include slogans like, "Hear the dawn chorus three miles off shore" and "Kick tieke out of the way". But, most importantly, what is required is a "communication strategy." MEG wish "to be informed of the DOC and EW activities happening and issues arising in the Northern Coromandel that may impact on their work. This was agreed upon by all present." Attendees note rats are high maintenance and that toxin use in the area is a worry. And, oh yes, iwi will need to be consulted at some stage.

With all in agreement, assignments are handed out. EW will send MEG a list of landowners and a map. DOC will provide iwi/hapu contact details to MEG and EW. And DOC staff will "locate words from Sir Logan Campbell's diary/Dermont Dervil *(sic)* re being woken up by the noise of birds offshore and forward to MEG."

The DOC/EW/MEG summit meeting moves on to the thorny issue of so-called Key Ecological Sites. "Peter Russell gave a brief on the previous difficulties with the KES Project. There were a number of inaccuracies with the land-based information used to identify landowners for the project, as a result a lot of wrong information was sent out causing confusion and consternation amongst landowners and Council alike.

"A Queen's Council submission was made from the upper Coromandel challenging the legal and enforcement status of the

KES project. As a result: 1) the project is entirely voluntary. There are no enforcement rules attached to the KES project; 2) There is some collective negativity towards the project from the upper Coromandel and other parts of the Coromandel, there is also collective support. There is full support from the EW council on the KES project and growing support for biodiversity initiatives in general."

Some landowners invite KES descriptors. It comes with cash incentives. EW provides 100 percent funding for initial predator control, materials and contracted services through annual operations and also provides funds for predator control materials for maintenance of those sites for five years, according to EW Biosecurity Officer Kirsten Crawford (November 2002).

The successful Queen's Council submission from the upper Coromandel that challenged the legal and enforcement status of the KES project reaffirmed landowner rights over regional government descriptive categories. EW had been planning to unilaterally impose those KES descriptions. The ruling gives landowners the right to decide whether or not to designate some part of their private land a KES. But the predator-proof fence project would undermine the Queen's Council action as it would see the entire upper Coromandel turned into a Key Ecological Site.

All those living at the top of the Coromandel are indebted to Thames-Coromandel District Council, V McLeod, S Goudie, MC and AE Ward, OJ Hale, WR, GK and MW Harrison and DK Maraeroa, GR Geard, GR Lumsden, JM Ward, P and C Ward and TC Ward for their submissions in 2001 challenging EW on its KES proposals.

A few months pass and as summer approaches, a community "Open Day" takes place on 30 November 2002 to publicly bat around the idea of a possum-proof fence. The pace of action is picking up. A facilitator from Transpower Landcare Trust conducts the proceedings. The Moehau Predator-Free Zone is officially on the roadmap.

According to meeting minutes, "The bush is quite silent on Moehau, the aim is to bring birdsong back." Toxin 1080 is listed as one of the many risks threatening Moehau, along with commercialisation, disrespectful people and various animals and weeds. The nature of control of introduced animals needs to be in agreement with landowners, according to the minutes and mammals need to be left alone if they are not impacting native bush significantly.

It is clear from the recorded comments that many in the community are not "on board" with MEG's "think big" fence project. Participants list their own visions for the area. An "organic peninsula" is suggested and other comments and concerns include:

"We don't like the concept of things being 'locked in'

"What can the fence achieve?

"What is the objective of the fence?

"What are the costs of the fence and buffer, versus the costs of other coordinated management techniques?

"What is the proposed budget?

"Where is the money coming from?

"Is the fence a feasible option?

"What is MEG's and other stakeholders roles in this whole proposal?

"Who will 'own' the fence?

"What is the effect of the Mayor's proposal to put a predator proof fence further south in the Coromandel?"

It is clear that the community is not buying the MEG fence plan. So a feasibility study is a sensible next step and EW will oblige by funding a study for MEG by a Waikato University graduate student (who will eventually become an EW employee). The DOC Biodiversity Fund will soon receive a MEG application for administrative costs over the coming three years valued at $108,000. Of this amount, $20,000 is estimated for landowner liaison, another $12,500 for "advisory" work, and volunteer coordination starts out at $7,500. Accountability (whatever that is) and reporting require $5,000. And education and "up-skilling" in year one will cost the taxpayer $5,000.

Back at the community hall, residents are told a Steering Group will be set up to move things ahead. DOC will be invited to provide a representative, as will Thames-Coromandel District Council, EW, local iwi, local residents and the Ministry of Agriculture and Fisheries (MAF).

After the meeting, MEG's Peter Buddle writes an upbeat letter to DOC Hauraki area manager John Gaukrodger claiming, "unanimous agreement was reached to define an area from the Colville valley north to the Cape, and to eradicate all possums, stoats, rats and magpies there. Other feral animals to be controlled include goats, cats, pigs and stray dogs." Buddle goes on to state, "the goodwill expressed at the meeting would attest that it definitely *has the community's support* [emphasis added].

But wait. Only eight people list possums, stoats and ferrets as a problem. And all other introduced species get fewer than eight votes. There was no consensus at all on popular hunted species pigs or goats and definitely none on cats and dogs. The claim that the community is generally on board for this well-intentioned but unfeasible project is clearly incorrect, if not completely delusional.

Action 2003

"All conservation of wildness is self-defeating, for to cherish
we must see and fondle, and when enough have seen and
fondled, there is no wilderness left to cherish."
Aldo Leopold A Sand County Almanac

In January, the chair of MEG writes to the mayor of Thames-
Coromandel District inviting a representative of council to join
the pest fence Steering Group. "Participation in this programme is
to be voluntary, and the goodwill expressed at the meeting (30th
November 2002) would attest that it definitely has the community's
support."

Eleven farmers and landowners are in attendance at the
February 11 meeting—Marcus, Ann, Simon, Theodora and Anthea
Ward, together with John Goudie, Alan Barnett, Kelvin Mouritsen,
Catherine Brown, Brian Bassett and Graeme Macrae. Seven iwi reps
attend – Oho Nicholls, Tui Nicholls, Roy Piahana, Liane Ngamane,
Betty Williams, Pauline Clarkin and Rawinia Brownlee. Five MEG
members are in the room, joined by DOC representative Carol
Nanning, EW pest contractor Roger Smith, Kirsten Crawford from
EW and Nicki Green from Landcare Trust. TCDC does not send a
representative.

According to verbal reports, some in attendance are more
than testy, and the minutes tend to support that interpretation.
The November community meeting minutes are questioned, in
particular the characterisation of the undertaking as a "restoration
project of all land to original state". A Hauraki Maori Trust Board
representative and others raise issues of process. Appropriate
protocols for communication and consultation are requested.
Everything grinds to a halt.

At this meeting a map is displayed showing two possible fence
routes. If the southern of the two suggested fence lines is adopted,
the barrier would cross no streams, encompass the Colville School,
and "may dilute the stake of the few major landholders around
Moehau". This last statement acknowledges the possibility of
contradictory opinions extant and suggests the best method for

dealing with conflict is to "dilute" it. To marginalize people who farm for a living, who have been conservationists their whole lives and whose families have inhabited the area for over 100 years, is a definite step in the wrong direction.

As autumn approaches, DOC's Nanning proves an invaluable asset, as supporter for further funding from EW. She attests "MEG is made up of a highly committed group of volunteers" and affirms she has "absolutely no hesitation in recommending the MEG as worthy of support."[17] The DOC/EW/MEG triumvirate is evolving as an effective mutual admiration and back-scratching society.

At a meeting in DOC headquarters on June 23, only the following are present: EW's Roger Smith (pest officer) and Peter Russell (biosecurity); DOC's Finn Buchanan (pest officer), Nanning (pubic relations), and John Gaukrodger (area manager) and MEG's Wayne Todd, Letticia Williams and Kathi Parr. No landowner representatives are invited.

In exciting new business, DOC and EW learn that "MEG wish to support/create an infrastructure to support dispersal of pateke ducks if Condition Funding available." Either funding arrives pronto or DOC has a surfeit of ducks because 40 or 50 brown teal ducks (pateke) are released in Port Charles shortly thereafter. A bunch that were to be released in Okarito, South Island, not far from where they were raised, is flown all the way to the Coromandel because a rimu mast season on the West Coast has supposedly resulted in a stoat increase. When the birds are finally released, one of those conferring blessings remarks, "They're only ducks!"

But as for predator control in the north, the minutes record DOC as stating there is "no money available for possum control next year…Rats are the major problem now…Racumin is the toxin to be trialled…Eight-year project, started last week (June 2003)… Roger strongly recommends phosphorous as a rat toxin… Rats will be post-monitored annually…Rat control continues elsewhere… Mist Trust was going to do a rat programme with DOC but that has fallen over due to excessive Mist Trust conditions…Technically not easy to monitor blocks less than 300 ha…May even have to let possums go to avoid statistical bias…If finances are tight, Finn recommended dropping any pre-testing…DOC's interests lie in a boundary line of Pt Charles/Pt Jackson junction on road and all North." So much for sensible possum and rat control.

What MEG's Wayne Todd really wants, however, is "suggestions for dealing with iwi." And here is where the meeting gets interesting. "Finn said that DOC tended to inform rather than consult with Iwi for MoH approval. John Gaukrodger talked about the value of working with Danny Hitchcock and Te Moehau Nga Tangata Whenua. Tamatera in particular are very good value."

Yes, one could call DOC's advice a bit patronising, if not downright cynical. But a more revealing summary of DOC's "consultation" process could not be found— just inform rather than consult! It is no wonder so many community members have lost confidence in DOC's willingness to listen.

Around this same time, MEG comes up with a *Partnership of an Understanding Proposal* to all iwi or hapu having influence over, and spiritual connection with, Moehau. And knowing where the big money will be, MEG zeroes right in on the cross-peninsula fence. The statement reads:

"We the Moehau Environment Group, having been given a mandate by the residents and ratepayers of the area Colville/ Waikawau Bay to Cape Colville, to investigate the implications and feasibility of an animal (vermin) proof fence…seek partnership or an understanding with those Iwi or Hapu wishing to influence this vision…We seek no authority over nor imposition on any lands, rather the promotion only, of sustainable land management, taking into account the concerns and wishes of all involved parties."

In July, MEG's newly employed coordinator reports, presumably tongue-in-cheek, he is coping successfully "with a free computer…travelling expenses paid for…It's really good 'cos all the other members of MEG can now sit around reading books, taking holidays and watching DVD's and stuff while I do all the work…Forced to do intensive counselling I have now overcome my shyness and am out pestering farmers and local landowners to get permission to carry out pestering *(sic)*…control. Gathering information and identifying toxin preferences…putting together a funding proposal for 2,000ha of pest control." His report explains EW is providing "some financial support to MEG projects". This includes "bait stations and toxins; maps and other data free, with the promise of paying for the feasibility study buffer-zone vs pest-proof fence (around \$5,000). They will also support the cost of facilitators at the next Hui we have."

But the really serious money is out there, as MEG was assured back at its game-plan meeting with DOC and EW in July a year earlier. And now is the time to go for it. EW's Peter Russell, writes a letter of support for MEG's mega-money application to the Department of Conservation's rich Biodiversity Condition Fund. The ambitious project is now defined as the "Creation of a Predator Free Zone in Northern Coromandel." The fence, according to MEG's application, is scheduled for completion by June 2007. No one in the community would be made aware of that.

The actual grant application requests no less than $571,365 to be spent over the next four years. The proposal clearly states the money is earmarked for a predator-proof fence to be built across the peninsula with construction to start in 2005. The application states how costly the current work has been. "This work has been expensive, for instance the level of funding invested includes: control costs of $420,000; mapping of pest control network = 5 days @ $600-$3,000; co-ordination of volunteers = 240 days @ $250 = $58,000; Environment Waikato staff time on the project of $21,600." The application brings into focus the big money picture. It is the first glimpse of how expensive it is to coordinate volunteers. Some "volunteers" actually pay to work such as Global Volunteers

No money is requested for poisons in year one—2003-04, but nearly $100,000 for each of the next three. Three lots of $5,000 for cyanide licenses but no names are supplied. The coordinator's work may be ramped up to "full time employment to support other landcare groups in the area". Everyone knows their position and has a role to play—on September 8 DOC's Nanning is writing again, and it's all about PR… and finding a good price for "rack cards".

This is not the end of applications to the Biodiversity Condition Fund—a deep cash well from which MEG learns to successfully siphon. Later, hundreds of thousands of dollars are granted to MEG for a rat control experiment on private land, including that of several MEG committee members and a handful of others in Port Charles. But this is well down the line.

Meanwhile, discussions with landowners about toxin use are proving a challenge. Documents released to UCLA by DOC in 2006 following an Official Information Act (OIA) request, reveal that owners whose land would be required for the pest barrier overwhelmingly reject both 1080 toxin and the anticoagulant brodifacoum. Terry Whitehouse, Amede Moreel, Vi Brown and Alexandra Sutherland, Waikanae pt 3, Te Kauae o Maui, and Karuna Falls are all opposed to both toxins, while Les Ward and Tokowhero Pt Scenic Reserve oppose use of 1080.

And of course there is the matter of actually dealing to predators. In September, MEG's Pete Buddle contacts Alistair Fairweather of DOC in Hamilton to introduce the fence plan. "Our group is coordinating a Predator Free Zone at the top of the Coromandel Peninsula, planning to eradicate all predator species and seal off the area with a predator fence. We have the support (so far) of 85-95% of landowners, many iwi, the Department of Conservation and Environment Waikato." Buddle writes, "encapsulated cyanide is the toxin most acceptable to most landowners up here". There is the vain hope to "eradicate rats entirely." As apparent head of the toxin team, he is keen to learn the residual, selective and effective nature of poisons including warfarin, Racumin, pindone, diphacinone, coumatetralyl, bromadiolone, brodifacoum, flocoumafen and difethialone, so "we can eliminate pest animals at least cost to the native flora and fauna."

DOC's reply, from Andrew Styche for the Waikato Conservator on 1 October 2003, is quite helpful. "Apart from the use of brodifacoum for island eradications and very restricted use on the mainland, the department does not currently support the use of second generation anticoagulants (brodifacoum, flocoumafen and bromadiolone). This is due to their extreme persistence and consequent risks to non-target species.

"Three of the products (toxins) you have listed (warfarin, pindone and difethialone) are not registered as rodenticides in NZ and cannot be used as such, though pindone is registered for use in the field on possums. Diphacinone is currently in use in a limited capacity, sold under the trade name Ditrac All Weather Block. This toxin is being tested for its efficacy against rats in two further bait formulations, which do not yet have full registration. Results of these trials will not be available until late 2004.

"The only anticoagulant registered for use in the field that is commonly available is coumatetralyl. This toxin is a first generation anticoagulant and is available as paste bait, sold under the name Racumin. Racumin has only been used in the field (by DOC staff) during the past two summers, and as yet there is no best practice for its use. We have had considerable success in reducing rat and mice populations using this bait (achieving tracking rates of 0%) but few Post-Operational Reports have been completed, which would support this. The other alternative rodenticide that we commonly use is 1080. If you decide to proceed with Racumin, contact Finn Buchanan or Eddie Murphy of the Hauraki Area Office for advice as to sowing rates."

As talk of the fence continues to percolate through the community, many still assume the plan cannot succeed and will eventually die a natural death. What they are not aware of is the big money at stake and the total commitment of DOC, MEG and EW to make this plan happen and make it happen now.

This train has definitely left the station.

2004-05 The Report

"The creation of these sanctuaries enclosed by predator-proof fences often creates small expensive zoos surrounded by degraded habitat that will never be able to sustain the animal and plant species contained within the fence."
R Paul Scofield, Canterbury Museum & Ross Cullen
and Maggie Wang, Lincoln University.[18]

The news is out. Or is it? MEG has commissioned Waikato University to undertake a project to provide information on the cost effectiveness of options identified for achieving a pest free status of the northern Coromandel.

An Analysis of the Costs of Pest Control Options in the Northern Coromandel, produced in April 2004 by graduate student Sandra A Barns of the Economics Department in the Waikato School of Management, is ready for all to consider. Well… not quite.

No one in the public arena is made aware of the report's existence until 2006 – and we soon find out why. To her great credit, Barns starts at the beginning and dives into her analysis without apparent preconceptions or questionable assumptions.

The study defines the potentially fenced area north of Colville as 22,000 ha, of which only 9,100 ha is DOC public land. Approximately 6,500 ha of the DOC land lies directly around Moehau. A further 275 ha of private land carry QEII covenants, and 3,874 ha are designated by EW as Key Ecological Sites.

Barns reviews current conservation efforts including pest species being targeted and current spending. Identified pests around Moehau include rabbits, cats, goats, pigs, hedgehogs, rats and mice. But identifying specific conservation goals and appropriate means to achieve them through pest control is not so straightforward.

As Barns points out, "Large gaps exist in the knowledge of the range and population of endangered and rare species in the area, and the extent of habitat damage caused by exotic animal pests. These pose questions for which answers will need to be sought to allow effective management of the area."[19] As for the seemingly simple matter of poisons, Barns reminds that, "Bait aversion, resistance to toxins and neophobia compromise the ability to put all of the pest species at risk."

But possibly the most significant issue of all is, according to the study, roughly 44 percent of the total land area is used in pastoral farming. Removal of all stock for months while toxins are dumped and remain deadly would be a necessity, but most likely "unacceptable" to farmers. But stock removal is worth investigating, she finds, "as costs saved from ground-based operations may cover some of the cost of stock removal".[20]

Other "complicating factors", according to Barns include non-target species deaths and adverse impacts on soils and waterways through misuse of pesticides. Non-target species that may be affected include "humans, domestic livestock and other non-native and native species," she points out. "Strong local public opinion is the only reason toxin 1080 has not been dropped on Moehau."[21] Barns vastly underestimates the objections of farmers to the prospect of their homes, paddocks and farm structures being carpeted aerially with one of the deadliest toxins ever developed – one which can kill cattle, dogs, cats, and yes…people many months after being laid.

The report raises the issue of adverse ecosystem responses to species removal that "may involve unwanted or unexpected consequences, such as the release of non-indigenous plant species. The presence of exotic pests in an environment creates its own balance, frequently upset by the removal of that pest."[22] Barns notes that rat increases due to stoat and cat control may lead to "more damage to native species populations than would have occurred in the absence of stoat and cat eradication. (Thomson 2004) Explosions in mouse populations may be another unexpected outcome, as might the release of exotic plant species in the absence of feral goats."[23]

Further into the report, the rubber hits the road when it comes to the critical matter of costs and benefits compared with current expenditures. With millions of dollars of ratepayer and taxpayer at stake, money is no small consideration. Over time, Barns finds that costs will converge – but "not within the expected lifetime of the fence". As they say in the world of pinball, the basic message Barns delivers about the fence is: "Game Over—Tilt". Or if one prefers tennis, "Point, Game, Match". As a practical matter, Barns points out, the costs of maintaining a "pest-free zone" behind a "pest-proof fence" would be ongoing. If "eradication of the various animal species were to be chosen as the preferred option, reinvasion will be inevitable."[24] She concludes, "A pest proof fence is not cost effective at currently available fence establishment costs."[25]

It is abundantly clear the Waikato University report by Sandra Barns does little to advance the interests of DOC and EW and thoroughly undermines the ambitions of MEG. As a result, the study does not see the light of day. It is only by obtaining documents under the Official Information Act, that UCLA discovers the existence of this publicly funded study almost two years later.

But with the Barns report under wraps, the fence boosters carry on behind the scenes.

DOC Area Manager John Gaukrodger writes to MEG in August with his own comments on the Barns Report. "You cannot guarantee eradication of some species, just as you cannot guarantee re-invasion of some species. Reaching for the stars could invite failure that merely strengthens the arm of the skeptics. Little failures to learn by are fine. You cannot afford big ones. There is far too much at stake." He advises, "It is the job of the promoters/ supports to 'grow' the idea in the skeptics' and non-believers' minds over time. This process can be tiring and full of knock-backs. Some individuals will undoubtedly require some positive coaching and possibly a bit of a push." Gaukrodger knew of DOC's past negative community engagement on the issue but still concluded, "The report does not provide the answer". He does see a fence/ buffer possibility along with some "pest specific eradication and some pest specific sustained control."

MEG now organises a September meeting in Colville to share their vision of a "predator free zone". With cash a big challenge, the World Wildlife Fund and UN Biosphere Reserve are suggested as two possible funders of the otherwise cost-ineffective predator fence. Still questions persist and the community is far from convinced. On 27 October, DOC signs a Memorandum of Understanding with MEG giving the eco-entrepreneurs authority to operate on 40 percent of the land in the zone south of the DOC Moehau Kiwi Sanctuary. The agreement allows the use of DOC's all-terrain vehicles (ATVs), offers trapping and other record keeping on the DOC data base, and reasonable staff time to manage the information. The agreement is for an initial 12-month period.

MEG's December *Hochstetter* newsletter to members rhetorically asks the question whether "eradication is possible?" Answer: "Need eradication to make the fence option viable." Other concerns, questions and suggestions follow: "Traps can create trap-shy animals and if not positioned well can harm kiwi. Could create fur industry. Biogro have ok'd Talon if in fenced area. Concern among some people about *Silent Spring* scenario. What are the toxins and what effects do they have? e.g. possum dies in stream or rats getting eaten by birds…Advantage of Talon is that public can use without a license. Also that it takes out possums, rats, mice-and stoats, through secondary poisoning. There is concern of ongoing use in large quantities. Has residual effect so needs to be used strategically." The question of toxins and organic farms is mentioned as a "dilemma and will continue until alternative technology is found." The member newsletter warns the predator-free zone project "can fail if not 100% landowner support, therefore need for continuing consultation."

In the February *Hochstetter*, DOC's Waikato Conservator Greg Martin gives MEG a bit of support, thanking all those involved in the creation of another kiwi sanctuary south of the proposed Moehau predator free zone. Martin feels "the area has huge potential for World Heritage Site status, especially if it includes some of the closer off shore islands."

MEG's profile apparently needs boosting as some funding applications are denied. "It seems that to go for significant funding we'll need to get a little more professional in our approach. We have hired a graphic design group—Studio Kirsch—to help us with branding and (to) develop some consistency across everything from logo and t-shirts, to membership brochures and eventually our web-site."

The strategy pays off, because by July DOC hands over $12,000 from the Exacerbator Fund which means, according to the newsletter, "that MEG's partnership with EW's predator control programme—the 'Stage Three Key Ecological Site Predator Control on Private Land', is secured and on target." MEG members visit Maungatautari to check out the fence progress across the Waikato.[26] MEG members are oblivious to the fact that the Maungatautari Ecological Island Trust will prove to be a financially floundering operation, living on millions of ratepayer and taxpayer life-support dollars far into the future—and still home to pests.

2006 Out of the Frying Pan

*"A woman's dress should be like a barbed-wire fence:
serving its purpose without obstructing the view."*

Sophia Loren

The job of predator control has been central to MEG's vision and work since the group's inception, and bush work costs money. As summer peaks, committee members report new funding from EW and the Bank of New Zealand (BNZ) Kiwi Recovery Trust to support work in Colville, Little Bay and Tuateawa. Another grant supports two new hires for track cutting and trapping. Trapping expands in Kennedy Bay and Papa Aroha.

This is all good work. Trapping stoats is a sensible conservation tactic. Stoats cause kiwi deaths – as do dogs, transmitters and road traffic. Killing off stoats however pleases rats and mice that now have less competition when seeking to dine on eggs and chicks.

In March, the MEG coordinator's annual report details "significant gains…especially in the supportive relationships with regional and local council, and with the DOC…More formal partnership arrangements have been negotiated with government agencies, and a detailed operational and strategy plan for biodiversity enhancement is being drafted between MEG and DOC for the northern Coromandel. This covers three to five-year immediate operational funding requirements, and ten and fifty-year strategy planning for projected outcomes." Most importantly, according to this report, Environment Waikato is preparing to sign an agreement with MEG and DOC that explicitly includes the pest proof fence proposal. The idea of promoting a Biosphere Reserve philosophical approach to the project also has been well received.

But accurate information is not always guaranteed. The coordinator reports that, "Significant changes in the overall management of their own reserves has seen the MEG coordinator in an advisory role (together with two others) for TCDC Reserves in the northern Zone. The mayor is keen to promote the MEG vision…There has been an assurance from the mayor that new compliance procedures for restricting cats and dogs will be built into future subdivision developments…" The mayor of Thames-Coromandel District subsequently denies the coordinator's claim regarding new compliance procedures.

As for the really big money, the coordinator reports two organisations have registered interest in submitting for the full development of a business case suitable to attract "both local and offshore funders to invest upwards of $5 million into the projects long term. AgResearch and MWH New Zealand are both keen to look at aspects of the development. Boffa Miskell are also interested once they have seen the brief." AgResearch later refutes the published information and require for it to be corrected.

MEG has been working the cash register and, more recently has been maintaining a newsletter link with absentee landowners in Little Bay and making visits in Tuateawa and Waitete Bay—all well south of the planned pest free zone. Representatives of the Little Bay Ratepayers Association support the fence and hope it can be located further south to include their patches. Still absent from recorded interactions is the personal engagement with the people who would soon be fenced in at the top of the peninsula. Their views on the proposal are never properly heard. These families have not even been properly asked. But that would all change in a matter of weeks.

When the April 13 edition of the *Bay Beacon* newspaper hits letterboxes, everything changes for locals north of the steel barrier line. The provocative article (*Pest-Proof Fence Will Protect 20,000 Hectares of Land North of Colville*) in the Whitianga-based weekly is a red alert to those who will be expected to live and work inside the coast-to-coast fence. The concept is presented as if it were a done deal.

In its heady anticipation of final funding and with confidence in the clear support from their behind-the-scenes backers at DOC and EW, MEG leadership has unfortunately jumped the gun. While celebrating in print the backing of a majority of landowners over whose property the fence line would run, they have somehow forgotten to consider the need for support from the people who would be fenced in. Had the "face" of the pest proof fence plan heeded the advice of DOC management and their own Waikato University study they would have made the agreement with affected residents their number one priority.

Every journey has waypoints. Should one ignore beacons and lighthouses at sea, one can end up shipwrecked. On land, ignoring signs can, at the very least, cause accidents. Ignoring landowners north of the barrier would prove more than a stumbling block or minor accident. This major oversight in planning, whether through arrogance or misunderstanding, was destined to doom the whole project.

The Tables Turn

"Do not protect yourself by a fence, but rather by your friends."

Czech proverb

Within days, and as a direct response to the public announcement of the barrier fence fait accompli, the Upper Coromandel Landcare Association is formed. The group's formal petition and Statement of Opposition is addressed to government authorities and declares:

"There is considerable and growing community opposition by residents in the affected area. These landowners would find themselves fenced into a newly proclaimed, sprawling DOC/EW/ MEG pest-management zone with new regulations and risky, ad hoc environmental tampering. "Concerns include: 1) extremely high cost of construction and ongoing management; 2) likelihood of continued reinvasions; 3) the inevitable use of extremely toxic 1080 poison over roughly 18,000 ha of private and public lands; 4) eradication of wild pigs, which have been a well managed food and recreational resource for many generations; 5) unintended adverse environmental knock-on effects of eradication strategies; 6) lack of agreement on what constitutes a 'pest' in the first instance."

Residents who live on, manage, and steward more than 18,000 acres of the area that would have been fenced—more than 85 percent of the private land affected – put pen to paper in opposition. With letters to editors appearing in local papers, simmering opposition to the fence plan starts spilling out into the open.

Meanwhile over in Raglan, MEG's coordinator is in full damage control, telling a Waikato Biodiversity Forum meeting—funded by EW, that "it is much more effective to have a paid worker to liaise with funders and co-ordinate the work needed to be done. There are 750 landowners to obtain buy-in for the MEG project and one strong opposition group can hijack process. Lobby politicians and agencies—have politicians visit the site. Projects could come to a standstill if the community does not want it. If there is no community support funders are less likely to support the project."

A UCLA member addresses the regional council's North Zone Biosecurity subcommittee to point out that MEG is in no way representative of the large-block land owner/occupiers in the area, and EW should not consider its positive working relationship with MEG as a substitute for full public involvement and for formal consultation with affected landowners. Regional council subsequently decides not to fund a MEG grant for pest fence demonstration signage. It is starting to look like MEG is being hung out to dry by its former 'silent' partners. On May 30, UCLA's concerns are laid out for all to see in an opinion piece in the nation's main daily newspaper, the *New Zealand Herald*.

Bitter Battle Brews Over Fencing an Inland Island

The Coromandel is a favourite getaway for thousands of Aucklanders, Hamiltonians and overseas visitors. It's an iconic Kiwi paradise. But there is trouble brewing. The basis of it is "environmentalists versus environmentalists". On one side is the Moehau Environment Group (MEG), a Coromandel conservation organisation which is active in pest and predator control, environmental education, and habitat restoration projects in and around the Moehau Range. For that, it is well respected and has the support of most residents.

But many Coromandel people now feel that MEG has overstepped its bounds by promoting a controversial plan to create what would be New Zealand's largest "mainland island," a sprawling 18,000ha expanse of public and private property to be managed as a "predator-free zone".

The idea is to erect a predator-proof fence—a 2m high steel barrier stretching coast-to-coast from Colville on the west to Waikawau Bay on the east. Intensive efforts would then be undertaken north of the fence to eradicate all predators (cats, rats, stoats, weasels, possums), pests and "habitat destroyers" (goats, pigs and deer) so that native species could thrive and others be successfully reintroduced. But the prospect of being fenced in has long-time residents and landowners alarmed.

What's wrong with the fence? Don't we all want to see the bush recover along with kiwi, brown teal, frogs and other endangered native species? Aren't we all conservationists at heart? Of course we do, and of course we are. But the potential ramifications of a predator-free zone are only now coming into focus.

The toxin 1080 is at the heart of the issue. Eradication of target species cannot be accomplished in an area so vast without widespread use of 1080. Banned in most of the world and classified by the World Health Organisation as "1A, extremely hazardous", 1080 not only wipes out target species but poses an environmental threat of its own to people, pets and a broad spectrum of organisms.

In a report to the Combined North and South Biosecurity Advisory subcommittee on 10 November, the MEG coordinator reports: "Negotiations with the Mahana commune over 1080 use are progressing well as are negotiations with another group in the North." MEG is clearly working to promote 1080 use on private land, and DOC already uses it on public lands despite deep national division on the issue. Landowners in the projected zone expect further pressure for 1080 to be widely applied if a pest-free zone is fenced. There is little more alarming to environmentalists than 1080. In the words of one Port Charles farmer: "If they think they're coming anywhere near my family's water supply with 1080, they better think again." And a Coromandel beekeeper said: "There goes my organic honey business."

The traditional Coromandel wild-pork dinner is also in the crosshairs. Pigs do a fair bit of environmental damage, especially to the kiwi habitat, and most conservationists regard the pigs as pests. But wild pigs have been a well-managed resource for over a century here. Pig hunters can make noise when they want to, so MEG has given this species a wide berth. Pig hunters know, however, that in the projected complete eradication of feral pigs is not a question of "if", but of "when".The essential question is whether the proposal for a huge pest-free zone is actually feasible. There are fundamental obstacles, according to the only published extensive report on the proposal, a Waikato University study commissioned by MEG in 2004 and funded by Environment Waikato Regional Council. Unlike every other location where a pest-free zone has been attempted, the projected upper Coromandel "mainland island" includes many family homes and farms - with cats and dogs and stock - thousands of seasonal visitors and constant traffic.

One thing is for sure. Where people reside, there will be rats. Where people reside, they will want to have cats and dogs. Where there are pet cats, there will be feral cats. Where there are dogs, kiwi will be killed. So the only strategy will be to introduce regulations, obligations and restrictions binding on local residents and visitors alike, encumbering property and invading private rights. Already, as reported in a recent MEG newsletter, the Thames Coromandel District mayor has agreed that "new compliance procedures for restricting cats and dogs will be built into future subdivision developments, especially in those areas of intensive species protection - particularly kiwi".

Do we envisage a total ban on pet cats in this Coromandel "paradise"? Do we want every visitor's dog to be checked at a fenced Colville border to see if the animals have had kiwi and frog-aversion training? Will there be a cat amnesty bin for holidaymakers? And what about that seaside picnic that so many Auckland-area boaties enjoy? On a "mainland island" there would have to be binding restrictions on shore landings and tie-ups.

In the end, the no-pest vision is not feasible, unless they eradicate from the Coromandel the biggest pest of all—people. And there is the nagging problem of cost. Leaving aside construction and early-phase predator knockdown, the continuing costs of attempting to eradicate those last few rats, possums, stoats and cats would be huge. Further invasions would be inevitable. An army of trappers and baiters and monitors and taggers would be required. It would be a dream come true for bureaucrats at DOC and EW and funded full-timers at MEG. But the money can come only from a few places. One obvious place is further targeted rates for Coromandel residents and taxpayers at large.

Conservation-minded proponents of a "Free Upper Coromandel" are to voice their concerns to district and regional councils and their friends in the conservation movement. We all want to knock down possum numbers and protect our kiwi. At issue, though, is how to do it. We are asking DOC and EW to end their tacit support of the MEG fence plan.

We are saying, loudly and forcefully, "Don't Fence Us In."

On the same day, with the *New Zealand Herald* story in council hands, a UCLA delegation comprising Anne Ward, Theodora Ward, Reihana Robinson and Geoffrey Robinson travels south to the offices of Thames-Coromandel District Council. The Mayor and councillors hear the following presentation after receiving their copy of UCLA's Petition and Statement of Opposition by landowners and residents representing more than 7,500 hectares of the proposed fenced area.

UCLA Presentation to District Council

Rarely does an issue galvanise residents coast to coast. But the proposal to fence off the Upper Coromandel and create a so-called "mainland island" environmental management area has done just that. Opposition includes farming families who have lived in the northern Coromandel for generations. It includes farmers of stock and crops, both conventional and organic. Opposition extends from the proposed fence line at Colville right up the west coast to the tip at Port Jackson. It extends over the hills right up the east side to the tip of Port Charles. Opposition includes smallholding landowners as well. And it includes workers whose jobs depend on viable farm units. These residents have not been heard from previously on the fence and "mainland island" proposal. And why is that? Their views have not been heard because they have not been consulted. Landowners whose active support and participation would be absolutely essential have not been asked whether or not they want to be drawn into such a scheme. They have not been surveyed as to their opinions on the use of 1080 poison on and near their land. They have not been asked whether new regulations, legal obligations, and restrictions would adversely impact upon their operations or property values.

No one has asked whether they would favour expenditure of vast sums of public funds on fence construction and endless years of ongoing management and whether they would favour additional targeted rates to fund it. They haven't been asked whether eradication of wild pigs would be a loss of a traditional resource. And despite their combined centuries of practical life experience managing animals and plants in a natural environment, they have not been asked whether, in fact, the whole idea of a pest and predator-free "mainland island" inhabited by scores of family and farm units with their stock and pets, hundreds of seasonal residents, and thousands of visitors is even remotely feasible.

Thames Coromandel District Council is hereby advised that the people most affected and who live, work and own land in the zone, vigourously oppose the fence plan going forward. These signatures are being forwarded to you as mayor because TCDC has been in discussions with proponents of the plan and because TCDC's support and cooperation would be required for the plan to proceed, including foremost the granting of rights-of-way for construction of the fence and implementation of various new policies. Council is urged to respect this broad and unequivocal public opposition by not making any commitments of public resources that facilitate the plan and by not implementing any policies that advance or support the plan.

Anne Ward, representing generations of farming families on the peninsula's northwest coast, pens the following letter on June 9:

Predator Fence Too Disruptive:

Contrary to the reports in last week's Hauraki Herald, there has been opposition to the predator proof fence since it was suggested, mainly because the idea is not soundly based, and also now is not recommended by the Waikato University report. Incidentally, a previous fence was planned and abandoned in the early 1990's. Mr Todd's statement that the fence proposal had full community support is not correct, and his survey to gauge support was carried out without the knowledge of our particular community. If you selectively survey some people and exclude others you can get the result you want! Having clarified these matters, may I emphasise that MEG's efforts to control predators by trapping and use of cyanide poison are applauded. However if they want to erect a predator proof fence perhaps they should ring fence their own properties. Fencing off the northern peninsula would be too disruptive to the many visitors and to the lives and businesses of those who would be fenced in rather than the predators fenced out.

Opposition to the fence is by no means universal. MEG has its supporters, and some come free of their moorings. Leonie Campbell of Colville suggests in a letter to the editor published June 23 that the UCLA spokesperson "goes to live elsewhere where she can enjoy the zoo-like atmosphere of goats, possums, stoats and rats south of Coromandel if she cant cope with the menagerie of birds we can now enjoy thanks to DOC and MEG."

Oh dear…

Meanwhile, residents start to sniff out the big money that is at stake for MEG. Many millions will be required to grade land, install and maintain such a contraption. The money has to come from somewhere, and ratepayers are the obvious sitting ducks.

In response to an Official Information Act request, UCLA receives a memo documenting an EW grant request for a whopping $1.2 million in relation to the fence proposal.[27] Once this figure is exposed, it is vigorously denied. Faced with the million-dollar embarrassment, MEG's backers at EW start to back and fill. A local weekly publishes *Mystery Memo Raises Fence Questions*, quoting senior council manager John Simmons.

"Someone has made a mistake. The document appears to have been generated through DOC, but my guess is there has been a mix up. I understand there was a grant of $12,000 applied for from EW, and the only explanation I can think of is that someone has read this wrong and put $1.2 million…I have never seen this memo and I am disturbed my name is on it. It is a bit of a mystery." From a senior government official, an explanation more lame and unsatisfactory would be hard to find. But money has been loose at EW and DOC and, after all, what difference is a million here or there…if ratepayers will be picking up the tab.

The prospect of a fence, however, still looms for anyone living north of Colville. That is because an actual section of Xcluder Pest Company's two-metre high steel barrier had been erected as a public display with promotional signage, on public land at the junction of Port Jackson and Port Charles roads just north of Colville. For some, this stick-in-the-eye is simply too much. UCLA lodges objections with the Coromandel-Colville Community Board and Thames-Coromandel District Council to the purely commercial use of council land for advertising Xcluder products and promoting a divisive and controversial private project. The TCDC manager in charge of roadside property cannot remember who made the request for placement of the fence display. Nor can he find any correspondence on the matter. The council's chief executive agrees to request removal of the large fence specimen. Then one winter night, it happens. While residents wait for TCDC to dismantle the fence display, someone does the job for them. As daylight breaks, the big green section of pest fence lies neatly on the ground, its supporting wood posts sawn low and clean. No culprit is found.

Angry charges fly. Port Charles Forest & Bird, in the *Hauraki Herald*, accuses UCLA of cutting down the sample fence. Having nothing to do with the vandalism, UCLA is offered an immediate retraction by editor Lee Foote. "*Hauraki Herald* apologises to the Association for any implication contained in an article on Friday. It was never our intention to imply any involvement by the Association…there is nothing to link the two and we would like to apologise." In retrospect, the night the fence went down may have marked the definitive beginning of the end.

With division rife in the community, MEG coordinator Todd admitted, "If there really is overwhelming opposition, then of course if could never work." And in a simple indication of where things were headed, he added, "We are not married to the concept."

Damage Control 2006

*After you have exhausted what there is in business,
politics, conviviality, and so on—have found that none of
these finally satisfy, or permanently wear - what remains?
Nature remains.*

Walt Whitman

Winter is not a happy time for fence planners. There is a chance that
years of behind-the-scenes planning and promotional groundwork
could be going up in smoke. DOC gets into gear to help struggling
MEG with damage control. Now that opposing views are gaining
traction, it is time for the big guns at the Waikato Conservancy in
Hamilton to assist with some professional public relations. Only
DOC does not want to be identified and certainly not seen as the
source of inchoate propaganda.[28]

On June 28, DOC begins its attempt to duck and cover. Amy
Hinaki, at the behest of Alisdair Craig and Greg Martin, writes
to MEG committee member Pim de Monchy advising, "It would
be more appropriate for this correspondence to be forwarded
to MEG from you." Mr de Monchy is given some coaching and
"key messages for inclusion in any membership or press release."
Alisdair Craig is Mr Public Relations—make that Community
Relations Manager, for DOC Hamilton. A bit of double-speak
would be helpful, and DOC suggests such verbal gymnastics
as, "MEG's stance on 1080 is neutral, with the group neither
advocating for nor protesting against its use."

The 1080 talking point is delicate, given widespread
opposition to the supertoxin throughout the Coromandel. But it
is a particularly thorny issue for MEG right now, since minutes
of the November 2005 EW Northern Zone Biosecurity Advisory
Subcommittee meeting quote MEG coordinator Wayne Todd as
saying, "Negotiations with the Mahana commune over 1080 use
are progressing well, as are negotiations with another group in
the North." Todd is caught out again as seconder to a committee
resolution to prepare "a submission *in support of* continued use of
1080" (emphasis added). As the 1080 issue erupts in public, the

Hauraki Herald quotes the MEG spokesperson saying, "It would be so bloody stupid for MEG to be seen promoting 1080; We are neutral on the use of 1080 and oppose aerial 1080..." The article suggests he had been in shock from the UCLA campaign against the fence. "It went completely out of my head at that stage; However, I am endeavouring to get it [the minutes] changed.'"

What is to be done? MEG's fulltime paid coordinator is caught promoting controversial toxin 1080 behind closed doors, while publicly denying it. So MEG committee member (and DOC employee) de Monchy is left to pass along spin from DOC headquarters such as: "These minutes were unfortunately mis-recorded but have remained confirmed. There is regret at the discomfort that this has caused. The group accepts that until each animal pest is eradicated it may be necessary to use toxins to control populations in key places...The group aims to discuss the issues with landowners north of the proposed fence line once a secure and feasible route has been finalised."

That final sentence is icing on the cake. Only *after* the fence route is signed and sealed will the landowners most affected be invited to "discuss their issues."

Meanwhile, DOC Waikato public relations staff are turning up the steam. They prepare a page of *True/False* statements that is reproduced by MEG and hand-delivered to area letterboxes. With credibility and transparency now an issue, MEG itself is in the headlights. Listed under *True*:

> *MEG neither supports, promotes nor discourages the use of 1080. MEG maintains a neutral stance on 1080,*

> *Landowners continue to have pet cats and dogs in the area. No attempt has been made to stop these landowners from having them,*

> *The Barns report (cost analysis) was funded through a $10,000 grant from the [DOC] Biodiversity Fund and a further $1,500 from private funds. EW provided a top up of $3,500 to cover cost overruns.*

In an effort to clarify the group's murky relationship with DOC and EW, suggested key messages for inclusion in any membership or press release are the following: "MEG is a non-profit, non-governmental, voluntary organization of 150 members aiming to carry out and support conservation activities within the working landscape that is the northern Coromandel. The group accepts that until each animal pest is eradicated it may be necessary to use toxins to control populations in key places." Obviously, toxin 1080 is one of those necessary toxins! With the fence project coming apart at the seams, DOC offers to act as facilitator "to explore possible alternatives", as they are "comfortable with MEG's proposal based on our experience of similar successful projects such as Maungatautari…" (see *Appendic I*)

But while DOC offers a helping hand, files received by UCLA in response to Official Information requests indicate the department might rather back off the project entirely to protect its own interests. "The Department has taken a neutral stand in respect of the fence…The issue is principally one for MEG to address. A partition *(sic)* against the proposal is presently running and has most of the significant landholders who have dealings with the Department as signatories. The Hauraki Area Manager is aware of this partition *(sic)* and will be developing strategies to position the Department appropriately with this group."

DOC notes the "wave of discontent mounting in opposition to the fence from various landowners. The Department has become partially implicated in this issue as two of our local staff members are also members of MEG…There is a risk of a conflict of interest between our local staff involved in the Moehau Kiwi Zone project, and the greater project of MEG's sanctuary." In fact, UCLA has publicly raised concerns with the Waikato Conservancy that a senior DOC project manager in the Moehau area (de Monchy) is also serving as a spokesperson and committee member for a private not-for-profit interest group (MEG) that is actively promoting a controversial project (the fence) in the area and receiving DOC funds. de Monchy subsequently states he will be relinquishing his "voting rights" on the MEG committee at the next meeting, having noted concerns about his conflict of interest.

Waikato Conservator Greg Martin appears to further distance the department from the Coromandel fence fiasco. In a letter to Geoffrey Robinson of UCLA, Martin states the Department is "not responsible for the fence proposal." However, in his response to Martin, Robinson takes issue with that and seeks to set the record straight on DOC's role with the fence project from the start.

> *While the predator-proof fence project has been on its face an undertaking of the Moehau Environment Group, DOC has been active in supporting the project from the start and in directing MEG's promotional efforts. In reality, the MEG group functions as a 'proxy' or 'front group' for DOC, ostensibly making the fence proposal a 'community-driven' rather than 'DOC-driven' plan. This is critical since DOC has failed twice previously*

in 1983 and 1992 to push forward fence plans for Moehau. The Department does not enjoy a positive image among long-time landowners and residents as a result, and any revival of such a DOC-sponsored plan would be viewed with little other than disdain. Wholly apart from the funding which DOC provides to MEG and the granting of access to conservation land for MEG programmes, DOC has assisted MEG by providing DOC-paid display sites at field days for MEG use to actively promote its fence plan. DOC also allowed MEG to erect and maintain a predator-proof fence display barrier on DOC land at Waikawau since December 2005. DOC has further facilitated the fence plan by provisionally agreeing to allow construction of the actual fence on public DOC land at Waikawau, despite residents' opposition.

Proving definitively that DOC has in fact been orchestrating and promoting the fence plan from behind the scenes, residents have just last week been shocked to learn that DOC Area Manager John Gaukrodger has been actually advising MEG Coordinator Wayne Todd on a strategy to promote the fence plan. Gaukrodger's letter includes general advice on how to advance the fence idea. Landowners are now appalled that, while DOC has been publicly maintaining that the fence plan has not been its own, Mr. Gaukrodger has advised that 'Some individuals will undoubtedly require some positive coaxing and possibly a bit of a push.' Mr Gaukrodger summarises DOC's commitment to the fence by identifying the need 'to advance the strategic planning that is now required.' His letter is full of advice on how to avoid actions that 'strengthen the arm of the sceptics.' He advises on how best to carry out 'the job of the promoters/supporters.' Rather, what is required is for DOC and MEG to accept that the people most affected by the fence plan are the most opposed, and unequivocally so. The fence plan simply cannot work. You make reference in your letter to 'polarising the community.' The community is indeed polarised on the fence issue. Largely, this is as a result of both DOC and MEG plainly over-stepping their bounds. MEG is a private environmental advocacy group. Nevertheless, it acts publicly as if it is a quasi-governmental agency, making public statements about what 'will' and what 'will not' be public policy in their projected eco-managemenet zone. That there is polarisation is undeniable. What DOC can do now to ameliorate this polarisation is to rediscover its independence from MEG, get back to its primary job of protecting the public conservation estate, work cooperatively with farming families and stop 'working around' them. The first order of business is for DOC and its proxy MEG to call a halt to the doomed plan to build the fence.

Further documents received by UCLA via the OIA process include *The Proactive Plan Regarding the Predator-Proof Fence— Objectives for Managing the Issue,* wherein DOC's Hauraki area office indicates it is "moving to separate itself from this community based project." In July, the local DOC office publishes what will be manager John Gaukrodger's final, somewhat contradictory, *Around the Traps* community newsletter. The message is a strange combination of regretful swan song, parental "tut tut", and General MacArthur's famous "I Shall Return."

> *The Whenuakite possum/rat control operation and the Moehau predator proof fence idea have captured the headlines across the Peninsula. In both instances the real activity generated is coming from **just a couple of people**. At Maugatautari obviously close to everyone is "behind" the fence. The same cannot be said for Moehau. Without a detailed cost benefit analysis, any position on the pros and cons of a Predator Proof Fence proposal are premature. A key element of any analysis will be a potential route that a fence might follow, along with a significant number of other factors requiring consideration. This information would provide for objective consideration of a fence idea by all parties, and a more reasoned way forward. Ultimately this proposal requires community support and a positive cost benefit analysis. In the meantime the people of Maungatautari are "stealing a march" on Moehau to the social, economic and environmental well being of their area. In ten years Maungatautari could replace Moehau at the top of the list... [added emphasis]*[25]

Gaukrodger appears unaware that professional planners charged with determining the final fence route for the Maungatautari Ecological Island considered inclusion of even a single farm unit within the fence perimeter to be too risky even though considerable construction and maintenance money could be saved by shortening the fence and including that farm. It was decided the single farm in question had to be excluded, regardless of cost, for the project to enjoy any chance of ultimate success. Furthermore, Maungatautari is a reserve where access is gated and controlled and where, in many instances, even tramper backpacks are inspected. That the Moehau fence proposal was even remotely comparable to unpopulated Maungatautari is preposterous.

Looking back a year later, Gaukrodger would still be refusing to admit the central role his organisation had played commenting the department (Hauraki Area) had not expressed support for the Moehau fence proposal because there had been no clear cost/ benefit analysis done. Apparently "transparency" was the key to all staff involvement in community projects. Environment Waikato regional council is also seen to be running away from the Moehau pest fence debacle, and just like DOC, leaving their good mates at MEG to holding the bag.

On July 7, the Hamilton daily *Waikato Times* (*WT*) publishes an opinion piece headlined *A Great Donkey of an Idea* by UCLA writer

Geoffrey Robinson. In response, local EW Councillor Arthur Hinds incorrectly remarks (July 14 *WT*) "the regional council has not taken a position" on the proposal to build a controversial pest-excluding steel fence across the northern Coromandel Peninsula. Robinson responds to Hinds on July 25 (*WT*) as follows:

"Nothing could be further from the truth. EW has been working actively behind the scenes to push the fence project ahead, and Mr. Hinds is either sadly misinformed or otherwise unable to level with the public now that the plan has blown up amidst a wave of public opposition. According to internal EW correspondence, 'EW have been working with Moehau Environment Group to help them develop the fence project.' Furthermore, a grant application prepared by EW's Strategic Development Manager supporting ratepayer funding for the fence states that the application 'should be seen as a precursor to a desire for greater Environment Waikato involvement with MEG and the fence project.'

Earlier this year, an EW manager reported that the success of an expensive EW goat eradication programme was, in fact, dependent on construction of the fence. Mr. Hinds would be well advised to read his own council's materials lest he continue to mislead the ratepayer in the future."

Arthur Hinds loses his councillor seat at the next local body election.

In August, John Veysey of the 309 Road addresses a letter to everyone involved with UCLA on the "right side" of the fence, " just to reassure you that you have a huge amount of support from 'south of the border'. Having battled DOC's aerial 1080 since 1994, we know what you're up against BUT you have every chance of success in your endeavour against the fence." This would be UCLA's introduction to the indomitable and courageous Veysey, who has worked tirelessly to rid Papatuanuku of toxins in our wilderness and back yards. Scientists and farmers Quinn and Pat Whiting-O'Keefe of Port Charles write in the Whitianga weekly *Bay Beacon*.

At the core of whether the upper Coromandel landowners should be fenced in by the Moehau environment group, EW and DOC proposal (opposed by 85% of the to-be-enclosed land) are the alleged environmental benefits. Notwithstanding the specious, ad hominum attack on Reihana Robinson by L. Gamble (July 27), the MEG projects have been of dubious (and certainly undocumented) benefit to the environment. Indeed, there is considerable circumstantial evidence that some have been harmful. MEG,

DOC and EW funding has repeatedly meddled in Port Charles' complex ecosystem without adequate forethought, proper scientific underpinnings, or scientifically competent scrutiny. These efforts (however well meaning) have been amateurish, expensive and environmentally irresponsible.

For example, four years ago MEG and DOC began trapping feral cats in Port Charles to support DOC's pateke introduction programme (a farce anyway since pateke interbreed freely with mallards). The results were predictable and obvious: massive explosion in rabbit and rat populations, possibly mustelids as well, and probably collateral damage to native species. Predictably, the cats eventually became trap-shy and the prey species populations consequently reverted. We are left with a healthy population of smart cats, a traumatized ecosystem and ongoing payments to MEG principals to trap feral cats.

One cannot witness such fiascos without doubting assertions of ecological benefit by the same triumverate (DOC, EW and MEG) for the current multimillion-dollar, publicly funded fence proposal that ignores their own commissioned independent study, the conclusion of which doubted both the efficacy and cost-effectiveness of the fence.

In the August *Coromandel Town Chronicle*, UCLA publishes its monthly report and fence *post mortem*.

Meg-a-bucks on Moehau

The "pest-proof fence" proposal for the upper Coromandel has received a resounding and definitive "NO" from the people who would be "fenced-in".

The fence is officially dead. Not because promoters will admit it. Not because their own research shows it to be unfeasible. It's dead because residents on 85% of the private lands involved don't want it. Initial reaction to the groundswell of landowner opposition started with the time-worn "shoot the messenger" response from MEG fence promoters, accusing those who do not agree with them of being "downright malicious", and claiming that well-reasoned concerns are merely the result of "misinformation". Their dismissive response reflected a fundamental lack of respect for farming families and other concerned residents who have lived in some cases for generations on the land MEG seeks for a new eco-management zone. In the last month, initial panic at fence headquarters has turned to denial. This is understandable. The wheels have come off a scheme that otherwise had the potential to be a significant money-spinner from both corporate and government sources. And a flurry of revised statements in the press sadly indicates that MEG intends to keep their doomed fence plan on life support.

How ironic it was to hear in June from MEG coordinators that now, after the fence plan has been rejected, that MEG hopes to seek out the views of those same landowners. Is it not just a wee bit condescending to be told by fence promoters that opponents of the fence simply need more and better information? The assurance from the MEG coordinator that his group intends to "allow landowners to make up their own minds" is surprisingly arrogant. Excuse us, but those same landowners have already made up their own minds…without getting MEG's permission! It is high time for predator barrier planners to listen to the people and not lecture the people. It is also time to stop the backtracking and denials on cats, on pigs, on 1080 and more. Truthfulness is critical. It's time to close the "credibility gap", recently underscored by the embarrassing "Case of the Mistaken 1080 Minutes". A quick review of the issues shows why landowners are concerned about a fenced-in future. The 2004 Waikato University report states that the barrier's two-metre height is only necessary so as to exclude cats. MEG's web site highlights pigs as a prime "habitat destroyer" and species to be eradicated in so-called "mainland islands." While they now deny these species are part of their plan, residents would seem to have good reason to be worried.

*As for concerns about increasing pressure for use of aerial 1080, are residents "misinformed" when the official DOC web site states Hauraki DOC area manager John Gaukrodger "would like to mount an aerial operation over Moehau? MEG insists it is officially "neutral on 1080". That keeps them out of the 1080 "hot seat". After all, you only have to be "neutral" when your main supporters with all the money and power (DOC and EW) are vigourously pro-1080 and can be counted on to force aerial drops on a divided public when push comes to shove.**

And when it comes to the possibility of additional rating demands connected with what was reported (March 2006 MEG annual report) to be a $5 million project: we've only seen the beginning. EW previously funded in part a fence feasibility study. Even now as this issue of the Chronicle goes to press, EW is considering yet another grant request from the group —an $11,982 handout to pay for future fence signage complete with $2,850 of dollars for "supervision" expertise. Already we have the public's money being funneled to the group for its fence plan. When the numbers are in the millions, might ratepayers expect to foot more of the bill? And with a multi-million dollar "investment" (the fence) to protect, is it not likely that landowners and visitors alike would be faced with all manner of new regulations, legal obligations and restrictions to support evolving pest control and eradication strategies? Of course it is. In responding to "fence" opponents, MEG has brushed off all these messy concerns. But who are they to tell us what regional government might or might not do in the future in a newly created environmental management zone? Who are they to assure us what policies DOC will or will not adopt in the future? Who are they to claim that all sorts of activities, from boat landings and campgrounds to bach ownership and permissible farming practices, will not be affected? Even government officials themselves would never and could never make such assurances as to the future.

Is MEG some new form of quasi-government agency? Will they be making environmental and pest-management policy for the Coromandel? Is MEG a proxy for DOC and EW? Surely MEG has nurtured a comfortable symbiotic working and financial relationship with EW and DOC. But did we somehow miss an amendment to the Local Government Act? Did we misplace a page of our last local body election ballots? We don't think so, even if that's what it is sounding like. So where do we go from here? Realising its fence proposal is dead MEG now assures us that it is working to develop yet another feasibility study. Luckily for all of us local residents, we do not have to wait for the results. We can be assured that MEG will arrange for the most favourable feasibility study money can buy! A few things will not change, of course, no matter who does the study. Financial projections that go out 30 years can hardly be substantiated…they are little more than guesswork. Total eradication without reinvasion of predator species is impossible (Barns report P 67). There is no guarantee on projected fence lifetime…and any such "guarantee" would be worth little more than the paper written on (Barns report P 51). Rules and regulations associated with a "predator-free zone" can change at the whim of the government…anytime.

MEG appears unable to let go of its big fence plan and with good reason. With a price tag in the millions, the cash flow to this outwardly "volunteer" community group will be massive. Creaming off thousands in "administrative" payments from each grant to pay $65 per hour MEG coordinator pay packets while "volunteer" overseas and local troopers tramp the bush is the name of the game. If financial projections for the fence turn out to be wrong, no worries—MEG gets its money. If the fence turns out to be ineffective in stopping predator reinvasions—no worries, MEG gets its money. If the fence lasts for 30 years as advertised, MEG gets its money. If it rusts after 10 years, MEG gets its money. With an upfront investment in massive hardware, there is hardly any way for this particular strategy to be amended or fine-tuned as circumstances change or as better information becomes available. MEG, DOC and EW get locked in to the fence plan and residents get fenced into their homes and pick up the tab. While no one begrudges a little eco-entrepreneurship and the ability to bring available conservation money into the area, the endless cycle of grant-grabbing, branding, packaging and business strategy planning can lead to an organization increasingly out of touch with the very community it purports to represent. Fortunately when objections surfaced, MEG said "We are not married to the concept" and "If there really is overwhelming opposition then of course it could never work." MEG has been presented with just such opposition. People have listened, considered, and made up their minds. MEG, DOC and EW have been told loudly and clearly, "We don't want to be fenced in." So now we see DOC in the wings, preparing its own exit strategy, now that they realise MEG is no barometer of community opinion. Wittingly or unwittingly MEG has been used as a front group for an old, worn-out, impractical DOC plot. MEG, DOC and EW need to publicly and clearly abandon the "pest-proof fence" project now. Not to be "revisited" in a year or two. Not pending further feasibility studies—but clearly and definitively. The *"predator-proof fence" project should be left for what it was…a well-intentioned but unworkable and unfeasible idea. But despite the fact that this project was not meant to be, we do think that great strides can be made on a variety of environmental initiatives if we seek out common ground and work together. On this, we are truly on "the same side of the fence."*

On a lighter note, UCLA creates a simple and entertaining test for readers of the *Chronicle*.

Test Your
Pest-Proof Preparedness!

The Upper Coromandel Landcare Association asks you to please take a few minutes to complete this easy multiple-choice test to see whether you and your family are prepared for a "Fenced-In Future" on the northern Coromandel. Remember…When it comes to being "fenced in" we're all in this together!!

When a local environment group gives firm public assurances as to future policies and regulations in a "Pest-Free Zone", it is able to do so because it is a:
    a) new government agency
    b) professional fortune-telling group
    c) front group for DOC and EW
    d) a little birdie told them!!

According to an extensive 2004 University of Waikato feasibility study of the proposed "Predator-Proof Fence", where eradication of a pest species is the chosen option, reinvasion will be:
    a) impossible
    b) a one-in-a-million chance
    c) unthinkable
    d) inevitable

A 2004 fence strategy memo from the DOC area manager to the head of a local environmental group (uncovered as part of an Official Information Act request this July) advised that fence "skeptics" and residents opposed to the idea of a "predator-proof fence" will need:
    a) 1080 in their plonk
    b) to be forceably removed from their properties
    c) re-education in special environmental gulags
    d) "some positive coaxing and possibly a bit of a push"

Which household pet, despite being a known predator of native birds, have we been assured will not "be taken off us" in a newly defined "Predator-Free Zone":
  a) canary
  b) alligator
  c) Tele-Tubby
  d) domestic cat

A local environment group will receive its "administrative" and "management" fee payments for construction and maintenance of the "predator-proof fence" if the fence:
  a) lasts for at least 30 years
  b) rusts unexpectedly after only12 years
  c) proves completely ineffective against pest reinvasions
  d) all of the above

Which valuable recreational resource identified as a "habitat destroyer", do predator-proof fence promoters absolutely, positively, cross-their-hearts, no interest whatsoever, never, ever plan to eradicate now or in the future…promise…:
  a) pheasants
  b) rabbits
  c) freshwater eels
  d) wild pigs

A two-metre high, steel mesh barrier from water's edge at Colville to water's edge at Waikawau would be:
  a) aesthetically pleasing
  b) a jewel in the Coromandel tiara
  c) paid for without any public funds
  d) none of the above

In a new "Predator-Free Zone", increased use of aerial 1080 (banned in most of the world) would be:
  a) the last thing on anyone's mind
  b) unnecessary…possums would just die of fright
  c) risk-free and beneficial for biodiversity
  d) none of the above

If a "Predator-Free Zone" is fenced off, there will never, ever, ever be any need to regulate boat landings, household pets, wild pigs, goat farming, campgrounds, farm activities or anything else, because:
  a) well, there just won't
  b) the people will be outlawed first
  c) all the wild animals and predators will just leave of their
     own accord
  d) the fence will likely rust and we'll just start all over again

If the "predator-proof fence" proves ineffective, who still gets paid to administer the failed project?
    a) Environment Waikato
    b) DOC
    c) Moehau Environment Group
    d) all of the above

When a fulltime Coromandel DOC employee sits as a voting committee member of an environment group to which DOC gives public money, it is a:
    a) blatant conflict of interest
    b) obvious conflict of interest
    c) mutual back-scratching exercise
    d) business as usual

When a "volunteer" environment group stands to cream off hundreds of thousands of conservation grant dollars for "supervision" and "administration", it is a:
    a) dream come true
    b) cash cow to be milked for years
    c) best thing since sliced rewena
    d) all of the above

Self-appointed "volunteer" groups know better than long-time farming families about the natural environment and pest management because:
    a) they have broadband access and the farmers don't
    b) farmers just know about sheep and cows
    c) well, they just do
    d) whoops, maybe they don't after all

What do you do if your group's own feasibility study shows your pest-proof fence plan is not feasible?
    a) bury the report for two years
    b) spin the bad results as best you can
    c) commission the most favourable study money can buy
    d) all of the above

Who wrote last month's Coro Chronicle/community mail-out "true-false" fact sheet for MEG?
    a) a Pirate of the Caribbean
    b) MEG's chairperson
    c) DOC's Coromandel manager
    d) DOC's Community Relations Manager based in Hamilton

What group has applied for a mind-blowing $1,200,000 handout from Environment Waikato?
    a) Colville Tennis Club
    b) Coromandel Yoga Freestylers
    c) Fantail Bay Pig-Busters
    d) Moehau Environment Group

$81,000 a year for the part-time MEG coordinator is justified because:

    a) it's hard yakker—those boring meetings
    b) the grant merry-go-round makes you dizzy
    c) community consultation deserves hazard pay
    d) it's hard work bossing around the real volunteers

To be eligible for this month's grand "Predator-Proof Prize", send answers no later than August 7, 2036 (after completion of long-term toxicity surveys and fence-deterioration dates) to: Upper Coromandel Landcare Association, RD4 Port Charles, Coromandel. Readers with the most correct answers will be in a draw for a fabulous "Wild Animal Pack", including a pair of possum fur nipple warmers, a pair of kiwi down slippers, wild pig-tusk earrings, a feral goat black-powder horn, and special domestic cat euthanasia kit. Good luck and good night!

Gone But Not Forgotten

"Do unto those downstream as you would have those upstream do unto you."

Wendell Berry

Within weeks, the Moehau fence is publicly abandoned. Left on their own to make a convincing case for the "pest free zone" – and the big spend to fund it – MEG leaders are simply not up to the job. And forced to pick up their fence and go home it doesn't take long for MEG's blame game to get underway.

An obtuse August 22 *Hauraki Herald* headline says it all: *Opposition Cans Pest Proof Fence.* "Promoters say an 'unfair fight' has felled the proposed 8km pest proof fence...the brainchild of the Moehau Environment Group...they made the 'heartbreaking' decision to can the fence after a battle that got 'too ugly'..." The *Hauraki Herald* also publishes a letter by DOC staffer Mike Donoghue now believes UCLA has a "mean-spirited attitude... and now its display of a smug sense of satisfaction at having derailed a bold initiative to protect Moehau's unique biodiversity." In the weekly *Bay Beacon*, MEG's coordinator complains that unfair accusations have meant no funding organisations will look at the project.

In the regional *Waikato Times*, meanwhile, the MEG leader reportedly complains again that "the fight" was unfair. "UCLA wouldn't talk to us, so we were not given the chance to discuss their concerns. Instead they went through the media with information that was not always accurate." Nowhere is any inaccuracy cited. Nor did residents consider the matter a fight.[30]

Through the autumn and winter of 2006 no substantive response had ever been offered to objections from the community. The Moehau fence project clearly died of its own defects. As explained by UCLA in the *Waikato Times*, "Fence proponents could not make their case because that case was fatally flawed from the start. And no surprise they buried their own feasibility study when it showed the project likely could not succeed as envisaged...In practical terms, a predator-free 'mainland island' that includes working farms, hundreds of households and pets, and thousands of visitors and vehicles is unrealistic. Nowhere has such a plan succeeded. Predator fences do not work where people live. Organisers, who stood to benefit financially, could offer no reasoned responses to well-founded community concerns regarding increased aerial 1080 use, regulations and restrictions affecting farmers and other residents, ongoing high costs, and unintended environmental consequences. In four years, they succeeded only in convincing the public that their idea was a costly and risky mistake. Environmentally concerned residents support workable, practical, affordable, sensible and safe conservation practice."

Several peninsula observers put the debacle down to other causes. Purangi resident Bill Axbey observed in the *Times*, "People woke up to what was going to happen... It was an expensive experiment, a huge waste of money for something quite unproven." Axbey said most people in favour of the fence lived outside the proposed area. Whenuakite farmer Arthur Attfield was relieved the fence had been scrapped. He said landowners were concerned "there was a wider agenda." Axbey, however, also sounds a cautionary note. In an unpublished letter provided to UCLA, the former DOC conservator warns, "Having won the day, my suggestion is you gracefully ease out of arguments with the losers but keep a wary eye open for the next try. It will be sure to come in one form or another."

In a further hint of things to come he adds, "One thing I have learnt in my many years of tilting at bureaucracy and stupidity is that you should always wear your old clothes and gum boots if you go out to fight for your rights and freedoms as the amount of crap you have to wade and fight your way through is unbelievable. For my money the Upper Coromandel Landcare Association had thigh waders and wet suits. My advice is to give them a wash but don't throw them away as hell has no fury like a bureaucrat scorned."

Bill Axbey has hit the nail on the head. In a *New Zealand Herald* article just weeks later, DOC ecologist de Monchy reaffirms the long-term agenda. "We still have a long way to go before any proposed pest-proof fence becomes a reality. DOC *supports its erection* because of its potential value in pest control. We're working with Environment Waikato and MEG on a ten-year conservation plan for the Moehau area. (*emphasis added*)

And MEG won't give it up either. In the September issue of local Colville newsletter *Panui*, MEG states it "will no longer actively pursue their Pest Proof Fence project just north of Colville. However, MEG still believes that the fence is potentially the best tool with the current technology, for achieving the vision of a possum, mustelid and feral goat-free environment in the northern Coromandel." A subsequent multi-year grant application to DOC to "attack rats" on private Port Charles land confirmed the fence project's heart was still beating. "The long-term goal of MEG is to have Moehau as a Pest Free Zone". Once again for the uninitiated…a Pest Free Zone means a Pest Proof Fence.

As for plans to revive the pest proof fence, UCLA writes its September *Coromandel Chronicle* report:

Residents of the upper Coromandel have learned that the plan to construct a coast-to-coast steel pest barrier and create a sprawling 18,000 ha eco-management zone north of Colville is on hold. However, they are aware that fence proponents at MEG have been careful not to abandon the fence plan. To most people, "not at this time" means "maybe some other time." MEG's public statement indicates that the group still feels the fence is the best way to go. Residents are also keenly aware that the Department of Conservation and Environment Waikato Regional Council have remained silent on the fence issue and, presumably, are ready to support it again. Both agencies are formally on the record as supporting the MEG fence plan, and neither has made any official statement to alter or amend that support, despite requests to do so. While MEG was the group which, for the last four years, publicly advanced the plan to fence off Moehau, long-time residents know that the plan was attempted by DOC twice previously (in 1982 and 1993-4) and DOC was forced to pull the plug. Local families rejected the idea both times when put forward by government bureaucrats. But this time was different. This time, DOC had a so-called "community group" to front the plan and push it ahead. For most people, it is comfortable, when required, to challenge government bureaucrats on controversial policies such as a predator barrier enclosing thousands of hectares of farmland that has as its goal eradication of non-indigenous animal life. It is extremely uncomfortable, however, to challenge a policy when it is presented by well-intentioned but misguided neighbours whose other work many may have supported. The puppet-puppeteer approach seemed to work well for MEG and DOC – until recently. With government behind it, MEG could take the credit for advancing a seemingly good idea and benefit from a large cash flow of public and private monies for administration. When fund-raising and grant seeking, MEG could say it had the full support of DOC. When challenged on messy issues like the increased 1080 use required for the plan, however, MEG could sidestep the issue and leave DOC to take the heat. Meanwhile, from behind the scenes, a senior Coromandel DOC manager would sit as a voting committee member of MEG to help direct the activity. And DOC's Hauraki area manager would write detailed strategy advice to the MEG coordinator on how to push the fence plan ahead and how to manage the certain opposition and "push" skeptics if need be. DOC's heavy involvement could be shielded from the public and DOC could claim, as it has, that the fence plan was not its own. And if the fence plan should implode, as it has, DOC could walk away, keep quiet, and leave MEG to hold the bag. DOC acted to prop up MEG's authority and public image in other ways. Residents were amazed when DOC's local manager admitted that MEG contributed no funds and no work whatsoever on the recent Moehau goat eradication scheme, despite receiving major credit on the project's publicly funded brochures along with DOC and regional council. No one has a problem with a bit of eco-entrepreneurship. After all, it's all for the good of the environment. But since MEG enjoys the public benefits of a not-for-profit group, it should be transparent and accountable to its membership and the public at large. It should not act as a de facto proxy of government bureaucrats in effecting public policy. And as for DOC, if it wants to push another attempt to fence off the Coromandel, it should come out publicly and say so. At least for now, the Moehau fence project has been roundly rejected by the community it would have changed. In the end, no arguments were advanced by fence boosters to sway those who did not agree with them. The disappointment of MEG spokespeople was understandable, and the "shoot the messenger" reflex undermined their position in the community. On Maungatautari or at Karori – where there are no farms, no pets, no residents, no vehicles, no boats, no baches, no campgrounds – fence plans may make sense. But as locals could plainly see, here north of Colville is a very different scenario. In practical terms, a predator-free "mainland island" that includes working farms, hundreds of households and pets, and thousands of visitors and vehicles is simply unrealistic. Nowhere has such a plan succeeded. Predator fences do not work where people live. Locals who may not have agreed with the fence plan are among the staunchest supporters of conservation efforts to preserve the bush, restore habitat, knock down stoats, possums and rats, and save our iconic kiwi. Most have worked hard and long for years in cooperation with DOC and regional council. They know the land well, in some cases farming the same hills for generations. They represent hundreds of years of collective experience in the bush and on the ground. They have common sense and know sound environmental policy… and they can spot a non-starter when they see it.

Best of all, there is general agreement among environmental experts that the native bush around Moehau is strong and getting stronger. UCLA landowners are happy to have had a hand in that progress. They uniformly support practical, affordable, sensible and safe conservation practice and invite their friends at DOC and regional council, as well as their neighbours in MEG, to hop the fence and join them.

As the year draws to a close, MEG coordinator Todd, still licking his group's wounds, revisits the train-wreck and continues to assign blame. The MEG organiser bemoans what he calls the "highly effective, extremely negative, but ill-informed protest against MEG and the predator proof fence project," implying that opposition was due, not to legitimate concerns, but to residents who were "forced/pressured to toe the line on goat eradication and didn't like it." According to Todd, "Their backlash has produced a campaign, breeding and inciting fear and mistrust." Yikes! The coordinator's hands-in-the-air lament starts to get comical. He admits his "communication with some landowners was obviously not as *effective* as hoped". But, hey, it wasn't his fault. "I insisted on a newsletter being sent out to all landowners during negotiations for the goat eradication as a part of the consultation process. It wasn't going to be done originally. I was told by John Gaukrodger to leave all negotiations with the landowners to DOC and EW and that MEG and myself should keep a low profile...None of us have any professional expertise in communications strategy or public relations and perhaps it is an area we are lacking in." Still smarting almost a year later, the group's May/June *Megaphone* member newsletter looks back on a "very challenging rollercoaster year, with the huge disappointment of having to drop the Predator Proof Fence project."

And continuing to point fingers, the group insists, "for those of you unfamiliar with what happened; a small, vociferous group of landowners, carried out a rather nasty campaign to discredit MEG, and the conservation work being done on the northern Coromandel...a sad state of affairs made sadder by their refusal to sit down and talk it through. The bottom line, however, is no corporate sponsor in their right mind is going to entertain investing $5 million into a project with this sort of stuff going on...The fence was...a way to reduce predators and poison use over time in a cheap, efficient and sane way. And contrary to the opinions of the anti-fence group would not have cost the ratepayer one red cent."

The Pest Proof Jack-in-a-Box
2010-11

> *"The myth of the wilderness as "virgin" uninhabited land had always been especially cruel when seen from the perspective of the Indians who had once called that land home. Now they were forced to move elsewhere, with the result that tourists could safely enjoy the illusion that they were seeing their nation in its pristine, original state, in the new morning of God's own creation."*
>
> William Cronon *Trouble with Wilderness*

The third attempt to raise a steel barrier across the Coromandel peninsula is laid to rest but is not forgotten. Nearly four years pass since the residents of the northern Coromandel put a stop – they thought once and for all – to plans that would fence in their homes and farms behind checkpoints and gates.

Anne Ward, whose family has worked the land north of Colville for more than a century, writes in the May 2010 *Coromandel Town Chronicle* in response to a new round of comments aiming to resurrect the idea of fence one more time. She starts where it ended the last time —"Don't fence us in."

The controversy of introducing a pest proof fence cutting off the northern section of the Coromandel Peninsula from East to West lives on. For decades it has been mooted as being the answer to the possum, stoat and rat problem. The most recent, though not the first attempt, was in 2006, when this same fence plan was abandoned because it was roundly opposed, by the very members of our community who would have been most affected. Nothing has changed their view that it is not a sensible method of pest control for this area. Certainly, predator proof fencing has been used to advantage in Karori Wildlife Reserve in Wellington. At Maungatautari also, though here the fence has incurred huge ongoing debts; Waipa District Council and all EW ratepayers are picking up the bill for the next two years to the tune of $2 million and then what?

But in both of these cases there are no residents within the fence, tending their business for farming, tourism, fishing, or with boats calling in along the coast. No tourists camping, or loaded trucks and service vehicles coming in and out. Also in Karori and Maungatautari brodifacoum was used to kill possum, stoats, rats and mice. And who is supposed to pay for this new fence project? Are we the ratepayers expected to fund the venture, or are the promoters of the idea relying on grants? The cost of building the fence is not the end of the expense. Subsequent maintenance and upkeep in a coastal climate would be astronomical.

Our Community Plan should reflect widely shared values, but with sound commonsense prevailing so we say once again, "Don't fence us in."

But the murmurs and occasional public letters keep the fence dream alive, as if by sheer persistence those who believe in a different kind of conservation and environmentalism – safer, cleaner, more affordable, more humane, and more effective – will eventually be worn down or just go away. The May 2011 *Chronicle* mentions a Colville Possum Fence Committee that has "decided to establish an Incorporated Society, and would like to hear from anyone interested in becoming a member...So far we have been offered donations of up to $1,000 from individuals who would like to see this project succeed. We have also confirmed the route of the fence with landowners for over half its total length of around 6 kilometres...A Possum Proof Fence and the eradication of possums from Moehau is the only long-term answer to the possum dilemma." As of 2015, nothing further had been heard from that particular "group".

UCLA's August *Conservation Update* for the *Chronicle* offers a few facts and figures for those who still fancy the fence fantasy. The report references an article by Paul Scofield of the Canterbury Museum and his two Lincoln University co-authors in the March *NZ Journal of Ecology*.[31] The report soberly evaluates predator-proof fences as responses to biodiversity challenges. Among its findings are:

A review of pest-exclusion fences throughout New Zealand shows that the goals of fence projects are frequently not achieved and cost-benefit analyses often do not adequately quantify ongoing costs...We believe that the rate of growth in predator-proof-fence building is out of proportion to its benefits. The rapid growth rate may well be fuelled by the ready availability of community grants to fund such visible, tangible projects...It is paradoxical, therefore, that in mid-2006 the New Zealand Government gave $5.5 million to help build a predator-proof fence at Maungatautari, while at the same time DOC was unable to secure the funds to buy a large rat-free island in Golden Bay from which it had paid the owners to eradicate the rats." The per hectare costs of such methodology are astronomical...We calculate that the mean cost per hectare protected of the 18 sites listed... is approximately $3,365 per hectare, which is one to two orders of magnitude greater than the annual cost of ongoing effective predator control using the unfenced-mainland-island approaches above.

New investment in fences will be required every 25 years – their estimated life.

To top it all, "…several overseas authors recently questioned whether fences are indeed the panacea that will solve the global extinction crisis (Hayward & Kerley 2008; Bode & Wintle 2010); with one paper going so far as to suggest that wholesale fence creation will restrict endangered species' evolutionary potential (Hayward & Kerley 2008)"

The annual commitment to the Maungatautari fence is calculated at "slightly more than the budget DOC Waikato uses to maintain endangered species programmes for the whole of the Waikato Conservancy estate (3.8 million ha)."[32]

The Maungatautari Ecological Island fence project, periodically touted by DOC and MEG as an example of what can be achieved on the Coromandel, is in reality a warning flag. MEIT has been plagued from the start by operational, financial, access, and treaty problems – while failing to achieve its pest-free goal. Projected to be self-funding within a few years, the programme is still, 10 years later, on financial life support of close to $1millicn annually from regional and district ratepayers and tax revenue. Waikato councillors have labeled the fence project a "financial black hole".

*

The Moehau pest proof fence plan lies dormant, not dead. Experience shows it may rise again like the mythological phoenix at any time, fueled by good intentions, irrational exuberance, and just a dollop of self-interest. If and when it does, the issues will be exactly the same. A similar story will unfold, but most likely with new characters…maybe the next generation…but just as passionate about the bush, the birds, and the clean waters of the sacred mountain.

While this sleeping dog lies, another beast raises its head for wholesale slaughter. It seems we live in a culture divided – the tribe of the city and the tribe of the country. Wild pigs are on the menu…

Part Three:

Save Our Wild Pigs

"With prizes for the heaviest boars, best tusks and a section for the kids to get involved, the event promises to be a huge community get-together and organisers hope to make it an annual highlight for the small rural township near Pauanui...The event helps efforts to rid the peninsula of pests like wild boar, possums and magpies but is also about fundraising, fun and the challenge of hunting. All proceeds will go to Hikuai School. Principal Brendon Morrissey says the students are excited about the idea and they're well aware of the natural environment and threats to native bush... He says the school includes environmental education in its programme and will look into the conservation angles of managing possums and protecting the bush from pests."

Hauraki Herald, March 16, 2007

Good Keen Men Wild at Pest Policy

"The first Māori may well have carried pigs with them to New Zealand, for Polynesians carried pigs throughout the rest of the Pacific as far as Hawaii. They also probably carried chickens, which are known as moa throughout Polynesia. Curiously, both pig and chicken were absent by the time Cook landed in 1769 and the bones of neither species, is found in the archeological record. It seems likely that, having seen a 'real' moa, the Māori did not bother keeping or caring for chooks or pigs and that their domestic animals were all eaten shortly after arrival."

Tim Flannery[1]

Local organic farmer Geoffrey Robinson writes: "After 200 years at home in the rugged Coromandel bush and countless thousands of succulent visits to Kiwi dinner tables, the Captain Cocker almost met his match. The Captain Cooker is New Zealand vernacular for the black wild pig descended from gift pigs brought by Captain Cook on his 1774 Pacific voyage.[2] However the potential demise of the wild pig was not due to some disease, or packs of wild pig dogs or a few too many good keen hunters…but local government. It was spring 2006 when wild pigs almost went off the menu in the Waikato thanks to a stealth attack by regional council. In a major shift of priorities, the regional council Environment Waikato (EW) planned to no longer recognise the wild pig as a traditional food resource and recreational asset. Instead, in its draft five-year pest management plan, EW aimed to actively knock out pig populations on what amounted to virtually all of the Coromandel Peninsula and much of the Waikato. The council's proposed rules described a plan to inspect and monitor all properties with suspected or confirmed populations of wild pigs and then order or undertake direct control and eradication by whatever means it deemed most appropriate and cost effective.

Quite why EW decided to target the Coromandel's renowned wild boar and its wide constituency was not clear. Some saw the push on pigs as a response to public rejection in 2006 of the controversial predator-proof fence for the upper Coromandel which had had EW's active support and financial backing. That plan originally called for eradication of wild pigs due to their supposed impact on kiwi habitat. But in the face of opposition, fence proponents and the council dropped wild pigs from their species hit list and denied they had any designs on the razorbacked bush icon.

EW's draft pest strategy, however, told a different story, and the wild pig was clearly in the council's sights again. Why was the wild pig, previously noted as a resource and a simple nuisance predator by EW, suddenly elevated to Environmental Enemy Number One? Was there new environmental science available on wild pigs? Had new production issues arisen? Had the ecological balance dramatically changed? Obviously not. But what had clearly changed was a shift in EW's focus from rural possum control to wider, so-called "biodiversity" plans. The fact that the wild boar had successfully scratched out a living alongside thousands of plant and animal species for centuries as part of the Waikato's biodiversity heritage seemed to be lost on office staff back at base.

Alarm at the new pig policy was not limited to hunters and wild pork connoisseurs. For farmers and other landowners who had done a good job controlling feral pigs on their own properties without the help of EW staffers, the proposed pig policy would have meant EW could act without land occupier consent. Environmentalists also saw the "least cost" language as a clear mandate for continued and increased aerial applications of 1080 toxin.

But for many regular Kiwis it was another issue. They may not have been hunters themselves. And they may not have lived in the back blocks. But they saw the basic fabric of traditional rural life once again under threat: that wild pork country ham could be scratched from all menus."

From Local Entities to Mega-bureaucracies

"Never wrestle with pigs. You both get dirty and the pig likes it."
George Bernard Shaw

With wide coverage in farming newspapers *Good keen men wild at pest policy* was the first of many articles penned by Geoffrey Robinson and served to awaken an otherwise uninformed population. Environment Waikato eventually faced hundreds of submissions from citizens who do not regularly participate at this level of local government politics. A lack of involvement comes from the accurate public perception that once a local or regional council produces a draft document, invited submissions are either ignored or changes are merely cosmetic. How did this transformation unfold?

Prior to 1987 local government was not designed to be a mega-bureaucracy with overpaid employees running the show. After the capital was moved to Wellington in 1865, floundering provincial governments were legally abolished in 1875. Norman Kirk's 1974 Labour government "enacted the Local Government Act, with the purpose of 'rationalising local government by regionalisation'. "While planning and civil defense were the only mandatory functions, any new regional functions were to be delegated to these new regional councils. However, democratically elected regional government was dealt a blow when Muldoon's government came to power the following year." The intention was to confine regional councils to Wellington and Auckland with the rural regions to be represented by united councils, "comprised of members appointed from the territorial authorities within the region."[3]

Up until 1987 local governance was distributed between District Councils and various Boards. District Councillors were elected and charged with caring for communities in supportive roles such as providing libraries, rubbish collection, clean water and local roading with central government supplying the infrastructure necessary for a functioning democracy built using national taxes. Roading, rubbish and rats were the original three 'r's designated to direct the work of District Councils.[4]

The system was not 'broke', when Treasury's 1989 fingers were to hook local government into the business enterprise machinery of light-handed regulation for big business and heavy-handed regulation for ordinary citizens with the creation of regional councils. Elected regional councillors must hold no unassailable beliefs, a system that contributes to the emasculation of the potential for elected officials to do anything other than rubber stamp central government directives. The process is well documented by Jeremy Agar in his report looking at the sell off of assets in Christchurch.[5] Agar points out it is the "embedded managerial culture that binds local councils...They're supposed to be a board of governors, rubber stamping the decisions of staffers. In a managerial culture the last thing that's needed is for politicians to represent those who voted for them. Local government seeks to take the politics out of politics by making the Councillors depend on reports from senior (ambitious) bureaucrats, without which nothing can be done." Contrary views "being routinely dismissed as evidence of a 'dysfunctional culture." And in 1996 the Local Government Amendment Act (No. 3) imposed user-pays on local government. Some proportion of every item of expenditure must be calculated to include a measure of private as well as public good.[6]

Waikato ratepayers began paying regional property taxes, (but not called by that name, rather these 'taxes' are referred to as 'rates') in 1989 to support hundreds of new salaries attached to a new layer of regional government referred to as Environment Waikato (EW). In 2011 the acronym EW was unceremoniously dropped in favour of Waikato Regional Council (WRC) coinciding with a new catchphrase gracing Annual Reports—*Competing Globally Caring Locally*. Given WRC's push to expand industrial dairy farming on what was once forestland, their support for Tainui Group Holding's inland port over hundreds of hectares of Ruakura research station's arable land, their promotion of dirty cage-fish farming in the already heavily polluted Firth of Thames and their accommodation of policies that distribute an A1 World Health Organisation poison—1080, from the air and into water and onto land, the word "environment" became embarrassingly inappropriate.

The droll name change has been interpreted as an attempt to get the ball rolling to take over all District Councils and to push for super-regional governance to adopt the SuperCity model for the

Waikato. However on the Coromandel in 2013 over 1500 signatures were gathered to support an investigation into the possibility of holding onto active democracy by creating a local unitary council with boundaries similar to the current Thames Coromandel District Council. While the majority of residents oppose regional government based in Hamilton there is only a slender chance Coromandel will be successful in its goal. If not absorbed into the Hamilton network it may well be stitched onto the more coastal Bay of Plenty Regional Council.

Most New Zealanders live in towns and cities and this naturally influences central and regional government legislation relating to nature. Given the weight of wild animal and wild plant propaganda emanating from both government and business, it is becoming a challenge for many city dwellers to gauge a rural perspective or to comprehend what it means to live next to wild life and wilderness. Yet in spite of the crowded airwaves and slanted news media, wild animal survey results show overwhelming public support for humane killing of wild animals[7] and hunting maintains its long tradition as a respected outdoor pursuit.[8]

Pest Management –
A Waikato Council Business Opportunity

"I never met a pig I didn't like. All pigs are intelligent, emotional, and sensitive souls. They all love company. They all crave contact and comfort. Pigs have a delightful sense of mischief; most of them seem to enjoy a good joke and appreciate music. And that is something you would certainly never suspect from your relationship with a pork chop."

Sy Montgomery[9]

Around the world, good women and men have differed in their views as to what constitutes a "pest". Due to circumstance, culture, and context, where one person clearly sees a "pest", another may just as plainly see "potential".

In provincial New Zealand, whether on small town sections or large rural blocks, animal and plant pests have traditionally been considered the responsibility of property owners, and regional councils across the country have generally taken a similar view — usually explicitly. An article in Environment Waikato regional council's *Managing Pests for Our Future* makes clear for instance that "noxious plants (are) a landowner responsibility". However, to ensure that local government could lend positive support where warranted, the Biosecurity Act of 1993 (Part 5, Section 71) declared each and all regional councils "may prepare a proposal for a regional pest management strategy" (RPMS) if they so chose. Adoption of a pest management plan was not mandated — it was an option made available to councils under the Bioscurity Act.

When council staff in Hamilton discussed their first five-year strategy in 1994 (subsequently adopted in 1996), they noted while "Regional Councils are not obliged to prepare a RPMS, EW is taking this initiative to ensure that the environmental and economic well-being of the Waikato Region and its residents are protected." The Waikato plan started small. In 1994, eight animal categories were proposed for inclusion – possum, rabbit, wallaby, goat, mustelid, rook, magpie and wasp. By 2007, that number had quadrupled to

32. As for problem plant species, while 17 species were identified in 1994, the number more than tripled to 57 in thirteen years.

Naturally, when you increase your target species, regional ratepayers are sitting ducks. Over the years, EW became known for maintaining one of the most costly and onerous regional council pest strategies in the country, with annual budgets for pest management quickly growing well into the millions with newly created staff positions in operations and administration. By 2014-15, annual pest spending stood at $7,555,126. In 2007, the Waikato council actually employed a senior manager for "business development" reporting to the CEO. What was once "public service" had become just "business", and pest management was proving a lucrative growth area too good to pass up.

To this day, the Waikato pest strategy contrasts sharply in scope, complexity, and attitude with those of other New Zealand regional councils. Environment Bay of Plenty (EBOP), Gisborne, Northland and Tasman councils have adopted typical strategies that are relatively inexpensive, reasonable, and supportive. Tasman's unitary council has adopted an RPMS that simply aims to "advise and assist the public" and to "promote the voluntary control" of mustelids, feral cats and possums.[10] The EBOP strategy for 2003-08 listed only a small number of animals – ants, catfish, feral cat, eastern rosella, feral goat, koi carp, magpie, mynah, mustelids, possum, rabbit, rat, rook, wallaby and wasp. In Gisborne, the 2010-15 pest plan lists two insect species, five plants and six animals – rabbit, rook, possum, and cats, rats and mice. To help with possums in Gisborne, "Council will provide advice, support and assist planning where possible, to community groups and individual land occupiers undertaking their own control work." Also provided is information about traps, shooting and how to get one's cyanide license. A Taranaki Regional Council submission to the 2006 Waikato draft strategy addressed the large numbers of animals and plants in the Waikato strategy, indicating that big differences in targeted species reflected "differences in approach".

Differences in approach also extend to the councils' relationships with residents. In the Waikato, EW rules were introduced in 2008 to penalize ratepayers whose preference was humane wild animal control and not aerial 1080 toxin. A council biosecurity subcommittee that year reported, "Legal advice on charging a landowner is awaiting wording of the RPMS which is currently inoperative due to an Environment Court appeal." It goes on, "There is also increasing concern about toxins and the differing levels of knowledge/ignorance are leading to **fear and paranoia**. There is room for advocacy and education to **counter misinformation**." [added emphasis]

Northland Regional Council's Biosecurity Senior Programme Manager Don McKenzie put his organisation's approach this way in July 2015 correspondence: "We provide advice at the beginning of the conversation, and let the customer know they could be eligible for assistance, often the aim is to develop some kind of plan that the landowner believes will work and from that financial assistance can be offered. The most important factor we have learned is to work in a humble way with communities—most are at different levels of awareness and are not ready to take on complicated plans or monitoring—for many groups it takes a while to build trust and by simply supporting a community led initiative we can demonstrate that the council believes in their intent and their ability to make a difference. Look on the 'backyard kiwi site' for a community initiative in Northland and how the council is supporting them." http://www.backyardkiwi.org.nz/

Behind the Scenes: The Drafting of the Draft

"We fully understand the recreational positives of pig hunting, and have no wish to halt this pastime."
Northern Coromandel *Forest & Bird*, November 2007

Despite their wide reach into the animal and plant kingdoms, Environment Waikato did not ruffle too many feathers with its first two five-year Regional Pest Management Strategies. While sweeping many more species into its control nets than other regional councils from 1996 to 2006, EW pest policy was not controversial when it came to individual species. There was the bureaucrat-engendered issue confronted in 2002 of Key Ecological Sites (KES) that would impact landowners but regarding common problem animals like rabbits, rats or ants, hardly an eyebrow was raised. With recognised predators like stoats, weasels and feral cats, there was little disagreement on active control measures. And as for those occasional nuisance animals that were also highly valued as traditional food and recreational resources—goats, deer and pigs – control was basically left to landowners and hunters as it had been for many decades. No arguments there.

But with plans now well underway to fence off the northern Coromandel Peninsula and to formalise rules for newly designated kiwi sanctuaries and other areas of ecological significance, EW drew a bead on the three large exotic hunting species. In its next pest management strategy, the council alone would decide when pigs and deer would be eliminated, where and by what methods.

Usually, if only the right people are asked only the right questions, a predictable outcome is likely, if not assured. And so it goes with the creation of local government Regional Pest Management Strategies. Council management in Hamilton start by consulting with industry colleagues and interest groups on a pre-draft pest plan every five years (recently changed to 10 years). This part of the process is seminal in that ideas submitted on a 'discussion document' have a reasonable chance of ending up in the official draft strategy that is finally presented for public perusal and official consultation.

Input prior to creation of the draft plan is critical. Invitations are sent to mandated iwi, industry and interested parties, but very few members of the affected public get a look-in at this stage of the process. In 2006, EW sent out requests to 183 parties for comment on its pest strategy discussion document. With the exception of several large corporations and a few individuals, the only parties asked for comment were those the council was required to consult by statute, namely ministries, agencies, local government entities and representatives of tangata whenua. Although the Biosecurity Act specifically states councils can consult with any party or individual that it may deem appropriate, EW chose not to consult widely, and barely more than required. Despite significant changes to the status of pigs, deer and goats, no local hunting clubs were consulted.

Predictably, with the pre-draft process tightly controlled, only 13 responses were received that commented on the deer and pig categories, with two more referencing goats. But even though there was limited comment on the three prized species, regional council managers did not get the answers they had wanted. One official agency respondent, the Department of Conservation Taupo-Tongariro Conservancy, supported the status quo—full stop. Three respondents supported moving pigs and deer to "occupier control/containment category." These were Auckland Regional Council, the forestry company, Ernslaw One and Waipa District Council. Most importantly, eight respondents specifically stated simply that the regional council "should not control pigs." This was a message EW managers did not want to hear.

Only one respondent to the early discussion document, the DOC Waikato Conservancy (the council's partner in the Coromandel fence project), supported a plan to integrate controls between regional council and DOC. The response suggested moving pigs and deer to the containment category, citing flood control policy as the basis for control measures, and declaring the entire Coromandel Peninsula a high priority conservation area with DOC (using the Wild Animal Control Act) and EW (using the Biosecurity Act), carrying out combined controls as with their 2006 "Wall of Death" goat eradication project. DOC Waikato suggests working "together on these species." And what exactly would the integrated DOC-EW pig/deer/goat policy do? By integrating control policies for both public and private land, DOC could ensure control measures the Crown favours on public land are also carried out on private land, and species targeted by the Crown on public land would also be targeted on private land, despite DOC and EW having responsibilities to different constituencies. DOC is answerable to the Crown, while EW answers to regional ratepayers. (In a ideal world given the small size of Aotearoa there is of course no sense in regional plans. This is just a matter of central government passing the buck to the regions to grow budgets for highly paid employees and toxic chemicals and poisons.)

The economic impact of the DOC proposal on Waikato ratepayers would be significant. By integrating control policies, DOC can benefit from funding contributed by Waikato ratepayers to support its activity on public land to directly benefit the Crown. Essentially, Waikato residents subsidise DOC and the Crown. Under the proposed 2006 plan, funding for regional biosecurity measures will quadruple in six years.

Of course there were many others whose ideas EW could have chosen to listen to—regional ratepayers, sportspeople, hunters, farmers, ecologists, conservation groups, botanists and pesticide activists for starters. A handful of respondents to the discussion document were not at all happy with the changes proposing that EW directly control (kill) wild pigs. Graeme Hayward of Whitianga wrote, "I have been hunting since I can remember, which is 25 years ago and my father before me…I wish to take more young hunters and my kids hunting pig for years to come…Pig hunting competitions in the Waikato region have donated thousands of dollars to charity over years." Alan Ludwig of Paeroa questioned, "What's happening to democracy? I do not see wild pigs as a problem. I am a keen hunter who owns a farm surrounded by native bush and pines. We have the odd pig turn up. The local pig hunters keep them well under control." Shane McLean, based in Tokoroa, shared local knowledge. "Pig and deer numbers are not very high…1080 is another waste of money, killing everything (birds, dogs, deer, pigs), possums have to eat heaps before dying an agonizing death, dogs and deer only need half a bait. I don't want my rates put up for pest control when people I know will do it for free…happily. Pigs and deer are not pests. They are a good source of food for the community. Give clubs permission to have night shoots for possums and rabbits…encourage the younger ones to go out into the forest and learn about survival and hunting. It will keep them off the streets."

John Sanford, president of Hauraki Coromandel Province Federated Farmers together with Bev Sanford wrote: "No deer are in the Coromandel and Tb has not been found for many years on the Coromandel so it is not an issue…Pigs wander over large areas and so culling from high value sites will not stop re-infestation shortly afterwards. 1080 kills smaller pigs but has not controlled pigs in the Coromandel even though extensive 1080 drops have taken place…Farmers already control pigs coming in as there is a ready supply of hunters prepared to help control pigs. Farmers then control good hunters and specify areas hunters can access away from stock especially those calving. Hunters with poor dogs do not get asked back. Over what area will pests be controlled from a high value site? The fear is, a farmer 2 kms away from a high value site, will be a target as pigs wander…Leave farmers to manage their own pig problems on the Coromandel as direct control will produce poor results for a high cost…"

Not hearing what they wanted to hear, council management chose to ignore this representative community input. Without a single request from any landowner, council employees decide to target wild pigs, going so far as to propose eradication in areas of "significance". Pig hunters and farmers have hunted wild pigs for more than a century with no assistance from government bodies, and with no requests for such assistance. Why the change now?

More Questions than Answers

"A peculiar virtue in wildlife ethics is that the hunter ordinarily has no gallery to applaud or disapprove of his (or her) conduct. Whatever his act, they are dictated by his own conscience, rather than a mob of onlookers. It is difficult to exaggerate the importance of this fact."
Aldo Leopold A Sand County Almanac

In the wake of an aborted pest-proof fence proposal for the upper Coromandel, EW proposes to expand its flexibility and authority to control feral animals—most notably wild pigs—cn a broad range of private lands. EW and fence supporters denied in 2006 that they had any plans to target wild pigs, but now they are giving themselves the ammunition to do so. Under current EW policy, wild pigs are acknowledged as a resource in addition to an environmental nuisance. EW's new policy completely eliminates all mention of the fact that wild pigs are a significant food and recreational resource as they have been for over 200 years. Instead, it only identifies pigs as an environmental and production threat.

On 2 May 2007 Geoffrey Robinson distributes a series of somewhat rhetorical questions throughout the farming and conservation and pig hunting networks.

Pigs a Problem? Pigs are a resource—a food resource and a traditional recreational resource. EW has recognized this in the past. The public has said so loudly and clearly. There are hundreds of keen pig-hunters on the Coromandel and thousands throughout the Waikato who enjoy a real kiwi wild pork dinner when they can.

Pigs an Environmental Problem? Everyone knows that pigs root about and disturb the ground. That's no secret. That's how they make their living. But native species get along fine with pigs. Right under EW's nose on Moehau, (an area with a fairly healthy pig population) DOC is proclaiming one of the biggest successes in all of New Zealand in reintroduction and survival of kiwi. Pigs are supposed to harm kiwi habitat. How can they be such a problem if kiwis are doing well and the native bush in the area is lush and thriving?

Why Is EW Doing This? EW has given no good reason for elevating the wild pig to Environmental Enemy Number One. They refer to biodiversity goals. But pigs are part of our rural biodiversity and coexist very well with countless native animal and plant species. It appears funding for possum Tb work drying up, the new catchword is ``Biodiversity`` and they propose to introduce a new rating structure clear across the region to fund projects in this area.

What Exactly Is Being Proposed? EW proposes to reclassify the wild pig from a resource and simple nuisance pest to a full-fledged eradication pest. Their stated goal is to reduce pig populations by direct control (i.e.killing them). They propose to inspect and monitor all properties suspected of having pigs, identify pig populations, and then order control measures or undertake those measures themselves. They state they do not need land occupier consent to proceed.

Where Will Pigs Be (Controlled) Killed? As the plan is written pigs will be killed virtually anywhere on the Coromandel and throughout most of the Waikato. At so-called `high-value sites, near those sites, and anywhere that may affect those sites, whether adjacent to them or 40 kilometres away.

Who Should Control Pigs? Pig hunters, farmers and landowners are already controlling pigs very well where required. They don't need office staffers to order them about. Of course, everyone is aware that pigs can cause localized environmental damage and affect production values. But capable landowners have successfully managed and controlled feral pigs for many decades. They do not need to be stripped of this responsibility by EW office staff looking to expand their patch. Feral pigs are well under control, thank you, and their numbers down in the opinion of hunters who know best. Five years ago: Intervention not required, not practical, or not cost effective. What has changed in the last five years? New environmental science? New production problems? Identification of new threats? Has the ecological balance dramatically changed? Obviously not.

Nothing has changed. What biodiversity problem? Pigs have been with us for 200 years. They are part of the fabric of rural kiwi life. Now promoted to environmental enemy number one. It will be the end of the Captain Cooker on the Coromandel for sure under this plan. For backblock old-timers and recreational hunters, this decision is a full-scale assault on the fabric of rural life. EW proposes to claim authority to act on actual sites, near actual sites, and anywhere that may conceivably affect control outcomes at those actual high value sites, whether nextdoor or many kilometers away. On the Coromandel and much of the Waikato, this arguably means all lands public and private, whether of actual high value or not.

For his next slightly more humourous presentation to the media Robinson crafted a press release: ***It's Goodbye Wild Pork Pie on the Coromandel.***

Forget the hangi plates. No more wild food fests or community hog hunts. Two hundred years of traditional kai is going off the menu. And the fabric of rural kiwi life is being shredded in the process. That's what Environment Waikato (EW) regional council planners have in mind in their glossy 2007-2012 Proposed Regional Pest Management Strategy just released to the public. EW plans to extend its authority to monitor and inspect all properties in the region, private and public, for suspected pig populations, giving itself the right to directly hunt, poison or otherwise destroy any pigs itself or to order landowners to carry out eradication themselves. EW says it can choose the most cost-effective means (1080 anyone?). And Council states that it does not require any landowner permissions to act as it sees fit.

Who picks up the tab under this plan? According to EW, every property owner across the region will be hit with a new, targeted rate based on capital value and scheduled to nearly double in only four years. With government like this, who needs foreign enemies? Last week, EW's front line spinmaster John Simmons was denying it all. He stated publicly that EW does recognise the resource value of pigs and that EW only wants to `control` pigs at a few high value locations. Not to worry, said Simmons. According to his spin, EW really has no intention of eradicating pigs in all the areas its new policy specifically states it will be able to do so.

But it's all down in the new plan in black and white. Either Simmons has failed to read his own policy document prior to its release. Or he must figure that those pesky ratepayers can't read anyway. Concerned ratepayers last week were wondering just who asked for this campaign to stamp out the new Environmental Enemy Number One? Who asked to pay new and soon-to-double rates for pest control? What has changed in the last five years to justify this about-face in Council policy? Is there new pig science we have all missed? Has the environment radically changed? Of course not. What has changed, though, is an emboldened rogue Council grabbing rates and expanding its patch.

Farmers, landowners and keen hunters have done a fine job, thank you, controlling pigs for more than a century—all without the help of EW staffers back at the office and at no cost whatsoever to the ratepayer.

They don`t need monitoring, inspections, mandatory eradication, or EW hunters and poison poppers on their land. Time is of the essence, as the EW submissions deadline is April 10. Copies of EW`s plan are available at (0800 800 401). It is 180 pages, so get a printed copy sent to you. Let EW hear it loud and clear: The wild pig is a valued food, recreational, cultural and economic resource. No EW destruction of wild pigs without the permission of landowners requesting assistance.

The Submission Process

"If the three prized feral food animals are removed from their habitats then the potential for some families already struggling becomes worse and hunting as a means of choice becomes unavailable, effectively removing the ability of choice from everyone of us. Our families and our communities both Maori and non-Maori believe they should retain the ability to choose to hunt…"

Ngati Maru Runanga

Waikato Regional Council found itself facing down hundreds of families and enraged citizens when they sent out their Draft RPMS 2007-2012. Hidden in this document were not only controls of hedgehogs and privet and wasps and magpies. The menace of the feral pig meant a reclassification from nuisance to the hardcore category: control species.

Many submitters chose to use Robinson's template that stated unequivocal opposition to Section 6.6 Feral Pigs.

"The description of the feral pig fails to identify the species as a valuable food resource and should include this information. The description of the feral pig furthermore fails to identify the species as a valuable recreational resource, which also provides economic benefits to the region, and should include this information. The feral pig has been a traditional food and recreational resource locally for over 200 years. This was acknowledged by EW Regional Council in its previous Pest Management Strategy 2002-2007 but has been omitted in the current proposal. The feral pig is an important traditional food source for tangata whenua who were gifted the animal before the country was established and who have been managing the resource since that time on their lands. Feral pigs are a time-honoured tradition at many public gatherings, celebrations, hui and other special events either as food or trophies. As a recreational resource, the wild pig provides economic benefits to the region, outfitters, retailers, lodging, guides, to name a few.

The submission raised "opposition to the inspection and monitoring of private properties by Council without the permission of the land occupier, opposition to any requirement by Council that any private land occupier undertake any specific control activity relating to feral pigs and opposition to the undertaking of direct control of feral pigs by Council on private land without the permission of the land occupier. Land occupiers have been successfully controlling feral pigs on their properties. They have done so at no cost to the ratepayer. Land occupiers presently have sufficient incentive to control pigs on properties dues to the food and recreational value of the feral pigs, and to limit any adverse effects on production values on their properties. There is no new scientific evidence of any significant increases in feral pig populations locally since the 2002-2007 Strategy was adopted; nor of any increased adverse effects on production values; nor any increased effects on the environment, so as to justify intervention by Council nor to justify change in the management of feral pigs from the existing 2002-2007 policy. The region's widely recognized improvement in diverse native bush, demonstrates that these successes are totally compatible with existing control strategies for feral pigs."

A separate major concern in 2007 is the limited time frame allowed for submissions. The public is invited to respond within a mere 20 working days. Formal requests to extend the submission time period are denied. However back in 1994/5 the council really wanted to hear from the public. They made a twelve-week period available, leading to 170 submissions. By 2007 it would appear the cast of characters on large salaries at EW no longer care to encourage contributions to their crafted RPMS masterpiece as they do not budge on the minimum time frame. They choose to follow the letter of the law that reads "not earlier than 20 working days after public notice of the proposal is given" (Biosecurity Act 1993 S 88 10, d). Numerous writers comment on the lack of time to make adequate submissions. There is sufficient time however for EW's own staffer David Spiers to pen 24 pages of neatly typed suggestions requesting staff to change, add, correct, delete and clarify sections of the RPMS written up by yet other well-paid members of the staff. From a ratepayer perspective it would have been preferable the draft document was proofed prior to going public.

Speaking for Ourselves

I've always loved pigs: the shape of them, the look of them,
and the fact that they are so intelligent.

Maurice Sendak

Submissions came fast and furious from throughout the region
to support the status quo and to combat change that were it
successful would have radically altered a way of life devalued
by office-bound bureaucrats. Colin Harris, Patron Whitianga
Pig Hunting Club explained how the club was formed in 1986 to
foster hunting, "especially among the youth. We currently have
70 members spread from Auckland to the Waikato and here on
the Coromandel Peninsula. Our main concern is the removal of
the feral pig from nuisance category to a pest (6.6) because of a
perceived threat to the environment and to production.. Obviously
the problems with feral pigs arise when they achieve high numbers
which would be rare with current hunting pressures in most of
the Regional Council's area. The danger with the change is that
with the current propensity to use 1080 as a control weapon for
all pests in Category 6 this could include the feral pig. We believe
any high pig populations could be reduced using hunting clubs
such as ourselves using aversion-trained dogs. Pests should be
graded according to the damage they do and their nuisance value.
Animals such as feral pig and deer have beneficial values to rural
areas that far exceed the animals or pests they are grouped with
in Category 6...If Environment Waikato were to proceed with the
alteration of categorization of pigs and deer our club would unite
with other hunting interest groups to mount a legal challenge..."

In the *Hauraki Herald* December 14 2007, Harris writes of life-
long hunting: "My father hunted. My wife hunts and my 11 year-
old son does too. Hunters go out to catch pork to eat, not just to kill
everything in the bush. You always leave something for next time
and as long as they are kept at a balance, pigs cause little problem.
Actually, they can help native plants spread through the bush
by eating the berries — karaka, nikau, tawa, miro. New plants
grow in new areas...Pig hunting clubs encourage young hunters

to go hunting, teaching them bush craft, gun safety and fitness. Isn't it better for kids to be out hunting than drinking alcohol or wandering the streets getting into trouble. I know what I would prefer my son to be doing."

Coromandel resident Bernard Davies declares that in his experience kiwi hold their ground amid high numbers of wild pigs in the "decades prior to the meat hunting era of the 60's and 70's. The taking of wild pigs and other game animals is a highly valued tradition that should be preserved. Many young New Zealanders gain their first bush experience by hunting. The social benefits from hunting are at least equal to other sports participation. Control of wild pigs by Environment Waikato would be a waste of money. EW should abandon this blatant attempt to eradicate the wild pig in all instances. Regional Council should not extend its authority to carry out or require direct control or eradication of feral pigs on any lands without the express permission of the landowner or land occupier. If EW or DOC staff want to go pig hunting they should wait for their day off and hunt unpaid" He suggests "A bounty on possums and mustelids would compliment continued work by EW and DOC and eventually reduce poison use."

Davies concludes his submission with the statement: "Flooding and erosion are caused by extreme rain and high wind toppling trees into rivers, causing dams which then burst."

This reference to flooding and erosion links with the unsubstantiated EW theory that poisoning off wild animals will help put leaves on trees thereby slowing flooding and erosion. After the coastal "weather bomb" of 2002 where one life was lost and much destruction wrought especially in Coromandel town, millions of dollars were squandered killing possums and goats and rats using this baseless rationale. It could be said that ratepayers were hoodwinked or chose to turn a blind eye to the poison programme. Now that necessary work on actual flood control to protect coastal communities continues to be underfunded eyes may be opening. This scam is called The Peninsula Project and is documented in *Voices of the Coromandel.*

Shane Walker of Coromandel writes "As a ratepayer I don't want a further rates increase to pay for this, when it will be unnecessary. I have a young family. I want them to enjoy the hunting of the wild pig and provide meat for the family like we have done in the past. What will kids enjoy in the future if there are not pigs to hunt?" Nikola Vukojevich, Thames comments "Pig hunting on the Coromandel is a healthy sport that has become a great challenge. Wild pigs are a great food source for our community. Listen to the ratepayers! It's our community and New Zealander's country. This is our voice! Councils are elected and should reflect what the people of the community want—not the views of only a few. Leave the pigs alone."

Julian Williams Environment Officer for the Waikato Raupatu Trustee Company Ltd. asks for recognitions of animals of value to their hapu and marae. "…Waikato-Tainui would like special recognition (of animals) as being of some importance to Māori. They include, but are not limited to: All deer, goats, pigs, rown bull-headed catfish. The purpose for noting these animals is that they play a role in our traditions, regardless of these species being introduced to our lands, they became a food source to our people." On integrated pest management at high value sites Waikato-Tainui state the following: "When an animal is determined to be causing harm to other more 'important' species and are required to be managed through culling or biological agents, Waikato-Tainui would like a 'first right' to that culling or the placement of the biological agents. This would provide assurance to our hapu and Marae that the agents are being placed in an area that will not be harmful to other species important to us. Also, the animals such as deer and pigs can be culled and used to provide kai to our marae or whatever purpose we see as beneficial for our people." On biological control programmes it is clearly stated that they should not proceed "without prior approval from iwi, hapu and marae."

Craig Solomon, Marutuahu Confederated Tribes of Hauraki Manaia, reminds councillors "Pig hunting is not a sport for whanau but a lifestyle and a food source. For generations it has been the same. My whanau owns thousands of acres in the Manaia Valley and we wish to make it clear to EW we will not tolerate any trespass of wild pig monitors of our land. Any breach of this trespass will result in legal and physical action. Respect our right. We are tangata whenua not EW." Chayne Reid of Thames has hunted for 40 years on the Coromandel and these days "we are lucky to catch a dozen a year. Why pay to kill these pigs when the hunters are doing it for you?"

In order to pay for all this extra work EW will build a sluice to siphon money right out of rate-payer's pockets based on capital value—everyone who owns two hectares or more (with horses or fruit trees or garlic crops) must acquiesce to even more rates. This equation does not even take into account so-called "targeted rates" that amount to $5,407,000 in 2007/8 but rise to $10,109,000 in 2011/12. Put this information alongside the entrenched opposition from EW to landowners controlling their own land and using animals such as possums and goats and pigs as a resource and you are bound for conflict. The biosecurity rate was charged on rating units two hectares and greater until the commencement of the 2007/2008 rating year when it changed to being based on capital value on all rating units across the region. Originally the rate was for pest control on what was largely rural land. A change of thinking about biodiversity meant that it covered more than just pest control and therefore should be applied across the region.[11].

Anthony Reid of Whitianga believes "dogs are branded, hunters registered. The pigs on the Coro Peninsula are definitely on the decrease and I know this as I have hunted the area for 50 years and have been made honorary life member of the Coromandel Pig Hunting Club and I am still hunting." Costa Peters of Coromandel thinks "this is an outrageous policy, I have been hunting for 35 years, not only for food, but for family activity, fitness, scenery, peacefulness…You guys sitting in your office all day would have no idea of what's happening in the bush, no one from EW, has consulted or talked to anyone in our club or community that I know of. Our dogs go through kiwi, dotterel, stock training to be able to go in the bush…if you take the pigs out you are just going to upset a tradition and a lot of people and take a lot of fun and food away. I would rather have my kids hunting pigs than walking around the streets, getting into trouble, or doing nothing constructive." Colin Pepper of Thames: "This proposal is going overboard. It infringes on private property rights and my heritage. Wild pigs are not a problem on the Peninsula and are kept under control. This is just another EW in bed with DOC, greenie power grab. Stop wasting my rates…"

Sharmayne Novis who resides in Port Charles writes "How can EW justify taking food from my children's mouths when wild pork is a major food supply for us!! We cant just 'duck' into the local Pac n' Save (2 hours drive away for us) and buy domestic pork/meat! My husband not only hunts as a family tradition and hobby, but to put food on our table. I am disgusted—but not at all surprised—that a government body would do this to my family. Tamsyn Nevin of Coromandel writes "As a young and upcoming pig hunter I do not think it fair for you to take this away from us, it is our hobby and a way for me to spend quality time with my dad!" Also from Coromandel, Nikki Nevin: "Leave the land alone! Landowners are more than capable of controlling the pigs by bringing in local hunters who do it as a sport and love---not a job!

Stalwart environmentalist and founding member of the Eastern Coromandel Landcare Association Arthur Attfield who farms in Whenuakite believes EW must engage with the people at a rural level as a partnership across communities. The "policy is too extravagant and ambitious, and is not sustainable economically, socially, and politically which will bankrupt the region. The recent policy on 1080 (aerial) and the predator fence infringe on property rights in rural areas and has left people disillusioned and angry..."

Thomas Mackenzie of Puriri Valley "EW has no need to have anything to do with controlling wild pigs on the Coromandel or anywhere else. The system with recreational hunting has worked find for the last 100 plus years with no cost to anyone. Being landowners and farmers in an area where our neighbours are both DOC and forestry and where pig numbers were quite high we have seen the pig numbers decline to very low levels in the last few years with hunting pressure. Why would EW want to start poking their nose in now? No one will ever be coming onto our property to kill pigs or anything else without my permission." Lynette Louden offers "I have lived on the Coromandel at Te Puru for 47 years. Part of the fascination with our visitors from overseas is the hunting in the Coromandel ranges. Four generations of Loudens have hunted these hills. The pigs are still a staple part of our diet and that of our many friends and visitors. The Environment Waikato should keep well away, they are ruining part of our heritage."

Lisa Louden comments "My husband has been pig hunting all his life, as his father and uncles have and his grandfather and grandfather's father. We have just had a son of our own and we hope to carry on this line of traditional hunting. Being on one wage we find the meat that we catch a huge saving in groceries. The pigs are far and few between and therefore I don't see the pigs as a major problem on the Coromandel Peninsula. I ask anyone from EW to come to one of the competitions held by CPC (Coromandel Pighunting Club) and see what a wonderful family oriented sport/

hobby this is." Frank Johnstone of Coromandel demands EW "abandon this brainless idea of controlling pigs. We have seen ideas like this in the past. They serve only to put more financial pressure on ratepayers and to endorse your policy of "We Will Because We Can". Wild pigs are a way of life on the Peninsula…" Evan Davies of Coromandel whose cogent statement is repeated in many submissions: "Destroying wild pigs will destroy our lifestyle. Have respect for local culture." Zane Evans farming in Colville on the upper Coromandel peninsula "Wild pigs are very much under control on this property."

Mockie Johnstone on behalf of the Coromandel Pighunting Club writes, "The Coromandel Pighunting Club oppose any change to Waikato Regional Pest Management Strategy with express concern over the wild pig. Wild pigs provide many valuable assets in an area like the Coromandel Peninsula such as food value, family hunting, and kid hunting instead of roaming the streets, which is increasingly happening to our young people dut to EW and DOC policies. Pig numbers are at a very low level on most of the Peninsula. Any area with a few extra pigs can be controlled by local hunters—at no cost to the ratepayer. Jill Davenport of Waihi: "As a tramper in the Coromandel and Kaimai Ranges we see very little evidence of pigs or pig rooting. We have very few wild animals in NZ. Do you want to eradicate everything? Leave something for the hunters. They are doing a good job. Better than burning up our streets with fast cars." Raymond Clark, Thames "Our family food source will be wiped out. That being the case, will the people sitting in the office making these decisions come forth and substitute what they intend to take away? I would like to meet the person who actually came up with this idea. I wonder if they will be brave enough to put up their hand."

A.K. Campbell of Thames is a little more forthright: "This is my sport and will be my grandson's as well. Why don't you pricks get a life? My father hunted pigs as did his father and also my father-in-law who is 70 years young and still gets out there and enjoys hunting wild pigs." Conservationist and farmer Carl Brogtrop of Thames declares the majority view: "If feral pigs are needed to be culled call/inform the local pig hunter clubs."

Longtime campaigner from Otorohanga, Trevor Addenbrooke is seriously concerned "As a landowner and farm manager, I feel that these extreme measures you propose are totally unnecessary and a breach of our ownership rights to be able to control feral deer, feral goats and pigs ourselves. As a keen hunter myself, and a member of a Pig Hunting Club for many years, I feel along with many others, that this is going to affect our basic right to hunt these animals and for the landowner to control the pests. A more effective way of dealing with the pest problem, if in fact a problem is identified, would be for EW to work with the landowner and with Hunting Clubs as a first line of response to deal with the problem. I feel strongly that there are already many areas of bush that have earmarked as sanctuaries for protected birdlife and that there are enough measures and controls for this already in place in this area…The other issue I feel strongly about is that this proposal is extremely culturally insensitive. The Maori people have had the right to hunt wild animals as a source of food for centuries and this should be allowed to continue."

The Upper Coromandel Landcare Association's first honorary member, conservationist Bill Axbey, now of Cook's Beach, writes "…I consider the proposals nothing more than empire building with the host of new laws, restrictions and reduction of the individual rights…The whole emphasis is on control by EW staff who under the new proposed management strategy make all decisions, monitor, issue directions and decide on future action. It also confers right of entry onto land be it section or farm block for inspections purposes and gives itself the right to charge for such. I am afraid I for one do not have the confidence in such a system or staff, no matter how many art degrees they have…Feral pigs are of particular interest on the Coromandel being a high priority recreational and food source. They have been present for many years and local utilisers and farmers have adequately controlled numbers. Just what present effect pigs have on the indigenous biodiversity values of the Coromandel is a debatable point. The whole Coromandel peninsula is a "High Value Site" to eco-fundamentalists and their judgement as to the value of sites and the dangers pigs represent can be clouded accordingly. There is also much concern that new additives have made 1080 poison baits more acceptable to pigs making extermination over large areas in conjunction with possums a possibility."

Researcher and conservationist Murray Dench of Te Awamutu opposes the inclusion of deer as new EW targets and shares the science that proves EW intervention unnecessary. "The Proposed

Regional Pest Management Strategy states in Part 2 section 6.4 'In forested areas deer will destroy the under-storey.' The science says:-'Herbivores removed little of the total annual forage production (1.1% for deer). Deer removed about 10% of the foliage in the browse tier. In addition as deer obtained much of their food as litter fall, consumption exceeded the amount of material produced in the browse tier. Although the consumption of litter fall does not affect regeneration, it does increase the amount of food available to deer...Neither possums or deer are likely to cause deforestation in the Waihaha catchment, or even cause major shifts in the abundance of the common species. Consequently, the overall diversity of the vegetation is unlikely to change in the longer term. Kamahi appears to be the only tree species likely to respond to moderate reductions in deer density.' (*Science for Conservation/50 Comparison of red deer and possum diets and impacts in podocarp-hardwood forest*, Waihaha Catchment, Pureora Forest Park. G Nugent K W Fraser and P J Sweetapple) Conclusion: In areas which are readily accessible to recreational hunters, deer do not destroy understorey as stated. The proposed RPMS states in Part 2 section6.4: 'Feral deer may also have significant impact on agricultural production values. Feral deer, along with possum, are a vector for bovine tuberculosis.' The science says 'Wild deer in New Zealand are not maintenance hosts for Tb. They contract the disease through some behavioural interaction with possums, most likely live ones ...the absence of Tb in fawns less than 10 months of age, even in areas where over half the adult females that bore them were infected."[i.e.mothers don't even infect their offspring] Deer control is not required in order to reduce transmission of Tb among wild deer and eradicate Tb from them.' Conclusion: Deer are NOT "a vector for bovine tuberculosis" as stated. (Source: Animal Health Board *Epidemiology of Bovine Tuberculosis in Wild Deer* G Nugent J Whitford)

Hugh Barr, National Advocate for the New Zealand Deerstalkers Association (NZDA) was integral in the struggle to articulate opposition to the RPMS. "NZDA opposes (wild) deer and feral pigs being listed as pests, and asks they be removed from the animal pest schedule because they are valued by many Waikato communities, as wild meat for the table, and for recreational hunting, and because they are a significant part of the Waikato's and New Zealand's outdoor activities and traditions.

We show deer numbers are probably in decline in the Waikato. Neither has any evidence been produced saying they are causing environmental damage, soil loss or flood risk. NZDA opposes aerial 1080 poison being spread on public lands in the Waikato region to control pests, because the high deer by-kill that often results eliminates recreational deerstalking for many years while the herd rebuilds. The Graf Boys' DVD *A Shadow of Doubt* shows a high deer by-kill, and low possum numbers in Whirinaki Forest Park.[12] This park is a popular recreational hunting area in the southern Bay of Plenty. Last winter it was part of an AHB aerial 1080 megadrop. Deer were not the target species, but they died anyway. The DVD also highlights the major animal cruelty issues associated with aerial 1080 use, as it kills indiscriminately – deer pigs, birds, possums etc.[13]

Shane Thomsen of Thames says he has "hunted on the Coromandel since I was a young boy and my father has done the same. I have three sons who have experienced the pighunting life since they were capable of walking through the bush. I always get comments about how outgoing and well behaved my sons are. My answer to that is 'instead of roaming the streets through boredom, and making trouble they keep themselves away from criminal activities by pighunting and respecting the land they live in!' I think we should be encouraging more young people to go pighunting on the Coromandel. If EW do their homework and talk to the older pighunters in the Coromandel, they will realize that the pig hunting population is declining, simply because of the hunting pressure from the local people who look forward to their weekly walk and hopefully bring home some food for the family on a regular basis. Hunting pigs is a tradition on the Coromandel, and has been for around 200 years. My ancestors have hunted and gathered food on their land for hundreds of years. These include the local tribes such as Ngati Maru, Ngati Tamatera, Ngati Porou, and Tainui. I am a direct descendant of King Tawhiao, my great, great grandfather. I'm sure he will be rolling in his grave knowing that we cant hunt for a feed anymore..."

Interestingly it falls to the submission from the Ministry for Agriculture and Forestry (MAF) to write from their Wellington perspective to remind EW that "Section 76" of the Biosecurity Act states that the proposal for a pest management strategy must specify "an analysis of the benefits and costs of the strategy"...Although the proposed strategy does state that this analysis was carried out it does not contain a reference to the data or where this information is available…This section (Effects on the Environment) should include an acknowledgement of the potential off-target impacts of pesticides and other methods of animal pest control and that care will be taken during the design of pest management programmes to minimize off-target risk…**animal welfare issues are becoming of much wider concern within NZ and internationally**. Pest management is coming under increasing scrutiny and pest management strategies need to demonstrate a commitment to animal welfare…should also include a statement recognizing EW's commitment to Animal Welfare and utilizing recognized humane methods of pest management in control programmes…Although pest welfare issues will likely not affect international trade, there are some marked concerns overseas with some of our pest control methods. With the growing awareness nationally and overseas of Animal Welfare issues, it is important that authorities are not only seen to be utilizing humane principles, but are also promoting these to stakeholders." [added emphasis]

Mike Grayburn Tokoroa read "with some dismay recently, in the *South Waikato News*, of planned culling, control, extermination of the wild pig population from public and private land in the EW region. The pig was described as a pest. It is a pest in some farm margins near forest boundaries. It may cause some damage to flora in native bush. I am a professional and came to Tokoroa in 1963. Four generations of our family have hunted, worked and recreated in the local forests. They are not overrun with wild pigs. Our community needs access to public and private land to chase wild pigs. This week I canvassed some local farmers on the subject, and to a one they agreed pigs were a pest in the "back paddock" but in the same breath they thought it ludicrous for EW to contemplate extermination. One farmer thought that the timing of the announcement might be an April Fools joke. The historic value of the wild pig to the South Waikato and beyond is massive. It has a sporting function every winter for over 1200 people who pay their Tokoroa Pig Hunting Club fees. There is a social importance for the people who look forward to the season every year, training dogs and sharing skills and tales. An economic function must not be ignored as winter meat supplements the household freezers throughout the region. Hangi without pork would not be right.

Hunting has a culling function in the winter season. The pig is not an environmental pest; it is a far more important resource to the area. Please reconsider this ill-advised option and leave the wild pig population as is."

Giles Bayley, Otorohanga "…If you are wanting to continue this form of control on land owners, I would suggest that you would need to purchase our property. As a farmer, we are always trying to make the best of the grass conditions within the present environment, which includes pest control. We don't like to see pests eating or rooting our ground up. Our farm is bordering onto State-owned native bush from which most of these pests come, and if you think you can come onto our property and point the finger at us as if it is our problem then you are mistaken. I know that in fact there is not a 'pest problem' with pig, goat and deer… It is a wish list by some dreamy idiot, who wishes to see every introduced species within NZ to be eradicated. In regard to this strategy being released for public submission I am disgusted in the way you have gone about trying to get it through without any public consultation, also in such a short time span, and over a holiday period. It shows how little respect EW has with its power trip type tactics."

Conservationist and pig hunter Craig Hodge of Whitianga "can find no current, relevant research that supports the change of the feral pig category from nuisance pest to pest. As you have stated, this decision to define an animal as a pest involves a degree of subjectivity 'and necessarily requires an element of political judgement' and since there is no real research to support this change we are left to believe the change is due to political influence that is unacceptable. We also note as part of the 'screening process' the Council has to be of the opinion that 'a) The animals are capable of causing serious adverse and unintended effects in relation to the Waikato region' and furthermore 'the regional impacts of an animal have to be ranked medium to high to warrant being declared a 'pest'. But by your own admission you accept that the damage done by the feral pig is relatively localized. Therefore there should be no need to change its previous status as the impact is not medium to high but relatively localized. The policy also states 'the benefits of having this strategy outweigh the costs.' As it is currently being managed for free and is under control I cant see how changing it will be beneficial. I would like to see the feral pig returned to its previous category of nuisance pest. I would also like to see the previous management strategies of raising awareness, promoting voluntary control and encouraging private land occupiers to control feral pigs returned. There is absolutely no reason for Council to get involved especially at a cost to ratepayers. I am happy to help with research and control whenever needed. We have kept feral pig populations under control for many years and can see no reason to change the current management of the feral pig. I oppose the description of the feral pig as it omits the fact that the feral pig is an important food and recreational resource. In the 2002-2007 RPMS this information was included and I feel nothing has changed for it to be omitted. This information regarding the feral pig is important to NZ culture and should be included. The feral pig is an important food source for many families, especially over the winter months, as in our region work is very seasonal and some families depend on the meat. It is also a traditional food at many celebrations and meetings...It benefits people's health (numerous kilometres walked), helps boost the local economy by supporting the butchers, retailers (clothing, guns, ammunition), restaurants, lodgings, and pubs and provides family activities especially competitions which also support fund-raising for the local schools. As a hunter on the Coromandel for over 30 years I can testify that the pig population is under control and is on the decrease...you cannot compare the Coromandel pig population with statistics taken from the Murchison area in the South Island 18 years ago."

Neil Stewart of Tokoroa reminds EW it "should not be responsible for possum control. The DOC should control possum numbers. Keeping possum numbers down to 5%RTC will involve 1080 drops that I oppose only because of the so-called non-target bykill of deer and pigs.... EW should encourage trappers to control possums. While prices are high for possum fur ($90 kg) EW should seek a Polytech or similar to hold courses for possumers." W.Petersen on behalf of Tainui Pighunting Club, Urenui declares "We are a club that operates mostly in Southern King Country, Northern Taranaki areas and we strongly oppose this proposal by EW. We feel 99% of private landowners...(have) their own preferred hunters on their phone list. We promote recreational pig hunting to the youth in these areas to help keep them on the straight and narrow...The wild pig is both a source of food and recreation to thousands of New Zealanders. Our club is so pro-active that we are promoting 'kiwi proofing' our dogs to enhance the pristine native forest. Where is your consultation?

Colville farmer and pig hunter, John Ward demands EW "Leave wild pigs to the existing pig hunters for sport and food. Pig numbers are under control and remain so if hunted regularly, which happens so long as 1080 hasn't been spread around by DOC and Regional Council. You can't even afford to control gorse properly. Why take on more so-called pests and waste more ratepayer's money?" Graham Wilson of Whitianga writes "Pigs were given to our tupuna by the captains of the early timber ships and are regarded as taonga...It would not be in the spirit of the Treaty to implement new legislation...Consult your Treaty partners." Marcus and Anne Ward, longtime farmers and conservationists from the western side of Moehau mountain, have stood up on behalf of rural dwellers from the very first RPMS. Their first documented submission is to the 1994 WRC document: *Managing Pests for Our Future* where Marcus and Anne Ward are submitters 86, John Goudie is submitter 119 with Mrs B Dench representing the NZ Deerstalkers Association along with Rangi Mahuta's submission on behalf of Huakina Development Trust. (HDT) HDT also contributes in 2006 highlighting serious concerns regarding EW dumping pesticides in the Waikato River alongside which they inhabit "five Marae...Huakina has in the past been outspoken regarding our objection to the use of 1080..." Back in 1994 David Taipari appears in slot 125 with a submission made on behalf of Moehau nga Tangata Whenua Trust Board in 1994 but this group does not appear to contribute in 2006.

Tokoroa submitters including Bruce Belfield, Sandi and Colin Cureen remind EW deer and wild pigs are not pests and that DOC is responsible for wild animal management under the Wild Animal Control Act. They question the squandering of ratepayer money. "Our Local Branch of NZ Deerstalkers is more than willing to work with EW staff to help reduce high numbers of deer and wild pigs in the region if and where they may exist...Browsing damage by deer is over exaggerated. In the Waikato region deer browse damage is hardly recognisable. DOC and Forest and Bird are totally over the top saying deer are damaging the forest. If this is true let them prove deer and wild pigs are causing all this damage. The fact is weather is the main cause of erosion and damage not only in the forest but in the whole country. Aerial 1080 is killing native birds and invertebrates indiscriminately and often in large numbers... This country prosecutes people who are cruel to animals. Who is prosecuting those who are dropping 1080 poison? Don't they know the cruel and heartless way it kills animals. Maybe these people should be watching an animal while it is dying after eating 1080 poison. It is hard to understand why DOC and Forest and Bird are condoning the use of 1080, when they should be protecting wild life not destroying it."

The issue of toxin 1080 use is thoroughly covered with the submission of Clare St Pierre but the toxin is not mentioned once in the final RPMS. This deception is maintained with 'control' being the euphemism as to how we kill wild animals. Terry Care, President Te Kuiti Pig Hunting Club spoke to their submission. "Te Kuiti Pig Hunting Club has 140 members. This year in June we will be celebrating our 20th anniversary. The club has been part of our local community for two decades. In that time the club has grown to a position where we now own our own clubrooms at Hangatiki (formerly the Hangatiki Hall). Our members have been part of countless pig hunting competitions organised to raise money for charities in our local communities e.g. schools, sports clubs etc. These competitions also have a children's section for small game such as heaviest possum, rabbit, magpie etc. We are getting kids out into the native bush participating in a unique sport that is part of our culture. We were approached by the Te Kuiti Centenary Committee to organise a pig hunting competition as part of the celebrations. This was one of the most popular and best patronised events during the centenary and is further recognition of the role pig hunting has played in the history of Te Kuiti and a large number of other towns in rural New Zealand...The Te Kuiti Pig Hunting Club strongly believes that the Proposed Pest Management Strategy in its current form will have a detrimental effect on pig hunting and the associated communities."

Nigel Keall, a committee member of the Te Kuiti Pig Hunting Club writes "We accept and support the control of a large number of pests for the benefit of our native bush and birds...Our club members and a large number of other persons in the community still rely on the feral pig as a major source of food and recreation. Pig hunting is part of our history and culture. Hunting is a recognised recreational activity that sees large numbers of people each week getting into our great outdoors, exercising and socialising. We find it frustrating that Environment Waikato does not recognise this. Feral pigs and native birds, although not specifically targeted, have also suffered a reduction in numbers from previous Environment Waikato 'pest control' operations where our native bush is top dressed with 1080. Each feral pig killed by Environment Waikato whether through direct control or as a bykill during other pest control operations is a wasted resource and a waste of ratepayer funds. This situation can only have resulted from misplaced idealism, a lack of consultation or ignorance. Pig Hunting Clubs and individual pig hunters have also been remiss in ensuring their views are heard at a regional and national level. This type of bureaucratic attitude is the justification many people are using when illegally releasing wild animals. These releases are generally undertaken to establish new areas for hunting or to replenish stock following control operations. We do not need to outline to you the threat these releases provide. Our club does not support the illegal release of feral pigs. Any localised damage from feral pigs or any threat to high value sites could be easily controlled with better liaison between Environment Waikato staff and pig hunting clubs.

"We also take issue with several "facts" as outlined in Section 6.6 of the proposed strategy. The feral pig has a minimal environmental impact. It is not a browsing animal. It's rooting of the forest floor and consumption of native fruit and berries, is quite sustainable. The very high estimates of feral pig densities referred to in the proposed strategy are not representative of the Waikato area. It is also unfair (and poor science) to compare the diet of feral pigs in the Waikato with those studied on Auckland and D'Urville Islands. The two latest 'scientific studies' being proffered relate to Aorangi and Lord Howe Island. Aorangi is a small island in the Poor Knights group and Lord Howe Island is in Australian territory. Both locations are islands that have different climate, terrain and biodiversity to the Waikato region. Both receive little or no recreational hunting pressure. Their relevance to our local situation is nil. There is no evidence that the feral pig is a threat to biodiversity in the Waikato region. We have previously assisted EW to collect feral pigs for TB sampling. There were no positive results from the fifty samples we provided. This is an example of what can be achieved when EW work in concert with the community rather than against them. Recreational hunters have and will continue to provide all necessary feral pig control in the Waikato region. There is no history of problems and with numbers declining it is highly unlikely that this will eventuate. In conclusion we believe that the feral pig is not an environmental or production threat in the Waikato. The fact that they have co-existed with 'threatened species' in 'high value sites' for centuries is clear evidence of this. We wish to have the feral pig relieved of its 'pest' status. It should not be included in the Pest Management Strategy. It should be recognised and managed as the community resource that it is."

A large group of deerstalkers mostly from from Te Aroha and Paeroa but also from Hamilton, Morrinsville, Upper Hutt, Auckland, and Te Puke oppose inclusion of deer, pigs and goats. Their robust submission concludes: "There is no need whatsoever for deer, pigs and goats to be changed to pests—this is a total sledgehammer to hit in a tack scenario. It is also EW's way of taking full and total control and giving them undeniable access to all land due to loose worded conditions. Hedgehogs are a red herring. Every property has hedgehogs so this will give EW/WRC an open mandate to enter properties at will and use the working 'high value sites' at its own discretion. Recreational hunters can, do and will continue to keep deer and pig numbers under control. WRC via using 1080 and anticoagulant poisons however, are making meat hunting a non-option with these poisons in the animal's system so hence, lack of hunting will create higher numbers and play into the lap of WRC's argument. Keep the poisons and the dictatorial attitudes out off our backcountry, work with the hunters (recreational) and promote a healthy community, healthy environment and healthy respect for all concerned...It is clearly pointed out that Transit will not be liable for its road reserves but local councils will—talk about greasing to another well funded and empowered body. This is simply because Transit would laugh in your face and tell you to complain to someone who cares! It is also of grave concern to all that WRC has written into this plan that they are not liable for any claims made resulting from the implementation of this strategy. This attitude is totally 'Hitlerish" and cannot be tolerated in the realms of democracy...Quite clearly due to the arrogant actions and behaviour of some WRC decision makers...we do not trust or respect your words and its time you thought long and hard about working with the communities and recreational hunters as opposed to doing the dirty on us time after time."

Brett & Suzanne Millward of Raglan "…come from a long line of hunters…believe your problem is feral cats and mustelids. Get onto that with traps and you will really make headway. (We) do not believe it is in the interests of the community to give more power to EW staff. Pigs are historically part of NZ culture. They were placed here by our ancestors as a food source and continue to be one. They are currently controlled adequately…EW have too much power now and already take huge areas of hunting away by their indiscriminate use of 1080. In short I don't trust them. EW need to consult in a far more open way with landowners and hunters…use of 1080 will come back and bit you. Talk to us." Mike Bailey Secretary of the Taupo Branch NZDA declares "Deer and pigs are not pests. They are a highly valued game animal and should be recognized for that. They are also a wild food source for many hunters and their families, myself included (I am) very concerned that EW intends to double its RPMS expenditure over the five years of the Plan for no worthwhile reason. With reduced incidence of Tb in the region, pest expenditure must be reduced. This Plan is an excessive example of needless poisoning and empire building by EW. Better control of contaminated stock movement will help reduce the spread of bovine Tb. The requirements of S72 of the Biosecurity Act to supply Cost-Benefit assessments (CBA) individually for all species named as pests, has not been complied with. So the draft RPMS does not adequately inform the public, and should should be withdrawn, re-written and re-issued to provide this information."

Maureen Coleman, President Thames Valley Deerstalkers Association, presented a well-crafted verbal submission on behalf of their nearly 300 members and voiced the "absolute disgust that our group as a whole has for the handling of this entire process and the shocking behaviour, dodging and falsities dished out to us and numerous other groups and individuals." Coleman attacks the frustrating issue of the limited time frame for submissions as well as the abysmal information distribution to ordinary ratepayers and addresses the patronizing responses from EW, the loose wording that contributed to uncertain interpretations, the matter of toxin distribution, the ill-defined high value sites, and the fact that EW cannot control the list of pests they already list, so why add more? She discusses the Nugent paper of 1988 and the Dyke Report of 2000, showing total numbers of active deer stalkers and pig hunters plus the dollar value put back into the NZ economy, and that does not even include merino mink, wild venison and possum products. This information she contrasts with the enormous rise in rates take for the burgeoning EW poison pest plan, a rise of over 100% in three years. The health and well being of rural NZ is questioned, as youngsters are encouraged through the local clubs to engage with the wilderness, learn about mother nature and to take responsibility for food gathering. Coleman finds then regional councilor, Arthur Hinds, amusing for his comments in the April 2007 *Envirocare* EW newsletter, as possum numbers are back to an all time high in the Whenuakite Kiwi Zone after 1080 was dumped just one year earlier, and pigs are also back because pig hunters will not go anywhere near there.

Locals are dubbing this 1080 poisoning a failure. Apparently Hinds is quoted in the EW puff piece as saying the poisoning was a great success. Bovine Tb (BTb) is not the problem: contamination from poisons is the problem. She discusses one of the helicopter companies (EPRO) involvement with toxin dumping. "It is a well known fact as often heard from EPRO staff, that BTb reactors will always be just around the corner where EPRO's next job is about to start. These people have, naturally for job security reasons, not put this is writing, however numerous staff have admitted that reactor animals from infected areas have 'found their way' into an area that is next on the poisoning list to give weight to the argument. It's amazing how far a deer can go stropped under a chopper or on the back of a vehicle—this wreaks of underhandedness and clearly goes on unchecked to back up your claims. Finally as I close my submission here, can I get from you please, an honest answer as to why, when all but fragments of this document are so totally loosely worded, that on page 168 under Compensation, that you can all of a sudden produce a firm, undeniably worked sentence that cannot be manipulated by anyone? That sentence reads: 'No compensation will be payable by WRC for any claims brought, for any matters, as a result of the implementation of this strategy.'" She writes elsewhere "Keep poison out of the big game food chain." Given this country's penchant for herbicides and pesticides, this slogan could work just as well as a chant demanding: Keep poison out of our food chain.

Terry O'Neil of Thames writes: "I'm the third generation O"Neil to hunt the Coromandel. Now my son and grandson also hunt pigs in the Colville, Port Jackson area. In the 1970's I could travel to Colville and catch 5 or 6 pigs on a weekend. Now in 2007 I could travel 6 times and catch one pig. There's no pig problem anywhere on the Peninsula…so why change?" The gregarious conservationist and Treasurer of the Coromandel Pig Hunting Club, Bill Lightfoot writes: "…I have been pig hunting for over 60 years…The wild pig is a main food source, not only for rural people but also for many pig hunters who reside in the city and enjoy the sport of pig hunting. Throughout the years many thousands of young people have been encouraged to take up the sport of pig hunting. They have been taught to enjoy it and at the same time, learn to respect and take care of their environment. If this opportunity had not been available for our young folk, many would have lived a wayward lifestyle. Who knows I could have been one of them. The pigs are fewer and fewer, not only in the Coromandel but it is a general trend throughout the country brought about by hunting pressure. I recently spoke to a farmer north of Colville who said, in times gone by, he shot approximately 100 pigs a year while working around his farm. But he says he has only shot one pig in the last 12 years. Our club has an annual competition that attracts 80 plus adult and 70 plus junior entries. The average number of pigs weighed in, in the last 3 years has been around 3 per competition. These figures show how low the pig polulation has become in the Coromandel compared with previous years. Coromandel town and businesses show support for the Pig Hunting Club by sponsoring virtually all the prizes. As an encouragement for the effort of enthusiasm and keenness put in by them, all junior entries receive a prize for something or another. The delight, pride and respect it brings to these young people, our future generation, is a wonderful sight to see. So tell me, why is EW spending millions of dollars of public money when hunters are doing the job for nothing! The impact that pigs have in your current policy, such as crop damage, stock damage, and pasture damage is misleading information, which by no means can, or should be, used to describe the current pig situation as it stands in it's present day form…About 10 years ago at a meeting in Papa Aroha the DOC propaganda machine told us when they were about to control the Blue Mountain area east of Papa Aroha, the poison Talon they were using was totally safe, totally biodegradeable and would not leave any lasting residues. They backed these statements by saying they had done extensive tests on this product and were 100% sure of its capabilities. We recently had a meeting with a senior DOC official about the effect of 1080 poison at which he stated that over recent yeasrs they have discovered Talon leaves poison residue in both animal carcasses and the ground…Now we are getting the same propaganda message about 1080 and its uses. Can we expect in a few years time the same message from DOC about 1080 as we have received about Talon…that is…'we are very sorry that further tests on 1080 have revealed that it is not safe as we thought and we must stop using it' is to come?"

Tony Pearse NZ Deer Farmers' Association Ltd on authority and on behalf of the NZDFA Executive Committee and the Chairs of the Local NZDFA Branches of Waikato (George Thomas), Waipa (Brian Wellington), Rotorua (Andrew Mitchell), Tongariro (John Derbridge), Bay of Plenty (Earle Wells) reminds EW that more than 150,000 people hunt something in New Zealand each year and access to hunting areas has been identified as a major contributor to hunter success and enjoyment of the outdoors. "There seems to be some confusion and muddling of the role of the department of Conservation and Regional Councils. Whilst in general terms regional councils have responsibilities under the Resource Management Act and where applicable, the Biosecurity Act, it is the Department of Conservation that is mandated by the Wild Animal Control Act 1977 to control deer and wild pigs on public conservation land. DOC receives funding from central government for this purpose. It is not the role of regional government to take over this role or to double the financial burden onto ratepayers for work that should be funded by central government. If DOC does not see the control of deer and pigs to be a priority then EW should not usurp this position…Eradication is an impractical objective for the widespread ungulate species particularly red deer. Many New Zealanders are unwilling to accept that their support for the conservation of native species and ecosystems must necessarily come at the cost of denying any place in New Zealand's wild lands for introduced species such as deer and pigs…Biodiversity by definition must include valued introduced biodiversity. Deer and pigs enhance our cultural heritage not derogate from it. The harvest of pigs has been an integral part of the New Zealand way of life…Regional goals should reflect the aspirations of ratepayers and in the case of deer; we do not for one minute believe that including deer in the strategy is pursuant to the aspirations of the hunters, farmers, and general public of the Waikato. Deer, nor pigs, are a threat to primary production…At densities existing in the Waikato Region what examples of the severe deterioration of forested areas exist?…We challenge EW to come up with specific examples in the Waikato Region…It concerns us that a regional authority is attempting to impose greater regulation in this area than a national policy and programme…The use of toxins will also have the potential to detract from our clean green image…Hunting has been very effective at reducing deer numbers and protecting native ecosystems in forested areas…"

Warren Jeffcoat President Peninsula Pig Hunting Club writes, "We strongly object to your intention to eradicate the feral pig from public and private land in NZ. Our membership includes a wide range of ages, from 16 to 79 but the vast majority are fathers and grandfathers…In our pig hunting club there is a strong incentive to take our children and grandchildren out hunting with us for some very exciting and healthy family experiences. It promotes good strong family ties and interaction." Sadly now passed on, Louis Ross of Whitianga required EW to "…Please note: The first law of the environment and evolution is all must contribute more than they take."

Bureaucracy Blows Up
Kiwi Sanctuaries on the Coromandel

"I'm only one in a long line of rabble rousers, as a critic once termed me. If we don't find more, then God help us. I still think we can win the battle, but we wont have a show if we continue to swallow the arrogant, self-serving attitudes of recent governments...At election times politicians are supposed to give an account of themselves, their actions and policies and we will be fools in the extreme if we do not take them to task."

John Henderson[14]

The very organization designed to promote biodiversity ends up destroying their fragile community support. No one originally opposed the idea of "kiwi sanctuaries". So how did the kiwi sanctuaries implode? DOC dreamed up the label Moehau Kiwi Sanctuary (MKS) to encompass the entire tip of the peninsula. No private landowner was consulted. The Department of Conservation advertises and takes credit for maintaining an 18,500-hectare unofficial Moehau Kiwi Sanctuary when in actual fact the DOC land comprises well under half that area. No neighbouring landowner has a problem with inclusion until the new RPMS comes along threatening eradication of wild pigs from kiwi sanctuaries and their surrounds. Almost overnight DOC's so-called "kiwi sanctuary" was reduced in size by approximately 10,000 hectares when many nearby landowners formally declared their properties were not, and had never been, part of any official DOC scheme.

The Upper Coromandel Landcare Association (UCLA) alerts the public via a press release dated 24 April 2007 under the headline: *EW Blows Up Map of Kiwi Sanctuary.*

"Conservationists who farm more than 15,000 acres on the upper Coromandel today notified the Department of Conservation in Thames that their properties are located outside the department's Moehau Kiwi Sanctuary (MKS). The notifications to DOC mean that the MKS is reduced by over 40 percent in total area, and its map resembles a Swiss cheese. Additional withdrawals are expected.

Farming families acted in direct response to a sweeping expansion of wild animal control powers announced by Environment Waikato (EW) in its draft regional pest management strategy and follow-up statements by EW officials in recent weeks. The Moehau Kiwi Sanctuary (MKS) is an informal label used to identify an operational area where these same residents, together with community groups and DOC, have been working cooperatively and voluntarily for years on a range of pest initiatives. There is no statutory or regulatory basis for the kiwi zone. There was no formal consultation process before its establishment, and no permissions were either sought or granted for inclusion. Of concern to landowners are EW plans to inspect and monitor all properties, without consent and particularly in kiwi sanctuaries, and to order destruction of any wild pig populations down to whatever level council chooses and by whatever means it deems most cost effective, including poisons. Farmers have successfully controlled wild pigs for generations at no cost whatsoever to the regional ratepayers. They also are active in possum and stoat control, in many cases at their own expense. According to Reihana Robinson, spokesperson for the Upper Coromandel Landcare Association, 'EW with its new pest strategy has blown up the Moehau Kiwi Sanctuary. But our commitment to environmental and conservation efforts in and around Moehau is ongoing.'

Landowners of thousands of hectares of land around Moehau signed a letter withdrawing their land from the designated 'kiwi sanctuary'. The letters were delivered to Hauraki DOC.[15]

But while the DOC kiwi sanctuary "shrank", the hard conservation work has continued. Families around Moehau have always been keen environmentalists, and these residents continue to hunt and trap possums, stoats and rats on their own land, on their own time, and at their own expense. Their efforts have been rewarded many times over by the sounds and sights of healthy kiwi and other native and non-native species. Credit is due for their sustained conservation efforts, without the benefit of grant money handouts, on thousands of hectares outside of DOC's own "kiwi zone".

Letters describing the unofficial MEG Kiwi Sanctuary (MEGKS) situated further south of Moehau were drafted and sent off by farmers whose private land would also be at risk. That area comprises, according to a DOC colour brochure, all private and public property south of Port Charles and Waikawau Roads to Amodeo Bay and then in an east-northeasterly direction to Kennedy Bay and Tuateawa. Meanwhile the Eastern Coromandel Landcare Association (ECLA) sent off similar letters to the Whenuakite Kiwi Care Group (WKCG) withdrawing private land from the so-called Whenuakite Kiwi Zone (WKZ). Shortsighted Hamilton bureaucrats who had imagined they were able to act with impunity with regard to crafting new definitions of private land encountered ineluctable opposition.

The Moehau Messenger 24 May 2007 begins "Although more than 6000ha of private land is no longer included in the Moehau Kiwi Sanctuary kiwi ranger Yuri Forbes, who has worked there for six years, believes people are generally supportive of what the group is trying to do…The staff at Moehau has recorded a 77% increase in kiwi chick survival…The sanctuary has existed since 2000 but has no official recognition." *DOC Denies Kiwi Sanctuary in Jeopardy* is the headline in the Hamilton daily newspaper the *Waikato Times* of April 27, 2007 where Martin Tiffany and Reon Suddaby pick up UCLA's press release: "The Conservation Department denies its Moehau kiwi sanctuary is in jeopardy, despite at least 20 farm families pulling land out of the project. Coromandel farmer Reihana Robinson said at least 20 farming families were in the process of withdrawing their support for the kiwi sanctuary in response to a 'sweeping expansion of wild animal control powers announced by Environment Waikato'. Their land accounted for about 40 per cent of the sanctuary's 18,000ha. Another 7000ha is a state forest park. The withdrawal is a response to Environment Waikato's draft regional pest management strategy. Proposed changes give Environment Waikato greater flexibility to control wild pigs 'but only if they are shown to be damaging high-value conservation areas or sensitive upper catchment watershed areas.' DOC spokesperson Des Williams said while the farmers' actions were disappointing, their land sat on the fringes of the forest park and the future of the kiwi sanctuary was not at risk…Department staff would meet the farmers to discuss their concerns, Mr. Williams said. 'It won't happen overnight, but in time we'll catch up with them and talk through the issues.' Environment Waikato's biosecurity and heritage group manager, John Simmons, said people had got the wrong end of the stick. The proposed changes were only 'subtle' and had no major impact. Farmers and hunters disagree, saying the draft strategy would give the regional council sweeping powers and that the policy was railroaded through without proper consultation. Mr. Simmons said today's hunters' meeting at 2pm at the Waikato Events Centre, would give him the opportunity to set the record straight. Ms Robinson, spokeswoman for the Upper Coromandel Landcare Association, said farmers had successfully controlled wild pigs for generations, at no cost to regional ratepayers. Despite formally pulling out of the sanctuary, they would continue pest control initiatives. 'Of concern to landowners are Environment Waikato plans to inspect and monitor all properties, without consent and particularly in kiwi sanctuaries, and to order destruction of any wild pig populations down to whatever level council chooses and by whatever means it deems most cost-effective, including poisons,' she said." What readers of the draft strategy find ominous EW defines as 'subtle'. Herein lies the division between the perception from an office block and that of people living on the back blocks.

Some History or Phoenix Rising

*1841 census: "European and natives' staple diet was pork
and potatoes"*

Dom Felice Vagglioli[16]

Back on September 31, 2000 certain Coromandel residents were surprised to receive a letter from EW's Peter Russell headed: *"Key Ecological Sites identified for Pest Control in the Thames-Coromandel District.* Environment Waikato has identified land you own or have an interest in as a Key Ecological Site in the Waikato Region, and assistance for pest control and fencing of bush and wetland areas may be available." Key Ecological Sites (KES) are in fact a phoenix rising once more in 2006 manifested in the RPMS, albeit sporting a new acronym—HVS or High Value Site. It will appear in yet another guise in 2012 as Significant Natural Areas or SNA's. Russell's 2000 letter continues "Ecological and pest management specialists, Gerry Kessels and Associates and EcoFX Pest Solutions Ltd, were engaged by EW in late 1999 to identify ecologically significant areas in private ownership and rank each site for priority for animal and plant pest control...Thirty-six Key Ecological Sites were identified in the Thames Coromandel District, and a further 110 in the Waikato and Franklin Districts. The Thames Coromandel sites comprise 14,400 ha, with the four largest sites covering 7000 ha." Cost to EW for the Coromandel KES report is just under the $50,000 limit for manager's discretion requiring no full Council decision. The letter goes on: "Incidentally you and the people who we have talked to about the KES programme, have interpreted wrongly the intentions of EW. We are not interested in land confiscation, taking land off people etc. Fencing may be an issue for some sites and some properties within sites but it is not a blanket policy decision by any means. The claim that no one has been consulted also is untrue."

EW's John Simmons writes on May 7, 2001 "As a consequence of the RPMS Hearings Committee deliberations and a legal opinion supplied by A. Logan of Ross Dowling Marquet Griffen Barristers and Solicitors it appears prudent for Council to extend the current RPMS for a further year. There are several issues that provide uncertainty to progressing the proposed RPMS until staff has completed further analysis, and it appears likely that Council will have to withdraw the proposed RPMS and propose a 'revised' proposed RPMS later this year. The issues that require further analysis to provide more rigour and legal substance to the proposal are a detailed cost benefit analysis for each pest species proposed, a review of the funding policy, detailed costs of the strategy for each species or category of species and changes to the Key Ecological component." This document is co-signed by the Group Manager Policy, A.M.D. Rennes.

The *2000 National Biodiversity Strategy* states "Landowners generally don't react positively to being told what to do on their land, therefore regulation is likely to be counterproductive and also risks losing many private 'conservators' across the country." This strategy remained unread or ignored by regional councillors and staff responsible for the draft RPMS and revealed their lack of sensitivity to rural communities. Farmers have long memories on the Coromandel so this material provides a backdrop and informs the coming confrontation with DOC.

Waikato Pig Hunters up in Arms

"Leave wild animals alone please, especially wild pigs"
Ngahere von Bassewitz-Wafer[17]

Farming newspapers, local papers and radio stations carry the story about proposed changes to the pest strategy out into the wider community. The largest pig hunter's club in the country then organises a public meeting at Claudelands Events Centre in Hamilton on Anzac Day, April 25, 2007. Martin Tiffany's *Waikato Times* headline of April 24 reads: *Hunters put pest plan in the gun.* "A proposed pest plan has put the future of a significant kiwi sanctuary under threat, and will see hundreds of Waikato hunters meet tomorrow in protest. The hunters head to the Hamilton meeting concerned that Environment Waikato's proposed policy changes will mean there will soon be nothing left to hunt. The hunters are expected in by the busload from around the Waikato and as far afield as Hawkes Bay for a public meeting to oppose the council's draft Regional Pest Management Strategy. It upgrades pig and deer to a higher grade of pest and proposes culling them in areas considered 'high value.'... Mr Fitzgerald and his club, which boasts a membership of about 1300, are behind the public meeting to be held from 2pm tomorrow at the Waikato Events Centre at Claudelands." The flyer for the meeting states 'The battle lines have been drawn and it is time for hunters to stand up and be counted and show that we are a united force to be reckoned with. We are not only fighting for our chosen sport, but the hunting opportunities of the future generations. A comprehensive legal submission has been lodged with Environment Waikato, but now your personal support is needed if we are to put a stop to this evil plan. Please come along, bring your mates and let your concerns be heard."

From as far away as Napier an article appears in the *Hawkes Bay Today* newspaper headed *Bay pig hunters trigger alarm* written on April 23, 2007 by Lawrence Gullery. "Hawke's Bay pig hunters are worried a harder line on culling feral pigs may reduce their hunting opportunities in the region's ranges. Waikato territorial authorities are looking at tougher methods to control the number of feral pigs in the Coromandel Peninsula that has pig hunters in Hawke's Bay asking whether the same methods could be employed here. The Hawke's Bay Pig Hunters Club will attend a public meeting at the Hamilton Town Hall on April 25 to discuss, with other hunting clubs, Environment Waikato Regional Council's pest management strategy. The meeting, organised by the Tokoroa Pig Hunters Club, has invited Environment Waikato to explain how it intends to deal with wild pigs. The strategy will allow the council to control pig numbers without land owners' permission, but only if the animals are damaging 'high value' areas."

Farmers and pig hunters and conservationists head off to Hamilton from the Coromandel. It is a sunny Anzac Day and hundreds of people turn up, whole families, old and young, pākehā and māori and the stage is set. After some negotiation UCLA is invited to be one of the speakers. From back stage it appeared the EW speakers were able to exert some pressure on the timetable. UCLA addressed the scant public information and timeframe for submissions:

"If you by chance saw the one-time ads EW placed in some local papers there was no mention of the major changes being considered for traditional pig and deer game resources. If you saw EW's mailout to homes, no mention there either. Most people were completely unaware the plan even existed and heard about the pest plan by word of mouth. How to get a copy? EW said in its adverts to go to the local library for a look-in. Or you could download all 180 pages and go blind trying to read it on your computer, if it doesn't crash. As a last resort, maybe EW would mail you a copy and you might have a few days to respond. Some of us here were able to get the document in time and were fortunate enough to have the time to review it. But to see that the public had an opportunity to have its say, we formally asked CEO Harry Wilson to extend the submission deadline by a few weeks. No way, Wilson told us. The law said no less than 20 days for public comment, and EW decided to go with the bare minimum… plus the long Easter weekend. Thanks for nothing, Harry.

And while an outraged public was getting the word out, out came so-called biodiversity manager John Simmons on radio and in newspapers, not to listen, but to tell us all we are wrong and we are extreme. Unbeknownst to most of us, EW had solicited input on a discussion document last year from more than a hundred interested parties. As it turns out, more than a third are government employees or EW contractors. Most people in this room would say they are interested parties and serious stakeholders. But how many people here today were asked their opinions of the major changes being considered? EW was not listening…except to its best friends. Over the last few weeks, EW went into damage control and spin patrol. It is not what the proposal actually states, we are told. It's how EW really feels that counts. Trust us, they say. Instead of listening EW has been out there telling us to calm down. They have been doggedly defending, when they should be taking citizen concerns on board. So much for an intentionally botched process.

On to the product: bad policy from beginning to end. EW`s catchy new marketing pitch for 2007 is `Maintain the Gain`. That`s right. Well to most of us it is more like `Maintain the Drain`…on ratepayer wallets. Or `Maintain the Pain`…for regular kiwis trying their best to make ends meet. But one thing is for sure: Environment Waikato has set out to expand its patch at ratepayer expense. Although they present no cost-benefit analysis as stipulated, EW does slip in a new, targeted pest rate to apply from Hamilton to Port Jackson based on capital value to fund the new scheme.

Who will pay? Anyone who owns or rents a home in town or out on the back blocks. And they have the nerve to suggest that this spending should double from $5 million to $10 million in only four years. How is that for fiscal responsibility? Of course, you cannot blame them. What do you do when your budget dries up? Most of us conserve, recycle, and maybe add a cup of water to the soup. What does a bureaucrat do when their budget dries up? In this case, we all know that Animal Health Board funding for Tb is supposed to be drying up. So lo and behold new pests are born and environmental enemies declared. The only problem is that EW is pinning the tail on every single ratepayer.

*As for policy relating to specific species, big changes were made to the status of wild pigs. These tough animals have been part of New Zealand bush for well over two hundred years. They are no recent accidental release from Oz or containership escapees. They were gifted to tangata whenua and have been a valuable food, recreational, cultural and economic resource for yonks. But all that has changed in EW`s new policy. Every last word describing pigs as any kind of resource have been eliminated from the draft policy. Pigs are no longer a resource. According to EW, they are now production and environmental threats .It has been astounding to hear EW backtrack when called on this issue. According to John Simmons and councilor Hinds, EW **really does** value pigs as a resource. Honest they do. That`s why they removed the language saying so. It is not what the document says that counts. It is what Simmons and Hinds say that we are to believe.*

We say if EW truly regards pigs as a resource, the document should say so in black and white. Wild pigs are a resource to be managed, not a pest to be controlled. And there are many other critical problems. To many residents across the region, EW`s aggressive expansion of enforcement powers is completely out of line. EW proposes to inspect and monitor all properties for the presence of wild pigs, with or without landowner consent. They furthermore intend to order or carry out the destruction of pig populations *down to whatever level they wish and by whatever means they deem most cost-effective (more aerial 1080 anyone?*

And where does EW intend to carry out its game animal eradication schemes? Well if you read the actual draft, the precise legally crafted language gives EW the authority to eliminate pigs in virtually all of the Coromandel and much of the Waikato. It is all there in black and white. Talk about expanding your patch! But when the public objected this month, once again EW went into damage control. At first, on public radio EW`s John Simmons told a porky. EW only planned to do some pig control in a very few special sites of high significance, not over large areas. But about a week later, Simmons took some truth serum and acknowledged that EW did intend to knock down pigs, but only in certain areas...such as in and near kiwi sanctuaries! Well now we know what we knew all along.

To give you an idea of what this means, more than 60,000 acres on the northern Coromandel has been designated kiwi sanctuaries with more popping up regularly. Allowing for the range of pigs and looking closely at EW`s document, this means goodbye wild pork pie on the peninsula. And EW has carefully drafted language that makes virtually all of the ranges subject to their pig eradication policies. If not because of so-called biodiversity claims, then by virtue of real or imaginary impact on catchments. There are problems on almost every page of EW`s proposed strategy. So the big question for many of us has been —Why? Why is EW doing this? How can they be so out of touch? Out of touch with tradition. Out of touch with public sentiment. Out of touch with fiscal reality. Out of touch with the environmental mainstream. One reporter recently asked Simmons if there was new evidence that pig populations had significantly increased in the region or that new production threats had been identified. To both questions he answered no.

Did anyone ask for these changes? Did farmers moan about production losses? Is the bush being degraded? We the public have been hearing just the opposite. To find out more we used the Official Information Act to learn this past Monday that all of the respondents to EW`s request for input last year urged that council not intervene in the control of wild pigs, all parties, (of the 15 responses in total) bar one: Department of Conservation. EW`s best friend when it comes to budget problems...DOC. DOC presented Hamilton its wish list for EW`s new five-year strategy to Santa Claus over at his workshop on 401 Grey Street. And boy has Santa delivered. As the documents confirm, EW has not written a plan for its ratepayers at all. It hasn`t written a plan for residents, farmers, hunters and employers, it has written a plan for DOC.

With regard to pigs, DOC states it had a problem with access to private property. So it calls on EW to step in and take over pig control for them... even though wild pigs are not the responsibility of regional councils. And there is plenty more to confirm that the hidden hand behind the odd behaviour of EW in this case is DOC. And were critics over the past couple of weeks off the mark when they pointed out that EW was giving itself the power to order pig eradications over virtually the entire Coromandel Peninsula? Not at all. They were spot on. In the DOC memo obtained this week under our OIA request, DOC states boldly and clearly regarding feral goats, pigs and deer 'we would like to see the entire Coromandel peninsula declared a high priority conservation area in recognition of the Peninsula Project and Waihou Valley scheme'.

So there you have it. EW`s process was flawed not because these guys are stupid. They are not. They are very clever…up to a point. And is this draft policy a disaster because EW planners have made some unfortunate errors? No way. The document reflects exactly what EW intended to put over on the public. A plan that creates new problems and guarantees huge budget increases.

There are steps we can take. First, because of process shortcomings and numerous problems with content —the entire 2007-12 Proposed Pest Management Strategy should be withdrawn. The public should demand this loud and clear. Second, Biosecurity Manager John Simmons at EW should resign. He has presided over a disaster and has failed to serve his real constituency. He has failed Waikato ratepayers Third, let EW staff, councilors, newspapers, talkback listeners know that we are fed up and have had enough of being lead around by a nose ring. It`s time EW got responsible with its budget and responsive to the public. Fourth, if EW does not withdraw this strategy or rewrite it in the interest of the general public, then please be prepared to join a range of groups and individuals who have pledged to take the matter right up through the highest courts. And we look forward to your presence in the week starting May 21 at the hearings. There is a place for everyone to express their individual concerns and an opportunity to stand together."

During the boisterous meeting in Hamilton a question was directed at EW's John Simmons wanting clarification of the statement made by dairy farmer and EW councillor for Thames-Coromandel, Arthur Hinds who had stated in *Farmers Weekly* April 2 2007 "There are places where pigs are a threat." However when John Simmons was asked at the Anzac Day Hamilton meeting to define locations where pigs or deer that are proving a production threat or an environmental threat he repudiated the statement and said that no one had suggested a location in the Waikato.

Alison Smith writes up the pig hunter meeting on May 1, 2007 in the weekly *Hauraki Herald* "Proposed changes to EW's draft regional pest management strategy would give greater flexibility to control wild pigs if they are shown to be damaging high-value conservation areas or sensitive upper catchment watershed areas. The changes have angered hunters and farmers on the Coromandel Peninsula, who met with EW on Wednesday to air concerns over the council's proposal to inspect and monitor all properties without consent and order destruction of any wild pig populations using whatever means they choose, including poisons. Farmers, landowners and hunters from the peninsula were among 500 people gathered at the meeting in Hamilton, where they told EW representatives that farmers had successfully controlled wild pigs for generations, at no cost to regional ratepayers. Whenuakite farmer Arthur Attfield said there was widespread mistrust over EW and the Department of Conservation working together on policies that did not consider the rights and recreations of landowners and farmers. 'It was a good hearing but a lot of people feel there's a hidden agenda,' he said. 'We're quite prepared for our rates to be used in a democracy not a dictatorship.'

On April 26, Geoff Taylor writes a story for the Waikato Times *Pig hunters take aim at council's pest plan* noting "Waikato pig hunters mobilized yesterday and threatened High Court action to stop an Environment Waikato plan which they say threatens their sport. Four-wheel-drives and utes covered the paddocks outside Hamilton's Claudelands Events Centre as about 350 pig hunters attended a protest meeting on proposed changes to the regional pest management strategy. Two EW staff members were given a fair hearing, although strategic development manager Kevin Collins—from Pennsylvania— was jeered and taunted for his American accent."

The same reporter then heads off on a pig hunt and writes a feature story published on 5 May 2007 called *New Zealand: Pig hunters up in arms featur*ing a hunt with President of the Tokoroa Pig Hunter's Club, Geoff Fitzgerald and Andy Wheki from Tauwhare, Bruce Garmonsway from Matangi, Mike Preston from Kihikihi and his 10 year old daughter Glenys plus dogs. Taylor incorporates news from the Anzac Day meeting where "hundreds of vehicles are parked on the grass fields outside Claudelands Events Centre, where the Tokoroa Pig Hunting Club has organised a meeting to protest Environment Waikato's plan. Four-wheel drives and utes dominate. Pig hunters have come to town. It's all down to two pages in Environment Waikato's 200-page proposed 2007-2012 RPMS. A new rule has been proposed giving the council the ability to control pig numbers on private property next to what it describes as 'high value' environmental sites - even if landowners don't agree. The present plan demands the council get agreement from landowners. They also don't like the fact the council doesn't seem to recognise pigs and deer are not just a pest, but have value as a resource.

On the far right at the front table sit Environment Waikato's two representatives, John Simmons and Kevin Collins. Simmons, biosecurity group manager, looks determined while Collins, strategic development manager, looks apprehensive. Tokoroa Pig Hunting club president Geoff Fitzgerald is first on and attacks the plan as 'flaky'. He says the club, with 1300 members, is the biggest in the country and has 400 junior members. 'Pig hunting is not only physical and character building, but it teaches traditional food gathering skills to the young.' He tells how the pig hunting club's efforts were applauded by Conservation Minister Chris Carter at a recent Recreation Summit, and says the club's efforts would be challenged by any meaningless killing of the resource. Reihana Robinson, of the Upper Coromandel Landcare Association, questions whether 'high value' sites will include huge tracts of farmers' land that have been voluntarily designated as a kiwi sanctuary. 'This means goodbye wild pork pie on the peninsula.' "She and her husband Geoffrey have been vociferous opponents of the plan. The day before the meeting, they announced they and other farmers had withdrawn their properties from the Conservation Department's Moehau Kiwi Sanctuary in protest. The sanctuary is a voluntary community effort to restrict pests. The loss of the protesting farmers' 4000ha would reduce the sanctuary by a third. 'EW, with its new pest strategy, has blown up the Moehau Kiwi Sanctuary,' Reihana Robinson said when she announced the withdrawal. Tokoroa club patron Garry Ottmann tells the meeting that while Environment Waikato may see the move as a minor change to the strategy, pig huntersdo not. He goes on to quote John Simmons who says the council does not want to eradicate feral pig populations, or even control them in most places and that it would be impossible to eradicate feral pigs anyway. He reminds the audience that there is no suitable toxin for killing wild pigs and that phosphorous is registered but is inhumane. Kevin Collins states repeatedly that Waikato pig hunters are controlling numbers well. Simmons says Environment Waikato has had a good relationship with pig hunters. For instance, the Tokoroa Club is able to release hundreds of disease-free pigs into Kinleith forest each season under the proviso it supplies pigs' heads to the council so they can be tested for bovine TB. Simmons say there has always been a lot of goodwill. 'This furore that has been stirred up is disappointing.' He says he feels pig hunters have been given 'bad information' and have been stirred up by 'one or two individuals'. Whatever the case, the argument may not go away in a hurry."

Meanwhile Back at the Kiwi Sanctuaries
—Collateral Damage

*"Ethical behavior is doing the right thing when no one else
is watching- even when doing the wrong thing is legal."*

Aldo Leopold

Not only did dogmatic, pedantic bureaucrats refuse to listen to any opposition to their contentious pest plan, they blew up the Coromandel kiwi sanctuaries. While notifications of landowner withdrawals occurred prior to the ANZAC Day pig hunter meeting in Hamilton, it took a few weeks for DOC to respond. Fortuitously a DOC staffer from the Tongariro conservancy was temporarily in charge at the Hauraki office so rather than any contumely diatribe, landowners received an uncharacteristically (for DOC) adroit letter from Nicola Etheridge (Acting Area Manager) acknowledging the new correct smaller land mass confined in the most part to the DOC land, and confirming all withdrawals from the kiwi zone. In response to requests regarding withdrawal of farmland from the Kiwi Sanctuary the following letter dated 3rd May 2007, from Acting Area Manager-Hauraki, Nicola Etheridge was sent to all petitioners.

"Thank you for your letter of 16th April seeking the removal of your land from the Moehau Kiwi Sanctuary. As you correctly state, The Moehau Kiwi Sanctuary is part of an operational plan for DOC, being one of five priority sites for kiwi management identified in the national Kiwi Recovery Plan.

The Sanctuary is a spatial concept only, not an area with legally defined boundaries, and no land deemed to be part of the Sanctuary has acquired any special legal status as a result of its inclusion. In view of this fact, and the fact that participation in the sanctuary has always been on an entirely voluntary basis, there are actually no inherent regulatory or financial implications, and no restrictions or obligations on landowners.

Notwithstanding this, we accept your request to ensure that your land will not be considered a part of the Sanctuary in the future. We therefore undertake to amend all maps of the area produced by the department so that they clearly illustrate which land is included and which is excluded from the Sanctuary. In addition, all future written descriptions will clearly state that not all landowners in the area are participants. Public records will be adjusted accordingly and other agencies advised as appropriate.

The map is currently being revised by our GIS staff at the Conservancy Office. I will send you a copy as soon as it is complete. It will clearly show land the department administers, private land with sustained trapping and private land with no sustained trapping. The title of the map will also be changed to exclude the words Kiwi Sanctuary on private land. That title describes the land administered by the department only. To date we have informed Environment Waikato and the District Councils of the change. You will appreciate that it will take a little while before all the old maps are disposed of and new ones replaced.

Finally, the department is grateful that you support the protection of kiwi and are implementing protection for them on your land."

Nicola Etheridge is the kind of DOC Manager we would like to see stay on the Coromandel.

Diane Novis of Port Charles pens a letter to the *Hauraki Herald* published on May 29, 2007 "…My family is part of the Upper Coromandel Landcare Association and one of the 'aberrant' group of landowners which have withdrawn from the Moehau Kiwi Sanctuary. We have done this because at no time was permission sought or granted to include our property in the MKS. Also, the inclusion of the property in the MKS could, if the proposed regional pest management strategy goes ahead in its present form result in the future imposition of toxic pesticides, herbicides and other animal and plant control measures on our land without our permission. If this constitutes "self interest" so be it. We, as a family, will continue our ongoing control of animal and plant pests on our property and do our bit for conservation in our own quiet way." This letter encapsulates the unacknowledged ongoing work by those who live and farm and work around Moehau with no fanfare and no government grants, or glossy brochures.

Further south of the DOC Kiwi Sanctuary a similarly invented mirage called Moehau Environment Group (MEG) Kiwi Sanctuary also blew up. There is no statutory or regulatory basis for this Kiwi Zone and there was no formal consultation process before its establishment but the kiwi sanctuary designation has been a helpful tool in the environment group's fundraising efforts. From Waikawau to Colville and further south, landowners signed similar documents used by the upper Coromandel landowners On May 5 the *Waikato Times* reports: "Landowners have pulled out of a second kiwi sanctuary as the backlash continues against plans to change

Environment Waikato's regional pest management strategy. Conservationists have also accused EW of being a Conservation Department puppet, but the regional council has hit back saying there has been a "gross misrepresentation" of facts. Coromandel farmer Reihana Robinson, spokeswoman for the Upper Coromandel Landcare Association (UCLA), said landowners had withdrawn more than 2023ha of private land from the Moehau Environment Group (MEG) Kiwi Sanctuary. She said this had reduced the two-year-old sanctuary by nearly a third in size and more withdrawals of land were expected. The withdrawals follow similar action last week by more than 20 landowners who withdrew more than 6070 ha from DOC's Moehau Kiwi Sanctuary, a separate area adjacent to the MEG area. Mrs Robinson said residents acted in response to a 'sweeping expansion of wild animal control powers' proposed by EW in its draft regional pest management strategy. 'EW is a rogue council increasingly out of touch with the community. Its breakup of the sanctuaries is but one symptom of faulty policy-making baked in a shell of arrogance. Rule changes were subtle but extremely significant.'"

The coordinator for MEG received a hand written note from UCLA clarifying that property owners wish to make it very clear that this action is *not* directed against MEG in any way, rather it has been forced upon them by EW, which has stated directly that properties in kiwi sanctuaries will be subject to new inspection, monitoring, and direct control intervention by EW. This has given residents no choice but to make sure they are withdrawn from the kiwi sanctuary. However the 2007-08 MEG *Newsletter* ignores landowners' concerns with regard to DOC's MKS and records the incident as follows in their 07-08 Report. "The Moehau Environment Group Kiwi Sanctuary is immediately south of the Department of Conservation's Moehau Kiwi Sanctuary which covers 16,745 hectares from the northern tip of the Coromandel southward, and therefore complements work there. It is bounded to the south by trapping programmes in Kennedy Bay (Harataunga Kiwi Project) and the Papa Aroha Environment Group. The committee decided early on to integrate operations between the Moehau Environment Group and DOC, and have signed a Memorandum of Understanding that outlines the respective roles of each. During the early part of 2007 a campaign against the Regional Council's proposed Regional Pest Management Strategy (RPMS) affected the MEG Kiwi Sanctuary. Members of the lobby group 'Upper Coromandel Landcare Association' objected to the way in which 'kiwi sanctuaries' were singled out by the proposed RPMS for more intensive animal pest control measures, particularly larger species. The UCLA wrote to individual landowners within the sanctuaries (not just the one we look after) and encouraged them to withdraw their permission for the conservation work in protest at the proposed RPMS. As a result of this publicity Environment Waikato changed the proposed RPMS, and landowners did not withdraw their consent for our trapping operation. However, the issue exposed just how vulnerable projects like this can be to changes in the socio-political climate."

Alison Smith writes *Kiwi sanctuary in tatters following mass withdrawal* in the *Hauraki Herald* of May 8 2007. Her story documents over 2000ha withdrawn from the so-called MEG kiwi sanctuary that covers the Colville region. She states "the proposed pest controls have widened a divide between authorities and landowners on the Coromandel Peninsula, many of whom were against a drop of 1080 poison by DOC last year in the Whenuakite kiwi zone at the southern end of the peninsula." Yet another so-called kiwi sanctuary on the peninsula takes similar action. At the Whenuakite Kiwi Sanctuary on the east coast near Hahei and Hot Water Beach landowners belonging to the East Coromandel Landcare Association withdraw their land in protest. *More angry landowners pull out of kiwi zone writ*es Alison Smith on June 29 2007

"Landowners whose properties comprise a total of 1386ha have withdrawn from the Whenuakite Kiwi Zone and formed an East Coromandel Landcare Association to give themselves a united voice. The group is concerned that including their land in a kiwi zone will leave them powerless to stop the use of 1080 on their properties and other pest management practices favoured by authorities but which they have traditionally avoided. Many peninsula landowners accuse EW and the DOC of working together to gain greater control of private property within a framework of new legislation. The concern and frustration led to heated debate and to thousands of hectares of privately owned land being withdrawn from kiwi conservation zones throughout the peninsula. 'Yesterday's hand of friendship has turned into today's legislation,' said Whenuakite farmer Arthur Attfield…Gary Wilson, who owns 72ha in Whenuakite where he has lived for 35 years, said authorities had forced restrictions on a subdivided area of his land by not allowing people to keep dogs. 'They've claimed our farm,' he said. 'They're getting out of control, suggesting coming onto your property and shooting your pigs without your permission.' Mr Wilson is among

nine landowners who have withdrawn from the Whenuakite Kiwi Zone and joined the newly formed East Coromandel Landcare Association. His property contains one of the largest collections of a rare native plant and he says pigs and kiwi have co-existed on his land for many years. 'We hear them (kiwi) squeaking when we're out hunting pigs,' he said. 'I say just leave things alone. Human interference is what creates the problems...' EW manager Kevin Collins said...it would only be in extremely rare cases that the council would take direct action without landowner's consent... "If everything is thriving, there is no issue."Alison Smith notes in this article that UCLA has called for an independent inquiry into the use of 1080 and a Royal Commission.

The Hearings Panel

Studying cows, pigs and chickens can help an actor develop his character. There are a lot of things I learned from animals. One was that they couldn't hiss or boo me.

James Dean

Locals from all over the Coromandel make the effort to travel to Thames in order to speak in support of their written submissions and to support others at the EW Hearings Panel held at the War Memorial Hall. William Peters Environmental and Heritage Manager for Ngāti Maru Rūnanga, speaks to their submission: "... As kaitiaki we have many duties to perform which include but are not limited to, the protection of our resources and environments. In this instance, food sources as a means of survival is far more important than an eradication strategy and with this in mind, those pests that are not food sources should be targeted first and foremost, as an immediate short term strategy. And don't think that it isn't a matter of survival for some families, because it is...As kaitiaki the simple reason we perform our duties is to maintain a sustainable resource not only for the future generations of Marūtuahu, but also those non-Marūtuahu people residing within our traditional areas. As the manawhenua people of this region we have certain responsibilities towards all non-Marutūahu people living here among us...as manawhenua we have traditional duties to perform and if we allow certain prized food sources to be removed from our native environment, this would reflect negatively on our tribal mana particularly when in this case it is our treaty partner this government, whether local and/or central government, that as the main instigator will be ultimately responsible for removing some of these prized food sources...Because of the long-term destruction of the natural habitat our native food sources have rapidly diminished and what remains, while scarce, has become very significant today and as a consequence, we have had to change our ancestral habits by changing to other food sources available...Today much of our hunting is done in the supermarket and while this is now the accepted practice many māori and non-māori enjoy the accomplishment and satisfaction of growing their food, trapping, hunting and fishing outside the supermarket environment. Surely with something like 93 pests overall, the edible pests particularly the 3 highly prized ones can be dealt with after the other 90…If the three prized feral food animals are removed from their habitats then the potential for some families already struggling becomes worse, and hunting as a means of choice becomes unavailable effectively removing the ability of choice from everyone of us. Our families and our communities both Māori and non-Māori believe they should retain the ability to choose to hunt…This proposal if granted, will adversely affect the relationship that we as Ngāti Maru and tangata whenua have with our culture, traditions, our ancestral lands, sites, wāhi tapu and other taonga, and also contravenes and undermines our kaitiakitanga status, which in the Act is a matter of national importance. Our rights and interests as guaranteed under the Treaty of Waitangi are also adversely affected."

Long time conservationist and 1080 poison opponents based in Reporoa, Graham and Anne Sperry point out "Environment Waikato is guilty of being part of the extreme environmental agenda of a minority…We do not believe that the rights and traditions of generations of New Zealanders to harvest wild animals from our wild places…should be removed by application of unnecessary and unjustifiable attitudes and regulations. While we have complete agreement with the need to control and even in some cases eliminate very harmful undesirable organisms, we do not agree that many of the introduced organisms can or should be classified as very harmful unless they breed or are present in very high populations. They can co-exist within and enhance our wild places…We point out, observe, comment and demand that animals such as hare, rabbit, wild pigs, deer, wallaby possum, pheasant, quail, trout, dama dama, turkey, geese, duck, trout/salmonids, perch, carp, tench, goldfish, honeybees, dairy cows, domestic pigs, peacock, guinea fowl, partridge, blackbird, sparrow, thrush, starling, dog and many other animals and insects, along with introduced flora such as peach, nectarine, sweet corn, maize, wheat, swede, sugar beet, clover, pinus radiate, many exotic firs, plums, gooseberries, strawberries, potatoes, onions, leeks, cabbage, peas, beans, hops, barley and many new grasses and herbs and flowers are useful, are part of our traditions, are managed or were introduced as assets and should continue to be managed as assets...Therefore we require that you manage these and other useful organisms as assets, that you use the term 'biodiversity' correctly, and that you recognise that preservation and reversion of so-called 'high value' areas is a subject prone to the whims of the interpreting body; in this case EW. We and we believe a majority of thinking ratepayers, do not accept that your interpretation of 'high value' is necessarily valid."

Dr D Wright who heads the local EW Catchment subcommittee states "the RPMS document is a long and complex document... It seems to be designed following a burearucrat's dream, and I wonder if any cost benefit has been undertaken to compare the cost of its preparation and review versus investing the dollars in achieving the region's goals...When is a pest a pest?" He also asks that a hierarchy of pests is identified and reminds EW that the time frame is too short "to prepare a considered robust response."

On May 23 Martin Tiffany writing for the *Waikato Times* quotes Te Awamutu deer hunter Murray Dench who at the second day of hearings on EW's draft regional pest management strategy in Hamilton tells EW "not to become a branch office of DOC but rather use 'enlightened' management methods to solve the pest management issues it faces. EW must not assume the mantra of DOC. Please be modern-thinking and develop modern management principles for an animal which has been a highly respected outdoor recreational asset for more than 150 years."

Roll Back the Pest Strategy

*"Hunting teaches all sorts of skills. Safety with firearms,
selective hunting, appreciation of nature and lessons that
to succeed you've got to put in a bit of sweat and toil. Take
a kid hunting now and again. You are doing that young
individual and tomorrow's society a lot of good."*
Tony Orman *About Deer and Deer Stalking*

On May 22 Martin Tiffany writes "Waikato regional council staff appear to be sticking to their guns over the inclusion of pigs and deer as pests in a controversial regional pest management strategy—but say monitoring and control methods need to be transparent. In a memo to the pest management review panel, which began hearings yesterday, Environment Waikato's Natural Heritage programme manager Kevin Collins said 'for example, the (strategy) might clearly state the requirement that landowners would be consulted before any monitoring was done and as part of any process to identify control methods'. In June 2007 *Hauraki Herald* the Hearings Committee chair Councilor Laurie Burdett "denied the council was backing down from its strategy but was looking at making it easier to understand."

The revelation that Council will not take into account the views of the general public while reprehensible does not come as a surprise. The second Parliamentary Commissioner for the Environment (PCE) Morgan Williams, investigated the nature of local government 'consultation'. The study was based in the Coromandel town of Whangamata and found the Local Government Act enables Council to create a document over a period of months with interested parties and that this 'discussion document' is re-formatted by staff to create what is somewhat disingenuously referred to as a 'draft'. The public is then invited to make submissions within a limited time frame and imagines their views may be incorporated into the final document. However where there is conflict with the status quo or the written 'draft', rarely are opposing submissions acted upon. This leaves ordinary citizens, the fraught task of appealing the decision in the Environment Court. Fortuitously on this occasion the work is undertaken by the effort, courage and funds of the Tokoroa Pig Hunting club. A number of Coromandel individuals who belong to UCLA join the case.

Later in the year UCLA releases the following press statement on November 5th aptly titled *'Conservation Group Calls for Rollback of EW Pest Strategy'*

"The Upper Coromandel Landcare Association (UCLA) today called upon the newly elected Environment Waikato Regional Council to immediately withdraw its controversial pest management strategy, in its entirety, as one of Council's first orders of business. In place of the new plan, UCLA called for a five-year extension of EW's operational 2002-2007 pest policies, which the conservation group termed 'sensible, affordable and acceptable to the community'. According to UCLA, 'the projected quadrupling of EW pest control spending called for under the 2007-2012 strategy is completely irresponsible, particularly as Waikato ratepayers have suffered the nation's highest increases in rates demands over the last five years. In addition to cost, the previous Council ignored the views of the wider community by extending to EW staff, in their sole discretion, the power to order destruction of recreational species such as pigs and deer virtually anywhere. These species, a traditional resource and part of our biodiversity heritage, have been kept in check for decades at no cost whatsoever to ratepayers', the group said. UCLA noted that the recently adopted EW pest management strategy has already resulted in an Environment Court appeal, which will mean even more ratepayer dollars wasted on defending 'a bankrupt policy opposed by thousands of residents from Coromandel to Taupo. Previous Council put the budget and career special interests of EW staff ahead of the general public,' UCLA said. 'Fortunately, EW has the opportunity to address the problem right now by simply reverting to its workable 2002-2007 strategy. In the future, EW can look at the strategies of Bay of Plenty or Tasman-Nelson regions as examples of pest plans which leave the management of recreational species to hunters and which keep pest spending to affordable levels.'"

Capricious Vagaries: Forest & Bird on Wild Pigs

*"A cat looks down on a man, a dog looks up to a man, but
a pig will look a man right in the eye and see his equal."*

Winston Churchill

The Upper Coromandel Forest and Bird group sends out an email in November 2007. It reads, "we believe that recreational hunting should be encouraged." They also claim "we fully understand the recreational positives of pig hunting, and have no wish to halt this pastime." So far, so good. However, in the same communication to local members, a guidance sheet is offered explaining how to fill out a submission form to the Game Animal Panel. Here we read the real Forest & Bird policy "protection of indigenous flora and fauna is so important that these animals (PIGS) should preferably be exterminated." F&B urge members to support their view and to include in their submissions the statement that "pigs do not provide any important benefits in respect of recreational hunting, food source or historic/cultural values." F&B's preferred method of control for wild pigs is "poisoning". However Dave Hansford in the *Forest and Bird* magazine of August 2014 has this to say about pigs "While nobody has any firm ideas about how to control pigs, most agree that using 1080 is out of the question. Māori communities … are precisely the sort of stakeholders DOC needs to keep onside. 'They simply wouldn't tolerate it,' says Julie Black, manager of Nga Whenua Rahui, (a Government fund to protect natural values on Māori-owned land). 'they would have issues about the use of 1080 around a traditional food source, and also with waterways and people's diets. It's about traditional Māori beliefs and values about upsetting the natural system with introduced toxins.' Furthermore farmers, who would be key players in any war on pigs, are not about to risk losing their farm dogs to 1080 poisoning. Quite apart from anything else, pigs are smarter than the average pest, and will simply regurgitate a1080 bait the moment they feel its effects. That creates two new problems, says Landcare Research wildlife toxicologist Penny Fisher. 'It increases the risk of them getting a sub-lethal dose and becoming bait-shy. Also the vomit itself can become a non-target hazard.'" Further on in the article Peter Williamson says "the (Conservation) Department generally has a 'very productive relationship with responsible pig-hunters and appreciates their contribution to pest control in the park.'… Wildlife managers must somehow curb the devastating impacts of pigs on biodiversity while accommodating their place in rural cultures this delicate juggling act may yet prove one of the biggest conservation challenges."

Pigs and Deer Lose their Pest Tag

"I firmly believe that in every man's soul, the instinct to hunt is deeply implanted. This primeval urge comes out sooner or later, early with some men, later with others."

Ken Cuthbertson[19]

Tokoroa Pig Hunting Club Inc v Waikato Regional Council

Case Number ENV-2007-AKL-000484

Topic: Waikato Regional Council Proposed Pest Management Strategy Review—decision to include wild deer and pigs as pets. *(sic)*

One has to wonder at the nature of the malapropism (above) in the official letter sent on 17 October 2008 on Ministry of Justice letterhead, signed off by Silua Fifita, Hearing Manager Auckland Environment Court Registry. Reference to deer and pigs as 'pets' would be humorous had the case not required the sacrifice of hard-earned dollars from the 1500 members of the Tokoroa Pig Hunters club and time-consuming legal work. To stay with the linguistic bouillabaisse momentarily, a misnomer is revealed in the proposed Regional Pest Strategy on page 111. Feral deer are given the scientific name Hydrocleys nymphoides. Hamilton City Council's CEO, A.J. Marryatt indicates they have labeled deer with the scientific name that "Pertains to water poppy." This flagrant, albeit potentially fragrant, oversight exposes haste and incompetence at regional council.

The Tokoroa Pig Hunters employ the legal firm, Cooney Lees Morgan of Tauranga.[20] The Appeal to the Environment Court was pursuant to Section 79D of the Biosecurity Act. Parties listed in the Environment Court case 2007-AKL-000484 include Maureen Coleman, Animal Health Board's Neil Blackie, Nardene Berry, Bernard Davies, D-G Department of Conservation's (Waikato conservancy) Susan Woodhouse, David Gardner, Reihana Robinson, Royal Forest and Bird Protection Society of New Zealand's (Waikato Branch) Philip Hart, Thames Valley Deer

Stalkers Assoc., Anne Ward, John Ward, Marcus Ward, Theodora Ward and Craig Solomon. Waikato Regional Council used our rates to pay Lachlan Muldowney of the Hamilton law firm, Tompkins Wake.

This factitious battle took place over the following year. The appellant's lawyer was involved in a serious accident requiring postponement of the negotiations. "As well as the ill health of the Appellant's representative, the main reason for requesting a four month lead in time for evidence preparation is that it is likely the experts the Appellant will instruct will be from overseas, and this length of time is required in order to manage the logistics of having such persons attend a hearing later in the year…The Appellant intends to continue to negotiate with the Respondent in good faith in the hope of resolving its appeal. Dated at Tauranga this 13th day of March 2008. P.H. Cooney/T.C.Waikato."[20]

The Tokoroa Pig Hunting Club Inc. state the "general public of New Zealand values game animals positively…The harvesting of game animals as a desirable recreational activity is compatible with the protection and maintenance of ecosystems in which game animals live. More than 50,000 people harvest large game in New Zealand, and over 150,000 people harvest small or large game at some time during each year. The Hilary Commission ranks shooting sports as the seventh most popular pursuit among adult males. Rugby is number five." The Club as been in existence since 1970 and has approximately 1300 members.

Jeff Neems writes (*Waikato Times*, Nov 10 2007) "Pressure is mounting on the newly elected Environment Waikato (EW) council to renegotiate or withdraw its controversial Pest Management Plan, with groups opposed to the plan joining together to fight the strategy. Three separate groups - the Upper Coromandel Land Care Association (UCLA), the East Coromandel Landcare Association and the Tokoroa Pig Hunting Club - believe the new council must address the Pest Management Plan issue as one of its first pieces of business."

On 10 October resolute *Waikato Times* writer Martin Tiffany reports "Wild pigs and deer are set to be taken off EW's pest blacklist in what is seen as a back-down by the regional council. An Environment Court hearing was to start on October 28, 2008 after the Tokoroa Pig Hunting Club appealed the inclusion of wild pigs and feral deer in the RPMS and took the fight to court…EW appears reluctant to admit defeat..." Councillor Laurie Burdett says it is a "successful compromise". She indicates "the success of ... managing pigs and deer would be evaluated over the coming three years, in time for the next scheduled regional pest management strategy review."

The *Wild Animal Control Act* 1977 is the fall back position which leaves things substantially as they were before the entire fiasco. Back in the northern Coromandel Peninsula settlements of Port Charles and Port Jackson, where the first alarm had been sounded and where the call went out to conservationists and sportspeople across the Waikato—to farmers and weekend hunters, to iwi and whanau and all who treasure the great outdoors and the best of kiwi traditions, a weary but satisfied cheer went up. UCLA said EW backed off because it looked like it was going to lose— "It was an indefensible policy and an aggressive overstepping of local government powers and it would not have stood up in court. Simple. The EW pest bureaucracy was out of line. The arrogance of EW council and bureaucrats who refused to listen to hundreds of submissions wasted both resources and time. The Tokoroa pig hunters put their money where their mouths were and won." In the Moehau local newsletter *Panui* UCLA sent out three cheers for the tenacious Tokoroa Pig Hunters Club for their successful challenge of the new rules. It is a good reminder that citizens can get involved and challenge authority where injustice is rampant. UCLA shares with the Tokoroa Pig Hunter's Club the vision of a healthy and diverse environment where human and wild animals co-exist for beauty, for health and for sustenance. In the *Report to Regional Pest Management Advisory Sub-committees* 31 October 2008, John Simmons reports "The strategy was appealed by the Tokoroa Pig Hunting Club because it identified feral pigs and deer as 'pests' that could be controlled under the Biosecurity Act. That litigation has been settled and the RPMS is expected to come into effect after it is adopted by the Council in December."

There is no accountability for those responsible. It would appear that those implicated have been exonerated. However rural dwellers have long memories and travesties of justice linger in the collective psyche. EW councillors could have avoided the lengthy and expensive impasse by listening to submitters rather than their employees whose only goal it seemed was to extend their domain and thereby justify further copious spending. Laurie Burdett lost her seat at the regional table at the next elections and John Simmons and his cohort no longer work for regional council. It could be said they were part of a broom sweeping exercise in 2014. The opposition to wild pig hunting continues to bleat unabated and there is no room to be complacent or inactive. The rural/town divide is feathered and groomed by inept reporting in radio, television and newsprint where anecdotal opinions receive wide coverage. Fortunately both digital and Māori media contribute more nuanced information.

A culture that celebrates unique qualities of upbringing including but not limited to wild food gathering, bush skills such as sustainable hunting and trapping, and the ability to survive in the wilderness with a healthy comprehension of nature in all her diversity, is a culture worth holding onto and sharing with town and city friends, family and strangers from near and far. The Coromandel offers this wild heritage and it requires nurturing by all who visit or live here.

Part Four:

Voices Of The Coromandel— Poison Peninsula

"When you see poison raining from the sky do you feel that this is right? When you read, "this is the only affordable way" do you feel clean? When you hear "there is no alternative" does your heart believe it? Do you think that a public relations campaign will make it right? Listen to the voice within you."

Fred Look *Coromandel Town Crier* 2007

"The Ngati Huarere ki Whangapoua Trust endorses the Coromandel-Colville Community Board's opposition to the use of residual poisons on the Coromandel peninsula. In the Trust's view the use of such poison is not consistent with katiakitanga and the Trust holds concerns about the long-term consequences of such poisons. The Trust supports the use of hunting, trapping and cyanide only."

Ngāti Huarere ki Whangapoua Trust Environmental Management Team

"The history of brushtail possums in New Zealand is bleak. The colonists who forcibly transported possums from their native Australia to New Zealand in the nineteenth century valued them as economic assets, quickly establishing a profitable fur industry. Over the past 80 or so years, however, New Zealand has increasingly scapegoated possums for the unanticipated negative impact their presence has had on the native environment and wildlife. Now this marsupial—blamed and despised—suffers the most miserable of reputations and is extensively targeted as the nation's number one pest. "

Potts, Annie[1]

Introduction

The Coromandel Peninsula of tourist literature is a fun-filled holiday location, replete with stunning beaches, lush indigenous forests and clean rivers—yours for the taking, on pleasant summer walks, in the surf and sand, or for extreme outdoor sports action. Just an easy drive from the country's largest city, the peninsula is a convenient and popular summer holiday home destination. The human population comprises long-time farming families, retirees and small communities of diverse populations and summer residents.

Promotional literature beckons…*"Renowned for its natural beauty, green pastures, misty rainforests and pristine golden beaches, The Coromandel is blessed with hundreds of natural hideaways, making it an ideal place to escape."*

But what shall we escape to? Some kind of pristine, pre-human landscape where no sign of human activity has sullied the views? If so, this would require annihilation of every invasive species by any and all means available. At present, people are not on the hit list. However, those who live at the top of the Coromandel Peninsula are aware their generations–long tenure on the land is in the crosshairs. For fundamentalist ecological zealots, why stop at ridding the land of rats and mice, stoats, ferrets, and possums? Wild pigs and feral goats—both favoured hunting species should certainly be eliminated. As should cats and dogs. Next stop, by any measure of logic…recalcitrant local landowners.

So far, the extremist conservation agenda to roll back the ecological clock has not come to pass (apart from the Wall of Death wild goat extermination programme). And while there remains a hardy and staunch community of civic-minded folk stewarding the land, raising families and food, that bleak future will be forestalled and the freedom to live alongside the Coromandel's native and non-native wild kingdom will be maintained.

Voices of the Coromandel: Poison Peninsula tells the story of grassroots opposition to government-sponsored poisoning of the peninsula's wildlife and way of life. With passion and reason, those who know the bush best denounce inhumane and irresponsible destruction of species large and small. They censure reprehensible official policy that promotes wanton use pesticides and herbicides that make a mockery of New Zealand's "100% pure" clean green brand. They demand that human health, social wellbeing, and environmental commonsense be placed ahead of greed and profit.

The stories follow the course of environmental actions beginning in the 1990s. Whether by picking up a pen and writing a letter to the newspaper, circulating a community-wide petition, presenting at council offices, or organising a major demonstration, each person's effort is part of the fabric of concern and action, the korowai/cloak woven into the social network of our community. It is a privilege to live on this small peninsula as all of those involved in the ongoing struggle for environmental justice know well. We understand why the journey is long and the battles seemingly never-ending. And so this final segment is a response to a question from the future…

"What did you do, Granddad, to help save the wild animals? What did you do, Grandma, to preserve our wild kingdom?"

If storytellers are not vigilant, stories can slip away. These tales of the Coromandel deserve not only plays and novels and songs; they deserve to stand, tall as kahikatea, as non-fictive narrative forming part of the backbone of our natural history. Voices of ordinary people striving to end indiscriminate toxin distribution on the Coromandel are to be found here expressing their fervent hope they may inspire new voices to join the "rabblerousers" so grandchildren/mokopuna are not left to inherit a marred landscape.

Coromandel—Poison Peninsula

Terry Tempest Williams *Pieces of White Shell*

There was a time when there were no people on the Coromandel, no rats, no possums, no pigs, no stoats, no cattle, nc sheep, no ducks. Indigenous birds, insects, bats, fresh water and ocean life welcomed the first canoe-loads of Polynesians who proceeded to destroy habitat as well as snare, hook, trap, catch and harvest the low-hanging fruit—the flightless birds and the plentiful sea life. Edible plants such as taro and sweet potato or kumara were tended. The Pacific rat, kiore, travelled aboard those first canoes and with surprising speed many native species (invertebrates, reptiles, molluscs and amphibians) became firstly endangered and then extinct. But it was not until well after the coming of the Pākehā, poison 1080 would spread its cruel wings over the Coromandel Peninsula yet no land on the Coromandel is deluged with unwanted wild animals. Possums did not even arrive on the Coromandel until the 1970's.

The Australian Brushtail Possum *(Trichosurus vulpecula)* a nocturnal tree dwelling marsupial, took its sweet time travelling north to the Coromandel from the South Island where they had first been released in the middle of the nineteenth century to aid the fur trade. Protected until 1946, possums were then singled out by government to be wiped out by hunting, trapping and poisoning by aerial and ground based toxin 1080. Members of the scientific community, hunters, farmers, the Nature Conservation Council as well as bird watchers belonging to Forest and Bird (F&B) all originally opposed the use of 1080 poison.[2]

A deal negotiated with a small chemical poison company in Oxford, Alabama, USA saw the government importing up to 80% of the entire world production of 1080 poison (2.3 tonnes of pure powder) by 2003. Once public funding was assured herbivorous possums were tarred with a public relations brush transforming them from a fur, skin and meat resource to an ecological enemy, a poster child of forest devastation and native bird predation that could be annihilated by poison 1080. Numerous native birds actually out-compete possums as predators of other native birds but this fact is blithely brushed aside in the vehement campaign to demonize the wild animal.[3] A government's job in this neo-liberal climate is to generate GDP so with this government-owned poison business over $100 million dollars of activity is created. All opposition to poison 1080 is branded by poison promoters as 'scaremongering' and 'misinformation' yet five decades of toxin drops have achieved no stated success. It is likely to have exacerbated the loss of native species such as the rock wren and the cheeky alpine parrot—the kea.[4]

Central and regional government 'conservation' policy over swathes of public and private land, is to helicopter-drop poison1080 laced food baits dealing protracted and inhumane deaths to all oxygen breathing creatures. Why? Their stated goal is to rid the wilderness of possums, rats and stoats. Meanwhile the deaths of non-target species including native birds, invertebrates and our only native mammal the bat, are rarely monitored. Accidents involving deaths of domestic animals are myriad, but many farmers are signed to secrecy when compensation is paid for loss of domestic cattle, horses, sheep or dogs.

Poison 1080 is not the only poison used by the New Zealand government but it is the only one dropped indiscriminately into water and onto land. When choosing such poisons to drop into the wilderness, proof of safety beyond doubt should be the responsibility of hazardous chemical producers. That industry is not required to prove safety is reprehensible.[5]

Calling a halt to this poison policy and supporting humane wild animal control has been the focus of many residents living on the Coromandel. Years of community action finally paid off, when at the end of 2009, the Thames Coromandel District Council agreed to advocate to the Minister of Conservation for possum control utilizing the only recognized humane toxin—cyanide, alongside trapping and hunting "where possible"— namely the whole Coromandel. Unsurprisingly, central government in the guise of the Department of Conservation (DOC) and the Waikato

Regional Council (WRC) refuse to heed local communities and continue to pump residual poisons, including aerial poison 1080.

Riding on the heels of government poison promotion is the Animal Health Board (AHB) an organization made up of government and farmer representatives. AHB has dumped tonnes of poison 1080 onto farmland and into forests in their vain attempt to eradicate bovine Tb in cows, by poisoning one of the vectors (possums). The Coromandel is bovine Tb free yet AHB in continues to haul levies, taxes and ratepayer dollars from Coromandel residents and farmers. Scheduled to wind up operations in 2013 AHB reinvented itself and morphed into OSPRI stretching its lifeline out to 2026. As they state on their webiste they are a "partnership" between government and primary industries administering two programmes—so-called TB-free and the national animal identification and traceability system (NAIT). Sensible solutions to the problem of bovine Tb include instituting strict stock movement controls and developing a vaccine for cows but bureaucrats running these animal 'health' organizations choose to keep their well-paid jobs and to continue to poison the countryside.[6]

With over a third of the Coromandel designated DOC land, aerial 1080 is dumped into forests adjacent to farmland and rural communities and into water catchments. DOC's inflated fear of possums leads to an irrational belief they can poison the countryside to a pristine future with forests empty of non-native predators. Thoughtful people can disagree about the best methods to control unwanted wild animals. On one side is the one hundred million dollar chemical pesticide industry backed by OSPRI, regional councils, the Department of Conservation, and more recently NZ Forest and Bird, all adamant that spreading toxin 1080 over vast tracts of land is the best way to prevent bovine tuberculosis and the best way to kill possums and rats.[7] Seeing things a bit differently, is a steadily growing number of farmers, tangata whenua, environmentalists, tourist operators, scientists, exporters, and even politicians who are saying the risky poisoning of New Zealand has got to stop as questions grow concerning the known impacts of secondary poisoning on native species, the potential human health effects, and the threat caused by the introduction of toxins into the local food chain.[8]

It is helpful to keep in mind that 1080 poison—or sodium monofluoroacetate, is not just another wild animal control product or substance requiring special care and handling. Poison1080 is exceptionally hazardous. Developed synthetically, first as an insecticide and rodenticide, this organofluorine compound is highly toxic to mammals and insects as it interrupts the Krebs cycle depriving cells of energy causing nausea, vomiting, abdominal pain, tachycardia, seizures, convulsions and sub-lethal doses attack the brain, heart, fetus, gonads and lungs. There is no antidote. It is used in small amounts in Israel, Mexico, Canada and Australia. It persists in the environment slowly decomposing in soil and water. The Australian SPCA has called for its ban as an inhumane poison.

Poisoning is only a temporary fix. The space created in nature by this shortsighted and inhumane policy is quickly replenished. Firstly, the mostly unaffected stoats that do not eat the bait, have a field day pursuing eggs and birds without the irksome competition of smart, pesky rats that then bounce back in far greater numbers than prior to the drop, to be followed by possums that stroll in from neighbouring scrub gullies or bush blocks.[9]

The co-evolution or adaptation of Western Australian bush rats *(Rattus fuscipes)* and western brushtail possums to the fluoroacetate-containing plants (*Gastolobium* species) that grow there (by developing a detoxification mechanism in the liver) has not transferred to the Eastern Brushtail Possum as fluoroacetate-containing plants were not growing in eastern Australia. It is the Eastern Possum that was translocated to New Zealand (NZ) and their diet consists of leaves, grasses, herbs, flowers, fruits and insects and in NZ eggs and birds are also occasionally eaten.[10] Synthetic poison 1080 kills birds, both those feeding directly on poison baits and those dining on poisoned insects and carcasses. It kills kaka and ruru and robins. It kills sheep and cattle and dogs and cats. It kills weta and fresh water crayfish/koura. It kills organisms large and small at all ecosystem levels. The preliminary review of the use of 1080 by the Australian Pesticides and Veterinary Medicines Authority (APVMA) released on 23 May 2005 documented the danger to non-target animals. The list of unintended victims expands but the official and pertinacious programme of 1080 poisoning across hundreds of thousands of hectares of New Zealand countryside each year goes on unabated.

Resistance by Coromandel conservationists living in the wilderness and in small communities has a long history and all question why alternatives to poison are not seriously considered. For starters, why not reinstate a bounty for hunters and trappers to encourage the gathering of healthy, valuable possum fur, meat and skins? Healthy conservation outcomes are exactly what Coromandel people seek, but with positive economic and social benefits.

Mutiny on the Bounties: Alternative to Poisoning

"A falcon is the perfect hunter."

Jean Craighead George

The possum bounty system was introduced for trappers and hunters in 1953 but halted in 1961. More than eight million bounties were paid for the two ears and a strip of skin. Why was the scheme halted? The official reason makes no sense whatsoever—apparently it was discontinued because trappers were blamed for 'farming' possums as they culled the so-called 'easy' possums from fence lines and farm roads. Assuming there is a shred of truth in their argument those are the very possums farmers would wish to have removed. Bovine Tb *Mycobacterium bovis* is a cow disease. The likely way a possum gets to be a vector is if it comes in contact with an infected cow. And the most common method for cows to get bovine Tb is from another cow. It is a great deal easier for bureaucrats sitting in offices in cities to contract one helicopter company to dump toxin 1080 than it is to pay numerous idiosyncratic trappers and hunters throughout the country. In 2009 Textiles NZ CEO Elizabeth Tennet described the possum/merino industry as worth over $100million a year and that the industry can "double its export growth in five years." She notes the main constraint is finding enough possum fur, "what is needed is more possum trapping and the collection of more possum fur. A co-ordinated system of permits for possum trapping would be a good start."[11]

Coromandel conservationist and writer Bill Axbey, promotes the bounty system and questions the money trail saying it "is a fair indication of how jealously guarded the possum control finances are…With regard to the Tb problem the very possums that would be killed for bounty are those that inhabit rural farm areas, road edges and small isolated scrub and bush areas…The inescapable fact is that a bounty will kill hundreds of thousands more possums for the same money…Quite frankly our clean green image is in greater danger from 1080 poison than it will ever be from Tb, that after all, comes from cows and is found worldwide. Official objections to a bounty on possums list the excuse that possums would be farmed —the very thing the present system is doing... What would be wrong with a bonus for every kilo of possum fur or a tax exemption for trappers selling fur? In China, Russia and many continental countries the armies use fur-bearing animals to supply them while we have 70,000,000 we are trying to get rid of that are classified as pests. I'd bet that no approach has ever been made at a government level to sound out the market and it is a certainty that no finance is available to sponsor and publicize the availability of high grade furs from a pest animal for use as a trade commodity. Even the animal rights people would be hard put to find a legitimate objection to the use of such furs. As long as the so-called pest control remains in the hands of a couple of government departments we will be faced with increased costs on what amounts to an in-house bounty system and a regular poison oriented control system that is nothing more than a type of farming."[12]

The bounty system continues to be resisted by DOC and the Waikato Regional Council on the Coromandel. From as far back as 1992, DOC intransigence and mathematical incompetence is reflected in their publicity material. Here is a spokesperson rattling unsubstantiated figures and negating the positive role played by bounties. "The DSIR estimates there were between 60 and 80 million possums in NZ back in 1988. Possums can reproduce at 30% a year so to work, any bounty system would have to remove a minimum of 20 million possums each year just to maintain the status quo...Money spent on bounties would be better spent on planned control as this gives higher returns on investment... Bounties had been introduced in the past for hedgehogs, ferrets, rabbits, pigs, deer, goats and even some introduced bird species but none had succeeded. Pest control to protect native species with high conservation values had to be totally effective, Mr. Buchanan said".[13] Possums usually produce one young a year.

To date, no single strategy can be said to have succeeded, however there is a stark example where bounties did 'succeed'. Toward the latter end of the nineteenth century kea (now an endangered native bird) were causing distress to sheep farmers. Starved of habitat and food, kea attacked live animals. In the 1920's the Department of Agriculture shelled out five shillings, with county councils and run holders each contributing half a crown. It is thought that over 150,000 kea were slaughtered in one hundred years from 1868. The bounty was removed in 1970. Journalist Philip Temple notes "this is one of the worst cases of avicide in history. That the kea survived this massive slaughter, and the continuing pressures on its environment, seems little short of a miracle."[14] By 2014 diminishing numbers of kea faced a new crisis, acknowledged even by DOC, to be poison 1080. Rather than halting aerial 1080 poison drops in kea territory, a technical advisor for DOC was to test repellents, by first dropping pellets designed to make kea so sick they would not eat from the following real poison bait drop. Apparently 155 birds have been monitored since 2008 during 10 poison drops. 13 percent, namely 20 birds were killed.

Now we are in the new millennium and while articulate, compassionate voices of opposition are many and widespread, opposition to bounties continues by regional councils and central government. Poison continues to be promoted as the perfect panacea, always with the qualifier "just another tool in the toolbox". In the farming paper *Country News* of August 2009 Steve and Sue Boot of Basically Bush Ltd in Opotiki state, "Commercial harvesting of possums has legitimacy as a viable method for possum management." Quite why bounties cannot be viewed the same way boils down to how the money is distributed. Possums live on to tell their tales, as no strategy over the decades has resulted in eradication.

1080 Toxin is on its Way to the 309

"Ever since it was proposed to drop 1080 on the Coromandel Ranges in 1994, I have tried to say at least leave the ranges free. 1080 is a deadly, tasteless poison, that has no antidote and kills birds, insects, frogs and mammals."

Charles Harsant[15]

The 309 Road is a windy unsealed artery that connects Coromandel town on the west coast to Whitianga on the east. It is here the struggle to halt the spread of toxins over the Coromandel began. The 309 Anti-Aerial 1080 group was formed in the early 1990s in response to DOC's proposed experimental dump of the toxin around the 309 Road. 24 of the 26 residents living in the affected area formed the new group. The correspondence from those early days could well have been written today, except in email form and therefore with more rapid interactions. The letters speak to issues such as damage to the tourism industry, concern the water catchment will be compromised, the fact of very low possum numbers and the growing lack of trust between ordinary citizens and DOC. I am indebted to stalwart environmental battler and farmer John Fowler for sharing the contents of his briefcase that was packed to the brim with hand-written letters, by himself and others, to politicians, scientists and newspapers.

Almost collegial in tone, the documents include a collection of correspondence between Shaun Ogilvie of Landcare Research and Tom Steel of the 309. The community's grave concern with the issue of sub-lethal doses of poison over the long term is recorded. Ogilvie explains he is working on the rate of leaching from toxic baits and says he will keep Steel informed. He states the highest concentration of 1080 measured in water was 3.4 ppb taken from streams between 1990 and 1994.

Independent researcher, Sean Weaver subsequently notes: "Of concern from an environmental toxicology perspective is the length of time 1080 takes to degrade in streams, surface waters and soils, and the concentrations that may persist, perhaps for a limited period, in these environments. Ogilvie et al (1996) examined the rates of 1080 degradation at different water temperatures... The research showed that the overall rate of degradation was significantly different at different water temperatures."[16]

Concentrations of fluoroacetate remained at 30% in the colder water (11 degrees C) and in deionised water little or no degradation at both temperatures, as there was an absence of microbes. Weaver points to a later paper by Eason et al (1999) that claims degradation "still occurs at less than 7 degrees within 1-2 weeks. The paper cited in substantiation of this statement is Ogilvie, et al. (1996). **Nowhere in the Ogilvie paper is there any mention of any experiment that tested the degradation of 1080 at or near 7 degrees C."** [emphasis added] New Zealand mountain stream temperatures are exceedingly low in winter when most poison drops occur.

Coromandel community members understand what it takes to kill an animal, namely the lethal dose (LD) but missing from all research is any data on chronic toxicity. "There are a variety of potential hazards associated with any partial persistence of 1080 including endocrine disruption, which can happen at very low concentrations, acute and chronic hazards to dogs, invertebrates, vertebrate wildlife, fish and other aquatic wildlife, aquatic and terrestrial food webs, and human drinking water supplies— particularly subterranean water flows."[17] In 1996 Helen Hughes the Parliamentary Commissioner for the Environment published a progress report called *Possum Management in New Zealand — Critical Issues* where she declares the "Ministry of Health has recommended lower maximum levels of 1080 in potable water from catchments treated with 1080 following an interim finding that relatively high doses of 1080 may cause mild developmental defects in pregnant rats (Eason et al, 1998)."

Ogilvie sends Steel a copy of Peter Notman's invertebrate study on 16 January 1996. "Compound 1080 is widely used in NZ for the control of wild animals. The tendency of 1080 to poison non-target birds and mammals is recognized, but its effects on invertebrates have gone mostly unnoticed...Poisoned insects provide a means of secondary poisoning for insectivores. Therefore 1080 should not be used where susceptible invertebrate species or rare insectivores are found."[18] Local researcher Dr Wendy Pond suggests "Keeping invertebrate numbers up may be more important to the survival of most native birds than keeping possum numbers down." In one letter Ogilvie casually alludes to dramas affecting his uncle—possibly a staunch poison 1080 supporter, who is living on the Coromandel at this time.[19]

Around the same time *Rural News* (1995) publishes a statement from DSIR ecological research scientist Mike Meads, "When dropping 1080 from the air…they (DOC) kill plant and animal communities. Forest litter is plant material that nourishes the forest, and insects and other invertebrates are animals which play a vital role in the health of the forest as well as being food for native birds and bats."

Tom Steel questions the lack of peer-reviewed research and challenges the use of aerial 1080 on moderate country suitable for ground control. He condemns the under-reporting of native bird deaths, the over-kill toxin quantities and the false water tests taken far from the area of poison drops well after the actual drop. He quotes Eric Spurr's research: "aerial 1080 should not be used in areas of rare birds." Would that include kiwi and falcon? Steel asks.[20]

Following reports of native robin and tomtit fatalities in the Pureora forest after a toxin 1080 drop, an article in Fowler's briefcase by journalist Kingsley Field reports the Animal Health Board (AHB) may no longer use 1080-poisoned carrot baits. Field notes AHB is worried regional councils are sloppy with their quality assurance of aerial dumping of toxin 1080 with few audit procedures.[21] In the same month Stella Penny, Regional Conservator of DOC, writes to John Fowler (November 1996). She includes a copy of a letter by DOC's Simon Kelton that lists DOC 'research' to prove efficacy of 1080. Kelton is concerned the strong AHB reaction to reports of robin and tomtit loss may jeopardize the programme. He worries "If the anti 1080 movement were to make use of the preliminary results from Waipapa, and the AHB were to state to the media that they would no longer use carrot as a bait, I feel the argument would not end there and that pollard could well be included. We would be playing right into the anti lobby's hands. (This particular operation has already been in the paper over the death of a number of bulls that gained access to the airstrip three weeks after the operation, and also via the letter to the editor from a disaffected deerstalker)…It is essential the research programme be resourced sufficiently to follow the recovery of the above populations." Kelton's comments are clear enough on the issue of funding 'to follow recovery".[22]

There is no accountability if non-target species are killed. Lack of intent abrogates DOC. If one kills a pedestrian while driving, one's lack of intent to kill or injure does not remove responsibility. The fact that more human beings are born does not discount culpability in the killing of one human. DOC's so-called lack of intent to kill native birds, dogs, bulls, sheep, invertebrates is currently not considered to be an offence.

The 309 Anti-Aerial 1080 group receive updates from the Ten-Eighty Action Network New Zealand (TANNZ) based in Napier. The National Secretary is Martin Brenstrum. Their update of March 1996 includes correspondence with the Minister of Health, Jenny Shipley, and a xerox of a *Dominion* newspaper article exposing the plan to sell millions of dollars of water to the Middle East with the writer questioning the dropping of toxin 1080 within 20 metres of the Featherston water supply and notes cyanide use conditions are now "far stricter than the conditions for aerially blanketing the country with 1080!" Their newsletter reveals results of the 1996 paired trials carried out in Eastern Kaweka and Matiri showing ground control achieved better results.

Coromandel town's inventive potter, sanctuary founder and railway conservator wrote to the Upper Coromandel Landcare Association (UCLA) with this very suggestion in 2013. Barry Brickell was keen to find a way forward.[23] No one on the Coromandel, including Barry, was aware of the paired trial. DOC chose to maintain the poison strategy so nothing positive came of the paired trial work. One must assume the money trail was committed to the chemical industry.

The TANNZ newsletter mentions the recommendation made by the Parliamentary Commissioner for the Environment (PCE) that asks, but does not require all local authorities to "develop a public decision making and reporting protocol which includes evaluation of control options and basis of costings, permits scrutiny of how decisions were reached, and produces documentation that is publicly available." Notwithstanding Wellington Regional Council "has not been able to provide at least one of its ratepayers with accurate details of how it spent its pest control money in 1994-1995." A summary of scientist Mike Mead's Whitecliff study on 1080 poisoning of invertebrates is published along with letters from Conservation Minister Denis Marshall and DOC's Murray Hosking that criticise the research.

The Hon Nick Smith, M.P. for Nelson and Minister of Conservation writes to Tom Steel on13 October 1997. His aides have come up with a few "facts" on sowing rates and apparently in the near future, sowing rates should drop to two or three kilos of cereal/pollard bait per hectare. Smith signs his name to the following fact: "the removal of these baits by pest mammals is expected to be almost **100% after three nights**, the vast majority of invertebrates (like weta) will not have the chance to encounter baits, let alone eat enough to present a problem to native predators from secondary poisoning…However, the paper by Bowen, Morgan and Eason (*N.Z. Journal of Agricultural Research*) raises areas of concern. I have asked the department for an evaluation of its significance for the current policy of allowing regional councils to use carrot bait on conservation land…I will keep you informed of progress with the issue." [emphasis added]

In the 1990's this correspondence took the form of hand written letters. As time passes the internet has the potential to speed up information exchange. But local activists regularly find DOC requesting the use of the Official Information Act (OIA) that allows them 20 working days to answer fairly basic questions. Tom Steel receives correspondence from Minister of Conservation, Sandra Lee, signed off by Phillida Bunkle on 26 September 2000, where Mead's 1994 study is referred to as "seriously flawed". These quoted papers from John Fowler's boxes and suitcases are just the tip of the iceberg of a treasure trove of correspondence carried out between Coromandel conservationists and all layers of government. It is all too easy to see how ordinary individuals are dismissed and ignored when the government, presumably hand in glove with the chemical industry, chooses to kill animals using toxins rather than employing humane wild animal control. Justice can take lifetimes to be served. Yet, there was a time when Coromandel was 1080 poison free and to share that changing story is 309 Hawk and Morepork Sanctuary founder, musician and historian John Veysey.

Coromandel the Beginning: John Veysey

"You can best serve civilization by being against what usually passes for it."

Wendell Berry

In the autumn of 1994 we knew very little about 1080. One day we looked up to see two DOC representatives, Fiona Edwards and Hazel Speed, standing on our doorstep. They had come to inform us that DOC was intending to use 1080 up the road to kill possums. Did we have any objections? Possums had devastated the orchard, eating every leaf from the youngest apricot trees, breaking branches and depriving us of any citrus the previous year, why on earth would we object to you killing possums? "Oh well" was the reply "Some people say that 1080 will kill birds and it has killed birds in the past, but we are using much more modern techniques nowadays. Some people are even afraid that the water will become contaminated."

"Really?" Our ears pricked up. This stuff kills birds and it might contaminate the water. "Test samples show that the water is quite safe. 1080 dissolves easily in water and breaks down into fluoride and carbon dioxide." "Oh?" We were wide awake by this time, being fully aware of the possible adverse effects of long-term fluoride intake and of Dr Eva Hill's battle to have it removed from Auckland's water supply. Dogs can die from eating dead possums. There is no antidote. No dogs in the poisoned area for half a year or more afterwards. The stream of information continued for more than an hour and all of it sounded frightening. Why were these women telling us this stuff? By the time they left we were thoroughly apprehensive and wondering what we were in for.

During the following weeks we tried to find out all we could about 1080. DOC held meetings informing local residents that a 1080-drop was proposed for the head of our valley—the Waiau valley. At the second of those meetings the regional conservator for DOC Stella Penny stated, "If residents were against the trial then it would NOT go ahead." When we heard this announcement we breathed a sigh of relief, as we now believed our destiny was in our own hands. By this time we had found out a lot more about 1080. Information had come from many different sources and most of it had been alarming. We listened to days of talkback radio. Callers who had lost dogs and farm animals talked about their horrendous experiences living near to poisoned areas and we learned of the inhumane death 1080 causes.

DOC pamphlets told us "naturally occurring 1080 found in Perth Australia was quite safe". Supposedly the man-made 1080 chemical reacted very differently to the "naturally occurring" 1080 and any comparison between the two was completely erroneous. The more DOC publications we read the easier it became to notice such misinformation. The propaganda sentences were carefully constructed, the words carefully chosen and the misleading seemed intentional.[24]

A petition was signed by 24 of the 26 residents of the Waiau valley saying "No" to the 1080 trial and sent to the regional conservator. We assumed that would be the end of our worries only to learn some weeks later, to our mortification the poison drop was going ahead despite Stella Penny's promise. We had been lied to. The Environment Commissioner in her report on 1080 mentions the disturbing psychological effect upon a person unable to say "No" to a bulldozing government department. Now we understood what she was talking about. No matter to whom we wrote or spoke nor how far up the chain of command they were, we could not make anyone see sense. There was no one we could turn to for help. We could think of nothing else but the poison drop. Would we dare eat the watercress again or the blackberries next summer?

We lay awake at night trying to think of some way to get through to the officials who were controlling this operation. The area did not need anything aerial, it was easy to drive to and walk through. We were shocked by the arrogance of the DOC staff, their high-handed treatment of country folk and the ease with which they could make promises and so quickly and publicly break them.

Without any further warning, on the windiest day we had experienced for years DOC dropped its 1080 and we knew, like many New Zealanders have learned before and since, how it feels to be crushed by an unstoppable power. On the day of the drop a DOC staff member told one of the locals that the drop had been a disaster. Vicious squalls had hit the helicopter from all directions.

The bucket operator had become so airsick he could no longer do his job. The pilot was left fighting to keep his craft in the air with one hand while trying to operate the spreader with the other.

After the helicopter had finished and the workers had departed, I entered the poisoned area and walked up the main stream. Bright green baits were easy to pick out lying on rocks and along the stream banks but I could not see any green baits in the stream water. We had been publicly promised: "No 1080 would be fed directly into waterways of any kind." Such a promise gave hope to those who took their water from the Waiau River. It took my eyes some time to adjust to the pellet shaped baits that were lying in the water. They had lost their green dye. These once green baits were now the colour of grain, almost white. They were in clumps. A clump here and another further upstream and the odd one or two baits in between. The poison had already washed out of the baits and been swept downstream just an hour or two after they had landed in the water. So here was another lie. The baits had landed in big numbers directly in the waterways. I tackled one of the DOC staff but was told "They're not waterways! It's gotta be 4 meters wide and 1 meter deep before it can be considered a "waterway"." I had a lot to learn.

The following day, accompanied by three neighbours, I walked into the area at first light. I walked along the top ridge. Bright green baits lay at my feet. A finch was pecking at bait and flew off as I approached. We divided up the area and each covered our own area looking for baits. Coming down off the centre ridge I noticed a pattern in the slope. A dying possum had been arching its back and curling up in its dying spasms as it slid down the slope. I looked for the dead possum at the base of the pattern but could not find it. When I looked up a large boar, white froth spilling from his mouth, was stumbling blindly towards me. He had presumably eaten the possum. I was in no danger but was moved by the pig's low agonising moans. There was a look of disbelief in his eye. The four of us, Jim and Stuart Edmondson, John Fowler and myself, crisscrossed the operation for five consecutive days looking for baits. After a week we sat down with a map to pool our knowledge. It soon became obvious that barely half the intended area had received sufficient baits to kill any possums. Much of the area was clear of baits. We did not find any dead possums.

After we had finished this monitoring I became very ill suffering heart palpitations, visual disturbances, hot and cold flushes, vomiting and severe headaches continuously for 10 days. All kinds of possibilities flooded through my mind but eventually I came right, weakened but alive. In hindsight I believe this frightening sickness was probably caused by stress — a type of secondary poisoning perhaps?[25] One month before the drop I trailed an old sheet in the stream below the drop area. Five minutes later I removed the sheet and counted 12 strong stonefly nymphs that I had to pull off the sheet before returning them to the water. One month after the drop I trailed the sheet in the same place again. This time a single nymph dropped off into the water as I pulled it ashore. There was not a single nymph attached to my sheet at a time when the nymphs should have been multiplying and strong. If the poison in the stream had affected these insect larvae what other poisonings had taken place downstream?

Weeks before DOC released its much-awaited report they (not independent monitors) stated they had counted 20% possums before the drop and 1.7% after the drop; a kill rate of 92%. At the beginning of September, a month after the drop, Jim came up with some traps and we laid our 3 lines out parallel with the DOC traps. In 3 nights we caught 20%, the same figure DOC had caught a month earlier before the drop. On 18 September 1994 DOC released their draft report of the trial drop. We were told that during the trial the Department surveyed vegetation changes, monitored frog populations and assessed changes to possum and rat numbers. In addition the Public Health Unit tested water from the Waiau River for presence of 1080. "The trial also gave the public an opportunity to scrutinise and observe an aerial application of 1080 baits." Numerous locals, Forest and Bird members etc., made their interest known to DOC but not one of us was told when the drop would take place. Stella Penny was informed that a protest would take place and maybe the drop was made in a hurry to avoid such a confrontation. Why else would they fly on such a windy day?

The first thing we noticed in the report was that two of the three pre-drop possum monitoring lines were placed in an area where no baits had landed. The rat monitoring tunnels also received hardly any baits. More than half of the monitoring had taken place **outside** the operation area. It took us some days to digest the report and to realise it left a lot of questions unanswered. Much of it was misleading. Forest and Bird members had been looking for dead birds and dead possums and remarked upon the way baits had landed in clumps with big gaps in between. We had been informed: "Pilots using GPS systems are able to achieve minimum standard coverage of 95% of target area". In this case the coverage was less than 60%. We knew. We had covered the entire area.The report makes no mention of the windy weather and continues as if all went perfectly. "While a computer can accurately plot flight paths, it is necessary to measure bait coverage on the ground". Two staffers carried out this bait coverage survey using the Morgan method: A 50 meter line was measured out with a hip-chain and two DOC staff spent five minutes looking 30 meters either side for baits. If no bait was found it was called a gap. If a single bait was found, no gap was recorded. "When no baits were found after 220 meters the line was abandoned due to time constraints."

The report was handed to us with apologies because the results of the bait toxicity samples were not back from the laboratory. However the report reads as if lab results were already back "Samples were collected until the baits were declared non-toxic by Landcare Research". Later in the conclusion we read: "Approx. 100 mm of rain is required before baits become non-toxic. In six weeks, over 250 mm of rain fell and the baits were non-toxic." No results to back it up; just a bald unsubstantiated statement. Read it quickly and you are supposed to feel reassured.

While digesting the report Tom Steel decided to get in touch with David Morgan at the government laboratories in Christchurch. The scientist was pleased to hear from Tom and sent him a copy of his bait distribution measuring method. Tom noticed the method required one man for five minutes max not two men spending so long they ran into time constraints before the half hour was up. How could they be so blase about such blatant inaccuracies?

What monitoring was carried out?
Vegetation Monitoring

According to DOC some trees have been so badly damaged they have only "45% canopy left". When asked to point out the damaged trees we found out "You can only see it from the air". DOC claimed to have high quality photos and even videos of this possum damage at the Waiau but so far have declined to show them to us. From the road you can overlook much of the "canopy" without seeing any apparent damage. All the regular walkers we spoke to had not noticed any possum damage in the area.

Kiwi Monitoring

Two kiwi experts were imported, at great expense, from Wellington. They brought their specially trained dogs intending to catch kiwi to attach radio transmitters. They failed to catch any kiwi however they did say they heard 3 separate kiwi calls before the drop was made. After the drop they listened for two weeks and heard no kiwi calls at all. DOC's conclusion: the Waiau kiwi was "either present and too quiet to monitor or had wandered outside the operational area". Not very convincing. DOC made matters worse when they later claimed that: "Conservation Corps volunteers found fresh kiwi probe marks in the operational area a month after the aerial application of baits." We had to laugh at that one.

Frog Monitoring

Once again we hear from very expensive frog experts. Nine Archey's frogs were counted before the operation and only 5 after the drop. The report tells us "a two factor analysis of Variance (Zar 1974 p. 164) of the above numbers shows there is no difference in the numbers of frogs found before and after the possum control operation." On the other hand 16 Hochstetter frogs were found before the operation and 21 afterwards and "a two factor analysis of variance of the above numbers showed there were more frogs found after the aerial application than before." No one has been able to explain how this two- factor analysis works. The final conclusion was that the increase was "perhaps due to different weather conditions." All the temperatures recorded at the Archey location were consistently 4 degrees higher than those at the Hochstetter location -—and the two locations are only 300 meters apart!

Rat Monitoring

90 out of 100 rat tunnels were placed in one of the large gaps that received no baits, making a complete nonsense of the results. No excuse was offered for this. Meaningless percentage figures were trotted out with their relative tracking indices.

Water Monitoring

Similar meaningless results as all the rest of the monitoring. I had seen the poison washed out of the baits within a few hours of landing in the streams and yet no water samples were taken until the following day long after the poison had washed downstream. No mention has ever been made about this well-known and widely accepted cause of pollution. The Health Board is well aware that there is a rush of poison in stream water under a 1080 drop. Their job is to keep it out of drinking water. Once the poison has washed past their particular uptake tap their responsibility for it ends. There seems to be a total absence of responsibility for this 1080 that has washed downstream below MOH's water sample point. At the Waiau in 1994, baits that landed directly in the streams had lost their poison by nightfall on the day of the drop and were still present in their same landing positions 10 days later. How long they take to disintegrate is irrelevant once the poison has been washed out of them. Disintegration of the bait has been willfully confused with biodegration of the poison.[26]

One thing that stood out in the report was the absence of costs. We, a small handful of local residents, knew exactly what a farce this aerial drop had been. We had taken great pains to find out. But nobody else outside the valley was interested. Even though DOC knew we knew and we knew they knew we knew, they were able to continue with their misleading, almost true but not quite, statements now known as pro-1080 propaganda. They were able to repeat their figures and continue to mislead others because it came down to our word against theirs and no one else took the time to find out first hand. On the face of it the pro-1080 propaganda sounds credible, all carefully phrased to give an intended impression without actually telling direct lies.

Today all the concerns are identical. None of the questions we were asking 20 years ago have been satisfactorily answered. More people are asking them today but the answers are just the same. They still use the "waterways" trick and people are still getting sucked into wanting to believe the best intentions of these agencies that still publish the meaningless number of Ministry of Health (MOH) clear water samples. They still state that 1080 breaks down quickly in water. They still give the impression that a GPS navigational device in the helicopter means you get 4.25 pellets per tennis court area spread. The possum is still the major target in the battle against bovine Tb. All media outlets print the poison promoter's press releases with no critique. And we are always just a handful of local residents. On the hopeful side I believe the day of the written propaganda is about over, soon to be pushed aside by the visual.

*

Around the same time as John Veysey and his 309 neighbours are battling DOC on the Coromandel, Helen Hughes, the Parliamentary Commissioner for the Environment (PCE) publishes two reports. Her *Summary of Findings: Possum Management in NZ* 1994 states, "we still do not know what the 'safe' threshold population level of possums is for either conservation or Tb control." It is in no poison promoter's interest to find the answer to this question and to illustrate the point, this question is still to be answered more than 20 years later. Hughes is also concerned that "continuing heavy reliance on 1080 or any other single toxin is not advisable over the long term". She requests "environmental impact reports" be provided after each aerial drop and the results be given to the NZ Fur Producers Association. It is blazingly obvious the PCE can only make "recommendations"—easy to ignore when it suits the status quo.

The NZ government had taken over the poison business in 1991 when it passed an Act of Parliament to create the State Owned Enterprise (SOE) poison company, Animal Control Products (ACP). One poison factory was in Waimate in the South Island and one is still operational in Wanganui. Somewhere in the time frame of 1987 and 1990 it seems clear deals were brokered with the Tull Chemical company based in the highly militarized and polluted town of Oxford, Alabama[27] as Tull then began exporting almost 90% of the world production of toxin 1080 to the clean green New Zealand shores. Relevant to sealing the deal may be the sudden increase in beef exports to the USA and the likely suppression of Japanese research into health promoting qualities of possum fur.[28]

The Department of Conservation was grafted onto New Zealand's political landscape in 1987 and with its creation came the demise of multiple government organizations including the Department of Scientific and Industrial Research, (DSIR) and the New Zealand Forest Service and NZ Wildlife Service and the loss of skilled scientists and wild life rangers. It has been said

DOC evolved to be a place of misery for those who had bush skills and were yet to retire, a place of mischief for those who are just in it for the money, and a hollow place for those who care about Papatuanuku. DOC staff know native species are killed and that 1080 is an inhumane way of death but contracting a helicopter company to dump a toxin causes fewer headaches (less administration, fewer accident compensation claims) for office-bound bureaucrats, than employing real trappers and hunters living in the wilderness capable of doing the hard work of track cutting, trapping and hunting.

1080 over Whenuakite and the 309

"This is one of the great difficulties of epidemiology and its role in public health policy, particularly in a culture where an agency producing a contaminant is innocent until proven guilty in a court of law."

Sean Weaver

The year is 2006. The 309 Road is in line for more poison. 13,500ha between Waiomu on the west and up to the 309 Road is designated for another 1080 dump. According to DOC this area includes rare coastal forest and a kauri sanctuary and has been "controlled" since 1995 resulting in low numbers of rats and possums as well as observed improvements in forest health and native bird populations. No rationale is given for another dump of toxin. One would imagine there would need to be an influx of possums to initiate yet another poison drop indicating DOC's strategy results in the 'farming' of possums, a factual interpretation never publicized. The Whenuakite block is to be doused with poison for the third time since 1999. The contractor EcoFX will drop non-toxic pre-feed during the next fine spell and follow it up with 2 kg per hectare of cinnamon-lured green 1080 pellets. In May 2006, local farmer Bruce Wilson questions DOC's plan to dump 1080 poison over Whenuakite on the east coast of the Coromandel where the risk to juvenile kiwi seem to have been ignored. He compliments the Whenuakite Kiwi group on a percentage increase for kiwi in the area (169% males, 92% females from 2001 to 2005) due to a track network for traps and bait stations. Wilson then wonders why this same group needs to support a 1080 poison drop.[29]

Bill Axbey, then retired to the Purangi in Cooks Beach, condemns the destruction wrought by human interference with the balance of nature by using poison as a panacea. "It is time that possum control and kiwi survival were separated by the system of poison laying…Kiwi zones should not have poison sown from the air… We are also faced with the enigma of the fact that stoat and wild cat kills are credited to those animals eating poisoned rats, mice and birds yet we are led to believe that kiwi and other birds are considered immune from eating poisoned insects?

"There is a thing called the "balance of nature" that is often quoted in conservation circles. In short it means a population of something that can maintain itself at a sustainable level by adequate food, shelter and breeding in the face of loss and predation by whatever. Whenever the rat and mouse population increases stoats and weasels that use them as their main source of prey also increase. When a poison campaign is carried out by air, the decline in rat and mouse population is drastic and sudden. A few stoats are killed at the same time but secondary poisoning according to DOC is not as deadly as the primary kill so many stoats are unaffected and to survive, turn to birds such as kiwi chicks. These drops regularly take place when such chicks are at their most vulnerable age. Result: adult kiwi may not be affected but juveniles experience a poor survival rate after bulk poison sowing that does not show up for some time and certainly not by adult counts…Possums do not eat kiwi, nor do rats but rats do eat eggs and chicks of smaller birds. Stoats and cats eat rats and mice as primary food and turn to kiwi chicks and other birds when the main food source is cut off by poison sowing. Cats like any predator take the easiest and most readily available food supply. After a poisoning rats and mice are only available for a short period as a secondary poison bait, the surviving predators turn to other prey. This would indicate that bulk poisoning is detrimental to kiwi populations…"[30] (The kiwi bird is the smallest living ratite, a family that includes emu and ostrich, and lays the largest egg in relation to its body size.)

Meanwhile on Moehau right at the top of the Coromandel kiwi are surviving beyond wildest expectations. The kiwi survival statistics for the Moehau Kiwi Sanctuary show sub-adult averages of 95% per year since the year 2000.[31] All of this has been achieved with no aerial toxins. Some of the success can be put down to solid hard work with trappers cutting tracks and setting stoat traps over the mountain. Still the poison pushers are dead set on spreading more and more toxin. Locals have vociferously opposed aerial 1080 on Moehau for decades and were successful in protecting the mountain and its fauna until the year 2013.

DOC's promotion of 1080 poison for Whenuakite prompts strong reaction from locals when readers of the local paper discover DOC's cavalier response to a request for a public meeting. Alison

Smith writing her story *Residents angry: no 1080 consultation* notes even though the majority of locals were opposed to the dropping of toxin 1080 it is clear their wishes would not have mattered in the least. "Asked why the department did not hold a public meeting, Mr de Monchy said: "I asked my manager a couple of times if we should hold a public meeting but his feeling was if you do so you give the impression that you will change the outcome. You can end up having more antipathy in a community when they can't actually change something. When slightly, or very frustrated people come together I don't know if you gain much."[32] Smith's story gives voice to residents' concerns: '"We haven't been notified, we had no idea," Whenuakite residents Karine and Gary Wilson say. 'We're a very small distance from the drop so it could affect our water and we're going to tanker water in. Where's the public meeting? Where's the consultation?' says Gary Wilson who owns a 72 hectare block in Whenuakite. 'DOC is setting itself up for eco-terrorism. We have no problem with bait stations containing 1080 because it's a form of pest control, but leave the kiwi alone. When they drop this and wipe them all out we'll just have to smile and say 'yes, they know best'.'" The locals say the excellent ground control in the area has contributed to kiwi numbers growing from 31 recorded in 2001, to 68 birds in 2005. DOC says the drop is to kill rats. Conservationist and farmer Arthur Attfield describes DOC as "neighbours from hell" His 133ha block adjoins private land where 1080 will be dropped. "These government agencies will go to any length to justify their policies. It's no wonder we don't trust them. When the population counts for nothing — that's bad."[33] Attfield's inspired description resonates with reporters further afield. A headline in *Country News,* reads *DOC denies being a 'neighbour from hell'* and the national daily also finds the colourful phrase arresting.[34]

DOC announces that two landowners "specifically sought the application of aerially applied 1080." Just two! A petition opposing the drop is signed by 400 locals and presented to DOC. The majority of people in the neighbourhood of the toxin drop do not support DOC's proposal. Once again majority local views are disregarded. Rather than respond to the concerns and wishes of 400 petitioners, DOC chooses to appease two landowners whose attitude to poison coincides with their own. Not one hectare of the land to be aerially treated by toxin can be considered "inaccessible" for trappers or hunters. The use of aerial 1080 toxin or accessible farmland near Whenuakite is an example of the misuse of toxin 1080 on the Coromandel. The DOC protocols for consultation with communities over poison programmes are presented under section *6.2 Public consultation process* where it states, "You must consider the need to canvas the views of recreational users, adjoining landowners, Iwi and NGO's and show you have considered ways of addressing any concerns raised." DOC fails again.

Visitors to the Coromandel are moved to put pen to paper as exemplified by this letter from a resident of New South Wales, Australia. Carolyn Dobson noted intense concerns regarding the earlier goat eradication, poison1080 and the wild animal barrier proposal: "DOC has repeatedly transgressed agreements made with landholders on the Coromandel and in other areas about access across and activities on private land for feral animal eradication."[35] David Green's front-page story titled: *1080: Where to from here?* The debate is already well underway on the Coromandel. The well-researched article uses the entire front page and includes: "Recent and proposed 1080 poisoning operations have fuelled strong opinion in Mercury Bay and Tairua... Before the drop, more than 400 locals, representing 75% of the landowners surrounding the Whenuakite area, signed a petition to oppose the drop. They say that over 1250 bait stations are already in place within the kiwi protection zone and that the recent aerial drop merely mopped up what was already a low possum population. The next line of conflict is likely to be between DOC and the residents of Kuaotunu who are already mobilizing a petition and written submissions to stop 1080 being used in bait stations in their area. New Zealand accounts for around 80% of the world market for 1080 and between 2.5 and 3 tonnes of the poison are dropped annually on up to a million hectares. Usually dropped in 12g green dyed carrots or cereal pellets...Purangi resident Bill Axbey worked for the Wildlife Service for 25 years and has had a great deal of experience working with 1080. He states the toxin does not break down as quickly as DOC claims and that 'what is really mad is trying to protect native bird species by blanket dropping a deadly poison during the nesting season...on top of birds being killed directly, the loss of rats from the food chain will only lead to stoats and weasels putting more pressure on young birds."

The story is illustrated with a photograph of six-year-old Ngahere Wafer, a visitor to the Coromandel, "who wants no more

1080. 'I know it kills things that are good for the earth like frogs, wetas and boars.' He reckons that a spotlight and a gun or bow and arrow are the best way to deal with possums."[36]

Kuaotunu Conflict

"We won't have a society if we destroy the environment"
Margaret Mead

The conflict in Kuauotunu is heating up—the original Kuaotunu Environmental Action (KEA) group is opposed to 1080 and Project Kiwi is supporting the use of 1080 poison. Conservationist and trapper, Victor McLean is pictured in a *Bay Beacon* story with his trained dog Cassie. Together they helped achieve an annual kiwi chick survival rate of 50%. McLean is now offering a unique bush experience of three-hour tramps to show visitors how a predator dog works.[37] In Victor's own words: "I worked for 8 years on a project where we had 50% kiwi chick survival using trapping only. This was a success. We had stopped 1080 in Otama. So we founded a new community organization—Kuaotunu Environmental Action (KEA). We are members of this community group and at present are doing the voluntary trapping for KEA. The community group works an area of approx 3500 hectares. We have just purchased 29 new Henry traps using the $5000 we got from EW. From yet another sponsor we have 10 kill traps for cats to use around Otama wetlands. There are two trap lines up and running that are checked on a voluntary basis. Possum control in 2009 was a success using feratox cyanide. Our company has been working with Social Services providing work experience over the last 12 months, offering training in bush craft, compass and map reading, trap variation and dog work for mustelids.

"Project Kiwi (PK) is the group that sacked me for saying no to 1080. PK now use residual poisons for rats. Project Kiwi released one kiwi back into the wild at 1000 grams, but they released it into an area with no trap protection from stoats, and no monitoring. A kiwi in captivity that weighs 1000 grams is just a fat bird that does not know how to move around in the wild, has not encountered any threats from stoats and it doesn't run when put on the ground it just sits. It does not have the muscle structure of a wild bird as it has not run up a hill or crossed a creek, so at 1000 grams it will have the strength of a 500 gram bird in the wild. Project Kiwi

"

did not monitor their Operation Nest Egg kiwi once the chick was released into the wild. Operation Nest Egg, (ONE) is a programme that raids kiwi nests, takes the egg into captivity to be cleaned, hatched, raised and released at 1000gms. The fact is Operation Nest Egg is a waste of time as you are releasing kiwi back into an area with no stoat traps. Trapping is still the only real answer. That was back in 2009 when they stopped trapping and went with residual poisons. Today (April 2014) they use poisons and traps. They monitor their ONE kiwi by call counts. They do not monitor their ONE kiwi by transmitter, they never have, so how do they know if they survive?"[38]

If we flash forward to March of 2014 we find the regional council pouring money into Project Kiwi for a "habitat and biodiversity inventory with a view to its operational area on the Kuaotunu Peninsula becoming a biodiversity hub...the Whau Whau Environmental Group pledged support." This article goes on to say that over 18 years "much of what we know about the trapping of predators and monitoring of kiwi has been developed and refined by the Project Kiwi Trust...in the past five years the trust has intensively trapped the core of the project (520 hectares)..."[39]

1080 in the Coromandel Town Water Catchment
2006-2007

"In one drop of water are found all the secrets of the oceans."
Khalil Gibran

DOC and EW plan to drop aerial 1080 into the Manaia and Coromandel water supply. There will be no independent monitoring of non-target species. The area is accessible to hunters and trappers. Local businesses are seriously concerned with any impact on tourism. Lorenza Devcich finds it unbelievable that yet again DOC is persisting in its plan to drop 1080 "even though the public is against it. Unsurprisingly DOC, the local MP, mayor and the leader of the Green Party have all just ignored our constant concern over the long term effects of this deadly poison." She asks town dwellers to take off their blinkers.[40] Mock Johnstone, Secretary of the Coromandel Pig Hunting Club writes on behalf of the club.

"This is a statement of disgust and objection to the wholesale poisoning of the hills and watersheds surrounding Coromandel town or any other town in the same situation. The effects of 1080 on wildlife in the poisoned areas are well known. What is not known for sure is how far down the food chain these toxins will travel before they stop. 1080 has devastating effects on wild pigs and dogs and anyone who has witnessed a dog dying from 1080 would not have seen anything so horrific. DOC is doing this operation in the name of 'flood control.' Killing the possums won't alter the fact that if it rains hard enough it will flood. It has always flooded: the only difference is that people have built more houses in the path of these floods, (poor Council decisions.) 1080 in bait stations is not a safe alternative as once it is eaten it is out of the bait station the poisoned animal can either find its way into waterways or die on land ready for any other animal to eat…. DOC wishes to do an aerial 1080 operation with rats as one of their main targets. Rats are not on the Peninsula Project list of pests to be destroyed…a simple cyanide and trapping programme of each of the native valleys would halt the pest problem, as these areas around Coromandel town are so easily accessible. So come on you people of Coromandel, the DOC propaganda machine (one of the best in the country) is about to swing into action to convince you that poisoning your food and water is just what you need. Make your thoughts your choice. The members of the Coromandel Pig Hunting Club totally oppose the use of 1080 or any other toxin which may affect our water quality or health, either present or in the future of any or all of the people of Aotearoa."[41]

The Upper Coromandel Landcare Associaton (UCLA) writes in support of those opposing the drop of toxin 1080 over the 309 and into the water catchment of Coromandel town. The story is illustrated with a photograph of a DOC toxin sign erected on the 309 Road. UCLA speculates what tourists will make of skull and cross bone danger signs. The information on the signs includes lethal dose information for a 20kg child. Only two, twelve gram baits containing 0.15% 1080 are necessary to kill a child, chronic poisoning is never raised as a risk factor.

The negative publicity does not bypass DOC and they endeavour to diminish the public health sign's impact by making the signs smaller, but are apparently thwarted in their ability to change the actual content, as the toxin is a World Health Organisation registered A1 Hazardous Toxin. Public health warning signs remain in use through the coming years but the size of the sign warning of poison dangers is reduced. DOC opines in the *Bay Beacon* of November 10, 2006 "Hysteria based on individual paranoia rarely reflects the facts." Once again, instead of presenting sound science to support their promotion of poison DOC makes extreme, unsupported and emotive accusations. And DOC wonders why their reputation is so tarnished on the Coromandel.

The official *Beware Poison* signage on the 309 Road suddenly gets a new date extension to January 31. This time period now includes school holidays directly contravening the provisions of the Hazardous Substances and New Organisms (HSNO) Act 1996 that clearly state with regard to aerial 1080, public holidays are to be avoided.

Colin Harris of Whitianga writes in February 2007 "It is totally frustrating and a little annoying listening to or reading the comments of the DOC and the Area Health Board about the benefits of 1080. The whole argument comes down to cost, which is a spurious measurement at best when applied to the environment. In 1990, when we still had a fur industry in NZ, the Fur Producers Association attempted to get the government to introduce a $2 per head bounty on possums. DOC vigorously opposed this. At the time a scientific study estimated a population of 70 million possums in NZ. Hypothetically all the possums could have been killed in one year for $140 million. Currently DOC and the health board receive $11 million annually of government money with no end in sight. DOC through their arrogance and ignorance missed a golden opportunity to mop up possums on all private lands that fringe the larger DOC reserves, by encouraging private individuals through the bounty system. Now that the horse has bolted, we are told that spreading 1080 like confetti from the air is the answer. How can we as a country honestly say that we are clean and green? Also, how can we preach, as we do to other countries, about the evils of eating whales when we are prepared to poison hundreds, if not thousands of organically grown pigs and deer in our forests without the slightest attempt to recover those animals before the poison drops?"[42]

Frank Foster of Tararu writes in the March Issue of *Thames Talk* "Government agencies do at times directly lie about issues, when it fits their political agenda… DOC seems to be simply shifting their opinion from categorically saying it is safe and harmless, to one now of more expediency and efficiency of possum eradication through 1080 application. Readers may be interested to note that a government State Owned Enterprise (SOE) controls the importation and distribution of 1080, owning in effect, the franchise, (Animal Control Products) and as such the Minister of Agriculture and Fisheries has an automatic seat on the Board alongside the Minister of Finance." By 2016 there seems to be a changing of the guard and the two ministers are the Minister and Deputy Minister of Primary Industries, Nathan Guy and Jo Goodhew. In the same issue of *Thames Talk*, Hemi J Parata writes suggesting "No one in their right mind would use 1080…When an SOE makes a good profit do the politicians not all rub their hands in glee, even if it has to sell tonnes of 1080 to make that profit?"

As one may imagine there is a counter attack in local newspaper letter columns by Forest and Birders now on the government poison dream team. Terry O'Neil of Waitakaruru responds: "Good on the Upper Coromandel Landcare Association, we don't all think like D. Ashby. I've worked and hunted all around Moehau mountain for over 30 years and the kiwi were plentiful and pigs even more so—they live in harmony. Since do-gooders got involved with trapping and poisons the kiwis have all but gone (I wonder where?). The silent majority does not go around trying to force their ideals on everybody else. Mr Ashby—nobody is being manipulated by anybody locally and they won't be manipulated by you or Forest and Bird."[43]

Charles Harsant, long time conservationist and respected farmer on the East Coast near Hahei writes the next letter referencing an editorial given over to a guest writer. "Regarding Evan Penny's editorial, it was for the most part untrue. Possums did not come onto the peninsula until about 1960, and as landowners we managed to control rabbits with night shoots without the need for help from a rabbit board. In the early years there was a bounty on wild pigs, paid by the Department of Agriculture, and farmers and young people kept the pig numbers down. At one time we could buy weed control chemicals through the Coromandel County Council at a reasonable price, so we controlled our own weeds. Our streams and farm ponds were home for frogs and it was always possible to see and hear skylarks in the sky. Now our bush and scrubland is covered with 1080 from the air and possums, birds, frogs, and insects are all victim of the ongoing 1080 drops. The road edges are also sprayed for weed control, so another frog habitat has gone. Mr. Penny states native animals can rebound and multiply. We have two species of native bat and it is about time the pig brought here by Captain Cook was classed as native, because the only native creatures we had that could browse the bush and scrub were moa."[44] Michael Daly's poem is published in the *Coromandel Town Chronicle (CTC)* concludes: "Stand united and stop DOC/From destroying our countryside/Don't listen to Environment Waikato/Because all they've done is lied."[45]

Ursula Walsh, a registered nurse, writes how she fell in love with New Zealand and its people, moving to the Coromandel a year earlier. She shows how activism can be motivated by beauty and is passionately articulate against the dumping of toxins into our stunning wilderness. She organises the *Coromandel Walk Against 1080* planned for Sunday 10th June 2pm 2007. Fred Look writes of the ethics of killing. "…We all feel some unease about killing. For some people this leads them to vegetarianism. For myself, I recognise that killing is fundamental to nature and that we are part of the natural world. So I kill to eat (fish etc.) or protect my sanity (rats!) or the environment (possums.). But I feel distress when I botch the job causing fright or pain or killing some other animal by mistake. The source of this distress is my conscience. So I am OK with killing that is done with care, respect and reverence. Shoddy careless killing is not OK with me at all. It makes me feel violated. I do not personally use poison because poison is dangerous and indiscriminate. But I accept the practice where trained persons lay poison and then go back and recover the carcasses and bait. So when I see DOC sponsored goat cullers working to reduce goat populations on fragile landscapes I am saddened but accepting. Likewise when I meet those who maintain the DOC trap lines (stoat and rat) that run across our land I am respectful of the work they do. In these cases individuals are taking personal responsibility to do the job right. When you see poison raining from the sky do you feel that this is right? When you read "this is the only affordable way" do you feel clean? When you hear that "there is no alternative" does your heart believe it? Do you think that a public relations campaign will make it right? Listen to the voice within you."[46]

In the same issue of *CTC* (May 2007) Gary Masters writes of his 2002 experience when walking the beach at Te Puru. He witnessed a "ghastly dog death." Following the massive flood of June 20, 2002 poisoned possums as well as debris, logs and sediment had been washed to the shore—DOC had dumped toxin 1080 up in the hills behind the coastal town of Te Puru. The usual safety assurances had been made. Alan Lowden, Grant Smith and Mr Johansen all lost dogs. The Lowden dog tested positive for 1080 poisoning. The test is extremely expensive and exposes yet another oversight by the Environmental Risk Management Agency (ERMA). ERMA when reassessing the toxin, should have laid the burden of the 'high cost' of testing for 1080 to those responsible for its distribution into the food chain. Sam Small of Coromandel asks "How can you call NZ clean and green if the DOC is going to drop thousands of tonnes of toxic poison into the environment? In my opinion, DOC should employ local trappers. There are many willing trappers who are keen to trap the possums on the peninsula. This will put money back into the community as well."

The *Coromandel Town Chronicle* is the only publication to dedicate unlimited space to the toxin issue. Editors Tom Look and Jennifer Greene joined with community opposition to provide well-researched articles exposing 1080 toxin dangers Look and Greene went out on a limb to give voice to our community. There would be repercussions that would lead to their eventual loss of editorship but they continue to be articulate conservationists on the upper Coromandel.

A picture of residents attending the local community board meeting to voice opposition to the 1080 drop appears in the June 7 issue of the *Moehau Messenger (MM)* to illustrate two front-page headlines: *1080: the debate goes on and the protests get louder* and *Residents tell the community board: stop 1080 drop.* An inset photograph of twelve-year-old Douglas Rauch is printed alongside his submission that reads: "I am against 1080 in the Coromandel because of what it does to us and our animals. It may kill the pests but will kill our native animals and after the drop the pests will come back 2X worse and with the native animals still recovering they won't stand a chance."

Numerous letters are published in all local papers opposing the promotion of toxin 1080. Activist and conservationist Lynley Brown writes "As a landowner on the 309 road I have just received Arthur Hind's EW letter assuring me I need not have concerns about the proposed aerial drop of 1080 poison in our area. After 12 years of researching the facts about 1080 I find the information sent by EW to be irresponsible. We are told we cannot fight pests without this deadly poison. This statement fills me with fear, not only for humans but also for animals that will suffer an agonizing death. It is widely known that the scientific quality of DOC's research is poor and does not support their statements such as '1080 breaks down rapidly in the environment' and 'in water and no one has ever been poisoned by 1080 in NZ.' There are many incidents of people becoming ill after a drop in their area and I therefore find those statements to be irresponsible. Why are DOC and EW so determined to poison our land, animals and birds and to feed us false information or do they naively believe this is the only solution? The future generations will judge them by their actions. Once we were told that DDT was safe."[47]

Moehau Poisoning 2007

"Live or die, but don't poison everything."

Anne Sexton

On May 21, 2007 DOC's Eddie Murphy sends a form letter to residents in the Moehau vicinity outlining a planned ground poisoning. Along with 1080 poison-laced baits, a suite of poisons will be used including pindone pellets and Decal pellets (cholecalciferol). Key facts are listed—residents must watch children at all times, not touch the bait and not eat wild animals from within a 2km buffer zone. Residents are reminded that poison baits or carcasses are deadly to dogs. Farmers and conservationists Chris and Dianne Novis are offered a map of the area. This is DOC's definition of "consultation". It is clearly not consultation. It is merely notification. The Upper Coromandel Landcare Association (UCLA) demand DOC cancel the proposed 1080 ground poisoning on Moehau's eastern block. At the same time UCLA casts doubts on whether DOC has undertaken iwi consultation. DOC considers they have "iwi blessing" from 20 years earlier.[48] The plan is to carry out a ground-based 1080 poisoning of more than 3300ha on the east block of Moehau to cover the entire mountain flank from the Okahutahi watershed that drains into Big Sandy, then past the popular Stony Bay campground and Coromandel walkway and mountain bike track, through the Muriwai and Holland Creek drainages toward Fletcher Bay and Port Jackson.

UCLA questions the impact of poison 1080 on the mauri of Moehau and on non-target species on Moehau. After DOC demands a fee to supply UCLA with evidence of 'consultation', local Member of Parliament, Sandra Goudie, requests copies under Section 12 of the Official Information Act 1982. Through Goudie's action it is discovered that all serious evidence registering opposition to the use of poison 1080 on Moehau was withheld from the Medical Officer of Health, Dr Dell Hood who is the first port of call by DOC when applying for permission to use a Vertebrate Toxic Agent (pursuant to the Hazardous Substances and New Organisms Act 1996). What Hood had been given as evidence of 'consultation' was a hand-written page confirming Murphy's form letter had actually been sent to locals **telling** them what would happen. She was also told Murphy held conversations with one or two farmers. No mention of UCLA's communications. Dell Hood lives in Waitete Bay on the Coromandel and one could imagine she was aware of local opposition to residual poisons. However Hood approved every 1080 toxin application prior to her retirement. Murphy's proposed start date is the first of July 2007 and the poisoning is to be completed within three months. 1.5g of 1080 poison will lace each kilo to be applied in bait stations as both pellet and gel to kill rodents and possums over 3300 ha on Moehau East block. Diphacinone encased in potato starch and stapled to trees will also be distributed until June 2008.

Meanwhile DOC's John Gaukrodger confirms, in his 2006 newsletter, the kiwi bird population on Moehau is improving. It "has increased dramatically from ten years ago, following decades of decline. A simple recipe of predator trapping backed by kiwi chick survival monitoring and hard work on the hill has produced this exceptional result, along with valuable knowledge of kiwi. Without protection, kiwi chick survival is around 5% in the wild. On Moehau the survival rate has been maintained at over 70% for the last seven years. Both kiwi protection and pig hunting are an integral part of the overall habitat, species and pest management strategy on Moehau." All this success—without aerial 1080? Is there anyone home?

Locals are distressed at the lack of consultation with the neighbouring community on Moehau. UCLA requests support— which is forthcoming from the Coromandel Colville Community Board (CCCB), to help bring an end to the application of toxin 1080 on Moehau East by DOC. Citizens continue to voice frustration at how the new Peninsula Project monies, to be utilized ostensibly to help reduce flooding, are being directed to poison operations. Residents continue to demand legitimate consultation in future wild animal control and to demand employment of local trappers and hunters. The community continues to inform DOC of their concerns including the potential threat 1080 poses to the mauri and wairua of Mother Earth.[49]

2007 Coromandel Citizens Take to the Streets to Oppose Toxin 1080

"In the beginning you must subject yourself to the influence of nature. You must be able to walk firmly on the ground before you start walking on a tightrope."

Henri Matisse

Coromandel Walk Against 1080 organizer Ursula Walsh invites one and all to join her making banners to protest 1080 in our environment and later, to gather outside the Information Centre on Sunday June 10, 2007 at 2.00 pm. On Sunday a simultaneous support demonstration occurs in the capital, Wellington, outside the ERMA headquarters located in BP House. Demonstrators in Wellington include students, deerstalkers and conservationists. They make use of the professionally produced Stop 1080 banner kindly supplied by long-time activist, writer and conservationist Kate Winters.

Hundreds of protestors take to the Coromandel streets in spite of the severely wintry weather. Blustery winds and bouts of rain in Coromandel town do not deter students and elderly, hunters and trades people, business owners and fisherfolk, all united against the poison drop in the Coromandel town catchment. Walsh addresses the gathering: "I emigrated to New Zealand for the beauty and the green image. I've been all over the world and this is the best country. I'm going to do everything I can in my power to ban this (1080)…In the Tauherinikau Valley, the Wake Trust used feratox- encapsulated cyanide- and trapping instead of 1080 to prevent weka from being wiped out. Ferratox kills possums quickly with virtually no risk to non-target species. Why can't we use this here?"[50]

Walsh was proud of the turnout especially given it was such an inclement day. Creative banners, a homegrown haka, donated hot soup and other food and drink formed a backdrop to the march along the main street. Maori television recorded the effort of estimates of upwards of 400 people—impressive numbers given the population of Coromandel town hovers around 1500.

The Thames newspaper also publishes a photograph of students who perform as the Possum Hottenanny at the Matatoki Possum Bust, an annual event that encourages possum trapping and hunting as well as providing a lot of fun. Nearly 800 possums were caught.

It is worth jumping a few years ahead to see how regional government distorts such events. In 2010 an influential poison promoter and Waikato Regional Council employee declaims "a **small** number of the Coromandel town community in particular expressed strong opposition to the possible use of 1080 toxin in the hill country above the town…A campaign was mounted by the antagonists which influenced several landowners to the extent they withdrew their consent…From a professional perspective staff are of the view that there is no rational reason why **conventional** possum control should not be carried out. However, there is such a prevailing bias against 1080 and other toxins because of **misinformation and** a concerted antagonist campaign, that alternative control (trapping only) may be the only viable option. If this is the case then the community needs to fund the additional cost of such control and accept the results." [emphasis added][51]

Following the demonstration a further town meeting is called and the Whitianga paper sends a reporter: *Town turns out for anti-1080 meeting* "A diverse group of 80 people turned up for the 1080 meeting at the Coromandel Area School on Sunday afternoon. Organizer of last weekend's protest Ursula Walsh was there to chair the meeting alongside Upper Coromandel Landcare Association spokesperson Reihana Robinson, scientist Quinn Whiting-O'Keefe, John Veysey and Coromandel Area School student twelve year old Douglas Rauch. Ex-Hamilton City Councillor and facilitator Annette Kaye said she had arranged a meeting with regional council staff in Hamilton on June 28.

Ms Kaye wanted two speakers with sound knowledge of 1080 to carry the message to Environment Waikato (EW regional council's brand) 'We want something productive to come out of this, if we can use an alternative, then I'm all for it. We say: let's not do the drop, let's get a plan and review.'…Mr Whiting-O'Keefe's main concern was planned aerial drops of 1080 by the Department of Conservation. 'There is not a single, credible study showing a mainland population benefit from 1080 treatment to any native faunal species, but there is lots of evidence that massive numbers of native birds are being killed by DOC's 1080 operations,' he said. John Morrissey (local police officer and district councillor) volunteered to air the views of the meeting at the public forum at the next Thames Coromandel District Council meeting on June 26."[52]

Jenefer Duane and Ron Spinhoven from Two Rock-Petaluma, California write how disturbed they were to discover their family retreat on the 309 is to be blitzed as part of a 400-tonne drop of 1080 poison. In the June *Coromandel Town Chronicle (CTC)* they write "an ominous cloud has parked itself over the 309 Road. Thanks to the internet keeping us connected to our friends and comrades in the area, we have been informed of what we consider to the frightening potential for an environmental disaster at the hands of the DOC."

DOC's Area Manager writes on the same page of the *CTC* that DOC are spending $4.7million of the Peninsula Project monies, and dropping 1080 is part of the plan. The Peninsula Project money was originally allocated in 2004 "to better protect people, property and essential services from flooding, reduce sedimentation in rivers, harbours and estuaries, improve water quality, reduce pests such as possums and goats, improve diversity of plants and animals, improve and stabilise catchments, sustain the mauri of the peninsula from the mountain range to the sea."

One has to question how water quality will be improved and how people will be protected through the use of aerial 1080 toxin. The background and impact of this bogus programme must briefly take centre stage to expose how rural discontent can grow when watered by government bombast and intimidation.

The Peninsula Project: How it all Began

*"When I see a bird that walks like a duck and swims like a
duck and quacks like a duck, I call that bird a duck."*
James Whitcomb Riley

In 2002 storms struck the west coast of the Coromandel causing
loss of life and homes, and massive environmental damage.
Two years go by, then on September 24 2004 the *Hauraki Herald*
carries numerous stories and one letter. First up, a large front
page photograph of a grinning pair—Prime Minister Helen Clark
embracing the TCDC Mayor Chris Lux. Why one may ask is there
such jubilation? Well the headline says it all *PM gives $10m flood
package.* This is the beginning of the disingenuous scheme dubbed
the Peninsula Project.

Locals could imagine taxes already collected would be used
for their benefit to help solve flooding problems. Those residents
who survived the massive flooding could imagine the $10 million
dollars would be utilised on the west coast (location of the 2002
devastation) of the Coromandel Peninsula to clear culverts,
build retaining walls, plant trees, relocate sewage plants on the
floodplain, move houses out of harm's way. However warning
bells start ringing in paragraph three of the story, as the money
"will be spread over four years and will go towards pest control,
property acquisition and engineering works." DOC is "spending
$365,000 this year, $1.366m in 2005/06 and $955,000 in following
years. The money will fund aerial and ground-based operations
to control goats and possums to prevent erosion, and establishing
healthy native forests." A total of $27 million will come from our
taxes and targeted rates to pay for wild animal control as part of
the flood control package.

Holidaymaker Dorothy Newall was swept out to sea after the
weather event referred to in all media and in local korero as the
"weather bomb", but millions of dollars will be dedicated to aerial
1080 poison to kill possums and rats and goats. According to the
September story, Chris Lux "was rapt...especially as it is getting
money for DOC." TCDC's CEO, Steve Ruru explains the new

money will be branded the *Peninsula Project*. It is to be a partnership between Hauraki Māori Trust Board, TCDC, DOC and EW. $690,000 has been allocated for property purchase. Environment Waikato's asset manager Scott Fowlds says, "everyone will get together to make the Peninsula Project work…We're getting close to cracking open the champagne." Frankly, beer could hold some agency on the West Coast of the Coromandel—perhaps further evidence of the disjuncture between city and country. In yet another news story *$10m flood package quells residents' fears* in the same paper we see "Flood affected property owners in Tararu are shelling out $3400 to pay for the Environment Waikato approved protection measures, which involves building stopbanks." The Peninsula Project continues to startle residents with its hunger for targeted rates to be used to kill possums and goats. Oddly, well outside the disaster region, the Moehau Environment group's rat killing project on the east coast of the upper Coromandel in Waikawau is financed by flood monies as well as duck repatriation in Port Charles—all documented in *Envirocare Peninsula Project highlights 2005*. Meanwhile landowners in flood-affected areas must pay extra hard-earned cash for real flood control.

It would appear the local council lost control of this project from the start. Forestry giant Ernslaw One Ltd states the Peninsula Project "appears to be oversold by EW as a workable remedy for flooding on debris, flood and debris avalanche prone fans on the peninsula…Individual Coromandel landowners, be they on the coast, on flood plains or in upland areas will individually accrue little if any relief from flooding" The project "is unlikely to alleviate future intense weather events."[53] EW remains in denial and publishes doc#1346156 that states killing possums "addresses the risks of large-scale canopy collapse in upper catchments. In turn, this assists in reducing long-term soil erosion and runoff." There is no hydrological study supporting their assertion, there are no photographs to prove "large-scale canopy collapse" but almost $5 million dollars are squandered just the same. The blatant promotion of the failed "pest control" segment should result in bureaucratic accountability.

Instead Julie Beaufill (EW) and Fin Buchanan (DOC) are rewarded with a trip to Hamilton to attend the Conserv-Vision Conference July 2007 to present their "paper" *A Partnership in Pest Control for Integrated Catchment Management: Working together to protect our people, property and the environment.* The Abstract begins "In June 2002 a life was lost and people were seriously injured when a weather bomb struck the Thames Coast of the Coromandel Peninsula." At exactly the half-way mark of the abstract we read "Animal pest control, aimed at possums and goats, will allow the forest to recover, improving the stability of the catchment and downstream river system, ultimately reducing the impact of flooding…The improved condition of the forest is already apparent with a notable increase in bird numbers." Their introduction confidently declares: "The Coromandel Peninsula has suffered three 100-year flood events since January 2002, so **something had to be done to address the high risks to life and property**". [emphasis added]

Yes, something had to be done to address the high risks to life and property and that is why Coromandel flood victims were initially pleased with the government package they believed would be used to decrease "the high risks to life and property." How delusional. Conference attendees learn DOC and EW have other plans…"The condition of large areas of the forest is poor mainly due to browsing animals…Possums are targeted because they are slowly killing the Peninsula's forests." $4.7 million would be handed to DOC in 2004 to "target possums and goats." This will be spent over five years. And going for the jugular, "Aerial application of 1080 is the preferred control method for the large, rugged areas." No substantiation or community consultation, just a bald bureaucratic claim repeating a belief held by central and regional government. But the writers note, "a Thames-based iwi was fundamentally against the use of pesticides on their lands and were seeking local employment opportunities for their young people. A pest control unit was established by the runanga. The unit was awarded a contract to trap on their lands…In the Tapu River catchment a private landowner, who works as a trapper, was **allowed** to trap possums on behalf of the Project on his own property, as well as on neighbouring land where the owners favoured trapping as a control option."[emphasis added]

From 2005 to 2007 aerial 1080 was dropped over 26,004ha, "a pest-free Peninsula for some key species may even be a possibility in the future" is proclaimed. The rat statistics are impressive, down from 98% to 5% in Tapu three weeks after the drop. Yet 2007 research shows rat populations more than double within 12 months of a poison drop, a fact surely known by the presenters.[54] In 2005/6 poison1080 was dropped in the Peninsula Project's name over 12,850ha of the upper catchments of the Kauaeranga, Tararu and Te Puru rivers. Goats were hunted through the Waiomuu and Waikawau catchments. EW's John Simmons reports to the North Zone Biosecurity Advisory Subcommittee on April 21, 2006: "We need to be able to demonstrate that goat and possum control is resulting in a healthier forest." So what do they do? Wildlands Consultants are contracted to establish 38 permanent plots to observe vegetation changes. What happens when UCLA asks for the report? Oh dear, it seems to be a disaster for a number of reasons—change of ownership of land not least of their worries. So yet more money down the tube for spurious goals.

The dissemination of an internal EW publication *Review of Thames Monitoring for Biophysical Benefits from Annual Pest Control*[55] repeats the mantra 'pest' control "potentially can deliver biophysical benefits including reduced peak flows and water yields (flooding), reduced erosion and sediment to streams and the coastal marine areas, debris reduction and improved biodiversity." With no supporting data. These same authors do mention the majority of increased run off and sediment is attributed to anthropomorphic activities. The glossy DOC 2006 report confirms the conference presenter's claim that some trapping has been approved: "a possum control contract, using only traps [is] let to Ngāti Maru Runanga." Ngāti Maru Pest Control trap "jointly owned Māori land". This and That Ltd and Wildlife Management Services also trap and/or ground-bait the Kereta East Block, 89 ha of private land in Tapu valley.

An alternative to poison 1080 is proposed by a local landcare group for Phase 3 of the Peninsula Project to embrace 10,00ha around Coromandel village. Corolandcare's John Veysey writes: "The plan involved three part-time trappers who would be assured of continuous employment and would be responsible for all wild animal control over the 10,000ha surrounding Coromandel town. They would set up a trap line to continue the stoat line which now stops at the top of the Whangapoua hill and maintain an encircling barrier round to Manaia to prevent incursions of all species from adjoining DOC land. This small team of bushmen would guarantee no dogs, no cats and no pigs would get poisoned accidentally as a result of their efforts. They would guarantee no poison would enter waterways. There would be no poisoned watercress or puha... And there would be no worries of poison washing out into our harbour. The way this team would work has nothing to do with the way DOC runs its pest control programmes. I would not expect any serious bushman to drop secure employment for a short three-month contract with DOC—that is not how to manage a successful trapping operation. If the Corolandcare plan were adopted, the cost of pest control would be halved. The absurd cost of $700 per goat is only part of DOC's unnecessary spending."[56]

By 2010, with a big push to support trappers and hunters and the use of the only poison considered humane—cyanide, John Veysey writes "Corolandcare lobbied hard with EW councillors to set up a locally run maintenance programme to ensure possum numbers were kept at a reasonable level all the time. They listened, promised, and then fell under the spell of EW staff and the sad fact is that there is no concept in either the DOC or the Regional Council camps of what "maintenance" might mean... The Peninsula Project possum and goat control scheme has now spent over $6 million. The reason given for the cost is to reduce the soil erosion caused by heavy rain. There is no evidence to show that this killing of goats and possums has, or ever will, make any difference to the amount of topsoil that washes down into our harbours during heavy rain. As one notable hydrologist put it many years ago: 'the idea that animals caused erosion was simple, intuitive and scientifically seductive, but hydrological studies have since proven it to be demonstrably false.'"

On November 19, 2012 John Veysey writes his 'final' report on the Peninsula Project. "It seems the Peninsula Project has come to an end. DOC has had a big spend up shooting goats and poisoning possums. Some say it has been a huge misuse of public money. A con. In order to justify the funds DOC sold the idea that by reducing the number of animals grazing the bush the amount of topsoil run-off would be reduced during heavy rains. After seven years we have seen no reduction of soil run-off; in fact we have experienced some of the worst flood damage in our history. There is no scientific connection between the number of possums and the amount of topsoil run-off and yet we have already spent over $6 million on this false premise... Many local properties have had possums streaming in from neighbouring DOC land. Why has DOC allowed possum numbers to get so out of hand? For years DOC has taken no action and now they tell us that trees are showing "signs of severe damage and other tree species have already died." Is this the right kind of management for our forests? It is clear that there are more suitable and publicly acceptable ways of controlling our pests, ways that are cheaper, greener and beyond DOC's present ability."

The *Peninsula Project Animal Pest Control Annual Report 2004/05* is disingenuously headlined *Thames Coast Flood Protection Project*. To call a multi-million dollar possum-killing spree a 'Flood Protection Project' means residents were insufficiently aware of how well they were duped. The report reminds residents "in 2004 EW and TCDC successfully sought additional funding for the DOC to carry out animal pest control along the Thames Coast… The Peninsula Project, and more fundamentally the TCFPP, is a collaborative project with the major players."

Looking at the money side and wondering who should pay for killing possums Peter Buckley in his role as chair of Waikato Federated Farmers writes to EW in 2006, "Possum control is largely a national conservation benefit…Possum control should… be funded through national taxes rather than regional rates."[57] Once in his comfortable role as Chair of EW he oversees a massive 20% hike in rates for wild animal control and supports additional funding of three-quarters of a million dollars to top up AHB possum control.

The Ongoing Struggle to Support Humane Wild Animal Control 2007, Royal Commission and 100%Pure

*"The world is a dangerous place, not because of those who
do evil, but because of those who look on and do nothing."*

Albert Einstein

Coromandel writer and conservationist Graeme Sturgeon comments on the east coast poison drop: "The bird nesting period was all but over when the Whenuakite air drop was completed on September 5 last year and there has not been a nesting season since. The reports of an increased bird population in the area cannot be considered a fact at all. Give birds at least one nest season before you claim such a miracle has happened, and a miracle it will be. This is part of the problem confronting both sides of the 1080 spectrum. Good, robust, peer-reviewed information showing any increase in the long-term bird populations is very scarce. Comments from farmers and local residents that they have seen more birds around is in no way good enough evidence to present to the public as a fact. I have on my screen at the moment a picture of Kevin Hackwell, the spokesman for F&B. He is holding up a bag of salt and vinegar chips at an interview on 1080 and the inference is that 1080 is no more dangerous than salt and vinegar chips. Should I take this as fact? Recently I heard about a pest control operator who, to convince farmers that they had no need to worry about 1080, would hold up a bait and lick it in front of them. Now I would not like to see children accept that as a fact either. It is hard to find this good hard evidence that I am looking for. Instead I find our bird population is in many places headed for extinction following successive 1080 drops."[58]

Young trapper Greg Sweeney is photographed with a heap of possums harvested from the Tairua forest. Sweeney hails from Opoutere and has cleared about 8000 possums from Rayonier's Tairua forest. He uses cyanide in winter and traps in summer. In 2007 possum fur is worth about $90kg. To pluck one kilo of fur requires approximately 20 possums. Sweeney loves the lifestyle, frequently sleeping out in the bush and he learned the tricks of the trade from Whangamata identity, Bill McCabe and Opoutere resident Ernie Evans. "There's no one breathing down your neck and I can work as hard as I want to."[59] In the Hamilton daily paper, Neil Stewart of Tokoroa writes about a successful Rakiura/ Stewart Island predator control programme that covers 31,700ha of the Rakiura National Park—all poisoned by hand returning a 0.2% trap catch, (two possums per 1000 traps). "To achieve a result like this in what is New Zealand's most southern and remote park with no road access, inclement weather, high crown fern, and sometimes steep terrain has to be applauded."[60] He points out how this result perfectly contradicts DOC's insistence that aerial 1080 drops are the only way to reduce possum numbers quoting their media release titled *Possum numbers crushed on Stewart Island*. He reminds readers, "EW totally refuses to consider widespread ground poisoning operations even though every area of bush in the Waikato region has road access and can be walked through in a day. EW's biosecurity manager John Simmon's statement that the 'big issue is educating landowners' shows the 'we are right, you are wrong' attitude of our regional council. The public own and use 90% of the region's indigenous forests and it is not us who need educating."[61] Bill Lightfoot writing from Coromandel argues the case for trapping and a bounty system, "as this has a snowball effect by creating employment, producing and exporting possum products, putting money back into the community and at the same time providing an activity for our young folk to enjoy and participate in. Don't let EW play Russian roulette with our healthy environment or take away our right to drink clean, pure water and destroy our clean, green image."

Supported by many conservation groups, UCLA gets the ball rolling with a formal request to the Prime Minister for a Royal Commission into toxin 1080. The distinguished organization, Soil and Health NZ and the renowned Pesticide Action Network (PAN) support the request. Soon-to-be Green MP, Steffan Browning writes a news item for the magazine *Organic NZ* supporting UCLA's call for an impartial evaluation of toxin 1080.

On 26 July the Hon David Benson-Pope, Minister for the Environment writes he does not "believe a Royal Commission of inquiry is justified at this time." This letter is copied to the Hon Chris Carter, Minister of Conservation and also contains the following: "You have stated that you believe the ERMA process and panel have been compromised by conflict of interest, limited scientific background of panelists, limited mandate, limited scope of scientific enquiry and political influence. I disagree." UCLA also lays a complaint to the Commerce Commission to censure Tourism New Zealand for their use of 100%Pure brand. New Zealand's poison use has attracted the attention of food safety management at several major international retail chains including Sainsbury (UK), Wholefoods Markets (USA) and Wild Oats (USA).

Coromandel activists Ursula Walsh and Annette Kaye, present two petitions to the regional council. One has over 1400 signatures and the second more than 80 local business people. Walsh writes in the local monthly, "Fantastic job, people of Coromandel. The march against 1080 was very successful, despite the rain and terrible wind. An estimated 400 people showed up. All the shop owners who were working came out in the street to support us. Some closed to join us. I was overwhelmed with the support from all parts of the community: old/young, Pakeha/Maori, hunters, teachers and workers and from the people that travelled from all over. Some of the media travelled two or more hours to cover our story. It was great to see reporters from Maori TV and National Radio. I would like to thank the business people who were so kind to all the protesters, Tere's who offered free hot soup and cake for the cold protestors—it was very welcome, Basic Café who also donated soup and Star & Garter provided us with a beautiful boil-up. This was the first time I've ever had boil-up and it was fantastic: warmed up everyone's cold bones. Thank you Carl. And The Top Pub gave free beer to protestors. Thanks also to McBreen Jenkins, Coromandel Quarry, our Police Department and other volunteers who helped us with traffic control. Thank you Kuaotunu for your support. Roi and friends, thank you for the song WE SAY NO TO 1080, and the haka. It was very beautiful. I will be demanding a public meeting between the people of Coromandel and the TCDC, DOC and EW. They have to listen. Now I know why I chose Coromandel for my new home. This is the most beautiful place and these are the most beautiful people in the world. I love you all. Thank you for believing in me. You give me courage to continue to fight against 1080. Keep your signs and watch this space."[62]

It is easy to see from this letter how much support the town offered up when faced with the relentless barrage of public relations by DOC and EW poison promoters. Supporters for the march came from the very top of the peninsula and from the west and east coasts. All Landcare groups were represented along with farmers, retirees and holidaymakers from the northern Coromandel. Jayden O'Neil wrote to the *CTC*, outraged at DOC's plan: "…1080 does not need to be used on the Coromandel Peninsula because there are heaps of people keen to trap possums." John Irvine wants to ban 1080 and reminds readers the government once provided ammunition and basic tucker that together with the bounty for ears and tails provided for a tough but healthy life. He supports bushwise and firearms-wise young people. "For the inconvenience of a damp backside now and then, he or she stands to earn a substantial income whilst aiding in the preservation of NZ's forests." He also points out that a licensed and proficient deer hunter back in the 1950's could apply to work a specific block of land where they could also live. The notion of living in the bush while caring for it is worthy of full investigation and could eventually see the light of day after Treaty of Waitangi negotiations between the Crown and iwi to settle land claims.[63]

Headlines in the farming paper *Straight Furrow* reads *Tension builds up as 1080 decision looms* and the story covers the Manaia residents who soundly reject 1080. The article also covers UCLA's call for an independent Royal Commission to " assure that all New Zealanders receive the benefit of the best science from an unbiased panel of experts" and reports DOC has "lost the confidence and support of many in the community…Coromandel Oyster Company owner Anne Louden…'It doesn't matter what the science says, if people are concerned there may 1080 in our oysters they won't want to eat them…Perception is reality. While science is safe today, tomorrow is another story.'"[64] UCLA disputes DOC's claim to have the 'blessing of tangata whenua, including trustees of the land'. Numbers of people representing iwi, including Toko Renata from Manaia, all say they know nothing of a 20 year-old blessing giving DOC all rights of caretaking Moehau mountain.[65]

The ineffectual follow-up meeting with DOC, EW and community members inspires a flush of letters to local papers following biased media coverage. "For three weeks prior to DOC's Coromandel information day they told us through the media that they had listened to us—the people of Coromandel town, and that they were coming to discuss our options. Around 1500 people (more than half the town) signed the petition. 400 people marched in shocking weather. We said very clearly that we did not want 1080. We said no 1080 at all. The information day told us we only have one option—to still have poison in our water catchment and in our pigs, still posing a threat to our children, dogs and birds. Not only will they use 1080, but also cholecalciferol, a poison that will last for years in the forest (according to Kiwicare) and even less humane in the way it kills its victims. ERMA's decision to continue the use of 1080 doesn't mean it is any less harmful than we know it is. It doesn't change the fact that the people of Coromandel do not want these toxins in our environment. So, yet again, we wait for DOC to listen." So writes conservationist Lynley Brown.[66]

Mock Johnstone, Secretary of the Coromandel Pig Hunters Club has his letter published in the same paper stating the EW and DOC Coromandel town meeting "was not as clear-cut as radio reports indicated. Anyone who left the meeting in a satisfied frame of mind probably did not understand the seriousness of the toxins being offered to take the place of 1080. It has been a worry to the people of Coromandel that the pressure they exerted on DOC not to use 1080 would result in the use of other toxins as bad or worse. Cholecalciferol has been offered and is to be used on much of the private land around Coromandel. DOC, in their own words admitted they know very little about cholecalciferol—they just don't know the effects of this toxin on animals or people. The next poison DOC is offering is brodifacoum (talon). This toxin is one of the worst there is for secondary and residual poisoning that we know of. DOC is not allowed to use it in many instances themselves, yet they are offering it to us. The NZ Food and Safety Authority set down a 36-month withholding period for consuming any wild game from areas where brodifacoum has been used and a 15 km buffer zone. We do not consider that DOC is making any concessions at all over what poisons are being used around Coromandel. There seems to be a policy of, if they can't get us with one they will get us with another. Don't just use what is being offered. Find someone you can trust and find the alternatives."[67] Johnstone is right to be concerned about other toxins. Charles Eason & Shaun Ogilvie later publish a paper looking into alternatives to toxin 1080 and brodifacoum noting while "1080 may not readily bioaccumulate it can persist in carcasses at hazardous concentrations that remain lethal to dogs and other avian or mammalian scavengers for several months. (Meenken and Booth 1997)" but that brodifacoum like

DDT can "bioaccumulate along terrestrial food chains" and that its "repeated use" is "unwise and discouraged". Their sub-lethal poisoning list includes "pigs, weka, morepork, harrier, pukeko, grey duck, robin, saddleback." Cyanide is described as the "most humane" poison.[68]

In *A different take on Coromandel 'pest workshop'* Geoffrey Robinson reminds readers "not everyone went away happy from Coromandel's invitation-only 'pest workshop' as was claimed by the meeting's organizers. Instead attendees reported that EW flabbergasted those in the room by asking if the community is prepared for even more targeted rates increases in order to avoid use of 1080 to reduce possums. When asked, neither EW nor DOC officials could document actual possum numbers in the first place. And neither could EW or DOC say what the numbers need to be to maintain a healthy ecosystem anyway. Officials admitted they have no hard data and they just don't know. But they would not budge from their insistence that there is a big problem requiring big spending, preferably on more poison. Another more public meeting is planned to follow up on 'options' for solving a 'problem' that may or may not exist. Hopefully this time EW will hear more clearly that 1080 is not acceptable to our community on any terms. Nor will we accept even higher rates demands for the privilege of our local government actually listening to us for once. When and if hard data actually shows that an exceptional pest problem exists, the Coromandel community is prepared to deal to it by locals hunting and trapping. And as for cost, we are paying our pest control levies already, thanks."[69] Ross Gardner of Port Jackson reminds readers "DDT was looked on as a wonderful invention…Agent Orange, billed as 'only a herbicide' was considered a valuable weapon for our soldiers and their allies in Vietnam. Many of those soldiers are now dead/dying from its effects and their descendants often have irreversible genetic damage…1080 has destroyed our game meat markets. In the 1970s I would receive more for one good wild pig than one and half weeks wages as a shepherd. Those who claim 1080 is only applied by air to targeted areas are sadly deluded. One example of a number of instances I know about occurred in the Kauaeranga Valley. After vehement assurances that inaccurate aim could never happen, due to the technology employed by the pilots, 24 baits were recovered from pastureland. A reliable source also informed me that baits were dropped in the very top of the

Thames water catchment. Hopefully EW will place a moratorium on 1080 use."[70]

No aerial drops this year blares one headline as DOC announces no aerial 1080 for pristine Moehau "this financial year." DOC's John Gaukrodger says "We have been in communication over the past 18 months in the Moehau area and this is still continuing. **We do not decide what is best for landowners; the choice is determined by the landowner.**" [emphasis added][71]. Is there a chance DOC is actually reading its own positive biodiversity reports on Moehau? Vain hope! At present there is an estimated "600 kiwi on the mountain with an annual increase of 15%"[72] Hand-laid 1080 pellets are due to go in the week of August 6th coinciding with Hiroshima Day. The short-term goal is to "introduce North Island robin, kokako and blue duck which may have once been present throughout the peninsula."[73]

UCLA in the meantime has called for the resignation of both the Waikato Regional Council chair, Jenni Vernon and the CEO, Harry Wilson. Claiming EW is out of touch and out of control, UCLA say evidence of toxins such as 1080 being forced on communities against their wishes smacks of a police state mentality. There is a need for competent representatives who will not squander ratepayer monies on a burgeoning poison industrial complex. Mock Johnstone writes in the *Hauraki Herald* on August 21 "The ERMA review on the assessment of 1080 has finally come out. Several months ago a spokesperson for the Environmental Risk Management Agency said ERMA would probably opt for the continuation of 1080 with a few more restrictions on its use. This statement was made before the submissions against 1080 were even heard so you might say ERMA let the cat out of the bag. On August 13 ERMA's official statement came out saying exactly what their man said months ago. I don't call that coincidence. I call that a case for the biggest liars with the biggest wallets winning one battle but not the 1080 war." DOC then announces on August 17 it will proceed with 1080 on Moehau as originally planned.

In September DOC denies UCLA's Official Information (OIA) request for the 1080 reassessment minutes of meetings, faxes, emails, memos, phone notes, and other printed records of the Steering Committee comprising representatives from DOC, ACP, AHB and regional council. In effect UCLA was requesting all records of all meetings held over the preceding four years where the poison promoters worked on their proposal. Eventually the minutes are received after an appeal to the office of the Ombudsman. This treasure trove, with fulsome redactions, is fully documented in volume two of *Rural Revolt New Zealand's State-Sponsored Addiction to Poison 1080.* In the original response sent to UCLA on 15 August 2007, DOC do not deny three years of poison 1080 are stored by Animal Control Products (ACP) "in the national interest." Deep in the mass of papers, finally received in February 2008 due to the intervention of Ombudsman David McGee, is the following information: "In Hauraki Area, DOC consults with the Hauraki Māori Trust Board." A somewhat enigmatic reference given the successful opposition to aerial 1080 on some māori land where the preferred method is trapping by Ngāti Maru Pest Control as referenced in DOC's own 2006 report.

Pete Hodgson Minster of Health writes to UCLA on September 4, "You ask about the sub-lethal effects of 1080 on humans. Conducting research of this type on humans is not allowed in NZ. I am informed that sub-chronic toxicity studies done in experimental animals at relatively high doses showed 1080 is capable of causing foetal malformations, adverse effects in male reproductive organs and cardiac effects. You ask whether the Ministry examines issues not addressed by the body of knowledge available through DOC supported research. Although the Ministry does not grant permits, international studies are also being reviewed."

UCLA reports in the September *Coromandel Town Chronicle* (*CTC*)"One way for Coromandel residents to improve our environment is in the upcoming local body elections…It's time to Dump Arthur Hinds, the peninsula's number one 1080 poison promoter. Residents are reminded that in late May it was Hinds who shocked and amazed Coromandel/Manaia residents with his letter and brochure promoting the use of 1080 in and around our community and water catchment. It's safe and effective, he said… Adding insult to injury, Hinds used our rates to pay for his poison promo." The report notes DOC's shiny new fleet of utes appears at precisely the same time as their refusal to engage trappers on the grounds they are "too expensive". The UCLA report ends on a positive note offering congratulations to the creators of the *309 Morepork and Hawk Sanctuary.* The same issue of *CTC* publishes a *Green Blog* by T. Everth who remarks, "We cannot blanket spray our environment with a strong poison year in and year out. Let's be honest, we will not be able to eradicate possums, rats, and stoats on the Peninsula, but we do stand a chance of controlling them in a meaningful way. And if we can do this with trapping, bait stations and other measures that have a high degree of public acceptance and a proven species specific effect then do we really need to use the controversial aerial broadcasting of this poison? I would much prefer to see DOC and EW presenting a sustainable long-term pest control strategy that is acceptable to the vast majority of the population. Aerial broadcasting of 1080 seems not to fit this goal at present. By insisting on the unpopular aerial application of 1080, DOC and EW stand the risk of doing more damage to the goal of protecting our environment than good."

Longtime conservationist and farmer, Arthur Attfield, writes of the "belligerent attitude of DOC and EW toward the public" and how they fund their extreme policies, including the idea of the predator fence near Colville to incarcerate communities, the blanket use of 1080 poison and the latest pest strategy that threatens to violate private property rights. "The fact that only 40 people from a population of thousands turned up at the DOC/ EW pest management information day, and only 12 attended the AGM of the Whenuakite Kiwi Care group, clearly indicates the gap between the general public and the combined DOC, EW and eco groups.'[74] UCLA agrees with the DOC Hauraki manager that it is "socially unacceptable to dump rubbish" in our conservation estate but UCLA goes further proclaiming it is socially, ethically, culturally and environmentally unacceptable to dump 1080 poison in our forests. UCLA asks all employees of DOC to refuse to distribute toxin 1080. Readers are reminded of DOC's Pim de Monchy, who noted in his *2000 Field Report* "The forest canopy at Moehau, including the species most vulnerable to and preferred by possums, is in excellent condition."[75] *NZ Truth* weekly publishes scores of letters over a number of pages of its December 13 issue. Their page three headline reads *50 years of 1080 abuse!* Above the story is a photograph of a Moehau farm gate sign declaring: NO DOC NO EW

December 13th is prize giving day at Coromandel Area School (CAS). UCLA members present Room 17 and their teacher, Kimberley Wilkinson, with the *Certificate of Academic Merit* in recognition of their research and investigative skills applied in the study of a local environmental issue (poison 1080) and for their ability to critique conventional wisdom and to actively participate in a local issue helping to build a healthy community. The *Hauraki Herald reports* this event on December 28— a good note to end the year: "A class of students at Coromandel Area School has been recognized for its investigation into the potential dangers of 1080. The Upper Coromandel Landcare Association presented students from Room 17 with a Certificate of Academic Merit and a number of books for the school library. The class researched the potential dangers of dropping 1080 into the Coromandel area watershed and presented its findings to the Coromandel-Colville Community Board." Dr Meriel Watts inscribes her classic *The Poisoning of New Zealand* 'To Room 17 Coromandel Area School— with real appreciation for your work on 1080 this year. I encourage you to also look at the problems caused by other pesticides to the environment and human health. Kia kaha.'

2008 Censorship and the
Hawk and Morepork Sanctuary

*"You can't commune with nature just by taking a walk.
You have to actually live in it."*

Vine Deloria Jr.

2008 gets off to a rough start with a campaign by a handful of locals who attempt to silence debate in Coromandel's monthly. Writing in the January *CTC*, Port Charles resident and Forest and Bird agitator (since relocated to England) Tina Morgan suggests "Perhaps it is time that this subject was dropped from the publication's columns..."

Silence as we know is the great oppressor. Silence is the weapon of choice of fascism. One revelation made possible by the release of 1080 documents via the Ombudsman's office shows how DOC manoeuvres the media and how coercion of reporters can be bought with freebies such as helicopter rides and carefully manipulated information.

"The hostile comments in January's *Chronicle* by the spokeswoman for Coromandel Forest and Bird and official of the Moehau Environment Group (MEG) directed at the UCLA beg for response." writes Geoffrey Robinson. "Tina Morgan is correct to point out that UCLA members (all fulltime local residents in contrast to MEG 'membership') have taken an active public stand on critical environmental issues facing our Coromandel-Moehau community, often in opposition to the positions held by her two organizations. But rather than debate the issues, her suggestion is that local publications cut off discussion, silence critics, and simply drop the subject. It is true UCLA members vigorously support the Parliamentary Commissioner for the Environment's 1994 recommendations that hunting and trapping of possums and mustelids is the most sensible, safe and affordable control option. UCLA also supports continued management of important cultural and recreational game species at no public expense by experienced hunters. And UCLA members volunteer countless hours to wild animal control and native bush restoration, in some cases on land they have stewarded and protected for generations. It is also true that UCLA spearheaded opposition to the unfeasible $5million scheme to fence in the entire northern peninsula with a two-metre high steel "pest" barrier. UCLA members oppose DOC and EW plans to blanket the Coromandel water catchment with super-poison 1080 and opposed DOC's saturation 1080 poisoning of Moehau's eastern flanks. And UCLA has opposed EW's aggressive new expansion of poison-based control of wild pigs and deer. Forest and Bird actively support the expanded use of aerial 1080. Not only in the "remote and inaccessible terrain" of Fiordland we all hear about, but right here in places like our drinking water and beside Waikato paddocks. They flooded the airwaves and newspapers with pro-1080 messages in 2007. F&B also actively promotes the extermination of wild pigs and deer, preferably by poisoning. As for MEG, what can you expect from a virtual wholly owned subsidiary of DOC Hauraki? MEG says it is "neutral" on 1080. Of course it is. How could it ever oppose DOC's and EW's 1080 poison plans when it is dependent on hundreds of thousands of ratepayer and taxpayer-grant dollars to fund its staff and activities? And how can it oppose EW's aggressive pest strategy when the MEG coordinator actually sits on an EW pest committee? MEG has lost its independence from both DOC and EW and must support their agendas or risk losing most of its annual budget. Coromandel area residents would like to hear more (not less) from F&B, DOC, EW and MEG about why we should welcome one of the world's deadliest poisons in our water, why we should wipe out well managed traditional recreational species, why our EW flood control dollars should be squandered on poison pellets, and why our taxes should be spent by DOC to trap Port Charles rats for $180 apiece. Public debate is the backbone of a healthy democratic community." Around this time MEG is exposed as a 1080 toxin promoter with their coordinator seconding a motion at an EW meeting (held well after his public mea culpa) in support of EW's submission to ERMA to promote 1080 use.

Poison promoters often accuse those who do not wish to use poison of being too emotional or misinformed. Similar accusations are used against those who challenge the status quo whether it is toxin 1080 or any other issue that serves some corporate interest that has government under its thumb. Yet here is DOC's 1080 spokesman John Cumberpatch endorsing five-minute bird counts as valid science saying: "It's the **gut reaction** of experienced field operational staff who have been doing this stuff for 20, 30 years. We know that they can go to a forest these days, and they'll tell you that 10 years ago that forest was silent." [added emphasis] So "gut reaction" is good enough for DOC.

On the issue of bird call counts the *NZ Herald* chimes in with a headline *Morepork thrive in poison areas.*[77] All it takes is 45 minutes in 16 sites in the Waitakeres to find what poisoners want to hear. Oh if it were only that easy. This so-called study is actually published in the *New Zealand Journal of Zoology*. According to the 22 year-old ecology student, Elisabeth Fraser "More than twice as many calls were recorded in the poisoned areas."[78] Apparently that is all it takes to believe morepork/ruru do not eat poisoned rats or 1080 baits.

From Coromandel, Tim Fuller reports "Hunters are, at this moment, trapping in the hills behind Coromandel and making significant inroads into the possum population. Why take their livelihood as well as endangering the people of the region?"[79] Identifying herself as a Wellingtonian, Kate Clarke (no relation to the then Director General one assumes) writes in that she is "surprised at the anti-1080 attitudes being expressed. In my area, where 1080 and brodifacoum are both used quite extensively, we have increasing numbers of birdlife."[80] However no aerial 1080 is ever likely to be spritzed over the city of Wellington where tui and kākā thrive in spite of rats and possums. Tom Look points out "tea contains fluoroacetate in minute quantities, but 1080 is sodium monofluoroacetate, which is not the same chemical. Fluoroacetic acid does not have a sodium atom associated with it. The fact that toxins are present in nature is no excuse for adding to the problem..." and Brulia Walsh questions DOC's definition of 'consultation'.[81] Respected longtime farmer Charles Harsant writes, "Ever since it was proposed to drop 1080 on the Coromandel Ranges in 1994, I have tried to say, at least leave the ranges free. 1080 is a deadly, tasteless poison, that has no antidote and kills birds, insects, frogs and mammals." He reminds readers that most poisons used in the world are plant based. "The ranges are not real wild and have tracks and history covering every part— gum-diggers, bush-men, prospectors and hunters made these. My father, Horace Harsant, and his brothers owned a store and gum-buying business in Gumtown (Coroglen) and, with a team of packhorses packed supplied to the bushcamps and gumdigger camps...."[82]

Kuaotunu Environmental Action (KEA) announces a possum project on 1000ha of DOC and private land. Feratox (encapsulated cyanide) baits will be placed in biodegradable bags and the group is seeking funding to set up 600 new stoat traps throughout a 4100ha area. They will also target feral cats and 300 Timms traps will be made available to private landowners who wish to trap and remaining or invading possums.

Hawks thrive in toxin-free sanctuary headlines an informative article two photographs of John Veysey on the lookout for hawks flying over cleared forestry land. Both Australasian hawks and ruru are thriving. "Ernslaw did all the birds a real favour when they resisted DOC's push to use 1080 in 2007. Of all the things we can do for these birds, the most significant has been to keep 1080 out of the area. For the hawks 1080 would have been disastrous. DOC's Pestoff poison, which is being used along the edges of the sanctuary, may not be any better than 1080 but at least it is arriving too late to affect this year's breeding season. The 309 moreporks are still enjoying a relatively poison-free environment. Morepork are probably the most vulnerable species to all poisons, especially aerial drops...thanks to Ernslaw their life among the pines has become a lot safer than living in the native bush."[83]

By 2008 the successful Driving Creek Wildlife Sanctuary have predator fenced their 1.6ha of land gifted by local hero, conservationist and internationally regarded potter Barry Brickell. Only wildlife is fenced in and to the extent that the area is small and highly managed, this is an example of positive community action.

Kauaeranga Valley is in Line for Aerial Dosing of 1080

"The question is whether any civilization can wage relentless war on life without destroying itself, and without losing the right to be called civilized."

Rachel Carson

As 2008 moves along DOC is set to drop 27,500kg of pre-feed and 1080 bait into the Kauaeranga Valley with the assistance of helicopter company EcoFX. The drop affects 8,288ha behind the Kauaeranga Valley that is made up of "mostly kauri-podocarp-hardwood forest, changing to sub-montane shrub and mossfields as altitude increases. The top of Table Mountain, the highpoint in this block, is swampy scrub, as is most of the Coromandel Ranges." Land comprising 5000ha "in residential areas and around watercourses" will not be subject to indiscriminate aerial poisoning. This land "will be subject to ground control."[84] The job title is *DOC's Thames Coast **Flood Protection** Project 2008/09 Aerial Possum and Ship rat Control*. [emphasis added] The conservation outcome aims to increase the "density of the forest under-storey and canopy through the control of goats and possums." No mention of "flood control" or rats. The final report obtained by UCLA much later in the proceedings via the Official Information Act (OIA) exposes DOC's outcome target was "to halt possum induced mortality of canopy trees". DOC is very careful not to publish any photographs showing canopy damage. In fact there is no photographic documentation showing canopy damage in any of the publications made available to the public. Money that should have been utilized for real flood protection was cannibalized and divvied up to poison rats and possums. The threatened species listed for salvation are kiwi, kereru, kaka and king fern. The actual impact of possums and rats on these species is not scientifically quantified.

DOC believes the area cannot be worked from the ground as it is "too dangerous but also the sheer scale of it is too much. This is a very big block of country." The land is made up of portions of the Coromandel Forest Park and adjacent private land. Monitoring must however occur, prior to the drop and after the drop and this requires real people walking in the real bush —a minor hiccup or merely paradoxical? DOC warns hunters not to eat pigs within a two km radius, and no rabbits for the table within two hundred metres, for up to 8 months after bait removal. (25,500ha in the neighbourhood will be doused again in 2015—a never-ending cycle.)

Questioning why DOC needs to dump 1080 toxin up behind Thames in the Forest Park when they did the same job just three years ago, John Veysey wonders whether it is to keep the cash flow gushing to helicopter businesses? He points out how pre-poison monitoring is ineffectual (wax-tag monitoring gives no clear numbers) so no one really has a clue of possum numbers either before or after a toxin drop. The goal to reduce numbers to 5% is spun out of thin air. Poison pushers state categorically that dumping toxin 1080 achieves a 'better than' 5% Residual Trap Catch (RTC). Research by Nugent, Whitford, Sweetapple, Duncan, Holland in 2010 concludes "we infer that reducing possum density by 60% will usually be sufficient to protect most of the possum-preferred tree species we studied."

Somewhat surprisingly a handful of registered organic farmers actually support the use of poison drops in their valley. Elizabeth McCracken farming in the Kauaeranga Valley writes in the local paper, how her views in 1972 were of "overgrazed hills, serious slips and stock in the Kauaeranga River. Serious flooding in 1981 and 1985 destroyed the road access to the Kauaeranga Visitor Centre. Thames was a disaster area. With changing land use, tree planting and fencing the river from stock…flooding has been less destructive, native birds have begun to return. Since the 1080drop* and laying of bait stations, possums have almost gone. Now we have up to 25 tui on the ground at a time, along with many pigeons and kaka. As an organic farmer and orchardist (Biogro since 1993), my instincts are to avoid poisons, but I believe hunters alone cannot control forest-destroying pests…DOC is to be commended for attempting to restore our forest from the destruction of the kauri milling days…" *[Presumably McCracken is referencing the 1080 drop that occurred a mere three years earlier.] One wonders if there are "many pigeons and kaka" and "up to 25 tui on the ground at a time" could this be considered a healthy bird life? Calling oneself an organic farmer at the same time supporting poison drops (knowing honeybees and endangered native species are harmed) is confounding. The whole area could be trapped or hunted or cyanided. Poisoning does not halt flooding and years later, in April 2014, the road to the Kauaeranga Visitor Centre is washed out causing closure but naturally there is no accountability. 'Yes we will use your flood control money to poison possums, oh so sorry, flooding continues in spite of our best poison efforts.'

Meanwhile in the very same month we find McCracken's neighbour, Jeanette Fitzsimmons worried about the lack of birdlife. Maybe they live at opposite ends of the Valley. Fitzsimmons is the Green party co-leader at the time: "I'm as uncomfortable about aerial drops as any person is but I don't think we've got an alternative for the remote, difficult country we have. The Coromandel has so little birdlife left and we do notice the difference when we get rid of the possums, stoats and rats. I'm not a great fan of 1080 at all. It's one of those awful compromises we have to make but as long as they keep it away from farmland and water supplies it's something we have to do." Fitzsimmons fails to ask why 1080 must be dropped again in three years if it is doing such a good job. One could very well call this kind of control "farming" possums for the helicopter company's benefit. Allan Berry of the same Valley uses "ill-informed" and "scaremongering" to slander locals who favour trapping, hunting and cyanide. Percy Thomas of Thames asks, "What are the biggest pests? The possums, the rats or the users of chemicals and other poisons used so indiscriminately?" Gary Blake of Waiomu welcomes the debate and raises the biodynamic option. Writer, hunter and conservationist Graeme Sturgeon discovers "Kauaeranga residents had told DOC's (Erana Stephens) they were supportive of the drop. But the first person I meet from up the Kauaeranga states "nobody asked me or my auntie and she is a big landowner up the valley—we don't want the drop."

Locals and tourists will miss out on enjoyment of the park as DOC announce an eight-month closure for the Valley. Ngati Maru, Ngati Tamaterā, police, vets, Forest and Bird, Thames Community Board, Waihou-Piako Flood Scheme, the Te Puru Flood mitigation working party, the Waikato Conservation Board, TCDC, Medical Officer of Health, United Water are said to have been "consulted". "Consultation" in this context is mere notification, albeit with a smidgin of picnic party outings—"a helicopter day" held for "iwi and other stakeholders." No pig hunting, deer stalking or Landcare groups are notified.

After the poison drop the official *DOC Operational Report for ERMA* notes: "While a small minority of the community protested the 1080 drop, all in all the community was supportive of the control work." One could say this is evidence of being economical with the truth given the subsequent 4000 signatures gathered to demand an investigation into the misuse of toxin 1080 on the peninsula. The petition was initiated and coordinated by the Thames Landcare Association for eventual presentation to a Select Committee at Parliament. Coromandel farmer Ross Gardner, says he was forced to move all his cattle out of the Kauaeranga Valley due to incompetence on the part of DOC personnel. "Watching the pre-feeding for the last 1080 drop I saw the helicopter fly over pastureland on two Devcich properties. The reason for this was incompetent planning by the DOC organizer who had a $30,000 secure facility constructed. It could not be used, so 1080 was flown from the information centre instead. After watching this overflying and finding gates left open by DOC employees, allowing $1000 bullocks to escape up the Hihi Stream, the decision was made to remove all cattle from that leased property. Subsequently it was admitted that 24 baits were picked up from pasture, but I guarantee nobody checked in the gorse to see if there were any baits in there. No compensation was offered for the loss of grazing and no one would take the lease on again for six months—again no compensation for the landowner. I lost one (cow) from metabolic disorder brought about by moving her and a newborn calf away from the drop zone. I then witnessed another cow dying violently in distress. An autopsy failed to ascertain cause, as the chemical needed to test for 1080 was not in the country. A coincidence when its 1080 drop time? DOC employees attached bait stations to boundary fences and even on trees within paddocks—all accessible to cattle tongues. I'm afraid these problems are again in store for those settlers in the Kauaeranga as there does not appear to have been a change of attitude by DOC."

DOC issues assurances about water quality and TCDC water contractors, United Water are actively involved.* After the drop, phone conversations with a United Water contractor reveal no water samples were taken immediately after the drop. How many tests were undertaken? Just two. One water sample is from the intake on the Kauaeranga River and the other from the Mangarehu Stream. According to the DOC report the "1080 concentration found in the water samples were less than the method detection limit (MDL) of 0.0001ug/ml." Of concern to all Thames residents is the statement in the *Operational Report* that reveals "**Although level of sampling was minimal and in conflict with measures described in published protocols, MOH were happy with sample proposed. Lesson: work closely with regulatory authorities to find practical compromises**…No detectable levels of 1080 present around intakes when water testing taken." [emphasis added]. The samples were taken well after the drop, certainly not within the requisite 4 hours. The tests are designed to **not** find poison 1080 in the water.

Fifteen days are to pass between the dropping of brown-coloured pre-feed non-toxic baits and the poison — a strategy used to entice animals to switch diets from their preferred leaves and blossoms to cylindrical, green, cinnamon-flavoured pellets then the similarly flavoured toxic pellets that will land on branches and limbs of canopy trees and on the forest floor where the bush is less dense. 1.5g of poison are added to each kilo of cereal bait. Helicopters are loaded from "specialized bait loading trucks" into under-slung buckets with non-retractable legs with loads up to 1300 kg. Dumping 27,500kg twice — first the fake baits then the real stuff, is helicopter-intensive. The pre-feed flights take two days of hefty diesel consumption. John Owen, Operations Manager for EcoFX Ltd affixes the usual reminders to the public advertisement "Do not touch bait. Watch children at all times. Do not eat animals from this area. Do not allow dogs access to animal carcasses." Originally DOC states the Kauaeranga Park would be closed for eight months but now the park is to remain open with the above provisos.

Wax tag monitoring of possums is carried out prior to the drop as the "trap catch monitoring (was) not undertaken **due to cost**… Wax tag monitoring will not give an RTC; at this stage we are unable to convert wax tag % to RTC% given the newness of its use on the Coromandel." More importantly "No monitoring of non-target species was undertaken." [emphasis added] One could say this is an ingeniously irresponsible scheme to hoodwink ratepayers. To keep the aerial 1080 costs down, no RTC monitoring will take place. With no independent monitoring and in fact no useful monitoring whatsoever there is no accountability. The land is accessible for monitoring, *ergo* it is accessible for hunting, trapping and cyanide. However trappers are not paid until they achieve their RTC goal, whereas helicopter pilots are automatically paid.

Trouble seems to raise its head in the *DOC Operational Report*. "Due to the low sowing rate of toxic bait staff had difficulty detecting bait for bait coverage monitoring. May need to dispense with that method for performance monitoring." DOC staffers walking the "tracks" report "suspected gaps" and are charged with clearing any baits found on the walking tracks. In contrast to this report and the *ERMA Annual Report on 1080 poison*, EcoFX's Kevin Christie reckons "the public could have faith the baits would end up only where they were meant to be. The helicopter used a differential global positioning (GPS), and all data was double-checked on the ground after every half-hour helicopter run." DOC's Fin Buchanan confirms this by saying "throughout the aerial operation, people on the ground checked the distribution of baits."

DOC workers had been brought in from around the peninsula and the Waikato to assist. "They count and measure the distances between the baits, to make sure we get the right coverage. If an area was found to have too few baits, the helicopter would drop more into it."[85] Evidently the land is neither too steep nor too dangerous as DOC staffers can search for toxic bait. Green Party apologists cling to their belief the area is so remote and difficult that dropping toxin 1080 is the only option. The additional cost for employees driven in from all over the Waikato is not factored into the aerial 1080 budget—further evidence of the hidden and excessive costs of aerial 1080. The alleged environmental benefits are mere whimsical extrapolations yet it must be pure bliss for bureaucrats to dial a number and employ a helicopter company to dump an inhumane poison. Who really cares about our environment and anyway who wants to be responsible for the employment of numerous idiosyncratic, highly skilled trappers and hunters.

Complaints and Incidents were lodged with ERMA, Ministry for the Environment, Medical Officer of Health, Ombudsman about 1) consultation being undertaken in the affected region of Te Puru in a timely and appropriate manner, 2) permits and other information regarding the aerial operation being provided to complainant in a timely and appropriate manner 3) evidence of collusion of government departments, 4) buffer zones, 5) breaches of MOH consent conditions, 6) wind speeds on the days of the toxic operations, 7) 1080 pellets around the water intake of the Kauaeranga forest education camp.

In June 2009 a Foliar Browse Index (FBI) is undertaken—less preferred species such as hinau, mahoe and towai were "common, and well distributed across the FBI plots. Highly preferred species, such as kohekohe and whauwhaupaku, were not common along FBI plots." Presumably, this translates into DOC believing that in less than a year the preferred species will be growing. The outcome of the FBI surveys is presented to Peninsula Project aficionados and sadly the researchers were unable to establish any useful information. Re-verification of data collected to date with regard to the canopy will "need" to take place but no date has been made publicly available during the following seven years. How the FBI is to be paid for is not stated. Whether the 80% targeted rate for all Coromandel zone residents for the infamous Peninsula Project is further bailing out the 1080 drop is unclear.

* A risk management plan August-October 2008 is provided by EcoFX Ltd: John Owen, Stuart McNaughton, Kevin Christie, Mike Karl. DOC staff: Fin Buchanan, Erica Stevens, Kim Dawick. Waikato District Health Board: Dell Hood, David Cumming. TCDC: Darren Toulon, Craig Birkett. United Water: Steve Rumble, Steve Eyberg. David Beck of Beck Helicopters is on the phone list.

Draconian Regional Council Plans

"Money often costs too much."

Ralph Waldo Emerson

Around this time the Waikato Regional Council takes stock of community opposition to toxin 1080 and in a bold policy shift, staff propose to systematically charge communities and landowners who choose wild animal control methods other than those council believes are most cost-effective, namely poison 1080. Individuals who choose more humane methods of wild animal control will have to pay for alternatives even though Regional Council and DOC have known since the Parliamentary Commissioner for the Environment's 1994 reports that trapping is as cost effective. Employing trappers is, however, a lot more complicated for staff sitting on their chuffs in Hamilton offices.

The new plan is a coercive and intimidating tactic to force aerial 1080 drops on unwilling communities whose mounting opposition to council's expanded toxin use is getting under the skin of bureaucrats keen on poison use. The Moehau-based conservation group, UCLA says the charges are heavy financial penalties for communities who wish to exercise their human rights to enjoy clean water, clean food supplies and a clean environment and will fall on those who can least afford it.[86]

However it appears the writers of *Think Piece on the Future of Pest Management—background analysis and interview findings*, believe "The LGA (Rating) 2002 sets out the basis on which rates must be assessed. The rules for how rates can be assessed are quite prescriptive and are unlikely to provide for targeting of rates on the basis of pest management services provided to the individual landowner."

Troublesome for Moehau fauna and flora, is the existence of a group of local 'volunteer' eco-entrepreneurs who support residual poison use. The *2008 DOC Pesticide Summary* exposes the Moehau 'Environment' Group (MEG) as the group who will do DOC's dirty work—for a fee, naturally. MEG is put in charge of seven of the ten DOC poison operations on the Coromandel to be carried out between October and November. Poison generates GDP as we all know and it certainly brings money into the community but in this instance it shows how the MEG executive chooses to be in conflict with our community, a community that has repeatedly chosen hunting, trapping and cyanide only and is clearly opposed to the use of residual poisons.

In the *Report of the North Zone Biosecurity Advisory Subcommittee* 13 May 2008 the Regional Council is seeking "Legal advice on charging a landowner (and) is awaiting wording of the RPMS which is currently inoperative due to an Environment Court appeal... There is also increasing concern about toxins and the differing levels of **knowledge/ignorance are leading to fear and paranoia. There is room for advocacy and education to counter misinformation.**" [emphasis added] Not only are council employees deciding poison policy but they are making proclamations concerning PR to counter intelligent community opposition.[87] Their splenetic, discriminatory deprecation welding "concern about toxins" to ignorance, fear, paranoia and misinformation is nothing less than jaundiced and biased opinion.

C. Scott of Kaukapapa asks whether there really is a serious possum problem in NZ. He finds "The 'pest' culture is the result of attitudes based on (a) possums are introduced and (b) introduced animals are pests. It is selective in its choice. The 'anti-introduced' phobia is a myth. Humans, cattle, sheep, potatoes and petunias are all introduced. The whole pest culture has been accompanied by flights of fantasy by DOC and AHB with the ulterior motive of keeping empires and salaries intact. There are not 70 million possums. What's more, possum numbers are in natural decline—a trend over decades in all wildlife liberation cases. Road kills are now rare and that includes areas not subject to 1080. At night on backcountry roads only occasional possums are seen—often none. Possums are not the Tb vector claimed. Landcare Research evidence suggests ferrets are also a problem but more so is stock movement. Ask South Island West Coasters about cattle trucks moving at night. New Zealand's 0.3% Tb infection is insignificant compared to Northern Ireland at over 7% and other EW countries. So where is the basis for fears of a trade barrier? So the possum paranoia and 1080 programme have no sound basis. It is a squandering of public money with a toxin that devastates bird life and of course deer. The attitude should change from pest to resource. Possums are a resource and since possum fur fetches $105 kg compared to farmed sheep wool at $3, isn't it folly to use a toxin that renders the fur and meat toxic?"[88]

Bryan Ritchie reports trapping over 1000 possums over a five-week period in 800ha of the Waiau catchment. "Let's say DOC's 1080 drop achieved a 1%RTC. Say half of these are female. At best they can double their numbers every year, so can DOC explain how half a percent of females in Year One can get numbers up to 5%, let alone dangerous numbers, again by Year Three. Just what are dangerous numbers? Pine forests flourish best with 12-14% RTC (Weir & Couper 2007). Ordinary broadleaf are happy with 25% RTC (Nugent et al. 2001). Demanding an RTC below 5% is overkill using unnecessary poison and is a rapid way of using up public money."[89]

The December *Kararehe Kino* announces "It appears the benefits of pest control operations must be assessed at the ecosystem level if biodiversity assets are to be protected."[90] This 'news' comes after the ERMA review and after Port Charles scientists Pat and Quinn Whiting-O'Keefe's expose the lack of rigorous science. '"DOC is giving people misinformation. Their claim that you can drop food laced with 1080 indiscriminately into a semi-tropical forest ecosystem and only negatively impact one or two target 'pest' species is counterintuitive and scientifically improbable. There is no credible scientific evidence showing any native bird benefits from...1080...' While acknowledging a handful of studies are scientifically robust, Whiting-O'Keefe's say a recently reported study on invertebrates 'highlights an unscientific bias by scientists in favour of DOC's pest-control programmes in that it points to the *'benefits* of reducing predators...in Tongariro National Park,' rather than *'effects'* a term deemed scientifically neutral. Scientific methodology demands any experiment/study must be open to observations that may contradict those hoped for, and that the structure of the study allows for a range of possible outcomes. Investigation of only benefits clearly implies that not only are harms or damages to invertebrates not to be investigated, but they need not even be reported if encountered. This is counter to the very core of science.""[91]

2009 Cruel Death—
Even Black-backed Gulls to be Poisoned by DOC

"The sun is always shining. We have oxygen, trees, birds. There's so much good things on Earth still. We haven't got around to destroying everything."

Ziggy Marley

1080 gets blame for 'cruel' death of dog reads the headline in the *Hauraki Herald* of December 12. A photograph of Peter Findlay, with his surviving Rotweiller, beside the grave of his two-year-old male dog. Findlay's 11-acre property borders bush on the outskirts of Thames. DOC failed to meet its responsibilities to let adjacent owners know deadly poison had been laid. Bait pieces in one pile of vomit choked up by their beloved dog, was the first indication 1080 poison may be the cause. Peter Findlay is quoted as saying in all his 40 years of working in the bush he has never seen anything as cruel as his dog's death on November 29, 2008. The Peninsula Project Flood Control programme manager, Fin Buchanan is quoted as saying "It's unfortunate that this accident has occurred despite the extensive campaign we undertook to help owners keep their pets safe." This so-called "extensive campaign" was found to be grossly inadequate—breaching basic rules of operation. The heart-breaking story also raises concern for the long-term health of ten families who take their water from the local stream. Colin Harris offers condolences to Peter Findlay for the loss of his Rottweiler. "It is my understanding that DOC entered Mr Findlay's property without notifying him (which is trespassing) and accessed neighbouring property to place 1080 in bait stations without the appropriate warning signs on the boundary fence advising type of poison and date laid (again, illegal). This cavalier approach by DOC has come about because of the previous Government and its ally, the Green Party, giving DOC an open cheque book and legislation that put conservation at a level above all other considerations. It is becoming increasingly clear that ratepayers and taxpayers on the Coromandel Peninsula are subsidizing DOC in its attempt to turn the peninsula into a goldmine for DOC operations."

Conservationist Philippa Gavey who rarely misses a call out to anti-1080 gatherings is on the cover of the January 30 issue of *Hauraki Herald*. She is the first person to sign the Thames Landcare petition demanding an enquiry into the dangerous misuse of poison 1080 on the Coromandel. Gavey is quoted "While we support the development of civilization, we're opposed to poisons being put into our food chain." Graeme Sturgeon points to local dog deaths and deaths of native birds in Pureora, Little Barrier and Franz Josef glacier as examples of the collateral damage of 1080 poisonings.

The next month John Veysey reminds readers of the increase in domestic animal deaths since DOC began spreading 1080 in the early 1990s and how water samples show the poison is washed downstream within 12 hours. The instructions on the packet of 1080 toxin require poison distributors to collect all poisoned carcasses. No collection of poisoned animals ever takes place on the Coromandel. Dead animals are strewn like landmines waiting for non-target species to come along to eat either a chronic dose, or to die. The manufacturer's label declares emphatically: the poison is not to enter waterways. When resource consents are issued from regional councils they are deliberately worded to allow 1080 toxin onto land and into water.

UCLA receives a letter from Mike Bennett of Barrytown near Runanga on the South Island's west coast. He has been battling against 1080 for over 20 years. Currently he is fighting for protection of the Southern Black-backed Gull (*larus dominicanus*) as DOC is poisoning a nesting colony near Gore. He mentions the Hokitika Borough Council's bylaw banning "all aerial distribution of 1080 in the watershed/catchment of the quite large Lake Kanieri, a rather large block of mountain country. Lake Kanieri is Hokitika's water-supply." The hope is that more councils and boards will take this action.

Yet another poison to be used on the peninsula by DOC and regional council is diphacinone, credited with wiping out a native bat population in Pureora. No bat surveys have been carried out on Moehau where neighbours know of local bat populations. The possibility of secondary poisoning of bats consuming arthropods that have fed on 1080 baits has been recorded in a report for DOC.[92] Wild pigs may not be eaten for more than 160 days after diphacinone sub-lethal exposure.[93]

Matt Philp investigates the use of poison 1080 in a balanced investigative article for *North & South magazine* and UCLA's letter (April issue) is published in response: "Mission creep by DOC and the Animal Health Board explains the widening gulf between advocates of 1080 and those conservationists who are opposed to poisoning our environment. Originally used in inaccessible areas, aerial 1080 poison is now used indiscriminately and close to human habitation, causing many communities to rebel. In the Waikato, we have a regional council that in 2006 used nearly 50% of all the 1080 dumped in onto our country for non-Tb purposes. Only as a result of a massive street protest and numerous petitions was Coromandel town spared 1080 in its water catchment. Still Environment Waikato continues to push poisons onto our communities. DOC used to be populated by fine conservationists like the great Bill Axbey, individuals prepared to do the hard yards, but now its so much more comfortable for office workers to direct pilots to dump poison. The Parliamentary Commissioner for the Environment in 1994 stated it was more cost-effective to use hunters and trappers over large areas of country and suggested DOC train more. Reflecting concerns over "significant effects on non-target organisms, unused baits and poisoned carcasses", the Nature Conservation Council (1962-1990) stated "no 1080 in national parks or sanctuaries". Toxin 1080 certainly has not brought possum numbers down. It has poisoned our wilderness for 50 years, yet DOC and Forest and Bird believe there are 70 million possums out there. We all love the bush and its time bounties and skin subsidies were reinstated. It's time DOC, regional councils and AHB woke up: 1080 is not working."

Whenuakite Action—
Halting The Helicopters and the Te Mata Debacle

"Pest-control is of course necessary and desirable, but it is an ecological matter, and cannot be handed over entirely to the chemists. The present campaign for mass chemical control, besides being fostered by the profit motive, is another symptom of our exaggeratedly technological and quantitative approach."

Julian Huxley Preface to *Silent Spring* 1962

Gerry Church writes in his Whitianga publication *The Informer*, September 2009 how the 1080drop proposed for 1200ha in Whenuakite was disrupted. "Police were called but with the landowner unavailable, trespass orders could not be issued against the 23 protestors. However police did block additional protestors from reaching the site and despite police saying that there would be no further drop activity that day, the protestors planned to stay until almost sundown to ensure that there would be no further drops. A member of the group, John Allen, explained why they were taking such strong action. 'It's gotten to the point where we're not being listened to. We've done the phone calls and letter writing and DOC just doesn't want to know.' 1080 isn't the only target. 'Basically we want all residual poisons gone – not just 1080 – because they're killing our native species.'" The story goes on to mention the dead dolphins washed up in the Hauraki Gulf after the brodifacoum aerial poisoning on Rangitoto. Aerial photographs accompany the article showing the Whenuakite helicopter landing area with locals and parked vehicles. One shot shows the loaded bucket ominously swaying beneath a flying helicopter. Lloyd McQueen sporting one of UCLA's "Stop 1080" T-shirts is photographed for two stories including one for the *Waikato Times*. He is shown standing his ground, along with other members of the community including farmers, iwi representatives, conservationists, pig hunters and landowners, who blockaded the farm road and were successful in stopping the drop by occupying the helicopter clearing on the Wallace land at the end of Boat Harbour Rd.

Simultaneously a group occupied the road near the Tapu Water Gardens where another projected drop had been planned on the Thames coast. However DOC resorted to using a different helicopter landing area further south in the Kauaeranga Valley and proceeded to dump poison over 800ha. John Veysey has a long letter in the same edition of *The Informer* where he clarifies Suren's water research carried out in 2004/06 showing how water samples are taken to ensure no 1080 poison is found. All poison is washed out of the physical bait and flows downstream. When and if water samples are taken within 4 hours of a drop they all contain poison 1080.

Paul Harper and Jeff Neems co-write *Protesters stop Coromandel 1080 drop.* The story is dramatically illustrated with the aforementioned photograph of McQueen and other 1080 resisters occupying the helicopter pad at Whenuakite. Vehicles are used to block access to the site. Colin Harris, a Whitianga hunter, landowner and farmer, is quoted saying the protest was about registering strong opposition to the use of 1080. "'We believe they have not followed due procedure,' he said. 'In the end we've got frustrated. We just feel this was our last action. The people here are concerned with the detrimental effects of 1080,' Mr Harris said. 'There needs (to be) a change of focus. It is truly feasible to do ground-based operations to protect our animals.' Mr Harris described the situation as a "Mexican standoff…Hopefully we'll hold them up all day,' he said.' About a dozen 1080 opponents had already gathered over the hill in Te Mata to disrupt DOC efforts to follow through with the Thames Coast aerial drop. 'We are here to perform a citizen's arrest and remove them from the Coromandel,' protestor Graeme Sturgeon says. He said the poison's guidelines said it should not be applied less than 150m from residential properties, recognised camping areas, tramping huts, bivvies, picnic areas, public toilets, public road lay-bys, tracks, public roads, watercraft landing points, streams, rivers, lakes, ponds and reservoirs.'"[94]

Meanwhile yet another 471ha of native and pine forest known as Te Mata Forest formed part of an EW poison1080 plan. The owners of the forest offered to conduct their own control to meet the required target however their tender for the job failed and an EW approved contractor got the job using traps and feratox. The contracting gang blazed the trees with an axe or machete for a better trap set and many trees were found damaged by driven nails. Independent forest assessors calculated the damage at $750,000 plus legal costs. Three years later EW has to pay out $300,000. The original aerial 1080 costing according to Sturgeon was $13,700 while the trapper was paid $4,967—an expensive, wasteful exercise.

Waiheke Call for Action

*"If you think you're too small to have an impact, try going
to bed with a mosquito in the room."*

Anonymous

Support comes from far afield and a nationwide call to show opposition to 1080 toxin is sent out from Waiheke Island. Hundreds of people protest on the Coromandel peninsula in Thames, Coromandel and Whitianga on the chosen day—November 14. On November 13 the *Hauraki Herald* previews the Sunday demonstrations to be held throughout the country. The focus of the demonstrations is a call to halt the use of poisons for wild animal control. Poison Free NZ, based in Waiheke, has inspired 16 marches across the country as far north as Auckland and as far south as Te Anau. A statement from the group said the demonstrations would protest the continuous, indiscriminate aerial dropping of the poisons 1080 and brodifacoum on our so-called 100% pure, clean, green country. The *Peninsula Post* emblazons its front page on November 19 with photographs of the demonstrations. Opposition to all residual poisons forms part of the campaign on the Coromandel as residents become more familiar with the array of inhumane toxins designed to keep on killing.

Organizer of the Whitianga demonstration, Victor McLean, believes the action to be a success, saying trapping has been proven to work on the Coromandel and that the lack of councillors speaking at the event shows the need for councillors who represent the people on this issue. A front page story, complete with photograph of numerous Whitianga residents marching in opposition to 1080 poison, has a headline: *'Don't poison' lobby marches.* "Around 300 people took to the streets of Whitianga on Sunday to protest against the use of poisons to control possums and other pests." Victor McLean, the organizer says, 'A trapping regime works and enhances the environment. I worked for 10 years on a trapping scheme and we had a 50% survival rate of kiwi chicks. Trapping is the most efficient and effective method of enhancing our environment. The government need to pay trappers for possum eradication and the fur becomes a perk—you cannot survive on money from fur alone…A lot of people on the Coromandel rely on wild game to supplement their diets…from the wild pork to the pheasants and rabbits.'"

Music teacher and long time conservationist Stephanie McKee is quoted saying she is opposed to 1080 drops because they are "indiscriminate, inhumane and indefensible. The case against aerial poisoning our forest for pest control is overwhelming from many angles including scientific, ecological and economic and on spiritual grounds."[95] The weekly *Informer* carries multiple photographs of the march. "We don't want 1080 on the Peninsula regardless of whether it's aerial drops or in bait stations."[96] Victor McLean reminds readers how government has funded trappers, via Ngā Whenua Rāhui, a funding programme under DOC that "exists to protect the natural integrity of Māori land and preserve mātauranga Māori" in Kennedy Bay and they proved trapping works.[97] One has to ask why trapping is not supported on the rest of the peninsula.

The large and colourful demonstration, replete with homemade creative signs and a dedicated haka, has as an intention to take their message to the Mercury Bay Community Board. The same issue of *Informer* reports the "haka was a message from tangata whenua to all NZ government departments that tangata whenua still retain the mana, kaitiakitanga and rangatiratanga jurisdiction over the ancient rohe and this particular eastern seaboard coastal stretch. And that they are responsible for the retention and protection of all quality water sources, streams, lakes, springs, etc."

Moehau on DOC's Hit List

"Rats and roaches live by competition under the laws of supply and demand: it is the privilege of human beings to live under the laws of justice and mercy."

Wendell Berry

UCLA obtains documents from the Department of Conservation disclosing the west side of Moehau is on a list of aerial 1080 super-toxin "operations" scheduled for May-June 2010. The internal DOC memo notes the upper Coromandel is "a controversial area" and that the drop is "possible but dependent on the outcome of consultation". UCLA asks for the precise location and boundaries of the poisoning; more precise dates of the poisoning; confirmation that 1080 will in fact be dropped from the air; names of the contractors to be employed; previous accidents in which those contractors have been implicated; where and when in our community the 1080 super-toxin will be stored and how it will be guarded; the dates, method and routes of transport of the poison in and through our community; and a summary of all potential health risks and adverse effects on local residents, recreational users, and native and introduced species. In response to the request, UCLA receives a five-sentence letter from Mr Gaukrodger refusing to supply information. Also stonewalled by DOC is John Veysey, our community's representative on Environment Waikato's Coromandel Catchment Subcommittee. He also sought information on behalf of residents about the planned drop. UCLA continues to strongly oppose any plans for the use of 1080 on Moehau and urges DOC to immediately cancel any such plan that may be in the pipeline.

Refusal by DOC to provide information on the planned May 2010 Moehau drop is bad news for concerned local residents. And thumbing its nose at reasonable requests by concerned residents is not a sign of positive community relations by these public servants. The potential effects of a 1080 operation on Moehau are wide-ranging. Landowners on the west flank may well be affected due to their uptake of water from mountain streams, as will visitors who may access the DOC estate or take drinking water from the streams or frequent the adjacent coastline and sea. Poison carcasses are likely to end up on the beaches. Thousands of livestock units get drinking water from creeks sourced in the area to be blanketed with the poison. With every one of those Moehau creeks being very fast flowing in times of flood, baits and dead carcasses are likely to come down onto farms and beside houses. Working dogs and the pets of both residents and visitors would also remain at high risk for months. Farmers and visitors alike would have to keep dogs muzzled at all times for fear of them even sniffing a carcass.

Also of critical importance on Moehau is the impact of any 1080 poison drop on Māori, who kaitiaki the mountain. DOC's John Gaukrodger told UCLA in 2007 that his poison work on the mountain is based on a 20-year-ago "blessing" from tangata whenua. Amazingly, he implied 1080 poisoning is part of "bringing back strength to the mauri of Moehau." That's not what UCLA understands from tangata whenua.

Quite how the blanket poisoning of our sacred mountain with a super-toxin known to impact invertebrate populations, kill numbers of insect-feeding native birds and devastate countless other species—from wild pigs to weta from ducks to deer—can sustain the mauri/life force of Moehau beggars belief. And in the meantime hundreds of thousands of taxpayer dollars are to be expended by DOC to reintroduce the insect-eating north island robins on Moehau.

Poison Poison Everywhere and Local Council Action

"I look out at my mountain surroundings and what do I see? Since the 1080 operations here in 2008 the small birds have been very slow in coming back but the most devastating loss is the number of native falcon that were part of our lives here."

Ron Eddy, Wairau Saddle

The biggest news continues to be the controversial Whenuakite and Thames coast 1080 poison drops. Despite widespread and growing opposition to its plans DOC pushes ahead with its indiscriminate poisoning of thousands of hectares. No matter—poisoned carcasses find their way onto neighbouring paddocks for dogs to feed on. No worries—by-kill of moreporks, hawks, pigs, weta and so many other critical links in the fragile ecosystem. If Tapu School is alarmed at the possibility of dilute super-toxin in its drinking water does DOC care? Even poison promoter Wren Green has to acknowledge that years of poisoning is not working: "Despite gains via intensive management (there are) serious declines for many acutely and chronically threatened species"[98]

Meanwhile, on the Upper Peninsula DOC reports ongoing use of the anticoagulant rodenticide, diphacinone over thousands of hectares of the east flank of Moehau. This huge block was ground-poisoned with 1080 in 2007, but rat populations are known to bounce back dramatically after such operations. This means more and more rat poison is needed just to stay even. The Moehau environment group (MEG) is actively poisoning (diphacinone), the Paeroa Block and the Knox Farm block at Waikawau. A quick review of the literature confirms that, in addition to killing rats, diphacinone is moderately toxic to fish and slightly toxic to birds. Animal studies confirm it may concentrate to varying degrees in the liver, kidneys and lungs. DOC and its contractors are increasing use of the poison and warn the public not to consume any game from poisoned areas and two kilometers beyond. In the case of pigs, which can range over many kilometers, it's anyone's guess whether local meat is tainted.

Problematically, studies now implicate diphacinone in large-scale deaths of one of New Zealand's most endangered species and its only native flying mammal—bats. Not only do individuals die, diphacinone kills colonies. A DOC poison operation due to take place in the Nelson Lakes National Park in mid-September is halted in response to concerns by a Nelson scientist that diphacinone could also kill the rare short-tailed bats that may inhabit the area. Endangered bats are present, mostly in remnant forests, throughout the Waikato. They are present on Little Barrier and fragile populations could well be threatened on Moehau.

MEG employees are laying one poison after another—funded by DOC and EW grant money. MEG promotes itself as a 'volunteer' organization at the same time running a bank balance of close to $200,000 annually with their "accounts person"—one of their founding members, receiving an 'honorarium' of $5000 annually. At this time the very large business of running Wellington's Karori Sanctuary, rebranded as Zealandia, operates with accounting work provided *pro bono*. Reported in November's *Panui*, MEG has set itself an admirable goal—to double the number of kiwi over the next 10 years. Quite how they intend to achieve that is anyone's guess but Red Admiral Ecology's Paddy Stewart of Coromandel and his team of kiwi listeners brave the elements on Moehau in pursuit of kiwi screeches. From this less than adequate, perhaps even fantastical methodology of counting kiwi in the wild, they believe kiwi numbers have already doubled in the previous nine years. The good news is, as reported by Stewart, kiwi birds are increasing with "predator trapping". Not a word about poisons. Stewart presents the *Moehau Kiwi Survey Interim Report* on October 23, 2009, noting that in 2000, 131 kiwi were heard, 92 male, 39 female and in 2009, 260 kiwi were heard, 174 male and 86 female.

The MEG 'Ecobase' that belongs to DOC hosts a two-day meeting of kiwi care groups from throughout the Coromandel. The intention may have been, from the perspective of visiting environmentalists, to co-ordinate activities and funding applications, however MEG is the only organization that gets a huge handout (close to $400,000) from regional council and the exclusivity of this grant leaves other kiwi groups somewhat miffed. The actual word used by Whenuakite Kiwicare lobbyist, Arthur Hinds in his member's report to the Coromandel Catchment subcommittee meeting in May 2016 is "confused", however it is not regional council's problem that MEG made a non-inclusive application for mega-bucks leaving other kiwi groups in their tail lights.

On the positive side of 2009, the Taupo District Council, under the able leadership of Rick Cooper, is lobbying all councils to end support for1080 toxin. No less than three District Councils support this initiative but Regional Councils have been legislated to control the consenting process. About 50 people attend the November 4th Thames Coromandel District Council (TCDC) meeting to express opposition to the recent aerial drops near Thames and Whenuakite. Councillors request a report from their staff in response to a proposal by one coucillor whereby council undertakes a determination of public views on 1080 with the possibility of joining other councils in Taupo, Kaikoura, Westland and Dunedin in actively advocating against further use of the poison within their boundaries.

Around 4000 people have signed 1080 petition that's on its way to Parliament, headlines the *Peninsula Post* on November 15. A copy of the petition will be presented to the TCDC at its next meeting. Graeme Sturgeon shares the hope that TCDC will follow Westland District Council and Taupo District Council to take an active stand against the use of 1080 toxin. Mayor Philippa Barriball states what is needed for the Coromandel is a solution that is unique for the Coromandel community. She also reminds readers that TCDC can take a position but they "do not have the power to stop the use of 1080 except on Council reserves." John Veysey reminds *Peninsula Post* readers on November 19 flood control money is being used to carry out wild animal control work as part of the Peninsula Project—totally inappropriate for the purpose of flood control.

Coromandel Colville Community Board Positive Action for a Healthy Environment

"Te Uringahu o Ngati Maru supports the Coromandel/ Colville wards resolution regarding the issues of community concern. We are a Hapu that has interests all over the Coromandel Peninsula and we do not support the use of 1080 poisons on any of the Tribal or Forest Parks throughout the Coromandel we have interest in."

Craig Solomon

Coromandel residents have urged an end to the increasing use of poisons that slaughter hundreds of non-target species, taint drinking water, cause secondary poisonings, kill pets and working dogs, accumulate in the food chain, kill inhumanely, and threaten tourist and export related jobs. UCLA members address the Colville Coromandel Community Board (CCCB) on December 1 to comment on the DOC/EW admission in their power point presentation to the community meeting in November that hunting and trapping possums is both less expensive and more effective than aerial 1080 poison. UCLA enumerates the added benefits of clean drinking water, no dead dogs, no slaughter of robins, tomtits, weta, bats and countless other species as well as fur recovery and new jobs. To their credit the local board responds positively and pass the following resolution:

"That the Coromandel-Colville Community Board:

1. Invite the Minister of Conservation and the local Coromandel Member of Parliament to attend a meeting in Coromandel to discuss the use of 1080 and other residual poisons on the Coromandel Peninsula with a view to seeking a Policy review

2. Advocate on behalf of the Coromandel-Colville community that all animal pest control be undertaken by trapping, hunting and non-residual poisons

3. Advocate that the Coromandel-Colville Ward be used as an example of how effective animal pest control can be using hunting, trapping and non-residual poisons."

The decision is made in response to a formal request presented jointly to the board by UCLA and the Corolandcare Association. An intrepid group of experienced and conservation-minded community members attend the meeting to answer questions from board members. UCLA takes the opportunity to congratulate Moehau resident and longtime farmer, Anne Ward, on her election to the Community Board. "Decades of conservation and farm work and voluntary contributions to our community along with impeccable integrity and fortitude for the coming meetings reflect the person we have all helped to elect. We offer hearty congratulations. Also we are pleased to offer congratulations to our new TCDC councilor. UCLA looks forward to working with you."

The Board can be sure its decision is broadly representative of public opinion. Over 1500 locals have signed petitions and hundreds have marched (twice!) on our streets protesting against the use of poison 1080. Residents have urged a hunting and trapping policy in countless submissions to council plans, letters to editors, and at many official meetings. The community board vote, although non-binding carries considerable political weight. The decision puts the Coromandel ward in step with the Taupo Council, as well as councils in Marlborough, Westland, Kaikoura and Dunedin, all of which have recently made similar decisions relating to the use of toxins. And it may help the Coromandel start to reclaim its somewhat tarnished image on environmental issues. Most importantly, the board's advocacy of a more responsible wild animal policy will be an important step toward protection of the fragile and complex ecosystems and make communities healthier places to live and work.

Meanwhile East Coast residents present a similar set of resolutions to the Whitianga Community Board. Their delegation asks for wild animal control to be limited to hunting and trapping and only non-residual and non-bio-accumulating poisons be utilised. Victor McLean explains Māori are unhappy with DOC's management on the Coromandel and that Māori need to take back the kaitiakitanga. Duncan Farmer expresses the concern regarding a lack of independent research especially with regard to sub-lethal poisoning, Colin Harris dramatically compares life on his farm surrounded by aerial 1080 to living in a war zone, only it is poison not land mines in the valley. Shelley Balsom points out her local tribe, Ngati Hei, has withdrawn support for 1080 and are re-negotiating wild animal control methods on islands iwi co-manage with DOC. A group of approximately 30 area residents attend the meeting in support of the policy change that would end the use of 1080 for possum and rat control on the east side. However Whitianga's Mercury Bay Community Board merely listen to the information presented and agree to discuss it at a later date.

Thames Council Success
for Flora and Fauna and Citizens

"Success is not final, failure is not fatal: it is the courage to continue that counts."

Winston Churchill

About 50 people are in attendance at the December TCDC meeting. They are there to support anti-1080 poison speakers and include representatives from East Coast iwi. Victor McLean urges Council to follow in the footsteps of Westland and Taupo District Councils that have adopted advocacy roles despite DOC's use of 1080 not coming under council mandate. "Other district councils have accepted they have a role to play. Do not let your community down." Duncan Farmer tells councillors it is their "job to advocate for our health and wellbeing." One councilor suggests a review. Mayor Philippa Barriball assesses the situation and takes the bull by the proverbial horns. "The use of 1080 is a national policy so can only be changed at a national level. We don't need to do any more research to take an advocacy position. We can do it now." Following the defeat of the review motion, a phoenix rises from the ashes as Barriball presents the following resolutions: "Council advocate to the Minister of Conservation that where possible animal pest control in the Thames-Coromandel District be undertaken by trapping, hunting and non-residual poisons.

—Resolves that council further advocate to the Minister of Conservation the potential for economic development in the growth of our possum fur exports.

—Resolves that council further advocate to the Minister of Economic Development the potential for economic development in the growth of our possum fur exports and the benefit of the job opportunities that are provided by the expanding market of possum fibre.

—Resolves to ask the Hauraki Coromandel Development Group to pursue feasibility funding from NZ Trade and Enterprise to develop the possum fibre market."

UCLA comments on council's action as a "huge step toward safe and sensible" wild animal control on the peninsula. While TCDC has no actual power in the decision-making process the resolutions contribute nails in the coffin of poison promoters. Some agencies claim 1080 is non-residual which is obvious game playing. A dog or a hawk or a weta that eats a poisoned carcass winds up dying a cruel death. Even DOC claims stoats as by-kill.[99] The *Coast and Country* newspaper reports, "In a surprise move just prior to Christmas the TCDC has become the third District Council in NZ to support 1080 protestors."[100]

2010 Stopping the Runaway Ahb Gravy Train and Green Party Culpability

"In Georgia where children work night and day in the cotton mills they have just passed a bill to protect songbirds. What about the little children from whom all song is gone?"

Mary Harris Jones

Bill Lightfoot, Treasurer of the Coromandel Pig Hunting Club writes in the *Coromandel Town Chronicle* January issue "…The main reason we recommend the use of cyanide, is because not only does it kill within seconds so the animal does not have a lingering death, it does not cause secondary poisoning as animals and birds etc. can eat parts of the dead possums without the risk of being poisoned themselves." He goes on to say, "approximately 300 plus people turned out, in the rain, for the protest march and of that 300 only 5, myself included, were Coromandel Pig Hunting Club members. The majority were local residents who do not want 1080 and all residual poisons spread on our peninsula. To prove a point, nearly 1500 signatures opposing 1080 use were collected in the Coromandel town alone and in excess of 4000 for the entire peninsula. Now what does that tell us?" In closing he suggests the poison promoters organize their own march in Coromandel.

Ban1080 graffiti on 20 official DOC signs require repairs. Two signs disappear completely. UCLA is contacted for comment and we offer: "No one condones thoughtless destruction of personal property. However given DOC's ongoing refusal to heed the public's legitimate health and environmental concerns about continued poisoning of Coromandel watersheds, the mounting frustration of residents is completely understandable. The graffiti is simply a reflection of DOC's own bullying."

In a positive move Port Charles resident Tina Morgan changes her tune and is on record saying the community should get the predator control they want and if they don't want 1080 toxin "maybe we should go all-out on a trapping programme. Would it really cost more to employ a team of trappers than it would to hire a helicopter?" EW councillor Pat Gregory holds the minority view on Regional Council that trapping is worth considering and says trappers have offered to kill possums for free in return for the fur. But Conservation Department Coromandel area manager John Gaukrodger says ground baiting was physically grueling and time consuming.[101] WRC refuses to acknowledge landowners can do their own wild animal control. Regional Council is actively maintaining their budget allocation and growing it exponentially over the long term.

UCLA's spokesperson is invited to write a column for the *New Zealand Farmers Weekly* in their *Pulpit* column headlined, *Stopping the runaway AHB gravy train*.[102] The article results in a flurry of denials from AHB's top brass. Audacious conservationist, Thames resident and artist Diana Halstead, responds to their attack, "The alacrity with which William McCook rushed to defend the Animal Health Board's expenditure following Reihana Robinson's intelligent re-evaluation of where this less than successful organisation may be heading, should possibly raise alarm bells on another front apart from that of bovine Tb eradication. Our exports of prime beef, lamb and venison to European and other northern hemisphere markets could cease totally once the knowledge of our continued large scale use of 1080 is fully realized abroad. After all, we are speaking here of a substance so ecotoxic that most countries in the world chose to ban its use long ago. Robinson is not advocating a ceasefire on pest control, she is merely spelling out what should be obvious to all, that there are less costly ways for us as farmers and landowners to achieve Tb eradication. This means methods that do not cause the devastation and long-term damage to our fauna and flora that has resulted from AHB's crippling obsession with 1080 at any cost. And what a cost, if our entire export market could also be jeopardized. This is something with the potential to impact on all our lives."[102] Ron Eddy of Wairau Saddle points out the *Pulpit* article "sure got the Animal Health Board gravy train huffing and puffing…AHB boss William McCook added nothing to the mix that hasn't been said countless times before. None of his statements were real facts either. They were generalisations only. This applies to other letters that supported his views…I look out at my mountain surroundings and what do I see? Since the 1080 operations here in 2008 the small birds have been very slow in coming back but the most devastating loss is the number of native falcon that were part of our lives here. They are now gone.

The bush on the slopes of the mountains is exactly the same as it always has been so those 1080 operations achieved very little apart from killing our falcons. There weren't any possums here anyway, those two 1080 operations just kept the gravy train moving."[103]

In a local paper Geoffrey Robinson writes of Green Party hypocrisy: "Lukewarm support on the Coromandel for the Green Party in its anti-mining campaign… should come as no surprise. Environmentalists, who have been natural allies of the Greens in the past, are turning away from the party in increasing numbers. These conservationists are let down, turned off, shocked and disgusted at the complete failure of the Greens to take a stand against the biggest environmental scandal of all—namely the ecocide and threats to human health posed by super-toxin 1080. At every turn in the growing local movement against 1080, the Green Party has been conspicuously absent. While thousands of marchers, petitioners, and campaigners young and old have battled against the poisoning of our Coromandel drinking water catchments and bush, the Green Party has failed to lift a finger, let alone speak out. When the Greens popped up with their big push against mining, they took active backing from the broader environmental movement for granted. But their call to arms smacks of hypocrisy. If the Coromandel is "Too Precious to Mine", surely it is "Too Precious to Poison".[104]

In March the *NZ Listener* publishes UCLA's letter: "In *Fiordland Fling*, December 26, Gareth Morgan flings about an oft repeated myth: 'possums have left their indelible stain here: white skeletons of rata that interrupt the canopy.' The Department of Conservation, Forest and Bird and those with a vested interest in the 1080 poison business do nothing to rectify this nonsense. Extensive research by forest ecologist Peter Bellingham, of Landcare Research, Lincoln, shows dieback of the southern rata is likely to be the result of natural causes such as high rainfall causing rapid depletion of soil nutrients. We can't blame possums for killing those trees."[105] Eleven years earlier a thesis presented for the degree of Doctor of Philosophy in Ecology at Massey University in 1999 by Kim Suzanne Mc Breen shows "Forest dieback is a complex area of study that has led to the development of a number of theories or models which purport to explain it…The experiment found no evidence that possums, pinhole borer, or Sporothrix were affecting the health of kamahi at this site…Possums, pinhole borer and

Sporothrix are not having a large effect on kamahi health in this area. "[106]

Gareth Morgan's mantra is repeated the following year in a *NZ Listener* letter (March 13, 2011) by local Thames councillor Bill Barclay whose South Island visit includes a helicopter ride where the pilot points out dying rata "to the north, and the brilliant red and green rata carpet stretching away to the south of the two rivers. He then volunteered, unaware of my interest in the matter that only south of the river had been subjected to 1080 control measures—principally aimed at protecting the rohe (kiwi) habitat. Without entering into all the other anti-1080 arguments, it was at least a convincing demonstration of its effectiveness." The science says otherwise, "Many believe possums cause dieback because they browse rata and kamahi. However, dieback occurs in forests where there are no possums. It now appears natural factors: the regeneration of rata, natural disturbance, and changes in soil fertility, all contribute as the main causes of dieback…Comparing several Westland valleys, dieback occurs independently of when possums colonised and irrespective of whether or not there has been possum control. Dieback is scarcely apparent in stable, very infertile granite areas but is pronounced in unstable, more fertile schist valleys."[107] Barclay's helicopter flight over Whitcombe Glacier and down the Whataroa River northern boundary of the South Westland DOC conservancy no doubt occurred. Anecdotal experience versus scientific research? And it is not clear whether the pilot had a conflict of interest, as helicopters are the vehicles used to dump poison 1080.

2010: Moehau, Poison Consents, Clyde Graf for Regional Council, Maori Party Effort

"Under the principles of kaitiaki or guardianship, I fail to see how residual poisons such as 1080 fit into these principles. In regard to Maori land administration, it is my understanding that 12 local iwi have withdrawn their approval for the Hauraki Maori Trust Board to speak on their behalf. I fail to see how the Hauraki Maori Trust Board has the mandate to authorize the poisoning of this land with a poison with so many detrimental side effects as 1080."

Colin Harris

There is a temporary reprieve for the ecosystem of Moehau as well as the many threatened native species like wetas, bats, morepork, hawks, and countless insects that make the mountain their home. UCLA obtained an updated internal document from DOC that lists all planned aerial 1080 jobs for 2010, and the drop on the west flank of the mountain, previously proposed by DOC for May-June, has been eliminated from the schedule. On behalf of local residents, UCLA has been seeking information on the Moehau 1080 drop from the DOC Hauraki office for months, but has faced obstacles every step of the way. Finally, in response to a complaint filed in January with the Director General, Waikato conservator, and local Thames manager of DOC, written confirmation is received that declares the aerial 1080 assault on Moehau "for May/June this year is not occurring". UCLA understands this a postponement and not a cancellation. Basically, DOC is now re-starting the process and says it is "unable to confirm this work until we have consulted with iwi, our adjacent landowners, and key stakeholders." DOC says, "specific details for the proposed operations will not be known until consultation and detailed planning has been completed. They indicate further information will be released once it has "obtained consent from the Medical Officer of Health if required." This means one and only one thing – aerial 1080.

UCLA maintains every resident in the Port Charles and Port Jackson area is a key stakeholder when it comes to poisoning this sacred mountain and condemns DOC's total lack of real consultation and their intimidating insistence on the use of poison1080 as part of their ground control operations on Moehau and in Kennedy Bay. Their plans to dump poison on Moehau are temporarily shelved and DOC's Steve Bolton says the department ran out of money to complete the required consultation. "The level of opposition to the use of 1080 was also a factor, Bolton says. We have to be squeaky clean in everything we do. We go through a rigorous consultation process, which we start about two months before an operation." An operation is planned and then consultation with residents occurs? UCLA reminds readers Moehau is criss-crossed with tracks available to hunters and trappers alike.

The often-repeated mantra extolling 1080 poison as the "cheap alternative" is blatantly untrue. Consultation was going to prove so expensive 1080 could not be used, but the money it takes to sell the idea to landowners is never included in the publicised budget when 1080 is the toxin of choice. Monitoring of wildlife is also not accounted for, and in fact rarely takes place. The 'consultation' eventually on offer in 2012-13 includes helicopter rides and free lunches for a select few with an emphasis on iwi. This aeronautical feature must really push up the cost of poisoning Moehau. Eco-entrepreneurial group MEG, in the meantime receives over a quarter of a million dollars to catch rats in the neighbourhood.

Peter Bacchus, long time biodynamic farmer of Paeroa writes "1080 would not be my poison of choice either domestically or in the bush. There is data showing that rat populations rapidly increase after aerial 1080 drops. They respond to food and space opportunities, as do many other pest organisms. If 1080 was the answer we would have been rid of our pest animals decades ago... Those who have observed animals dying of 1080 poison attest to a slow and agonizing death. For those fortunate to have not seen it personally, the Graf boys documentary shows the process."[108]

Throughout the winter of 2010 locals begin the campaign to dethrone Simon Friar from WRC and to elect documentary filmmaker and longtime environmentalist, Clyde Graf. This proves a lively aside to the ongoing campaign to end 1080. Together with his brother Steve, Graf has made award-winning documentaries including *A Shadow of Doubt* and *Poisoning Paradise*. Graf's posters proclaim him as "the People's Voice, a life-long environmentalist and international award winning film maker." He eventually wins in 2013 and fortuitously has the inestimable Taupo representative Kathy White alongside. The attacks on Graf extend to Waikato Regional Council employing law firm Brookfields to investigate a complaint by Waitomo District Mayor Brian Hanna who alleges Graf's filming of a farmer whose cows were poisoned by1080 was a 'conflict of interest'. In 2014 lawyer, Linda O'Reilly, found he acted in a way that is "inherently critical of the council, but he is entitled to be critical of the council". He is thus vindicated.

Straight Furrow features UCLA's nationwide campaign opposing the 10 and 20-year resource consent applications to WRC by two helicopter poison companies, EcoFX and EPRO that are seeking permission to dump toxin 1080 onto land and into waterways.[109] Kevin Christie, once a Key Ecological Sites (KES) contractor for Regional Council, runs EcoFX, and Roger Lorrigan of EPRO bought out parts of the regional council's pest control business in the late 1990's. Over decades serious money (in the millions) is to be made. The *Sunday Star Times* interviews Taupo Mayor Rick Cooper on June 27 and he "points to multimillion-dollar contracts awarded to a local firm, EPRO Ltd, to spread 1080 from the air. Its director and co-owner, Roger Lorigan, used to work at Environment Waikato, which issues resource consents for 1080 work, in its pest management unit. A former colleague, Kevin Christie, also has his own firm, EcoFX based in Otorohanga, which has also won big contracts. Their boss at Environment Waikato was John Simmons, now the biosecurity and natural heritage group manager at the council, in charge of pest management. In the late 90s, the council sold its possum control business to Lorigan and Christie, and Cooper claims they have been milking it ever since."

UCLA argues consents should only be granted for one year only, as there would be no luck attempting to eliminate them altogether. With this strategy UCLA is successful.

Many organizations join the coalition to demand EW not renew these consents for 10 and 20 years. Coromandel Landcare groups, NZ Soil and Health, Pesticide Action Network Aotearoa/New Zealand are among the many conservationists who join the campaign. A supercilious EW response finds no "special circumstances" to allow public notification. The report by Sheryl Roa, a Senior Resource Officer at EW, outlines the assumptions upon which the decisions were made to grant the consents and what conditions would be applied to the consents. Some disturbing highlights: "I consider that *iwi* are not affected parties…I don't consider that there are any other parties affected.

Animal welfare: Not applicable.

Storage of toxic baits: Refuse to consider.

Transportation of toxic baits: Refuse to consider.

Security of any aspect of operations: Refuse to consider.

Effects of toxic baits falling into drinking water: Less than minor.

And last but not least *Adverse Effects on desirable fauna*: Routine".

According to EW, if a 1080drop is planned for a pristine block of bush that has never been poisoned, EW does not consider the baseline for that block to be its actual pristine state, but applies instead as its baseline the environmental conditions of poisoned blocks elsewhere in the region. EW concludes, therefore, that in applying poison to the pristine block, it is not increasing any adverse effects above the existing baseline level.

Straight Furrow's reporter, Rachel Breckon was able to lay her hands on earlier consent conditions, one of which highlights the extent of legal protection for EW when it comes to "significant accidental discharge of 1080 baits into water." The article comments on TCDC's position on toxins and notes "The Maori Party issued a press statement in relation to the Prime Minister's comments that there was 'no alternative to 1080' with a statement calling for a large scale trapping programme. Tensions have also been running high around the country. The *Waikato Times* reported a Trade Me forum (which has since been closed down) that verbally abused John Gaukrodger, the outgoing Coromandel Department of Conservation manager. Thames-based staff has been physically and verbally abused by anti-1080 campaigners, according to the article."[110] Peter Bacchus writes his "possum ash is available for any landowners who would like to try a different method to get rid of the furry menace."[111] This methodology was pioneered by the Austrian philosopher Rudolf Steiner, and is referred to as 'peppering'. "Mr Bacchus says the method works by 'picking up the dynamic of the ash and transferring it to the sand and transferring it to the land and it radiates out. It's not associated with smell or taste, it's not poisonous, they just feel very uncomfortable in that area."

Around this time the Maori Party's Rahui Katene states the current policy is both lazy and shortsighted. She is to draft a member's bill to ban 1080, to transfer kaitiakitanga of DOC land to tangata whenua and to support investment in large-scale trapping projects. As time passes the government jumps on her plan, appoints a new Parliamentary Commissioner for the Environment (PCE) who subsequently writes a puff piece promoting more poison 1080 and undermining Katene's initiative.

Spokesperson for East Coromandel Landcare and long-time conservationist Arthur Attfield writes in the *Peninsula Post* of July 29, "Your paper clearly shows the deep divisions that seem to be prevalent between mainstream conservation groups, and other extreme elements of conservation, e.g. MEG, Kauri 2000, Forest and Bird and Whenuakite Kiwi Care who believe results can be achieved only through the use of 1080 and other toxins. By now these groups must be drowning in the constant self-adulation of success. The public certainly knows the other side of the issues. These groups have tried to elevate themselves for the purpose of denigrating the mainstream conservation image in the eyes of the public. They have been ferociously supported by DOC and EW." John Veysey documents the work of "secret poisoners" referencing MEG now spreading poison in Tuateawa and Waikawau Bay. "Most of the pro-poison propaganda turns out to be untrue; the threats unfounded…More and more landowners are managing to stand up against the poison drive, like the Waikato farmer Simon Beveridge who, sick of the unnecessary poisoning of non-target wildlife, has refused any more 1080 on his land. He faces huge legal and financial threats but has stood firm. He is a brave man and this kind of landowner resistance seems to be the only way to slow the DOC/E.W. poisoning Juggernaut." The *Coromandel Town Chronicle* under new management refuses to publish his report.

Dick Featherstone writes in a farming paper on August 9 "Here we have a Minister of Conservation, Kate Wilkinson, jumping up and down as if she has just sat on a swarm of bees, calling the Norwegian hunters that visited NZ a few months ago, disgraceful killers for shooting two native pigeons, that died instantly and humanely I might add. I blame DOC for not educating these hunters as to what not to shoot while in NZ. Here's my point: DOC will go out the very next day with their helicopters loaded with 1080 pellets and spread this cruel poison all over our forests and in our rivers and streams like confetti at a wedding. DOC end up killing not just two birds, but hundreds of birds — morepork, weka, tomtits—along with pigs, deer and a few possums. All of the above will die a very slow and cruel death. It's a bloody disgrace what goes on in NZ, especially considering we are supposed to be 100% pure clean and green. What a load of bullshit. 1080 is a lethal poison and it should not be anywhere near or in our waterways— it should be banned in NZ, the same as it's been banned overseas. End of story."

2010: Kennedy Bay Police Activities

I'm not against the police; I'm just afraid of them.
Alfred Hitchcock

The Kennedy Bay story starts late summer when DOC unveils plans for a 1080 ground operation on both public land and several large private properties. Seventeen hundred bait stations are to be stocked. Before long, the community is severely divided between those few allowing the 1080 poison to be placed on their land and the majority of residents who point out the hazard cannot be contained within property boundaries. Iwi and community leaders declare their vehement opposition to the poisoning plans, holding public meetings and issuing statements to authorities. The bush telegraph turns out rumours of possible actions to peacefully stop the poisoning. Requests for face-to-face meetings with officials are ignored. In the end, the Kennedy Bay 1080 poison operation goes ahead on schedule, but only after the flummoxed manager of DOC Hauraki is forced to purchase an unprecedented, last-minute full-page public relations advert in the local newspaper in an embarrassed attempt to justify the job and placate an irate community. What she fails to mention in the process is that official monitoring shows Kennedy Bay possum numbers prior to the poisoning are below the level that requires poisoning elsewhere in the Waikato region.

For his part, DOC Waikato Conservancy chief Greg Martin is aware of the widespread anger his plan has engendered. A nervous Martin calls out more than five police vehicles and numerous DOC strongmen, with dozens of ninja-outfitted riot cops put on alert able to respond to potential civil disobedience. On the day, the police callout was completely unnecessary. The poison was distributed. No violent protesters were anywhere to be found.[112] "The Coromandel has been a battleground between DOC and anti-1080 activists in the past and Mr Martin said the police had been asked to attend in anticipation of a possible protest by opponents of the poison." DOC had hired Kennedy Bay residents to lay the pre-feed. The new leader at DOC Hauraki explains the Residual

Trap Catch (yet another ineffectual methodology that only counts possums and does not look at biodiversity) for the area prior to the poison plan, is 5.8%, a figure that by 2013 is no longer considered sufficient to trigger WRC work on the Coromandel.[113]

Shenagh Gleeson reports with the headline: *Police not needed for 1080 operation at Kennedy Bay.* "About 30 DOC staff and contractors installed toxic-laced baits containing 1080…over an area of about 1100ha from the eastern side of Kennedy Bay to Pukenui Pt, north of Tuateawa…One landowner George Hovell, says it was great to get the job done. 'It all went smoothly. There were threats but nothing happened.' It's the first time 1080 has been used on the family's property and he has no concerns about it. Bush on the property has clearly benefited from earlier work, he says. "You look at the bush on our side of the bay and it's just beautiful and you look across the bay at the pohutukawa dying."[114] Wait a minute, there has been no 1080 used on the Hovell land but the bush is thriving due to "earlier pest control" one may assume was trapping, hunting or cyanide. Is there anyone home?

Meanwhile back on the Moehau front, Colin Harris writes "It was with considerable disappointment and a certain amount of anger that I read the article in this publication about the proposed 1080 operation from Sandy Bay to Māori land on Moehau. Under the principles of kaitiaki or guardianship, I fail to see how residual poisons such as 1080 fit into these principles. In regard to Maori land administration, it is my understanding that 12 local iwi have withdrawn their approval for the Hauraki Maori Trust Board to speak on their behalf. I fail to see how the Hauraki Maori Trust Board has the mandate to authorize the poisoning of this land with a poison with so many detrimental side effects as 1080. As patron of the Whitianga Pig Hunters Club I resent the inference that because hunters were given a few month's access, rat and possum numbers have exploded out of control. In discussion, some of these hunters informed me they had to work extremely hard for their solitary catches. It is news to us that there is now a huge pig problem. Why couldn't DOC direct the hunters to where the problem lay? As an ex-possum trapper, I also fail to see how rat and possum numbers have increased during the winter months, which is at odds with all known facts of the breeding habits of these species in NZ."[115]

The final word on the Kennedy Bay fiasco is published in the *Hamilton News* as part of the Robinson Report. "Conservationists often take different approaches to the same problem. But when one strategy in addition to its basic costs requires fighting ever-growing community opposition, notably the invigorated protests of tangata whenua, and when that same strategy requires expensive public relations campaigns and now even dozens of armed police for protection, that strategy is doomed. What Kennedy Bay showed is that pests and protesters aren't the problem. Last week's tense fiasco proved instead that official national pest control toxin policy is at a crisis point and major change is inevitable." Later in the year Karuna Falls resident and long-time environmentalist, Stephanie McKee researches the poison company Animal Control Products (ACP) annual reports and publishes a witty, intelligent analysis.[116]

2010: And it is off to
Wellington and the Select Committee

"Political language…is designed to make lies sound truthful and murder respectable, and to give an appearance of solidity to pure wind."

George Orwell

Anti-1080 groups to be heard in capital trumpets the headline in *Hauraki Herald*, October 15. So it is off to Wellington with a delegation of conservation volunteers from the Coromandel to argue against the prevailing poison policy for wild animal control. Thames Landcare are there in force with Diana Halstead, Graeme Sturgeon, Val and Peter Findlay and Dick Featherston. Together with Reihana Robinson all are invited to address the Local Government and Environment Committee on December 9, 2010. "Also set to be heard at the same time is a petition from Westland District Mayor Maureen Pugh which has 1660 signatures opposing the use of 1080 in that district." Filmmaker and conservationist Clyde Graf also attends. Chair of the select committee, Chris Auchinvole, who signs off on the letter declaring the date of the hearing, writes that DOC, AHB and ERMA will also be heard. We can predict the outcome. The status quo is to be maintained at any cost. In fact the eventual report repeats unsubstantiated claims by poison promoters such as "without 1080 our ability to protect many of our unique native plants and animals would be lost" and possums "are responsible for most TB infections in cattle and deer herds" and "trapping is not practical on a large scale or in rugged terrain." (Three years down the line in 2013 AHB will catch and test 2500 possums and mustelids and find startlingly, no positive results. Their archaic skin test has a 20 per cent error factor.) And the new PCE, who did not appear at the hearing, "told" the committee at some stage in the process that because public concern had not abated she thought "this may be partly due to either, or both, insufficient and ineffective communication by Government agencies."

Striving for the absurd DOC reminds the committee that the Peninsula Project was established to "improve the health of the environment and reduce flood risks" and that they are attempting to control goats and possums not because they want to save unique native plants and animals but because "they are major contributors to soil erosion, which increases the flooding risk." The committee deigns to note the $100 million fur pelt and fibre industry.

Both Coromandel weeklies print a photograph of the Coromandel delegation. Dick Featherston displays his banner proclaiming "NZ 1080 World Leader in Animal & Bird Cruelty". UCLA's representative lays out the misuse of poison 1080 on the Coromandel including the "regular failure by government officials to monitor pre-poison and post-poison pest numbers, failure to monitor non-target species deaths and secondary poisoning consequences…consistent failure to properly dispose of poisoned carcasses, failure to properly consult with tangata whenua and regular aerial use of 1080 in flat and easily accessible farm land, forestry blocks and rolling terrain on the Coromandel." The Select Committee listened to the following, "Conservationists, farmers, teachers, scientists, mums and dads, school children, pensioners, tourist operators, exporters, pakeha and tangata whenua – people from across the political spectrum – are asking that this government put a stop to the heavy use of one of the world's deadliest poisons where we work, where we live, and where we raise our families… this committee may be surprised to learn that precise pre-operation pest level monitoring in fact IS NOT routinely performed. As an example, the massive 2008 Kauaeranga Gorge aerial 1080 drop near Thames was undertaken without such documentation. That is misuse of 1080 on the Coromandel.

"Committee members would also be confident that after every 1080 poisoning operation is undertaken on the Coromandel Peninsula that there is precise monitoring of remaining levels of targeted pest species. But this committee may be surprised again to learn that precise post-operation pest level monitoring also IS NOT routinely performed. After the Kauaeranga Gorge drop in 2008, no such monitoring was performed…That is misuse of 1080 on the Coromandel. But let's leave brush-tailed possums for a moment. Hard research, including studies commissioned by our own Department of Conservation indicate aerial 1080 toxin applications cause high mortality among non-target bird species, both natives and non-natives, including robins, tomtits, kaka, ruru, harriers, falcons and others. Surely, given that many of these species are protected and some are endangered, committee members would be confident that monitoring of non-target species, both pre- and post-poisoning is undertaken always. However, this committee will be surprised to learn that on the Coromandel, as elsewhere, no such data is collected -- ever. By-kill is assured. But DOC and regional council avoid documenting it. That is misuse of 1080 on the Coromandel. But your committee can at least be confident that 1080 toxin is used in accordance with the manufacturer's label instructions.

"Tull Chemicals in Alabama USA instructs all users of their raw 1080 product to make sure that all poisoned carcasses are collected and disposed of properly. This will be to minimise any chance of secondary poisoning of non-target species and to assure that water supplies are not tainted. On the Coromandel, as is the case elsewhere in the Waikato, collection and disposal of poisoned carcasses, is never undertaken. They are left to poison scavenging birds or dogs or to decay with toxin-laden entrails in or beside streams. That is patent misuse of 1080. Meanwhile, DOC and council officials have assured us that 1080 poison is intended for use in those steep, remote or otherwise inaccessible places. But on the Coromandel, 1080 has been dropped by helicopter over thousands of hectares of accessible country. It has been dropped on massive stands of plantation pine, land that is criss-crossed with vehicle tracks near Coromandel Town. It has been dropped on farmland and in paddocks at Whenuakite, on flat terrain, on easy hillsides outside Thames, in bush only metres from public roads like the heavily touristed "309 Road" to Whitianga. This is misuse. And would any committee member feel comfortable with 1080 toxin being dropped into their family's drinking water catchment? Would they be comfortable with a toxin, banned in California as a potential endocrine disrupter, being present in however low or undetectable levels in their own or their wives' or their daughters' glass of water? But on the Coromandel, 1080 poison is in fact dropped into public and private water supply catchments, on a routine basis. This is misuse.

"And what about tangata whenua? Local iwi spokespersons on the Coromandel have expressed their firm opposition to 1080 operations on the peninsula in both formal addresses to the Thames-Coromandel District Council and in public statements through the press. They have made clear that 1080 use is an affront to cultural values of Māori and may represent treaty violations. They have described the negative impact of 1080 on the mauri, of life force, of the mountains and ecosystems. The policy is based on dogma, anecdote, informal observation and research that does not meet even the most basic scientific protocols. It does however support a hundred million per year 1080 industry. There is no research to show net ecological benefit. On the Coromandel, there have been extensive public expressions of opposition to current DOC/AHB/ERMA/Regional council 1080 operations. Farmers and conservationists made the trek to Hamilton in 2007 to personally speak to their submissions. Hundreds of individual protesters have marched in the streets in our communities. This and other petitions have been presented to government officials. Some have taken up what they believe is their only remaining option – civil disobedience. As the use of 1080 has increased in our region, so has the opposition. We have traveled here today to ask your help in stopping this practice. Not in 10 years. Not when some other poison is ready for trial. But now. This is what our communities are asking. This is what they deserve. Hunting and trapping is the answer. It is effective, safe, cost-effective and environmentally clean, a jobs creator, an export dollar protector and it is what the people want. The Coromandel is Tb free and is accessible country to trap and hunt. We all support conservation so let's do it without residual poisons."[117]

Accompanying the delegates to Wellington and contributing to the case are the tabled statements by Coromandel conservationists and farmers Theodora Ward and Arthur Attfield. Environmental scientist Sean Weaver provides comments along with his published research. Steffan Browning on behalf of NZ Soil and Health and Dr Meriel Watts, co-ordinator of Pesticide Action Network Aotearoa provide statements.[118]

Questions to DOC and AHB came from MPs Nikki Kaye, Dr Cam Calder, Rahui Katene, Nicky Wagner, Louise Upston and Kevin Hague. DOC Director General Al Morrison and his marketing team, AHB executives (including $400,000-a-year-plus CEO), and the ERMA officials who orchestrated the 1080 sham review in 2007 were present at taxpayer expense and were on the defensive.

The Coromandel petition to parliament asks for an investigation into the misuse of toxin 1080 on the Coromandel. DOC 's written response to the petition includes such juicy tidbits as "When the Department receives formal requests for information from members of the public on its operations these will be acknowledged and best endeavours made to provide the information, where it is available, in a timely manner." This becomes moot over the years as nearly every request for information results in a lengthy wait period, as each query is ratcheted up to OIA status. With regard to wind speed on the day of the dump DOC offers "While the wind speed on ridges was undeniably greater, this did not affect bait distribution" Water concerns were addressed as follows, "Additional conditions were placed on the Thames Coromandel water supply in the Mangarehu Stream; and a point on the Kauaearanga River where the helicopter was permitted to cross in performing the activity" and the "uptake of water to the reticulated water supplies was disconnected during the operation and was reopened three days after the last day of bait application." So there is no problem with 1080 toxin in water BUT they turn off the water anyway? In their earnest denial of water pollution they quote Suren "while cereal pellet baits take 3-4 days to disintegrate in running water, 1080 rapidly leaches from the baits…no 1080 detected in baits after 36 hours." The information missing in action is Suren's recommendation that sampling should be collected within 4 to 8 hours of potential contamination to detect presence of 1080. Nothing disclosed about where the 1080 toxin travels.[119] The technology required to detect poison 1080 at very low parts per billion does not exist in New Zealand.

2011 Action and the Silencing of Debate at CTC and Launch of Peninsula Press

"The first time it was reported that our friends were being butchered there was a cry of horror. Then a hundred were butchered. But when a thousand were butchered and there was no end to the butchery, a blanket of silence spread. When evil doing comes like falling rain, nobody calls out 'stop!' When crimes begin to pile up they become invisible. When sufferings become unendurable, the cries are no longer heard. The cries, too, fall like rain in summer"

Bertolt Brecht

On 22 March 2011 the Coromandel-Colville Community Board passed the following resolution to "reiterate its opposition to the use of 1080 in the Coromandel-Colville Ward and its support for alternative methods of pest eradication eg; hunting, trapping and cyanide." In April John Veysey asks the question: "Does DOC think they're going to put the clock back? Do we want them to put the clock back? If so, how far do we want it put back? 100 years, or 200 years? 200 years ago the place was already swarming with pigs. Does this give pigs a greater right to be here than a creature which arrived 100 years later? There has always been an underlying belief behind all our ecological restoration visions that there is something called a 'native'. Up until the Wildlife Service was disbanded in 1987, the way forward was to 'flatten the native, sow grass and graze sheep'. That became known as the kiwi way." Veysey's comments were in response to DOC's intention to release another 30 robins, after a supposed absence of 100 years, on Moehau this autumn. The translocation is part of DOC's "wider ecological restoration programme on Moehau". Is it just another experiment? Time travel to 2014 and DOC's so-called Kiwi Recovery programme alights on Moehau. They will uplift an initial bunch of 10 kiwi from Moehau to populate Motutapu Island. Quite how this equates to an "ecological restoration programme" for Moehau baffles.

UCLA is advised the *Coromandel Town Chronicle* will no longer accept any articles that refer to 1080 toxin—an issue of extreme interest and concern to thousands of Coromandel-Colville residents. The new editor makes it clear this editorial ban extends to all toxins. Since wild animal control operations by the Department of Conservation, Environment Waikato and other groups regularly involve residual and persistent toxin use over thousands of hectares of Coromandel native bush and farmland each year, this censorship is problematic. Stephanie McKee presents one of the last comments in the May issue before, it would appear, poison promoters are able to convince the editor to muzzle debate on the topic for six months. "Resorting to 'argumentum ad hominem' by using emotive and insulting language is often a sign of the absence of sound arguments to back your case, as is calling for a topic to be censored from community discussions … So congratulations to the editors for publishing opposing views about 1080 use—thus allowing the readers to make up their own minds and do their own research on this fraught topic. Many readers probably remember how vitriolic insults were hurled at those of us who opposed both the establishment of nuclear power in NZ and the aerial spraying of the dioxin containing 245-T around Coromandel. The Ministry of Works had working drawings for a nuclear power station in Colville! Imagine that. Thanks to the grassroots anti-nuclear movement that was supported by people from all sections of society, Cabbage Bay will never face what Fukushima is now facing—nuclear meltdown and disaster. Favourite insults back then were to call someone "hysterical" or "emotional". In fact those environmental campaigns were based on robust scientific research together with deep ethical concerns. While time proved us right on those issues, along the way we had to battle well-funded pro-nuclear public relations campaigns, as well as pro-245-T plain scientific ignorance. So thank you again CTC for allowing vigorous discussions in your pages. But let us argue over researched facts and informed opinions rather than resorting to 'argumentum ad hominem'."

A positive event in the world of newspapers occurs in Thames (in July) with the publication of a new free weekly called *Peninsula Press* offering the opportunity for local articles and letters challenging the status quo on a number of topics. Peter Bacchus exposes how much 1080 science is carried out at the behest of poison promoters. "We have not had truly independent science since the demise of the DSIR and Ruakura Research Station. I therefore tend to look carefully at who the funder is when I consider a scientific paper." He comments that one writer suggests the anti-1080 lobby is well funded. "I would like to know his source of information as most of those I am aware of who oppose the use of 1080 live on very modest incomes and spend considerable time in the bush hunting for food, pelts, and fiber." Within two years the paper will lose local advertisers after speculation that various approaches were made encouraging businesses not to advertise. The editor will be removed from his job in 2013 and not long after, the paper ceases publication. Prior to the paper's demise, Peter Findlay submits his dog's Vet Report: "This is to certify that lab testing of a vomit sample obtained…was positive for the poison 1080. This result, along with clinical signs consistent with poisoning, confirm 1080 as the cause of this dog's death." Findlay asks "Why did the department pay out compensation if they were innocent and free of blame? There's little wonder people don't trust them." In a government press release of July 25 the Minister of Conservation, Kate Wilkinson brands anti-1080 activists in the Coromandel with "a history of intimidating and threatening DOC staff". Surely it is her responsibility to find out the root cause and mediate.

2012 KEA Action in Otama,
a PCE Puff Piece and the Mana Party

"If voting changed anything, they'd make it illegal"
Emma Goldman

Victor McLean, Chair of the Kuaotunu Environmental Action group (KEA) writes to Eddie Murphy regarding DOC's plan to use1080 toxin at Otama. He reminds DOC, that KEA represents the community and works along side Ngati Hei and Ngati Tamatera Hapu ki Kuaotunu and "The majority of this community has made it clear that we do not want poisons to be used as pest control in our bush. Local farmers, hunters, trappers and residents—the people who live here are part of the ecosystem believe there are other, better alternatives." DOC is invited to discuss trapping with KEA but ignores the invitation. KEA writes again in May 2012 "Your operation that is to take place on public conservation land in May and June this year is an operation *not wanted* by majority of the Kuaotunu/Otama community—the people who live here. KEA represents the community's aspirations for a poison-free environment, for sustainable environmental practices and alternative methods rather than 1080 and other poisons. In July 2011 KEA proposed a trapping regime instead of poison for the Otama block and invited you to a community meeting to discuss this option further. DOC declined to meet. To say the people most affected by this operation have been consulted prior to its finalisation is *not true*. Not only have you ignored the community, you have *not* consulted Iwi Hapu of Ngati Hei nor Ngati Tamatera of Kuaotunu. Therefore we request that your poison operation stop immediately until DOC fulfills its own operational planning rules and regulations, which are first to meet with the people and Iwi of Kuaotunu and Otama". A full-page DOC promo in the *Peninsula Post* May 10 2012 announces, "DOC makes no apologies for using pesticides to control introduced pests." There is not a blush of pretence regarding "consultation" and residents of Otama are instructed to note the Waikato District Health Board must consent to the use of toxin 1080 and a "detailed assessment of the risks involved in the works" has been completed.

DOC ironically credits the Thames Landcare's petition for inspiring the Parliamentary Commissioner for the Environment's review — "an independent report from the PCE evaluating the use of 1080 (**written as a result of a petition from the Thames Landcare Group and others**)..." [emphasis added][120]. No consideration of Maori MP Rahui Katene's new Bill that may well have played a major role. The PCE's report achieved the poison promoters goal, chilling political opposition as Katene's bill was dropped.

The PCE's report is an absolute whitewash for the poison industry. Writing as a team called the *Robinson Report*, Geoffrey and Reihana Robinson's opinion piece is published in *Hamilton News*

"In true Orwellian fashion, the Parliamentary Commissioner for the Environment has manufactured a faith-based pitch for saving New Zealand wildlife by expanded poisoning of our fragile bush ecosystems. Billed as an "independent investigation", the report by Jan Wright is an unapologetically political document designed to head off potential legislative controls or a parliamentary moratorium on use of supertoxin 1080. With a $100m pest control industry under fire, Wright produced a lightweight document that is stunning for its lack of factual substance, its booster tone, and dismissive attitude toward those who disagree. And it's easy to see why the current PCE belched up the government line on 1080 policy.

"Wright, a career policy analyst and consultant, is the consummate Wellington political insider, with past board positions at Transit NZ, ACC, and Land Transport NZ. As for her advertised "independence" on the issue of 1080, one of Wright's former clients was none other than the pro-1080 Environmental Risk Management Authority. The report lacks any new information but is most notable for what it fails to consider. Wright refused to consider Maori cultural impacts, views of local communities, accidents and specifics of operations. The report makes numerous unsubstantiated claims giving the misleading impression her conclusions are fact-based. After carefully referencing a single study on kiwi populations, for example, she makes a highly emotional warning that six vastly different species of native birds "will almost certainly disappear". In actual fact, there is nothing cited in the scientific literature to back up her assertion.

"Even worse, Wright's Forests Under Attack scare section features a major factual error. She highlights tui and bellbirds (korimako) as examples of native species certain to "decline further". However, a close reading of the 2010 Journal of Ecology predation study Wright uses to buttress her 1080 sales pitch reveals both tui and bellbirds are actually expanding

their range across New Zealand and are not classified as threatened to any degree whatsoever. She warns of "loss or decline" of these seed-dispersing species and "cascading ecological changes in native forests" but the hard published data shows the exact opposite trend for these species. It appears Wright has not read her own sources. Furthermore, much of the so-called "science" and "research" upon which the PCE bases her opinions, has been produced by individuals with direct or indirect financial and career relationships to DOC, tainting their findings with the potential for bias. Readers searching the report for any new evidence to support her wacky conclusions find it's simply not there.

"Despite growing scientific opinion opposed to current 1080 policy, Wright ducks the issue, stating there simply are no good arguments against. She makes an absurd claim that 1080 "scores surprisingly well" on humaneness. She ignores well-documented, disastrous explosions in rat populations after 1080 drops. She fails to seriously address rural community concerns. The report is astounding in its failure to acknowledge well-established dangers of 1080. Even the 2007 ERMA report concluded that the effect on non-target animals exposed to 1080 is significantly adverse. A 2007 Landcare Research summary of 1080 possum and rat control warns of "negative long-terms consequences for robins and ground invertebrates." Wright's report flies in the face of recommendations by the Nature Conservation Council and distinguished former PCE Helen Hughes.

As seen from popular destinations like the Coromandel, Wright is a one-woman wrecking crew for the multi-billion dollar tourism industry, as disillusioned tourists increasingly attack New Zealand's fraudulent green branding. Export industries from shellfish to timber to fur to meat face potential catastrophic losses as well. But the PCE report fails to figure that in. Opposition to 1080 continues to mount. Regional councils and DOC are under increasing pressure from an informed public. Despite a born-again pitch from PCE Jan Wright, the tide of public opinion can't be stemmed. Decades of 1080 drops with no net ecosystem benefit have simply poisoned the well.'[121]

Meanwhile in October the *Mana Party Policy Statement* includes the following goals:

* Ban the use of 1080 poison and invest in alternative methods (and employment opportunities) to control the spread of tuberculosis by pests and rodents.
* Ban the growing and experimentation of GE and GM crops and stock in Aotearoa to protect the whakapapa of the food chain and indigenous plants and animals. We support GE-free, nano technology-free, pesticide and chemical-free food production.

* Promote and resource organic food production, including hua parakore foods (tikanga Māori system of food production), and extend current funding for the establishment of māra kai by whānau, marae, and communities.

2012: Local Landowners Unite, Northland's Possum Project, EW Withdraws Funding, CCCB Valiant Work

He manga wai koia kia kore e whitikia
It is a big river indeed that cannot be crossed

In October John Veysey chronicles the relentless, invasive strategies of Regional Council. "Last month (Sept 19) local landowners received a letter from Peter Russell of Waikato Regional Council telling us he was coming onto our land to get our possum numbers down below 5%. All the work will be done by contractors, he says. Council has budget approval for possum control to cover the entire area. This may not all need to be done. Certain properties may already be below the required 5%...Maybe you have already received a visit and been told that if you opt for poison in bait-stations it will be free and if you opt for trapping it will cost you extra. There is no reason for this. In 2007/08 the trapping in our hills cost less than the bait-stations and was more effective and long lasting. Trapping took place in the very inaccessible parts of the Matawai valley. If you have already been conned into agreeing to poison-filled bait-stations on your land and wish to change your decision to trapping only on your land you may do so. Why Regional Council should be so determined to spread poison on our hills is not understood. What is understood is that it is up to all local landowners to stand up against bait stations and insist upon trapping. If all stand together there is no reason why we cannot keep poison out of our hills. If you want any help or advice please get in touch." This is the beginning of a successful campaign to end a ratepayer funded EW 1080 drop but when the option to trap the area is raised EW funds dry up.

Hands-on possum control for students in the farming paper, *Rural North* documents the inspirational story of Enviroschools Northland Regional Council (NRC) coordinator, Susan Karels, who works with DOC and the local possum industry to set up training for more than 80 Northland students to gain qualifications in trapping, fur and pelt recovery through NRC's "Project

Possum". Cantrain's Geoff Allinson runs and designs the courses for participating students who can potentially earn NCEA Level 2 and 3 credits. Initially 81 students from more than a dozen schools jumped at the chance, mostly from Year 11 to Year 13. They learn the biology of possums, how to use different traps, how to pluck, skin and to prepare fur and skins for sale. Apparently a similar initiative with the same name has been proposed in the Manawatu to provide opportunities for young people to help them stay in the area once they leave school. Vision Manawatu's economic development manager Mark Maxwell "said the market, currently valued at $120 million, is forecasted to grow by 300% over the next five years if supply remains available. Revenue from fur sales will build a sustainable fund for future project expenses and course graduates will be provided with the opportunity to run their own businesses...It's an exciting initiative for both youth and industry."[122] Attempts to initiate a similar scheme with WRC meet solid resistance as there remains an aversion to considering possums as a resource. By 2015 staff opposing such an idea have either been made redundant or left WRC so residents on the Coromandel imagine bush skills may yet find support in their region. But no, 2016 arrives and there is nothing to show but an unsupported scoping report.[123] Wonder why? New staff just happen to be ex-DOC employees!

In May John Veysey and Reihana Robinson are invited to speak at the Coromandel Colville Community Board courtesy of the Chair John Walker, soon to be fittingly honoured in the Queens Birthday list. Regional council employees travelling from Hamilton and Whitianga discover, much to their evident consternation, they must actually listen to local input. Trialing trapping for industry purposes is the goal for the local community.

The brief cycle of aerial 1080 drops repeated every three to five years is "not economic" as noted in research summarised in the June issue of *Kararehe Kino Vertebrate Pest Research* by Chris Jones. According to this study, all it takes is a subsidy of $13.40 per ha and all of the Coromandel could be trapped. Jones writes "Aerial control does not deliver any socio-economic benefits to local communities, whereas a harvest industry could provide secure long-term employment where it is most needed and support local communities' kaitiakitanga (traditional guardianship/duty of care) of their forest environment."

Local councilor Tony Brljevich is the TCDC representative on the community board and he subsequently takes the request for support for trapping in the Coromandel/Colville Board area to the regional council's Coromandel Catchment sub-committee as he is TCDC representative on that subcommittee also. "Carcasses are being exported to Taiwan, Hong Kong and Malaysia, where the meat is being promoted as a healthy, low-cholesterol dish and pies and pate are produced commercially at Pukekura. Local trappers are already resolving most of the issues around possum control in the Manaia block and this needs to be encouraged, he says. If the WRC goes ahead with its programmed possum control of this area this industry will relocate and an opportunity to save valuable ratepayer dollars and create a sustainable industry will be lost. The budget for the trapping trial would only require sufficient funds to allow for monitoring, some training and possibly some traps and a discretionary fund for a subsidy if required, Mr Brljevich says."[124] Brljevich together with the other members of the CCCB is a force for good in the face of ongoing Regional Council opposition. How will regional council respond? Will they support locals? Will they ignore locals? Of course it doesn't take long for WRC to rip out any potential support. On July 12 *Peninsula Post* Tony Brljevich asks "regional council's Pest Management Committee to defer expenditure on the Manaia block for one to two years to allow the Coromandel community to trial a mixture of commercial and private trapping…We're concerned if the WRC goes ahead with the programmed possum control of the area then the industry will relocate. The opportunity for a sustainable industry will be lost here."

Radio New Zealand announces on 24th July, "Waikato Regional Council says it has not yet made a decision on any proposal for possum control on the north west Coromandel Peninsula. The Coromandel Colville Community Board and the Thames Coromandel District Council are against using residual poison and are instead supporting a locally based possum trapping industry. Earlier this year, Waikato Regional Council sought submissions from suitably experienced operators about undertaking possum control in the northwest Coromandel Peninsula. The Colville-Coromandel Community Board has put forward a proposal to the council to allow the community to trial a mixture of commercial and private possum trapping. The council says it has received a range of submissions and each is being assessed ahead of a staff report being prepared for the next regional pest management committee meeting in August. The council says it will consider the Colville-Coromandel Community Board's proposal, but it's inappropriate to comment on individual submissions."

Fortuitously on July 19 the *Peninsula Post* follows up on the June *Kararehe Kino* research with a story entitled *New study says possum trapping could be effective in some locations if it was subsidized*. Chris Jones from Landcare Research who together with a group of scientists including Graham Nugent "set out to find out whether possum fur harvesters could make a living and protect forest biodiversity…Working with Tuhoe harvesters around Ruatahuna, researchers found that the density and frequency of trapping needed to protect forest habitat made it uneconomic for a harvester. 'Either there would need to be some sort of subsidy, or trappers would have to lower their expectations in income' Mr. Jones says."

2012: Regional Council May
Pull out of Some Possum Control

"After all is said and done, more is said than done."

Aesop

The *Peninsula Press* runs stories in two September papers on the decision by WRC to withdraw from part of the Coromandel. It doesn't take long to discover WRC's strategy. Rather than support local initiatives to hunt, trap and use cyanide, they choose to opt out and come back in a few years to test the results. For three years Regional Council is to pull out of an area south of Coromandel. Council is abandoning possum control because "there's too much opposition to the most cost-effective option of 1080." The $115,000 allocated for the job, instead of going to support local trappers or hunters or licensed cyanide users, will be allotted to "support DOC operations in the southern Manaia/Kereta regions."

The local community board hoped to trial harvesting fur and meat but the "council doesn't **believe** this will be effective and is unwilling to subsidize it. The community wanted fur and meat harvesters. We don't **think** that will achieve the desired outcome in biodiversity protection, Mr Simmons said." [emphasis added]. Simmons, WRC's Group Manager Biosecurity-Heritage continues, "However the Community Board is free to continue with the trapping trial" without any regional council funds of course. Over $100,000 is siphoned off to trap a much smaller area of Māori land in the Kereta block and Tihiouou near DOC poison action.

The *Peninsula Press* September 6 issue headlines with a question: *Areas of Coromandel to be poison free?* There follows an in-depth story explaining how $500,000 was spent in the same area in 2007—presumably Peninsula Project monies. EW's John Simmons pontificates: "For the next few years, **there will be no council spending on possum control in this area.** This means no guaranteed results and no effort to control the rats, stoats and ferrets that also plague our forests." [emphasis added]

UCLA comments on the pyrrhic victory given how little is known about long-term effects of poisons in the environment. On

September 13 *Peninsula Post* declares WRC "is set to pull out of possum control in an area south of Coromandel town for the next three years." $115,000 allocated for the original poison work is handed to a specific set of landowners adjacent to the DOC poison block. And the community better watch out because Big Brother is coming in 2015 to count those possums. (It will not be Mr Peter Russell doing the counting because there appears to be a minor regime change in WRC's poison department, and along with John Simmons, Kevin Collins and Dave Hodges, Peter Russell is no longer on the payroll. But who can tell? Is it out of the frying pan into the fire with new employees straight from DOC?)

2013: Moehau in the Firing Line
Along with the Poison-Addled 309

"It is impractical to try to restore ecosystems to some 'rightful' historical state," a group of American researchers wrote a few years ago, in Nature. "We must embrace the fact of 'novel ecosystems' and incorporate many alien species into management plans, rather than try to achieve the often impossible goal of eradicating them"… Kiwis refuse to "embrace" novel ecosystems.

Elizabeth Kolbert, December 2014 *The New Yorker*

In the winter of 2013 DOC proposes to drop poison over the hills between the 309 and the Tapu/Coroglen roads and from empyrean heights over Moehau mountain. DOC pays for full-page colour ads in two local newspapers (November 2012) advertising their political agenda to dump poison where it has never been dumped before—on Moehau. The advertisements do not use the commonly referenced batch number (1080) to identify the poison, just the chemical name sodium fluoroacetate perhaps in an effort to defuse and distract? Locals want to know why there is a need to dump 1080 toxin after years of successful work using traps and ground-based poison on the mountain. A question that remains unanswered throughout the campaign. There has been no possum or rat monitoring at this stage, in readiness for this poison dump. Readers are blithely told that "this method has been chosen as it is the most effective and cost efficient method when used over extensive and rugged terrain and has the additional benefit of reducing both ship rat and possum numbers to a very low level at the same time."

Those in the community who continue to claim 1080 toxin is non-residual will be alarmed to read that DOC believes "through poisoning rats we also indirectly poison stoats." By the time the next full page ads (April 19, 2013) are published to update the readership, DOC appear to have pulled back from dumping toxin adjacent to one of the campgrounds and the DOC road leading to the campground, although the walking track north of Stony Bay is still to be liberally doused.

By the time these full-page ads appear DOC revises its map and blandly notes, "As a result of positive discussions with landowners the operational area now includes some additional areas of private land." Not an outright lie, just a blurring of the lines. The landowners have indeed agreed to add their land to the mix—approximately 700 ha of privately owned MIST Trust land but, and this is not disclosed to the newspaper readers, the poison of choice is not the inhumane poison 1080, it is cyanide. Thia information is affixed to a DOC letter sent to landowners on May 6, 2013.

The cost-effectiveness of toxin 1080 is highlighted in the initial advertisement yet further funds have materialised to cover cyanide and it is to be used on private landnot even. Costs also cover a mailout to landowners around Port Charles and up the West Coast—a colour brochure detailing, "what has been decided so far."

The effects of a 1080 operation on Moehau are potentially devastating—affecting water, indigenous and exotic flora and fauna, livestock and livelihoods. This would not be a one-off drop. Aerial toxin 1080 drops must be repeated at three-yearly intervals, in part due to exploding rat populations and possum reinvasions. And the DOC Hauraki office has spent tens of thousands of taxpayer dollars supporting the reintroduction of the insect-eating north island robin right on Moehau. As previously noted, robin populations are decimated by 1080 operations. The strong opposition against the planned 1080 drops includes pickets at popular tourist spots like Cathedral Cove. There is no justification to change strategies and dump poison on Moehau. Either DOC's new Hauraki Area Manager and its even newer Pest Programme manager, Brigitte Maier, have not reviewed the history of community opposition or have purposely adopted an aggressive and provocative new stance. UCLA strongly opposes any plans for the use of 1080 on Moehau and urges DOC to immediately cancel any such plan. A 2009 DOC report presented to the Coromandel community meeting, confirms hunting and trapping as being less expensive and more effective than 1080 poisoning, even in difficult terrain.

2013: What is to be Done?

"A person with a clear heart and an open mind can experience wilderness anywhere on earth."

Gary Snyder

Back in May 2007, shortly after the controversial ERMA 1080 re-assessment, Coromandel residents marched, hundreds strong, in the streets and petitioned DOC against planned 1080 drops on the Upper Peninsula. DOC management listened and the operations were cancelled. The very next month, DOC consultant Wren Green addressed the Forest and Bird AGM on the problem of public "concerns about 1080". Noting recent events, Green's advice to 1080 backers was simple—**"initiatives need to be created—starting in Coromandel"** [emphasis added]. So here we see the origin of a grudge campaign against the Coromandel now revealing itself in all its glory with a 2013 planned toxin assault on our sacred mountain Of course the poison promoters have not been idle in the interregnum. The intervening years have snared hard-earned ratepayer and taxpayer dollars to appease so-called environment clubs who agree to be 'neutral' on poison 1080. No one begrudges funds spent on shared community resources such as possum plucking machines or traps or even firearm and cyanide licenses, but PR? Just go to the charities website to see the financials for the wee eco-group MEG to discover how the money wheel spins.

On February 22, 2013 a formal complaint is sent to DOC asking that their proposal to dump toxin 1080 over Moehau be indefinitely suspended. The Waikato conservator Greg Martin receives the complaint. Residents state the bush is healthy, there is no justification for such a drastic change in policy and residents have concerns including hopper dust, water supplies, honey production, loss of organic status, long-term effects on non-target species and tourism. DOC refuses to budge. UCLA asks the Coromandel Colville Community Board to urgently request a meeting with the DOC Hauraki Area Manager and pest control staff to discuss alternatives to the announced aerial 1080 on Moehau and Manaia and to demand DOC suspend plans for the May aerial poison drop pending an acceptable agreement. The CCCB is on record supporting hunting, trapping and cyanide but in light of this new development it would be supportive of the community for the Board to re-state their implacable opposition to the Moehau and Manaia 1080 drops.

International visitors have responded on their blogs, twitter and facebook accounts, recording their outrage on discovering the planned dumping of toxin 1080 onto the peninsula's wild places and into the water supplies of many townships including Whitianga. They learn there is no evidence to show aerial 1080 is necessary for Te Moehau — tracks exist all over the mountain and have been put to good use over the past decades. This mountain is completely accessible — it is not a Sunday walk in some areas but as all trappers know, possums come to the bait. The only extant DOC Field Reports state the canopy is in great condition as recently as 2005. Nothing has changed — if anything the bird life and forest have improved. "The forest canopy at Moehau, including the species most vulnerable to and preferred by possums, is in excellent condition" according to Pim de Monchy's 2000 and 2005 Field Reports.

Bronwyn Eaton-Matheson from the Moehau Community in Sandy Bay calls to offer active support. She draws up a petition and gathers more than 400 names. Over 70 signatories reside either full-time or part-time around Moehau. They are all opposed to toxin 1080. The grim reality of the ruthless DOC machine strikes home as all attempts to communicate the community's opposition are spurned. An invitation for DOC personnel to receive the petition in Port Charles/Sandy Bay is initially agreed to, then cancelled. Letters, local community board resolutions, and press releases are ignored. This passive-aggressive DOC behaviour is the *modus operandi* for DOC in rural Coromandel. Long-time conservationist, farmer and 1080 opponent Ross Gardner, who works the Te Hope Valley adjacent to DOC land, speaks to a number of journalists exposing the distressing truth of a Department of so-called Conservation that no longer employs qualified bush people and wants an easy fix called toxin 1080. Gardner also accompanies a Te Arawa Lakes Trust visit to Moehau. Professor Peter Tapsell is among the party and he agrees to write a letter to the Minister of Conservation (2 April) opposing the drop. The letter is signed by Trust chair, Mr Toby Curtis: "…during a recent ascent and descent (of Mt Moehau) we were pleased to note no apparent sign (traps, baits, nests or tree damage) of any opossum, stoat, cat or weasel activity within the reserve, nor beyond in the surrounding DOC managed forest, reaching down to the coastal farmlands of the Ward family…We are therefore surprised to hear that DOC is planning an aerial drop of 1080 poison very soon that will spread across the whole Moehau reserve when there is no apparent reason…(we) urge the Crown to cancel its upcoming 1080 poison drop on the forest of Te Moehau o Tamatekapua and direct DOC's attention to establishing exactly where the predators are currently active and target them there." So much for 2007 DOC claim their poison work is based on a 20-year-ago "blessing" from tangata whenua

DOC can't even keep their story straight about their objectives and the problem. Is it rats and mice and pigs? Is it stoats? Is it canopy collapse? Northern rata, robin or kiwi survival? Reports confirm kiwi, robin and the canopy are all doing well. With no recent independent monitoring DOC's confused goals mean they will never be held accountable for any results when the operation fails, as it inevitably will. DOC's confrontational behaviour appears geared to break the back of community opposition to aerial 1080, a dream of the Hauraki office for decades. Former Area Manager John Gaukrodger was a definite 1080 promoter through the years but he interacted with the community and altered course and adopted a ground-based pest control strategy on Moehau. The cynics among us hear tales of behind-the-scenes communication battles aimed at convincing different parties through those long years, culminating in picnic lunches and free helicopter rides as well as funding for traps closer to home—anything to gain approval from affected parties. DOC publications claim the Hauraki Māori Trust Board deals to all iwi issues on the Coromandel. In contrast, new Manager Melissa King-Howell is keeping a low profile. She dished the responsibility for fronting the 1080drop to those further down the totem pole. King-Howell and the Hauraki DOC office thumb their noses at local communities. There is no legitimate consultation. DOC is *telling* locals what they plan to do. They will not listen to any opposition and refuse to consider alternatives that are safer, cheaper and entirely doable. They ignore the position of the Coromandel/Colville Community Board that has voted twice to support hunting and trapping and cyanide.

In spite of their inability to listen to our local community the erstwhile Director-General of DOC, Alistair Morrison is contacted. His assistant received the following email and forwarded it to the D-G. "...we live in a flawed paradise where government bodies refuse to listen to our communities. Of real concern is DOC ignoring iwi and our local community. Te Arawa Lakes Trust have written to Nick Smith Minister of Conservation urging the cancellation of this 1080 toxin drop. Victor McLean has authority from his "kaumatua and kuia to stand firm, NO 1080 in our Rohe" on behalf of Ngati Tamatera Kennedy Bay, Kuaotunu. I have been given responsibility to present Te Uringahu o Ngati Maru, Ngati Hei and Ngati Huarere opposition to an aerial drop of toxin 1080 on Moehau. The Upper Coromandel Landcare Association, for which I am the spokesperson, represents the tribe of Moehau dwellers who are in Sandy Bay, Port Charles and down the western coast who oppose this drop of toxin 1080. 74 locals and abutters have signed a petition opposing this drop. The mountain has been successfully trapped and hunted and baited for the past 13 years. Perhaps DOC does not know that a certified organic bee keeper must face moving over 500 hives, or how closing the mountain for eight months will have a negative impact on the tourist businesses that operate out of Coromandel taking visitors up to the tracks. Perhaps DOC does not realise that farmers take their waters from mountain streams and have offered no alternative water supplies. Our Thames-Coromandel District Council is opposed to aerial drops of 1080. DOC has ignored our petitions and keeps pushing poison. DOC is economical with the truth—they have told iwi they will accept alternative pest control on Moehau if it can be shown to work! Trapping and bait stations have been working for 13 years. DOC's Pim de Monchy's last field report in 2005 remarked on bush health. If DOC has no employees who can work on Te Moehau, let others in our community take over. Your budget of tens of thousands of dollars could pay trappers instead of Skyworks Helicopter Ltd. DOC is overstepping the line. Should they ignore iwi, the damage to the mauri of this mountain will be on their heads. Who does this mountain belong to? Who belongs to this mountain? We all respect DOC workers who know how to handle a rifle, trap, cut tracks, build huts and do the hard yards. If Moehau is the jewel in the crown of DOC land in the Waikato then it behoves DOC to put resources into Moehau. You may find it of interest that one of your employees on the Coromandel, in response to hearing of Nugent's rat study concerning the 5-fold bounce back of rats within 12 months of a 1080 drop said "all animals killed bounce back within three months." The people who live around Te Moehau love the mountain. No one wants it carpet-bombed with 1080.

The D-G responds: Reihana, I have had your email requesting a meeting before I go on leave next week. I have read your email and thank you for it. I do feel I should meet with people who share an interest in conservation outcomes and work hard in their communities to achieve them. But on some issues where discussion has taken place over many years and no resolution is reached, there does come a point where there is little point in continuing. The department's use of 1080 is such an issue. I respect your right to hold a contrary view, but I do not think any amount of talking will help us reach agreement and we need to just respectfully agree to disagree. I base that on the fact that this issue has been thoroughly tested independently by the panel set up to do that, and again by the Parliamentary Commissioner for the Environment. Neither supports your fundamental view, though recommendations for how we operate have been made and taken in to account. Notwithstanding that, you maintain your opposition to 1080, as of course you are entitled to do. I do not think a meeting between us will have any impact on either your opposition or my continued support for using 1080. Kind regards, Al Morrison

Eaton-Matheson's petition, signed by more than 70 Moehau locals and hundreds of visitors who oppose the expensive and ineffective and unsafe toxin 1080 drops on Moehau, is handed to the DOC office in Thames on March 4 after an invitation to meet in Port Charles is declined. DOC is asked to suspend its plans to proceed with the announced May-June 1080 drops and to organize public meetings in Coromandel town and Colville to reach consensus and to discuss alternative acceptable strategies.

2013: John Veysey on Water, Industrial Chemical Company Bayer AGb Bond with DOC to Rob Kiwi

Nature never deceives us; it is we who deceive ourselves

Jean-Jacques Rousseau

In March John Veysey writes "The results of the 1080 poisoning in Whenuakite related in the last *Chronicle* raise many concerns for everyone living near to the coming 1080 drops over Papakai, Manaia and Moehau. The Whenuakite block has received three aerial 1080 drops in the space of 5 years. In terms of 1080 absorption Whenuakite has been saturated. At a community meeting at Manaia recently we were reminded of the known dangers of 1080…Once the 1080 poison has been released into the environment it may spread through every waterway, every living creature and every living plant. You may not eat or drink or touch it without some kind of risk. DOC only tests for parts per million. DOC has no interest in diluted doses that do not kill you straight away. Parts per million can kill rather quickly but the long-term 1080 damage is being done by parts per billion and even parts per trillion.

"The only part of a 1080 poison drop that is of interest to the Ministry of Health is the poisoned water. Under every aerial 1080 drop poisoned baits land directly into stream waters. There is a rush of poison downstream within an hour or two of the baits landing in the water. Every water sample taken within 4 hours has tested positive for 1080. ALL the water samples that tested over the legal limit for 1080 were taken within the first four hours. The MOH switch off all drinking uptakes until the poison has washed away and the water is "clear" again and presumably, the baits in the streams no longer have any poison in them. The MOH then take clear water samples and open up the drinking taps again after three days have passed. Many more baits, land in trees or on the forest floor. Dead bodies may lie around everywhere but the trusty wild pig is a marvellous vacuum cleaner and within a couple of days pig bodies are all you can find. We all remember how seven fully-grown boars were found dead in a tiny block of privately owned bush after one of those Whenuakite drops. If seven mature males were killed in such a small area it is clear that over the entire drop area, scores of wild pigs were killed—a long, agonising death which is not pretty to watch."

The chemical industrial giant Bayer AG, major promoter of toxins as well as GE maize is the new corporate partner in what should be a crime—robbing kiwi from the Coromandel to pose with the CEO of Bayer AG Australia for cute publicity shots, then to hijack those same kiwi to Motutapu Island. The kiwi theft was supposed to be from Whenuakite. However the kiwi robbers couldn't find any birds there at all and had to head up to Kuaotunu to achieve their quota, and on the way, destroying family relationships as kiwi are known to be monogamous. DOC's Christine Friis attempts an explanation as to why kiwi were not uplifted from Whenuakite—apparently DOC suffered a "miscommunication" that resulted in members opposing the removal of kiwi.[125] However in 2016 despite numerous attempts it was yet again impossible to locate the desired number of kiwi planned for robbery.[126] Whenuakite conservationists could well be asking where have all the kiwi gone? In a hail of 1080, known to ravage young kiwi?

Later in May the *Peninsula Press* reprints a DOC promo that reports 1500 kiwi living on the peninsula so now DOC need to move lots to Motutapu to "save them". So far there are seven kiwi on the island and the goal is to transplant 40. If kiwi screech nearby locals need to keep quiet because lickety-split DOC robbers will be on the doorstep hunting down innocent birds for translocation programmes.

The Waikato Biodiversity Forum Circus

"Nonconformity is the highest evolutionary attainment of social animals."

Aldo Leopold

A Waikato Biodiversity Forum (WBF) meeting is planned for April in Colville. Many in the community look forward to discussing alternatives to the toxin 1080 drop on Moehau. After local conservationists known to oppose the use of toxin 1080 register to attend, the meeting is unceremoniously cancelled. Local rates contribute to the salary of the biodiversity forum organiser Moira Cursey, who seems to brazenly lie in response to local residents querying why the event was cancelled. She states it was due to insufficient interest. Email communications (released via the OIA) between the WBF and staff of DOC, WRC, and local contractors reveal how the public was misled as to the real reason for cancellation of the one-day workshop. Both DOC and WRC staff were aware of this fabrication at the time, so UCLA asks Waikato Regional Council and all Waikato district councils to withdraw financial support for the biodiversity forum. Cursey's email messages disclose her real concern was the prospect of discussing aerial 1080 use on Moehau. Why one would be afraid of discussing wild animal control at a biodiversity meeting boggles the mind. An email from Cursey to DOC, WRC and the Moehau Environment Group sent well before the registration deadline named several individual participants and read, " I don't want the day to cover any 1080 debate with <a resident> and will shut this cown if she tries to use the day for this agenda."

Later that day, Cursey emails DOC to say she had talked with "everyone involved" and that "all have concerns". The email states she had decided to simply cancel the workshop entirely, despite an offer of "support" from the DOC Hauraki area manager. Cursey added the cancellation "feels very comfortable for me". The next morning, Cursey messaged insiders that her public excuse for the cancellation would be "lack of community groups and landowners registered".

The email disclosures are extremely troubling because here is a lobby group, publicly funded by regional and district ratepayers, displaying anything but honesty, transparency, and integrity. Worse still, neither DOC nor regional council staff uttered a peep about the deception. With release of these emails, the Waikato Biodiversity Forum loses all credibility. The cutoff of ratepayer funding should be a no-brainer. As for DOC and WRC, they have a lot of explaining to do. Their collusion in silencing any discussion of wild animal control options is very worrisome — if not frightening.

NZ Police Join the DOC 1080 Team

*"When good people in any country cease their vigilance
and struggle, then evil men prevail."*

Pearl S. Buck

Hamilton News publishes the April 2013 *Robinson Report.*
"Chilling conservationists across the Waikato, the Department of
Conservation is now working hand in glove with the New Zealand
Police in a coordinated effort to quell opposition in advance of
controversial possum control operations underway this month. As
a result of ongoing information gathering by police and the Hauraki
DOC office in Thames, officers last week contacted by phone a list
of individuals known to oppose aerial 1080 with a stern warning
not to engage in illegal activity in relation to this month's drops on
the Moehau Range and further south on the peninsula.

The calls come out of the blue. Those contacted on instructions
from police Senior Sergeant Graham Shields include a 70-year-
old retired medical doctor and his PhD wife, who co-authored an
extensive statistical review of DOC "research" on the topic of aerial
1080 and related environmental outcomes. Their review is highly
critical of the quality and credibility of DOC "science" on the
subject. Others contacted by police included the Robinsons, who
have written critically on DOC toxin policy in several publications
and have addressed meetings urging district council intervention.

Although police refused to divulge how many individuals,
or who, were on their warning list, the Robinsons confirmed at
least one other person contacted by phone and another visited at
home by police. Several more are understood to have received the
warnings. Which agency initiated the warning call list and what
criteria were used to compile it remains fuzzy. So far, opposition
to 1080 alone seems to have attracted police attention. Police insist
the calls were not made at the request of DOC. A police spokesman
in Thames said the calls were merely a standard effort to prevent
"civil unrest", "maintain law and order", and keep people from
"getting too emotive".

According to DOC Hauraki manager Melissa King-Howell, her office did not request specific calls be made. But King-Howell did admit her office and local police "share intel" regularly. Explaining "intel", she said her office maintains comprehensive files and records of "everything" relating to its 1080 operations, from contacts with the public, to rumours, newspaper articles, letters to the editor, and information on community anti-1080 meetings. She explains DOC has received threats in the past and, as a result, works very closely with police now. King-Howell said she could not explain why particular individuals received police warnings. Another DOC spokesperson confirmed names of people who "could pose a risk" are passed to police. Examples she offered were those who had made threats or received restraining orders.

But for those who received police warnings for no apparent reason, it is simply harassment and intimidation based on their political views and vocal opposition to DOC's aerial 1080 plan. They find no other explanation—no police scrapes other than traffic tickets, no restraining orders or threats of violence —and no reason to be singled out by police. Since police say the warnings list was compiled to help "prevent violence", one could conclude that, according to DOC-Police "shared intel", those called are considered potentially violent or otherwise posing a substantial risk. And that does not sit well with retired physicians or columnists.

Police insist the calls were not meant to intimidate. But winding up on a police list and getting a personal warning call is serious business for anyone on the receiving end. And well it should be. The assumption is that, by making it onto that warning list, one is considered (by DOC or police) as more likely than the next person to commit a crime, break the law, or threaten public safety. If not, everyone in the phone book would be called.

With protests against mining on the Coromandel ongoing and likely to intensify given present government policy, the question arises whether NZ Police are compiling other such lists of those they consider potential "risks" and "threats" and whether individuals outspoken on other contentious public issues will also be targeted. According to Sgt. Shields, the police respect absolutely the right to protest. They are just trying to avoid confrontation and illegality, he said.

But for Coromandel residents active in the struggle to protect native biodiversity and ecosystems without the damage and dangers of aerial toxin 1080, their peninsula is feeling less and less like a relaxing holiday destination. After last week's targeted police warning calls, it's feeling more like the Urewera.[127]

Bee survival, Colville with Clyde Graf
and Occupy Moehau Statement

"The common ground is that we are all passionate about the health of our precious forests."

Stephanie McKee, May 2013

DOC will drop one to three kilos of poisoned bait for each hectare over 14,707 hectares of Moehau, Papakai and Manaia forests. Graeme and Julie Sturgeon write: *Does anyone care for our own bees?* "For without them we are lost… The EU has just placed a two-year ban on bee-killing pesticides. (1080 is a broad-spectrum pesticide/insecticide and it is fatal to bees and other insects, Meads.)[128] In 2008 we monitored and filmed the aftermath of the aerial 1080drop in the Kauaeranga River. We noted the poisoned pellets not only were present in the Kauaeranga River (Thames Water Supply) in quantity, but they had been sown right across a significant number of beehives in the area. These cereal baits are made up of about 20% sugar so they were literally crawling with bees. This careless broadcasting of a deadly poison wrapped in an attractive food is an unsavoury practice in more ways than one. Penny Fisher (Landcare Research) in a paper notes that in Dec 2002 and Jan 2003 three honeycomb samples tested from the Taumaranui area after the Tongariro aerial drop were found to contain 1080 residues. This dangerous practice is a sure way of destroying our export base when this poison is found in our products. One of our organic beekeepers on the Northern tip of the Coromandel is faced with an immense problem from the 1080 aerial drop due this month. What does he do with his five hundred hives? If any of his hives are within 3km of a 1080 drop his honey does not meet the organic qualities required for importation in many countries. Not only is this a logistics nightmare to move all the hives but also his bees will probably go hungry because there arejust not that many good places left on the Coromandel for bees. Many of the wild hives in our forest will not survive this attack on them by the Department Of Conservation."[129] Research by Notman [130] and Hutchison [131] confirm insects are at risk.

The local papers run stories in May including a reminder the Coromandel/Colville Community Board says there is "no need" for toxin 1080 and that "the community don't want it, residents don't want it and iwi don't want it, but DOC aren't listening to their constituents." Coromandel District Councillor, Tony Brljevich is quoted "I firmly believe that DOC management have the discretion to employ safer methods of possum control and are hiding behind national policy which allows aerial 1080 as an excuse to not look at other ways." At this point DOC's Rebecca Duffin responds to Brljevich's OIA request for "'all the correspondence between the Hauraki Maori Trust Board regarding the operations at Moehau and Manaia' and the amended request of 'only the correspondence from the Hauraki Maori Trust Board that approved the 1080 drop on Moehau…'

It reads as a farce. "No formal approval from the Hauraki Maori Trust Board was required therefore there is no information that falls within the grounds of the narrowed request." So the Hauraki Māori Trust Board (HMTB) has written not a word to approve the poison drop and Duffin continues, "in terms of your wider request the correspondence to Iwi regarding the 1080 operations comprises of approximately 100 emails. On these grounds I am refusing your request under sections 18 e (that the document alleged to contain the information requested does not exist) and 18 f (that the information requested cannot be made available without substantial collation and research) of the Official information Act (1982)." So the first document does not exist, yet HMTB is touted (in official publications) as DOC's number one 'go to' for poison negotiations as cited in minutes received by UCLA from the Ombudsman where it states "In Hauraki Area, DOC consults with the Hauraki Māori Trust Board and in Maniapoto, the Maniapoto Māori Trust Board."

Over 50 residents of northern Coromandel attend a meeting at the Colville hall organized by music teacher, gardener, poet and conservationist Stephanie McKee of Karuna Falls. Clyde Graf is the invited speaker. One of the Graf brother's documentaries on poison operations is viewed. The well-crafted *Moehau Declaration* is presented to the meeting who vote to support local iwi opposition and to ask DOC to stop the drop. **Occupy Moehau statement** *We all support healthy and humane wild animal policy appropriate for our peninsula. But DOC ignores local community concerns, refuses* *to train hunters or employ trappers long-term or use the only humane toxin, cyanide. DOC chooses poison 1080 that poisons all wildlife. Since 1987 DOC have been losing highly skilled staff who know and love the bush and now DOC is a third-rate tourist business, contracting out and privatizing animal control to helicopter companies who drop poison with no science to prove eco-system benefit. The Occupy Moehau protest is a huge effort involving people from all over the peninsula who say "If the Coromandel is too precious to mine it is too precious to poison."*

Residents Reject 1080 Drop, Dr Beasley's Medical Research

Look deep into nature, and then you will understand everything better

Albert Einstein

The organiser of the Colville meeting, Stephanie McKee, pens a press release (May 3, 2013) noting "There is also concern about risks to the endemic Archey's Frog whose population numbers have plummeted to critical levels in recent years. International and local eco-tourists will be greeted by the red skull and crossbones warning signs on the walking tracks for up to eight months that makes a mockery of our so-called " 100% Pure New Zealand" tourist slogan. If the Department undertook to follow its own guidelines, then there is hope that this issue could be resolved. Maybe with new management at the top, there will be a shift in the culture and an increased willingness to genuinely consult with communities to work out possum control methods that are acceptable to all. After all, the common ground is that we are all passionate about the health of our precious forests."

The headline in the *Hauraki Herald* of May 10, 2013 is an attention grabber: *Protesters plan disruption*. This follows UCLA's correspondence with the Ministry of Health sent on 04 May to Dell Hood and Thomasin Bright concerning the potential public health risk to individuals who will be tramping, camping, surveying and studying on a regular and daily basis throughout the planned aerial 1080 drop on Moehau. There is definite cause for concern with the possibility of ingestion of toxic baits by adults and children if the operation is approved and allowed to proceed with the usual blessing granted by the Waikato District Health Board. UCLA requests the permits requests be denied.

Dr Michael Beasley, of Otago Medical School and the National Centre for Poison, whose 1080 research remained incomplete at the time of the ERMA review into the reassessment of poison 1080, continues to investigate levels of 1080 poison in factory worker's urine and blood. His recent research indicates demonstrable levels of 1080 in urine and a high degree of risk, dependent on level of exposure. Landcare Research is the only facility with the capacity to carry out such tests.[132] Correspondence with Dr Beasley on 28 June 2013 includes results of work carried out in 2009. "The initial work was carried out by Landcare Research, and I was involved in writing it up. Subsequent to the setting of the provisional BEI (which occurred three or four years before the above paper was eventually published), further monitoring of workers in the industry (e.g. by DOC) began to occur. I have not been much involved in this area since 2009. However I understand that DOC, for example, and possibly other organizations, have continued to be involved in monitoring workers (e.g. 1080 in urine tests). Further documents on management of 1080 exposures were developed by these organizations (e.g. DOC), and these may be available to you. I believe that in recent years there has been suitable emphasis on exposure reduction measures, which seem to have been effective, as urine testing has given very low levels of 1080, often below the limit of detection."

Fire on the Mountain is the evocative title published as the *Robinson Report* in the April *Hamilton News*.

"The Department of Conservation is attempting to break the back of New Zealand's anti-1080 movement once and for all—right here in the Waikato on the flanks of iconic Moehau mountain at the northern tip of the Coromandel Peninsula. The catalyst is an extraordinary DOC decision to undertake precedent-setting aerial 1080 operations over 4,500 sloping hectares bordering settlements at Sandy Bay and Port Charles, residences and farms along the coastal Port Jackson Road, popular campgrounds at Stony Bay and Fantail Bay, and the Coromandel Coastal Walkway. Drops are planned for May to June. Aerial 1080 has never been used on this sweeping landscape. Te Moehau is no ordinary mountain. Moehau is the final resting place of Arawa chief Tamatekapua and is held sacred by both iwi and the wider Coromandel community.

"Although DOC manages conservation estate on the mountain, tangata whenua and neighbouring residents take their roles as kaitiaki and guardians just as seriously. For many years successful predator control on Moehau has been managed by trapping and ground baiting utilising an extensive network of established tracks and some hard yakker. DOC now says aerial 1080 is a more efficient way to meet its goals. But the plan happens to mean toxin pellets in the drinking water of neighbouring farmers, threats to rare native frogs and endangered birds, risks to stock, economic losses for the local honey industry, and severe affront to spiritual and cultural values. DOC's Hauraki office has been holding low-key meetings with individual residents and chosen iwi members to meet

minimum "consultation" requirements. It is also spending thousands
of dollars on helicopter overflight rides for "guests" in an attempt win
support for its operational policy shift. Opposition, meanwhile, is fierce
and confrontation looms. More than 70 immediate abutters and local
residents have petitioned DOC to abandon its plan. The Coromandel-
Colville Community Board has registered its opposition, seeking an
urgent meeting with DOC management.

"Now strong iwi opposition to aerial 1080 on Moehau has emerged, as
the situation moves past "simmer". In an April 2 letter to Conservation
Minister Nick Smith (released to the Robinsons), the Te Arawa Lakes
Trust stated it "will take offense to any violation of Te Arawa's wahi tapu"
without its permission. The Trust explicitly "urge the Crown to cancel its
upcoming 1080 poison drop on the forest of Te Moehua o Tamatekapua".
A spokesman for Ngati Tamatera, Kennedy Bay and Kuaotunu, confirmed
his iwi's position – "No 1080 in our Rohe". Representatives of Ngati Hei
and Ngati Huarere and Te Uringahu o Ngati Maru have also confirmed
to the Robinsons their respective iwi opposition to aerial 1080 on Moehau.
Iwi support hunting, trapping and cyanide, widely considered the most
humane toxin.

"Why such a confrontation on the Coromandel now? Back in May 2007,
shortly after the controversial ERMA 1080 reassessment, Coromandel
residents marched hundreds strong in the streets and petitioned DOC
against planned 1080 drops on the upper peninsula. DOC management
listened, the operations were cancelled, and the backdown served as
inspiration to 1080 opponents around New Zealand. The next month,
consultant Wren Green addressed the Forest & Bird AGM on the problem
of public "concerns about 1080". Noting recent events, Green's advice
to 1080 backers was simple — 'initiatives need to be created – starting in
Coromandel'. The unspoken grudge match between DOC and its pesky
opponents on the peninsula was underway.

"After a controversial Coromandel regional councillor known for
vocal advocacy of 1080 was voted out that October, he was handed the
Waikato Conservation Board chairman job (which he holds today). Then
DOC's Hauraki area manager in Thames was replaced by a Hamilton-
based administrator. It seems the former had made the fatal mistake of
occasionally listening to the community and respecting its wishes. In
contrast, his replacement has kept a low profile and avoided community
engagement, even as controversy smolders. Responding to Coromandel
community concerns from his perch in Hamilton recently, Waikato
Conservator Greg Martin insisted the Moehau 1080 operation "will not be
cancelled". DOC's top man, Al Morrison, last week refused a meeting in
Wellington to discuss the drop with a Moehau community representative.
Hauraki area DOC indicate the decision to press on with the Moehau drop
is, in fact, coming from Hamilton and Wellington.

"In the face of growing opposition, DOC management could still stop
the drop and instead work with iwi and neighbours on a mountain pest

strategy acceptable to all. If the operation goes ahead, potential harm to the department itself could be far-reaching and costly, for many years to come.'

Much like drone operators, DOC officials are sending in the toxin aircraft from remote offices in Thames and Hamilton and insulating themselves from the people and the collateral damage to non-target species and our tourist economy."

Living in Hope

Naku te rourou nau te rourou ka ora ai te iwi
With your basket and my basket the people will live

Despite DOC's insistence the poison drop will proceed, residents remain hopeful an agreement could be reached to continue ground-based control. Failing that, occupation of the mountain has been mooted. A growing number of people feel a permanent rotating presence inside the mountain toxin drop zone may be the best way of protecting native species, fragile ecosystems, and the health of our community against any aerial operation.

Port Charles residents have taken DOC conservator Greg Martin to task over his point blank refusal to reconsider the operation.

Dr Pat Whiting-OKeefe said people were extremely concerned about the planned poison drop. "We own a farm and a residential property in Port Charles at the foot of Moehau and we and our neighbours are wholly and vehemently opposed to DOC's aerial 1080 drop here and also the one that will take place on the portion of the Coromandel that includes the 309 Road." In a letter to Greg Martin Pat and Quinn Whiting-O'Keefe wrote, "We run cattle and have a dog, both of which are very susceptible to monofluoroacetate (1080). Moreover and more importantly, by dropping food laced with 1080, a universal extremely toxic poison into the entire ecosystem, you are in effect indiscriminately scattering poisoned food for all the animals in our ecosystem to consume. Hence you will kill not only rats and possums but many of the native species as well. Even carnivores will be affected when they consume poisoned carcasses. These effects have been amply documented in numerous published research studies most of which were sponsored by DOC." Responding to their concerns, Greg Martin made reference to the Parliamentary Commissioner for the Environment's "exhaustive" 2011 report on the use of 1080. He said Dr Wright "reached her conclusions, and her recommendation for the continued use of 1080 (where appropriate) only after a thorough study of the mountain of scientific material and research that is available."

Dr Pat Whiting-OKeefe, a California Institute of Technology qualified PhD chemist discredited Dr Wright's work: "please do not quote Dr. Wright as an authority in this regard. She has a doctorate in public policy. Her only science degree is in physics. She has no background in biology, ecology or chemistry. She is wholly unqualified in this arena. In her opening report overview Dr Wright emotively suggests that: 'Much of our identity as New Zealanders, along with its clean green brand with which we market our country to the world, is based on the ecosystem these pests are bent on destroying...'" Whiting-OKeefe and many other anti-1080 campaigners the length and breadth of NZ differ, saying it is the conservation agencies that are bent on destroying New Zealand's unique ecosystem.

The resourceful and dedicated Wendy Pond, Secretary Manu Waiata Restoration & Protection Society writes on May 13 "Aerial drops of 1080 poison require consent from Waikato Regional Council as an arm of government. Under the Local Government Act, Council has a duty to promote the wellbeing of communities. Boisterous meetings with the Community Board have demonstrated that a large number of ratepayers consider poisoning the local environment is not a wellbeing. Under the Resource Management Act harm must be "avoided, remedied, mitigated" (s5c). Observers have reported that possums and other animals poisoned by 1080 die in prolonged agony, up to 40 hours. I do not wish this unnecessary harm on any creature. 1080 drops are an unskillful means and as the harm cannot be avoided, remedied nor mitigated, the Act requires alternative methods to be investigated (s88, Schedule Four, 1b). So far, Council consents condone a lawless activity: the community's voice is not given weight, and harm is not avoided. In Coromandel, bushrangers, conservationists and school gangs have demonstrated that trapping is an alternative method promoting wellbeing. Children learn bushcraft; science and technology are practised with conscience; and the bush is safe for public enjoyment. An excellent range of traps is sold by James & Turner. 4 Square offers a choice of peanut butter, Chesdale cheese, and Marmite as spreads. To avoid dangerous substances, give me marmite over 1080 every day."[133]

Coromandel Voices and the Sorrowful Deluge

Whatungarongaro te tangata toitū te whenua
As man disappears from sight, the land remains

District Councillor Tony Brljevich pens the following for the *Coromandel Town Chronicle* in May:"In response to widespread community concerns over the proposed aerial 1080-drop around Mt Moehau planned for May or June this year, the Coromandel Colville Community Board met with Department of Conservation staff on the 16th of April to advocate for an alternative pest control programme. The Board was approached by residents of the northern Coromandel earlier this year when many landowners near the proposed drop voiced concerns over the possibility of poison being dropped in, or poisoned animals dying in, streams from which they source drinking water for human and livestock consumption. Other issues with DOC's proposal include the necessity of moving large numbers of beehives to safer locations, dying animals wandering onto farmland where working dogs may feed on them and the possibility that the programme will result in an explosion of rat numbers in the area or harm the poison may do to endangered native frog communities in the drop zone. The Community Board was very clear that it did not want to debate the science of 1080 but was opposed to the drop due to the reasons stated above. The Board has been consistent in its stance on 1080 and holds the view there are safer and more humane methods of pest control than spraying deadly toxins over the environment. The outcome of the meeting was that the Department of Conservation staff have policy to follow and the Board should be lobbying Wellington to change policy rather than advocating at a local level to get reform. DOC holds the position that aerial 1080 is a legal activity and one of the tools in it's pest management tool bag that it must use from time to time as necessity dictates. The Board will discuss this matter further at its next meeting before releasing a public statement."

UCLA continues its correspondence with the Medical Officer of Health officials based in Hamilton. The visitor list to see DOC's King-Howell includes the District Health Board's Thomasin Bright, who apparently has barely any time to respond on Dell Hood's behalf to UCLA's concerns but has somehow has managed to find a whole day to travel to Thames to enjoy the DOC chief's company. UCLA is inspired to invite her further north. We understand District Health Board employees do in fact head north but not to accept the local community's invitation. Rather they choose to fly with the poison team during the poisoning of Moehau.

Farmer and intrepid conservationist Charlie Harsant writes on May 24 *Hauraki Herald* from the long-term perspective of one who has lived here all his life. "Regarding the proposed 1080 air drop over the Papakai and central Coromandel Ranges, to me they are special places. They date back to stories my dad told me of his years with a team of pack horses delivering supplies to bush camps and gum diggers from Harsant Bros Store at Gumtown (Coroglen). The Papakai is a special place with amazing views over Mercury Bay and the Hauraki Gulf and a lot of bird life. The Lions Club put a track to the top of the Papakai as a project and it is a pity that DOC did not carry on and maybe continue to cut a walking track along to the Tapu-Coroglen Rd. It has been stated that if possum control were left to private hunters there would always be some left to breed. I note that DOC has been spreading 1080 by air every few years and even they must know that it will never eradicate all the possums. With 1080 they are also upsetting the balance of nature by killing off our natural predators like hawks and moreporks. In my lifetime we have done untold harm to our economy and bird life with DDT and Dieldren etc. We could easily wreck our beekeeping and tourism industry. We need walking tracks in the ranges and along the coast without signs saying '1080 poison laid for possums'."

Late on 5 June the Ward Councillor advised the Department of Conservation of several immediate contingencies and requested that the drop be postponed. The request was refused. DOC deluges Moehau in inclement weather, as conservationists protest in Stony Bay in a last minute effort to halt the poisoning of our mountain. Had the catastrophic weather event of June 12 2014 occurred precisely one year earlier an even greater calamity would have ensued, affecting humans and wild life. Extreme rain belted Moehau resulting in forest devastation that continues to dramatically impact farms and streams below. Fortuitously there was no loss of human life. Full knowledge of native wildlife loss is unknown but native eels and Archey's frogs were found washed up and dead.

It is tragic to realise DOC and EW, with their recumbent partners (Hauraki Māori Trust Board and TCDC) used Peninsula Project funds spending millions of dollars on killing goats and possums and rats in their deluded belief the work would help alleviate flooding and erosion on the Coromandel. It could be said that ratepayers were hoodwinked or turned a blind eye to poison funding while structural work on real flood control to protect coastal communities remained underfunded leaving local communities unjustly targeted for further rates. Had flood prone communities joined with Landcare groups opposing such wasteful and cruel policies, such monies may have been well utilized with flood solutions including engineering work and indigenous tree plantings.

A *caveat* to those who contemptuously "remain neutral on toxin 1080" or outright support dumping 1080 on Moehau is found in Pim de Monchy's *Moehau Forest Condition 1999/2000 Field Season Waikato Conservancy Monitoring Report.* "Possum densities have been low since control began, calculated as possum captures per 100 corrected trap nights (see Warburton 1997) typical catch rates since 1994 have been less than 6% prior to control and less than 2% afterwards." de Monchy's data shows 0.3% in places like Stony, Pahi and Fantail. Absolutely zero percent in Ohinewai/Waitoitoi and 14.9% at Tangiaro pre-control 2000. Since 2000 tracks have been cut and possum killing regularly undertaken. There never was a justifiable rationale for dumping poison on Moehau and the mountain weeps.

The final sagacious words on the traumatic days on Moehau and Papakai are left to Wendy Pond who points out DOC gave adjacent, concerned landowners only 24 hours notice of their intention to drop the WHO's A1 listed toxin 1080.

Matariki over Moehau : Wendy Pond

"The aerial drop onto Mount Moehau was made into a sodden forest, on a day of strong wind on 6 June 2013. A staff member from the Waikato District Health Board was aboard the helicopter. Baits were observed being sprayed along the coast where they would be retrieved by seabirds.

The permit did not require the Department to have regard for wind and weather conditions, nor to desist if unnecessary harm was foreseen. The helicopter dropped its load into the headwaters of the Moehau catchments. This terrain is a network of headwater streams that only ground trapping can avoid. And there was another contradiction. How would DOC staff retrieve poisoned carcasses from waterways whose inaccessibility is the justification for aerial broadcast?...An enquiry to a DOC officer received the response, "Carcasses will be removed from public tracks and thrown back into the bush. There will be no other collection of poisoned carcasses. We don't care if we poison the pigs. Carcasses will not be removed from the forest and will not be burnt or buried. " (DOC staff to Naomi Pond, 8 June 2013)...Thus there were no precautionary measures to avoid long-term poisoning of wildlife: kingfishers eating poisoned mice, moreporks eating poisoned rats, eels eating poisoned carcasses in streams, hawks and native falcons eating poisoned possums, pigs eating poisoned carcasses.

"The Health Protection Officer who authorised the permit failed in a duty to protect the health of New Zealand's forests....Moehau, the final resting place of Tamatekapua, is a sacred mountain. The descendants of Tamatekapua had made known their opposition to aerial dropping of 1080 poison in the Moehau range...

"The purpose of the Hazardous Substances and New Organisms Act 1996 s7 to take into account the need for caution in managing adverse effects where there is scientific and technical uncertainty about those effects was not served. The purposes of the Resource Management Act to avoid, remedy, mitigate harm s5(c), and to have particular regard for Kaitiakitanga s7(c) were not served. The purposes of the Local Government Act s78 to give consideration to the views and preferences of persons likely to be affected by, or to have an interest in, the matter, were not served. The purposes of the Biosecurity Law Reform Act s63 to consult with local authorities ¹(b), and with tangata whenua ¹(c), and with persons likely to be affected ⁵(a), and to consider their level of opposition ²(c), were not served...

"Managers failed in their responsibility to provide for "the use, development and protection of natural and physical resources in a way, or at a rate, which enables people and communities to provide for their social, economic, and cultural well being and for their health and safety." This fundamental principle of the Resource Management Act was not served. (RMA s5 Purpose of the Act.)...The Waikato District Health Board and the Department of Conservation failed in their duty to comply with the statutes. Such disregard invites criticism and contributes to public disaffection with government."[134]

The Great Moehau Kiwi Robbery

"Thus it is that wilderness serves as the unexamined foundation on which so many of the quasi-religious values of modern environmentalism rest."

William Cronon

Later in 2013 UCLA questions DOC management of the kiwi bird on Moehau. DOC plans to relocate ten brown kiwi birds from Moehau to Motutapu in the Hauraki Gulf, using highly publicised corporate sponsorship by global drug and pesticide manufacturer Bayer Inc, in a move they say will improve the long-term outlook for the species. Additional removals of 50 birds are planned. The numbers keep changing—those pesky kiwi birds avoid the trained dogs or just die for some reason. Citing conflicting statements from DOC on kiwi population health and the agency's failure to gain proper iwi approvals UCLA demands definitive, independent research on kiwi numbers and population dynamics on Moehau to guide management strategies, including any further translocations. The removal of kiwi from Moehau is also opposed by Coromandel conservation group Manu Waiata and the Thames Landcare Association.

DOC statements on population health are contradictory and unreliable. On the one hand there is the positive 2007 assessment by DOC's Hauraki area manager claiming more than 70 percent kiwi survival rates on Moehau. That report boasted, "the simple recipe of predator trapping and hard work on the hill has produced this exceptional result."[135] DOC kiwi numbers were increasing at a rate of 15 percent per year and the mountain was far below carrying capacity. The DOC Hauraki newsletter *Around the Traps* reported an impressive Moehau kiwi chick survival of 71.77% since 2000 with sub-adult averages of 95% per year and adult survival averaging 97.9%. The predicted "longevity is 47 years and therefore kiwi are now increasing at Moehau by around 14.8% per year." No mention, naturally, that this success has been achieved with no aerial toxins.

On the other hand, in 2014, one Coromandel iwi is told by DOC representatives, the kiwi population on Moehau is in decline.[136] DOC can't have it both ways. First they report a healthy kiwi population with more than 300 adult pairs and increasing, yet iwi are lobbied and told the population is dropping therefore kiwi need to be relocated in order to be 'saved'. DOC's attempt to prevail may well be replicating an old colonial trick to drive a wedge between local conservationists. The trick worked when Mackay wanted to open up Māori land for gold prospecting—one person was all he needed and he found that person in W.H. Taipari, son of senior rangatira of Ngati Maru Te Hauauru Taipari—the wedge used to prise Ngati Māru resistance.[137]

According to an independent surveyor of Moehau kiwi calls, "No one really knows how many birds are on Moehau"—in spite of the promise to carry out monitoring. No longer are there transmitters on birds so numbers are a matter of speculation. Young birds apparently don't even call until they are around three years old.

Way back on September 10 2010 the *Hauraki Herald* flaunts a full-page advertisement from DOC showing the new poison zone on the eastern flanks of Moehau. The ad also reminds readers how the North Island robin was reintroduced in April 2009 and the supposed goal is to bring kokako birds in 2012. (as of 2019 this has not occurred). The ad boasts "a healthy population of Coromandel Brown Kiwi" range over Moehau due to stoat trapping. The 77% survival rate for kiwi chicks reaching 1000gms is highlighted. The ad states this figure compares very favourably with a 5% rate for other North Island forests. "Population modeling shows an annual increase of 14.7% meaning the population is doubling every 5 years." It is estimated that adult kiwi on Moehau will live for an average of 47 years. Of interest is the proclamation there will be pre and post monitoring and that "this information will be made available to the public." That was 2010.

In 2014 a headline reads: *Moehau kiwi population has doubled in 14 years* declaring the reason for this success is due to trapping networks. One factual error relates to the size of the Moehau sanctuary as being "over 16,000 hectares at the northern tip of the Peninsula, two thirds of it is on private land and one-third on Public Conservation Land."

As be expected from the quality or lack thereof of New Zealand journalism, errors abound and no one challenges DOC propaganda. The "two-thirds" on private land reference is incorrect as private land was withdrawn from this so-called kiwi zone in 2006. Nevertheless the article proclaims the goal of this particular 'sanctuary' is to "establish a secure island population."[138]

UCLA also disputes DOC claims that the "Coromandel brown kiwi" is a distinct taxonomic unit that requires island relocation to survive. Whether the marginal genetic distinction is of any significance and whether inbreeding will contribute in any meaningful way to survival is highly questionable. The fact is no one at DOC can say what the so-called genomic difference actually is. In fact, they say, taxonomic status has yet to be formally determined. As of April 4, 2014 "The difference between Coromandel brown kiwi and those in the rest of the North Island has still not been formally described". The PhD student left university without completing her thesis! DOC has also failed to obtain proper and appropriate permissions for the translocation programme.

DOC could provide only two written confirmations showing iwi support for the translocation while claiming they had other 'verbal' approvals from unnamed representatives on what DOC claimed were 'unknown' dates. Of greater concern, UCLA has been advised by a Te Arawa iwi spokesperson that, 'As far as we're aware "NO" such permission has been granted from Te Arawa Iwi to DOC for the translocation of kiwi from Moehau to Motutapu'." In a letter dated 18 March 2014, responding to UCLA's OIA Chris Jenkins, Director Conservation Services, Northern North Island pronounces verbal approvals for kiwi removal from February 2012 through to August 2013 were given by the Hauraki Collective, the Hauraki Maori Trust Board, Ngati Hei, Hgati Huarere ke Whangapoua, Ngati Porou ki Hauraki, Ngati Tai ke Tamaki and Ngati Paoa Trust. No names and no numbers except for one letter from Ngati Huarere ki Whangapous and one from Ngati Porou ki Hauraki.

The conservation agency is engaged in an image-burnishing public relations exercise reflecting its new direction and focus on marketing opportunities with corporates at the expense of the mountain's resident kiwi population. There is local suspicion that DOC is mismanaging kiwi on the Coromandel.[139] If kiwi birds are in fact on the decline since 2007, it should be noted this is when the use of bait stations filled with toxin 1080 started on Moehau's eastern flank. In 2013, an aerial drop blanketed the entire mountain for the first time, and the poison is known to put juvenile kiwi at risk. DOC should leave the kiwi in peace, and the agency should continue the hard work of stoat trapping on our maunga.

The DOC plan to initially relocate 10 brown kiwi from Mt Moehau to Motutapu in the Hauraki Gulf, with highly publicised corporate sponsorship by global drug and pesticide manufacturer Bayer, is a move **said** will improve the long-term outlook for the species. Additional removals totaling 50 birds are planned on the peninsula. DOC knows the Coromandel kiwi is a taxon "currently recognised but not formally described" but no one at DOC can tell us whether the genomic difference is of any significance whatsoever.

Is DOC mismanaging Moehau kiwi? Red Admiral Ecology 2010 survey report for DOC quotes DOC's Pim De Monchy: "the population modeling suggests that if all dog related predation of kiwi was eliminated there would now be almost no need for stoat control to maintain a stable population of kiwi." In the *Peninsula Post* of January 5 2007 Pim de Monchy mentions 17 kiwi chicks have been radio tagged. That was back in 2007.

Around the same time central government provides $4 million for stoat research and given their penchant for kiwi eggs and young this could be seen to be money spent in the right direction for kiwi survival. However, the venerable Bill Axbey's offering bears consideration, "A hundred years ago one Richard Henry listed stoats as the major threat to New Zealand birds. Now after eighteen years of proving him right, monies previously wasted, are at last going into significant numbers of stoat traps. However work on a more suitable lure than a nice clean chook egg that can be bought in the supermarket and delivered by helicopter seems to be years away. I guess that is par for the course as stoats hunt mainly by smell and hearing so visual baits will be all that's required for the next ten years! Both kiwi and kakapo, particularly kiwi, produce a strong scent to and from nesting holes and there you have a well-marked trail to a stoat lunch. Imitated or taped rat or rabbit squeals, chick squeaks and several scents attract them, but of course those are practical ways and those who discovered them didn't have degrees or academic leanings, so there is little interest in pursuing them until they have been studied and at least two papers written on them. Some places like Pureora must be sodden with poison by now and the effects must surely be starting to show up on its insects and bird life as well as the target species…It is interesting to note that the areas where blue duck are vanishing are those that have received the most 1080 over the years. Possums however after 90% kills, are back to original numbers in a very short time and the puzzle of how vegetable-based possum baits are supposed to kill stoats and other meat eaters without the poison being residual is still to be explained. Likewise, how the trickle down of 1080 is prevented from affecting such things as the native carnivorous and vegetarian snails, the latter are quite partial to the actual baits."

Correspondence with the Senior Curator Natural History Canterbury Museum and author of the outstanding 2013 Yale press publication *Birds of New Zealand*, Paul Scofield includes the following email from 23 June 2014: "Dear Ms Robinson, Like Hugh I have no reason to suspect that Coromandel kiwi are genetically any different than other northern populations. Kiwi biogeography is based not on any recent geological phenomena but ancient landmass separations, and as such Kiwi have probably not been isolated in the Coromandel for long enough for any genetic distinctiveness to develop." Later he writes to say he does support DOC's intention to manage the population until "sound and substantial genetic work is done to establish the absence of any difference."

Christine Friis (DOC Hauraki) writes on 15 May 2014, "The tenth kiwi from the Moehau catch was a young chick which has been in care at the Auckland Zoo. Staff have been waiting for its health to improve so it could be released on Motutapu Island with its father and sibling. However this young chick has failed to thrive, lacked vigour and has been unwell since it came in. So the decision has been made to euthanize it. This decision was made after much discussion with zoo veterinarians and kiwi experts. The little kiwi's welfare was key in this decision as it could not survive without intervention." Without DOC's brutal removal of two chicks and their father (the mother has no doubt been abandoned, left without her life-long mate) this young chick would have lived and died on Moehau, its home, its turangawaewae. Human intervention saw this chick killed by so-called conservation interventionists.

Like Axbey, ranger and conservationist Sid Marsh repeats how human intervention (investigating kiwi burrows) assists stoat predation by making the track to the nest an easy passage way. Red Admiral Ecology's Patrick (Paddy) Stewart quotes Tommy Herbert in his 2010 report on *The Response of kiwi to predator control and advocacy, Moehau 2000 to 2009* — "disturbance during nesting periods has been shown to be a factor in nest failures at Moehau". Stewart also notes that "controlling stoats to low densities facilitated a strong kiwi recruitment result across the greater landscape at Moehau." de Monchy makes a personal comment to Stewart suggesting that if all "dog predation of kiwi was eliminated there would now be almost no need for stoat control to maintain a stable population of kiwi."

2014: Moehau's apocalyptic rains

*"Whether we and our politicians know it or not, Nature
is party to all our deals and decisions, and she has more
votes, a longer memory, and a sterner sense of justice than
we do."*

Wendell Berry

To the Upper Coromandel Landcare Association's members
who all live around Moehau, the June apocalyptic deluge on the
mountain was devastating. Fortunately no human life was lost.
Local farming families with support from around the peninsula
struggle with the aftermath, as do residents and holiday bach
owners on the west coast.

The recovery will take years. There was a huge effort and long
hours put in by machine operators during the first two weeks
following the storm restoring the Port Jackson road to a useable
standard and redirecting creeks back to their original channels.
Small crews worked from daylight to dark every day, some
travelling the full length of the Peninsula each night to be at home
for an hour or two before returning for the daylight start next day.
WRC, it must be said, have used rates for the first time ever in the
area.

Apart from respecting the awesome power of Mother Nature
there is another lesson to be learned. The tragedy again points
out the failures of regional government when it comes to its flood
control responsibilities. As Thames Coasters know only too well
from the weather bomb of 2002, flooding can cause tremendous
damage and in that case the loss of human life. However WRC
diverted millions of rates dollars with their phony sales pitch
"putting leaves on trees" wasting what should have been serious
flood control money to poison possums and rats and to massacre
goats instead of improving critical infrastructure to protect life and
property.

WRC used close to a thousand dollars of ratepayer money per
goat on its self-titled Wall of Death pogrom, leaving hundreds
of carcasses to rot on Moehau at a time when feral goat meat

was fetching over $6 a kilo. As for the bogus Peninsula Project spearheaded by WRC, residents on the upper Coromandel have been objecting from the start. Killing wild animals as an effective and efficient means to control flooding simply beggars belief. There is no science to support the idea.

Fast forward to June 2014. Had this storm and deluge occurred at the same time last year, right after the Department of so-called Conservation had carpet-bombed Moehau with tonnes of poison 1080 pellets, in addition to suffering massive erosion our neighbours would have seen those tonnes of poison 1080 wash down onto their paddocks and gardens, into their wells, and into their houses and homes. The major volume of material that caused the log and rock jams came from the State Forest Park—DOC country. In many cases, slips run from the top of the range. The sheer volume of matter and water flattened and uprooted everything in its path, right out to sea. Huge amounts of massive indigenous trees now clog or lie all along creek banks. The clean streams protection fencing—all demolished. Ratepayer's money is fixing all roads and creeks and access to DOC campgrounds. Regional Councillors, Clyde Graf and Stu Husband help immensely. Without them Moehau West Coasters would have felt ignored. The moral of the story for regional council is flood control money needs to be spent on actual flood control.

Sir Michael Fay's Romance with Poison
and the Te Aroha Declaration

"The secret of life is honesty and fair dealing. If you can fake that, you've got it made."

Groucho Marx

Government obeisance to poisoning continues to suppurate. In the winter of 2014 DOC collaborates with multi-millionaire Sir Michael Fay to dump tonnes of residual toxin, brodifacoum, over Great Mercury, his personal island, co-owned with Mr. Richwhite. Apparently after enduring years of ignominy in the business fraternity thanks to pocketing taxpayer money—"Fay Richwhite/Capital Markets acted as advisor and/or purchaser in the privatization of Telecom, Development Finance Corporation, Housing Corporation mortgages and Tranz Rail"[140] Fay and Richwhite appear to wish to burnish their public halos. *Appendix I*

The cost of the poison job is \$1.47 million, with DOC using taxpayer funds for their part of the job (\$750,000) which means New Zealand citizens are to pay to poison a walkable private island. Landowners could in fact be expected to look after their own land and of interest is one regional council— Canterbury, thought to be the first to recognize kaitiakitanga as a responsibility that comes with owning land.

Meanwhile international opprobrium for DOC's poison business appears in Maggie Sergio's column for Huffington Post.[141] Sergio states, "Lurking in the background is usually New Zealand's Department of Conservation and their Island Eradication Advisory Service Group selling a variety of consulting services, including the bait and helicopter pilots necessary. The practice of using helicopters to carry out poison drops, (be it brodifacoum or 1080), is only done by the government of New Zealand. No other country in the world engages in this macabre practice that is driven by a business model that demands that an invasive species "crisis" be manufactured whenever money runs low. As mentioned, money is also generated by New Zealand's export of these services around the globe. There is a close working relationship between New

Zealand's DOC and Island Conservation, as former employees of DOC are now employed by Island Conservation."

Around the same time (27 May) Stephanie McKee gathers conservationists from around the country to craft the following document:

Te Aroha Declaration:

As citizens of New Zealand/Aotearoa, we declare our duty to safeguard the vitality/mauri of ecosystems. Considering that nature is dynamic and evolution ongoing in ways that exceed full human understanding, we recognize that nany management interventions need to apply the precautionary principle. Therefore:

We support the right of humans and wildlife to a healthy, non-toxic environment.

We understand that any species deemed a problem may have yet unrecognized vital roles in ecosystems and may create opportunities for community economies.

We declare the right for communities/iwi to hunt safe game and to gather safe plants/rongoa māori.

We endorse the highest standards of animal welfare for all species.

We assert the democratic right of communities/iwi to participate in making policies that affect their environment.

We recognize the weight of citizens' observations and local knowledge.

We require ecosystem studies to meet international standards for experimental design.

We endorse the principles of the draft Ecocide Act 2010, which would hold to account heads of state, ministers, CEO's, directors and/or any persons who exercise powers over the environment.

The Wild Future Coalition that drafts this declaration is a group that includes scientists, teachers, researchers, hunters, botanists, historians, horticulturalists, trappers, healers, doctors, farmers, homemakers, gardeners, bird watchers, outdoor guides, documentary film makers, authors, poets, builders, musicians, business operators, artists, veterinarians and conservationists.

The swings and the roundabouts of community stories ravel and unravel threads to educate and inspire. We all share Papatūānuku, thus the struggle continues. As Sonja Davies told a distraught President of the Wellington primary teachers union after her loss of a remit to the national conference that would have seen the teacher's organization adopt the Working Women's Charter, "It is not for you dear, it is for your grandchildren." And she is right. Our work is for our mokopuna.

Encomium

Mary Oliver, poet

We end this journey with a farewell to a great conservationist who left the earth too soon. There will always be questions only Bill Axbey can answer. His knowledge gained, firstly with the Wildlife Service as a deer culler, field technician and then as Southland Conservator of Wildlife, meant his bush knowledge was unsurpassed. As a mentor for many, his bush skills are just part of his legacy. Bill's conservation writings in local newspapers and national magazines evidence his delight in acerbic rhetoric, always delivered with a twist of glee and a flourish of the poetic. Bill Axbey along with Mike Meads were honorary members of the Upper Coromandel Landcare Association.

At the end of 2013 we learn of the passing of Charlie Harsant, a totara in our community. These losses hurt but the light lit by their beacons accompanies all on the journey to protect, to kaitiaki Papatuanuku. We are indebted to all who journey on this path to kaitiaki mother earth.

Suggested Further Reading

Monin, Paul. *This is my place: Hauraki contested, 1769–1875.* *Wellington: Bridget Williams Books, 2001.*

Moore, Phil, and Neville Ritchie. *Coromandel gold: a guide to the historic goldfields of Coromandel Peninsula.* Palmerston North: Dunmore Press, 1996.

Orwin, Joanna. *Kauri: witness to a nation's history.* Auckland: New Holland, 2004.

Park, Geoff. *Ngā Uruora: the groves of life: ecology and history in a New Zealand landscape.* Wellington: Victoria University Press, 1995.

Endnotes: *First They Came for the Goats*

¹ *Weekend Herald* December 22 2007

² *Humane Toxins: Advancing the Best of the Old and the New* Poster created by Connovation Research Lincoln University, Charles Eason, Elaine Murphy, Steve Hix, Lee Shapiro, Duncan MacMorran, Shaun Ogilvie "Cyanide is the only registered poison that is proven to be humane."

³ *Future Eaters* Grove Press 2002 Tim Flannery

⁴ http://www.georgegrey.org.nz/TheCollection/CollectionItem/id/81/title/legend-origin-of-mana-of-thames-tribes.aspx *Legend - Origin of Mana of Thames Tribes*

Patupaiarehe or tūrehu – rendered 'fairy folk' have a privileged presence amongst storytellers, enabling renditions to be cloaked with mythical and mystical fog.

Margret Orbell's translation of the "Origin of mana of Thames tribes" in *Te Ao Hou* as *'The Fairies of Moehau'* (no. 63. June – August 1968. p.4.) *"...My friend, do not imagine that Moehau is now free from tapu – no, the peak is still tapu. No man since Tamatekapua has ever attained the peak, though it may be that Governor Grey will do so"*.

⁵ *'Hauraki–Coromandel region - Māori migration and settlement'* Paul Monin Te Ara—*The Encyclopedia of New Zealand*, updated 13-Jul-12 URL: http://www.TeAra.govt.nz/en/hauraki-coromandel-region/page-4

"Ngāti Hei descend from Tama te Kapua, and those descended from his grandson formed Ngāti Huarere. After approximately 300 years, invading Tainui defeated Ngāti Huarere. The Marutūahu Confederation was formed and subsequently two tribes, Ngāti Paaoa and Ngāti Maru were defeated in 1821 by the musket bearing Ngāpuhi causing a decade of depopulation."

⁶ *The Penguin History of New Zealand* Michael King 2003 P 83 and P 66

⁷ "Tama te kapua was the captain of the Te Arawa waka. His father was Houmaitawhiti. Houmaitawhiti was a chief and he had twin brothers Hei and Tia. Houmaitawhiti sent Tama te kapua and Hei to Aotearoa on Te Arawa waka. His poroporoake to them was " Go forth and seek a better life under the mantle of peace do not take up the ways of war for there is only useless death...." Tama te kapua's son was Tuhoromatakaka. Tuhoromatakaka's son was Huarere. Huarere was the direct descendant of Houmaitawhiti thus being the tuakana line. Moehau was claimed by Tama te kapua upon his arrival to Aotearoa. It is also his resting place. Huarere and Hei were the eponymous ancestors of the current day Iwi Ngāti Huarere & Ngāti Hei. Huarere held mana whenua, mana moana and mana tangata over much of the Hauraki region and also into Tamaki.

Marutūahu & Ngāpuhi invaded and due to this warfare Huarere numbers reduced considerably. Huarere was forced to retreat from the foreshores of Hauraki to live inland and became the tree people taking refuge in the forest. Huarere never left the Hauraki region contrary to claims that they were completely destroyed by Marutūahu. When the marauding tribes of Marutūahu retreated, the people of Huarere continued their occupation and cultivations thus retaining ahi kaa roa to the current day"*

*Information from Lucien Mangakahia kindly supplied by Wanda Brljevich

The narrative continues to be fraught with contention…http://ngatimaru. iwi.nz/history/ the Ngāti Maru history documents "a long war" that was waged on Ngāti Huarere and Ngāti Hako. "This war lasted four generations and in consequence the territory of Ngāti Maru and other Marutūahu tribes expanded. After this there was a period of relative peace." However this was not to last as once again "warring between the Marutūahu and the first peoples spread throughout the Peninsula and across the Plains of Hauraki." Eventually "the conquered lands were divided and settled by the Marutūahu and peace was made through the intentional interlinking of whakapapa lines in the customary Maori way… As told by Te Hiri Ngamane at the Hauraki Treaty of Waitangi Claims 2002."

8   *The Explorations of Captain James Cook in the Pacific as told by selections of his own journals 1768-1779* edited by A. Grenfell Price 1971 [6]

9   http://billbarc.squarespace.com/ http://www.scoop.co.nz/stories/HL1211/ S00010/finfish-plan-swimming-in- circles.htm http://www.scoop.co.nz/ stories/AK1304/S00404/regional-council-rebuts- fish-farming-claims.htm http://www.scoop.co.nz/stories/HL1304/S00049/murky-plan-b-for-fish-farming.htm

Sow Crates of the Sea Opinion piece for *Hamilton News* by Geoffrey and Reihana Robinson "You've got to admit it. The life of a fat, farmed Coromandel oyster or a tasty, cultivated green-lipped mussel isn't all too bad. Hanging for months on lines in the Firth of Thames or bedded down in warm washed mud flats, those shellfish pretty much live the lives they were cut out for. On the water, their conditions couldn't be much better. On the platter, there is no finer.

But picture another aquaculture scenario. Steel cages housing thousands of close-packed kingfish. Those strong, fast fighters, when running free are prized game fish, known for their strength, size and beauty. But packed into the world of industrial-style fish farming, they are just numbers in another profit-driven, Brave New World scheme. Sea lice, parasites, cankers, open rub-wounds, and bloated floaters never make the glossy brochures or menu blurbs.

For economically hard-done-by Thames, glowing industry media releases paint cage finfish farming as a jobs panacea, although no hard jobs data are on offer. And looking to display pro-development credentials, boosters at district and regional councils have been quick to jump in feet first. Over at Environment Waikato's fact-free public relations department, a fantasy figure of $1 billion in annual sales is tossed about freely, even though aquaculture experts suggest much less and a long wait. Lost in the politically motivated jobs hype is the simple fact that cage finfish farming is a dirty industry loaded with a long list of big environmental and biosecurity risks.

Start with the buildup of pest species and their spread to the environment and infection of native stocks that commonly follows from intensification. Consider accidental releases of farmed stock and their potential for devastating crossbreeding consequences in the wild. Degradation of the local marine environment is a given, as suspended fish cages mean massive, unavoidable deposition of waste material from faeces and uneaten food on the seabed. Food additives dish up another risk factor, including toxic zinc accumulation.

Not to mention those copper-based anti-fouling paints. Then there is the thorny matter of therapeutic chemicals like praziquantel and cleaning agents like hydrogen peroxide needed to treat closely packed and disease-prone fish. Just three months ago in Oz, tonnes of kingi were killed during gill-fluke cleaning when the chemical formula was flubbed.

And does our "environmental" regional council care about sustainability? Where exactly do they believe all those thousands of tonnes of fish feed would actually come from? Caged finfish farms take unsustainability to previously unheard of levels. It turns out that, depending on species and location, between four and six tonnes of wild fish are caught and processed to produce a single tonne of farmed fish. That's not just unsustainable, it's unethical. Even EW notes the global concern for depleted wild fish stock used as fishmeal.

Opposition from conservationists and local shellfish producers, whose clean waters could be fouled, is mounting. But finfish farming on the Firth of Thames is getting a free pass on its environmental risks and degradation. In the meantime, here's a business tip for wide-eyed promoters. In markets like North America, industrially farmed finfish is becoming a low-end commodity in seafood chillers, not the *poisson du jour* being claimed. Tonnes of unsustainably raised bulk fish, crated and medicated, from a half-world away just won't impress. And a dirty new Coromandel industry at the expense of a healthy sea is no bargain either."

[10] O Moehau Mountain (*How much can you love?*)

Red-haired denizens, so the old ones say
Bide their time beyond ordinary sight
Are mountain dwellers agile as fairies
Alive to temptation we're blessed
to feel their fairy fibrillations
as they rove the cloud-stricken summit
haunting our night passage
Bush scouts infiltrating
We who are neighbours

What to believe?

Pixies come gentle down your slopes
Pixies sleep on your forest pillows

Curious guerilla queens and kings
compose forest hymns

Patupaiarehe faerie floaters

Sleepers of mountain

Bind us as if with twine
Tie skillful sailor-knots
Tether us as if it were our destiny
We the ensorcelled
In your tiny hands we lean into enchantment
A tender brew humming oriori clusters
like lullabies

Tendrils creep around our bodies
We the befrienders link fingers
Bird talk and wind whispers reveal the saga
The skald
Putorino flutes bringing *Tranquility*
Mountain subdued beneath volcanic cloud
A daily shroud

No one own you
Like the great chief spoke
We belong you murmuring mountain

    Reihana Robinson

[11] Bill Axbey hand written script:

" Continual propaganda statements without factual basis such as; 'Thar are exterminating the Cook Lily, deer are responsible for the decline in takahē, all deer are noxious animals, 1080 poison is not residual, a bounty on possums would not work, there are 70,000,000 possums, NZ flora has never been subjected to browsing, lead poisoning kills thousands of ducks etc.' were allowed to go virtually unchallenged and legislation and finance provided to treat the so-called menace.

A hundred years ago one Richard Henry listed stoats as the major threat to NZ birds, now after eighteen years of proving him right, monies previously wasted, is at last going into significant numbers of stoat traps. However work on a more suitable lure than a nice clean chook egg that can be bought in the supermarket and delivered by helicopter seems to be years away. I guess that is par for the course as stoats hunt mainly by smell and hearing so visual baits will be all that's required for the next ten years!

Both kiwi and kākāpō, particularly kiwi, produce a strong scent to and from nesting holes and you have a well-marked trail to a stoat lunch. Imitated or taped rat or rabbit squeals, chick squeaks and several scents attract them but of course those are practical ways and those who discovered them didn't have degrees or academic leanings so there is little interest in pursuing them until they have been studied and at least two papers written on them. *(Bill is right on target. $4 million is given to stoat* *research. Bill's answer lies in the smelly, waxy brown substance from a rabbit's scent glands.)*

[12] *Moehau Forest Condition 1999/2000 Field Season* Pim de Monchy, Jennifer Hurst *Waikato Conservancy Monitoring Report 2000/18*

[13] *Around the Traps* July 2006 "Projected longevity is 47 years with adult survival averaging 97.9% and sub-adult averaging 95.8%."

[14] The Moehau Environment Group received a blood transfusion from some city transplants who set the original group of possum trappers on a whole new trajectory that took professional fund raising to an all time local high all the while claiming 'volunteer' status. Information from MEG's website (2006) talks of "habitat destroyers" being feral goats, pigs and deer and that their goal is a pest proof fence constructed to span the Peninsula. An analysis of the costs of pest control options in the Northern Coromandel was published in April 2004 by Sandra Barns, Waikato School of Management, Waikato University. Few people got to read it prior to 2006.

[15] *Kamahi decline in Tongariro National Park: a thesis presented for the degree of Doctor of philosophy in Ecology at Massey University* McBreen, Kim Suzanne 1999

[16] *Cost Benefit Analysis of Selected Pest Organisms* 2004 Simon Harris and David Skilton

[17] Tony Orman *Marlborough Express* 28 May 2008 quotint from his letter titled *Lady of Passion and Principle.*

[18] *Straight Furrow* 26 February 2013 letter by Garrick Batten, Caprinex Enterprises Ltd, Brightwater Nelson

[19] *Forest and Bird* Issue Number 315 2005

[20] *Goat Eradication Programme -- A Faulty Process*: Geoffrey Robinson:

[21] Model Code of Practice for the Humane Control of Feral Goats Sharp, T. and Saunders, G. Recommended reading

[22] *Use of Judas goats* prepared by Trudy Sharp & Glen Saunders, NSW Department of Primary Industries:

"Feral goats (Capra *hircus*) can have a significant impact on the environment and agricultural production and are a potential reservoir and vector of endemic and exotic diseases. Although often considered a pest, feral goats are also an important resource, harvested commercially, primarily for meat. Control methods include trapping, mustering, exclusion fencing, ground shooting and shooting from helicopters.

Radio-collared 'Judas' goats are used to locate groups of feral goats that are difficult to find by other methods. This technique involves attaching a radio-collar to a feral goat and releasing it with the expectation that it will join up with other goats. Goats are particularly suited to the Judas method as they are a highly social species and will seek the companionship of any other feral goats in the area.

Once the position of the feral herd is established, the goats accompanying the Judas animal are either mustered or destroyed by shooting...The Judas goat is usually allowed to escape so that it will search out other groups of feral goats. Once eradication is achieved the Judas goat is located, and then shot and the radio-collar retrieved."

23 Correspondence with regard to MEG's role in the goat massacre Geoffrey Robinson to John Simmons at EW 1 September 2005

24 *A Hydrologist's Contribution to the Debate on Wild Animal Management* by Patrick Grant published in the NZ Journal of Ecology 1989

25 *The Third Wave Poisoning the Land* Bill Benfield Tross Publishing 2011 (P 143)

26 *Managed Flooding Integrated Catchment Management Needed to Avoid Flooding and Pollution in Coromandel* Marjorie van Roon, published December 2003

27 *ibid.*

28 *Bay Beacon* December 1 2000

29 Report to North Zone Biosecurity Advisory Subcommittee 20 April 2006

30 Susan Timmins and Julie Geritzlehner, *Do weeds respond to pest animal control?* DOC Science Internal Series 121 2003

31 *The Importance of Feral Animals in New Zealand* M.R. Rudge

DSIR Land Resources, Lower Hutt

Abstract: Feral mammals are important on New Zealand islands for two different and sometimes conflicting reasons: They reduce the value of the island for conserving indigenous flora and fauna, but they also have an intrinsic value in programmes of livestock genetic conservation. Sometimes these conflicts can be separated (Pitt Island, Arapawa Island); sometimes they cannot (Auckland Island).

If they can, the interesting process of selection without domestication can be observed in the feral population. If the conflicts cannot be resolved in situ, management practices should allow for securing the genetic type before it is exterminated. The recent draft of the IUCN Feral Caprinae Position Statement offers a practical guide to issues and solutions for managers. This information is taken from: http://www.doc.govt.nz/upload/documents/science-and- technical/EcologicalRestorationNZIslands.pdf

32 Verbal presentation by Wiremu Peters to the Hearings committee on EW's Regional Pest Management Strategy 2007-12 on behalf of Ngāti Maru

33 *Waikato Times* May 4 2007

34 *Hauraki Herald* August 17 2007

35 Funded by the MAF Sustainable Farming Fund, Meat and Wool NZ, Mohair NZ and the NZ Boer Goat Breeders Association.

36 *Straight Furrow* December 18 2007

[37] USA: 410 tonnes, Reunion Island: 360 tonnes, Martinique: 147 tonnes, Trinidad and Tobago: 41 tonnes, Guadeloupe: 48 tonnes, Fiji: 26 tonnes and the UK: 20 tonnes.

[38] *Straight Furrow* November 13 2007

[39] *The Australian Geographic* March 2008

[40] A local historian noted the following after viewing *Country Calendar* featuring Graham Williams farming Maungaroa Station near Tolaga Bay. "One of his great skills is rounding up wild goats. He praises their intelligence. Well known for his skill, he musters thousands every year all over. The majority is sent to the works while any bucks with large horns go to Game Farms for the overseas trophy hunter to shoot. Numbers are pulled in from properties bounding State owned land. The proceeds are halved between the landowner whose property the animal has grown on and himself. Asked about the strong smell they exude: 'Marvellous… It's the smell of money' His turnover from this venture is considerable. Would there not be more sense in awarding someone like this who must have indirectly removed multiple thousands of goats from ravishing government lands without there being a bean of cost to the tax payer!"

Ka ngāro, i te ngāro, a te Moa "lost as the moa is lost"

Endnotes: *Don't Fence Us In*

1 R. Paul Scofield Canterbury Museum, Ross Cullen and Maggie Wang Faculty of *Commerce*, Lincoln University: *Are predator-proof fences the answer to New Zealand's terrestrial faunal biodiversity crisis?* in *The NZ Journal of Ecology* September 2011 P 33

2 Axbey, Bill Hand-written column for *NZ Outdoors* magazine provided to author

3 *Hauraki Herald* July 24 1993 *Readers Write Moehau Marsupial Myopia*

4 *Hauraki Herald* May 16 1992

5 *Bay Beacon* April 13 2006

6 *ibid.*

7 Barns, S. *An analysis of the costs of pest control options in the Northern Coromandel* P 25

8 *ibid.* P42

9 Upper Coromandel Landcare Association's Statement of Opposition. UCLA provided media statements and presentations to the Thames Coromandel District Council (TCDC), Environment Waikato regional council (EW) and the Department of Conservation (DOC). UCLA successfully campaigned to halt the well-intentioned faulty concept. Since our inception we have lost key members in John Goudie and Philip Ward. We miss their input, historical knowledge, wry comments and helpful guidance. Their long years of hard work on the upper Coromandel are reflected in the healthy farms they have left for children and grandchildren. Their participation in community struggles leaves a model for future generations.

10 *Bay Beacon* 22 June 2006

11 Axbey, B. *pers. letter*

12 This figure is revealed in the notes to the Queens Councsel appeal against the inclusion of such sites in the Regional Pest Management Strategy

13 Kevin Christie, formerly an EW employee, now running EcoFX earning what amounts to hundreds of thousands of dollars over the years to dump aerial toxin 1080. Roger Smith, pest officer who promotes anti-coagulant Talon (brodifacoum) to private landowners around Moehau.

14 OIA documents requested by UCLA

15 Date verified by EW's then Privacy Officer, Diana Palmer

16 MEG financial statements declare $227,126.09 in 2009, $214,043.88 in 2010

17 22 April 2003 letter of support signed by Carol Nanning, Programme Manager Community Relations for Area Manager Hauraki

[18] R Paul Scofield, Canterbury Museum & Ross Cullen and Maggie Wang, Lincoln University research *Are predator-proof fences the answer to New Zealand's terrestrial faunal biodiversity crisis?* in *The NZ Journal of Ecology* March 2011

[19] Barns, S. *An analysis of the costs of pest control options in the Northern Coromandel* April 2004 P 18

[20] *ibid.* P 41

[21] *ibid.* P 42

[22] *ibid.* P 45

[23] *ibid.* P46

[24] *ibid.* P48

[25] *ibid.* P 49

[26] Maungatautari Ecological Island Trust (MEIT) is aiming to be a predator free wildlife sanctuary —mice refuse to evacuate however. MEIT has faced conflict with pakeha and maori neighbours as well as ratepayers throughout the region. The national government forked out $5.5 million in 2006 at a time when DOC was unable to secure funds to buy a large rat free island in Golden Bay where they had apparently paid the owners to eradicate the rats. Based near Cambridge but well off the beaten track MEIT has so far failed in its dream to attract thousands of visitors. No families farm inside the fence. See Appendic I

[27] August 2004 ref NHT 02 04 25 + LSN 222/Doc#1120002 31st March 2006

[28] On a separate issue the following year *February* 15 2007 the minutes of the *Waikato Conservancy Board Te Papa Atawhai o te Rohe o Tainui* record the Auckland Conservation Board's concerns regarding plans for caged fish farming in the Wilson's Bay aquaculture management area located in the purview of the Waikato Conservancy. The Waikato Conservancy would appear to be without opinion. Remarkable, given the well-researched Coromandel written and verbal submissions from ex-DOC employees, farmer/conservationists and scientists.

[29] *Around the Traps Community Newsletter Hauraki area* July 2006 includes the following with regard to kiwi: "Moehau Kiwi Sanctuary's first five years have been written up in a report. Anybody interested in the results can request a copy from Pim or Trudy at the Coromandel Field Base. The basics are: chick survival has averaged at 71.77% since 2000; sub-adult survival averages 95.8% per year, adult survival averages 97.9% per year (so predicted longevity is 47 years) and therefore kiwi are now increasing at Moehau by around 14.8 per year. This compares with an annual decline of about 6% in 'unmanaged' North Island Kiwi populations." This great success is attributed to anecdotes with mustelid control receiving kudos. 30 breeding pairs of the North Island brown kiwi are encumbered with transmitters to discern nesting sites with up to 30 chicks are then likewise tagged. Later in the decade we learn that entanglement is one of the main causes of death for kiwi chicks and that is directly attributable to transmitters. Radio transmitters have been removed so monitoring is

more haphazard. Volunteers listen at dusk in early winter and count the haunting kiwi screeches.

30 *Waikato Times* September 20 2006

31 R. Paul Scofield of Canterbury Museum, Ross Cullen and Maggie Wang of the Faculty of Commerce, Lincoln University research *Are predator-proof fences the answer to New Zealand's terrestrial faunal biodiversity crisis?* in *The NZ Journal of Ecology* March 2011

32 The *New Zealand Journal of Ecology* 21 March 2011 publishes on line *Are predator-proof fences the answer to NZ's terrestrial faunal biodiversity crisis?* R. Paul Scofield, Ross Cullen and Maggie Wang.

These are independent researchers with no conflict of interest. Scofield is based at Canterbury Museum, Christchurch, Cullen and Wang are based at the Faculty of Commerce, Lincoln University, Canterbury. "While we applaud the idealistic goal of ecosystem restoration to its prehuman state, its implementation in NZ is problematic (Norton 2009). The keystone avian herbivores, the moa (Dinorthiformes), are extinct and so are crucial components of the prehuman biota, from the giant flightless herbivorous goose (Cnemiornis) to the tiny flightless avian mouse (Traversia)(Worthy & Holdaway 2002).

"We do not deny that a 'mainland island' will protect different overall biodiversity values than an oceanic island due to the wider habitat range available on the mainland, and this is especially true of montane and alpine ecosystems (Meurk & Blaschke 1990). We emphasize, however, that what is critically important here is the preservation of taxa that will become extinct without immediate intervention, not the somewhat illusory goal of the preservation of an exact copy of a prehuman functional ecosystem."

"We believe that the rate of growth in predator-proof fence building is out of proportion to its benefits." Their research lists all previous such papers including one by the managing director of the Xcluder predator proof fence company! DOC blissfully publishes this co-authored paper titled *Multiple-Species Exclusion Fencing and Technology for Mainland Sites* by Tim Day and Roger MacGibbon, Xcluder TM Pest Fencing Ltd. Cambridge. Included in the Abstract we find "The outcome of this research programme has been the commercial availability of two designs of XcluderTM pest proof fence."

Endnotes: *Save Our Wild Pigs*

1   Flannery, Tim *The Future Eaters* 1997

2   Cuthbertson, Ken *Pig Hunting in New Zealand* "French explorers also delivered pigs as gifts that had been bred from stock on various other Pacific islands.

3   envirohistorynz.com/2010/04/17/a-short-history-of-regional-government-in-nz/

http://envirohistorynz.com/2010/04/17/a-short-history-of-regional-government-in-nz/

4   Easton, Brian *The Commercialisation of New Zealand* AUP 1997

5   *Campaign Against Foreign Control Aotearoa* December 2015 publication *Watchdog.*

6   Jesson, Bruce *Only Their Purpose is Mad The Money Men Take Over NZ* 1999

7   95-98% find poisoning of deer and pigs unacceptable…88% felt that control methods should conform to some minimum standards for humaneness" "Poisoning is clearly seen by the public as an unacceptable control method for these larger species (deer, pigs, goats.) *Introduced Wildlife: A Survey of General Public Views, Landcare Research Science Series #23* Wayne Fraser 2001. The Wilkinson and Fitzgerald, Landcare study was published in 2006. "70% find the poisoning of possums with 1080 unacceptable"

8   "At present there are about 250,000 feral deer in New Zealand. These are pursued by about 37,000 hunters who spend more than $20 million annually harvesting about 70,000 deer." Nugent G. and Fraser K.W. *NZ Journal of Zoology – Pests or Valued Resources? Conflicts in management of deer.*

9   Montgomery, Sy *The Good Pig: The Extraordinary Life of Christopher Hogwood*

10   UCLA press release 24 May 2007 *Tasman-Nelson…A Model for EW Pest Plan*

A Coromandel environmental group this week offered what it said was a `way out` for Environment Waikato Regional Council (EW) from its bogged down pest management strategy against which a coalition of hunters, iwi, farmers and conservationists is digging in for a long haul of legal challenges. The Upper Coromandel Landcare Association (UCLA) has put forth a proposal whereby EW would withdraw its controversial plan and adopt in its place a five-year strategy modeled on the comparable Tasman-Nelson District. EW plans to triple pest management expenditures over the five years to 2011 and expand animal pest control to trophy species such as wild pigs and deer. Its strategy has drawn intense opposition. Submitters have likened the EW plan to a `Perfect Storm` of runaway rates, attacks on private landowner rights, and threats to traditional Kiwi values. EW, meanwhile, has defended what it says is a sensible pest control plan.

According to UCLA, the Tasman-Nelson District is a good model for the Waikato. The districts are comparable in many respects, and both include large blocks of conservation estate and sensitive coastline. Both must balance the requirements of city dwellers as well as rural communities. UCLA spokesperson Reihana Robinson urged EW's pest managers to take a step back from the brink and consider the alternative. 'We have been sold the TINA myth by EW…There-Is-No-Alterative. No alternative to skyrocketing pest control spending. No alternative to excessive ratepayer burdens. No alternative to knocking out wild pigs and deer. But Tasman-Nelson shows us there is an alternative, Robinson says. The five-year Tasman-Nelson RPMS, adopted this year, calls for no regional intervention to control pigs and deer. 'The people of Tasman-Nelson don't want it, so their council isn't forcing it on them, Robinson said. The plan calls for annual spending increases of 3%, in line with inflation, for the duration of the strategy. 'Tasman-Nelson doesn't want uncontrolled spending and rates, so their council isn't forcing it on them,' she said. 'Rather than inviting a legal showdown with Waikato ratepayers, Robinson said, EW should take a page from another district's successful song book.'

[11] Statement provided in February 2016 by Linda Bond, a team leader in the rates and finance department of Waikato Regional Council (WRC)

[12] *A Shadow of Doubt* is the first of two outstanding documentaries produced and directed by Steve and Clyde Graf. Their second DVD on toxin 1080 is able to be viewed at https://www.youtube.com/watch?v=yQRuOj96CRs and is called *Poisoning Paradise Ecocide New Zealand*. http://www.imdb.com/title/tt1588425/ The Graf brothers have also created documentaries on deerstalking and bow hunting. They are conservationists truly capable of presenting NZ wildlife and the consequences of indiscriminate poisoning of our beautiful wilderness.

[13] Excerpts from the NZDA submission written and presented by Hugh Barr

Though deer may destroy under-storey at high numbers, no evidence that this situation occurs in the Waikato Region is supplied. This information contradicts the information given in the Landcare (2006) document, which says: At current generally low densities, most groups comprise only 2-3 deer." No evidence is given that deer are a problem, let alone a pest, in the Waikato region…There is no case presented for making feral pigs pests in the Waikato. No benefit-cost analysis was supplied in the draft RPMS… This "study" completely fails to meet the requirements of S 72 [1] of the Biosecurity Act. As well, there is no specific assessment for deer and feral pigs singly. In my 40 years of business consultancy I have never seen such rubbish as this CBA.

NZDA proposes EW recognise wild deer and feral pigs as valued community natural resources for food for the table, and recreational hunting, and as traditional, longstanding community resources. Remove them as "pests" as no proof has been given that their numbers are such as to be pests, in terms of damage to native plants

That all aerial 1080 operations become discretionary activities under the Resource Management Act, so that recreational hunting stakeholders have the opportunity to engage with EW staff. At present aerial 1080 drops are a permitted use, in spite of the death they wreak on recreational hunting species and native birds including carnivores hawks, kaka, falcon, morepork, weak etc.

It is difficult to see the ham-fisted attempt by staff and consultants to hype up deer and feral pigs as anything else than staff empire building. As a former regional councillor myself, I urge the Council to cut back severely on this staff racket. The EW draft Annual Plan shows environmental pest management increasing from $2.5 Million this year (06-07) to $11.8 M five years hence (2012-13), and to $15.4 M in 2016-17 (9 years hence). Obviously the EW staff believe ratepayers have money to burn.

NZDA Proposes: EW total regional pest spend be reduced significantly over the next 5 years of this Strategy, because of the reduction now the Tb risk is diminishing. Give your ratepayers a bonus instead.

Definition of High Value sites: NZDA supports Geoffrey Robinson in his submission that High Value sites and high value catchments need to be quantitatively defined.

NZDA Proposes: That high value sites be decided and the RPMS then be put out again for public consultation. Especially the agreement of the owner would seem necessary. Otherwise EW should be required to buy the site at whatever the current owner wants to sell it for.

Soil and Flood risks and pests impacts – rubbish!: It appears some EW staff have been around long enough to remember how the NZ Forest Service (NZFS) made much of reducing soil erosion and flood risks by attacking deer. This was never more than another way for NZFS to vilify deer. It is even more so today. If EW wanted to reduce soil erosion and flood risk, it presumably has hydrological models assessing where runoff is fastest with rain, and where the risk of erosion of valuable topsoil, and floods is greatest. Check and you will find this is pastureland, used for economic production. Think too about the erosion and flood risk when pine plantations are cut down. Massive soil disturbance, massive destruction of vegetation, massive erosion and flood risk in the short term. Does EW intend to close both these industries down in its region? Presumably not. These are examples of risks EW has to accept. Beside them, a bit of deer browse and pig rooting has a laughably small impact. Indeed browse is a fact of life in New Zealand forests and grasslands. Only 600 years ago before they were eaten to extinction, up to 8 million moas browsed them. Not having forest browse is unnatural. NZDA proposes:

EW drop the connection between "pests" and erosion and flooding. The risk from pests is minimal compared to other risks such as clearance for pastoralism, or forest cutting operations. Holding ponds and other methods of trapping silt or water are far more appropriate.

Other NZDA concerns:

Farming Pests or killing them to waste: Real pests such as rabbits, rats, stoats, wasps etc are impossible to exterminate on a regional scale. No doubt it is a rather good living trying to do the impossible with loads of ratepayer money. Such subsidised poisoning to waste adds nothing to the community in the medium term, except wasted rates, costs and toxins. Alternatively the sustainable solution is to harvest the "pests" ie find something saleable one can get from the resource.

NZDA proposes: EW adopt the line of most community benefit. As EW cannot wipe out many pests, learn to live with them at the lowest community cost, by harvesting them, not poisoning them to waste...

NZDA proposes: Though bandaids may be possible to meet some of our concerns, the reality is the RPMS is so inadequate and inadequately argued. It needs to be withdrawn and revised with deer and pigs removed from being pests. Or preferably, given that EW has no reasonable arguments for deer/feral pigs being pests, that they be removed as pests, but recognised as valued recreational and wild meat species, and protected from aerial 1080 by compulsory mitigation eg using recreational hunting volunteers, ground control in significant recreational hunting areas, or possum trapping, or possibly repellent as a short term mitigation. NZDA also proposes EW completely change its RPMS to go down the valued harvesting alternative, and relieve its ratepayers of never-ending rates increases.

Harris Consulting: *Cost-benefit analysis of selected pest organisms* January 2007 Simon Harris, David Skilton Ch 15 (page 50) deals with Integrated Vertebrate Pest Control at High Value Catchment and High Value Biodiversity sites. Covers deer and pigs. Provides no Waikato regional info on either deer or feral pigs. No individual Benefit-Cost Analysis provided for deer or feral pigs. Totally qualitative, with assumptions that lead to EW staff's required conclusion. Not science but charlatanism. Story telling a la Forest and Bird, with no connection with the Waikato region. Talks about 100 year events. In recent examples of 100 year events (Manawatu-Wanganui (February 16 2004), it is farmlands that are the main sufferers from intense rains. If this is the criterion, then EW should be shifting people out of pastoralism. Native forest browsing has negligible effect compared with other factors such as pastoral farming. EW probably has hydrological flood models showing this reality. This assessment is bunkum, not a scientific CBA. Deer and pigs are an insignificant cause of EW flood damage in the last 30 years. Conclusion on CBA: This consultant rubbish does not meet the requirements of S 72 [1] of the Biosecurity Act. There is no specific assessment for deer and feral pigs singly.

[14] Henderson is quoted in Tony Orman's *About Deer and Deer Stalking*

[15] "This letter is in reference to the Moehau Kiwi Sanctuary (MKS), as designated by the Department of Conservation (DOC), and the status of private property said to be located within its boundaries. We note that recently, officials and spokespersons for DOC have made public mention of the Moehau Kiwi Sanctuary and in so doing have implied or stated outright that the MKS area comprises all public and private property north of Colville Bay on the western side of the peninsula and Waikawau Bay on the eastern side and north of Port Charles Road and Waikawau Road. The MKS is also illustrated in a colour A3 brochure with map, graph, illustrations and text published, apparently, by DOC. That map clearly indicates that the MKS includes all land in the area described

above. With specific reference to the apparent inclusion by DOC of my/ our property (listed below) in the designated MKS area, please be aware of the following:

My/our property is located outside the Moehau Kiwi Sanctuary.

No permission has been sought or granted to include the property in the MKS.

No formal public consultation process with landowners affected by the MKS has been undertaken.

No statutory or regulatory basis exists for inclusion of any property in the MKS without the express permission of its owners.

Inclusion of a property in the MKS may encumber that property and may result in the imposition of legal regulations, obligations, and restrictions binding upon the owners of that property.

Inclusion of a property in the MKS may result in financial obligations for the owners and may subject the owners to adverse financial consequences.

Inclusion of a property in the MKS may result in imposition of toxic pesticides, herbicides and other involuntary animal and plant control measures without landowner consent.

I hereby request that the Department of Conservation immediately:

Delete and remove the property listed below from all area descriptions of the Moehau Kiwi Sanctuary and all public records of the MKS.

Confirm in writing that the property is no longer recorded as part of, or as included within, the MKS.

Notify any and all public or private agencies that to its knowledge may maintain records of the MKS boundaries as to the correction referenced in this letter. "

16 Dom Felice Vagglioli University of Otago Press 2000, P 112 *History of New Zealand and its Inhabitants*

17 *Regional Pest Management Strategy (RPMS) submission 2007*

18 Orman, Tony *About Deer and Deer Stalking* 2002 Spring Creek

19 Cuthbertson, Ken *Pighunting in New Zealand* 1974 A.H. & A.W. Reed

20 Representing Environment Bay of Plenty at the Waitangi Tribunal "P Cooney and TC Waikato, closing submissions of counsel for Environment Bay of Plenty, 14 October 2005 (paper3.3.114), p9; Mai Chen and Lecretia Seales, closing submissions for Waikato Regional Council, 14 October 2005 (paper 3.3.112), pp 4–5

Endnotes: Voices of the Coromandel—
Poison Peninsula

"You have noticed that truth comes into this world with two faces. One is sad with suffering, and the other laughs; but it is the same face, laughing or weeping. When people are already in despair, maybe the laughing face is better for them; and when they feel too good and are too sure of being safe, maybe the weeping face is better for them to see."
Black Elk Speaks Being the life Story of a holy Man of the Oglala Sioux As told through John G Neihardt
(Flaming Rainbow)

[1]   Potts, Annie Co-Director, New Zealand Centre for Human-Animal Studies University of Canterbury *Kiwis Against Possums: A Critical Analysis of Anti-Possum Rhetoric in Aotearoa New Zealand* Society Animals 17 (2009)

[2]   *Moehau Possum Survey 1987* A S Garrick draft. "M Ward (pers comm.) commented his first sighting of possums within the area was in 1954 at Fantail Bay, and that possums appeared in the southern part of the region about 25 years ago. K Purdon (pers comm.) recorded possums at Sandy Bay in 1965. No other early reference to possums in other areas was obtained during the survey, suggesting that possums have only recently become more widespread. Moore (1973) noted that possums were not present on Mt Moehau, in 1971. However, while possum numbers have probably been very low for perhaps twenty or thirty years and peripherally distributed, their presence within the inner forests has been noticed within the last 6-7 years (P.Novis pers comm.)…"

[3]   Pietak, Dr Alexis 2014 *A Critical Look at Aerial-Dropped, Poison-Laced Food in New Zealand's Forest Ecosystems* p 23. Retrieved from 1080poison.co.nz "While possums have been listed as preying upon birds and bird eggs, their diets have been found to consist of only trace amounts (less than 0.5%) bird or bird eggs, and to consist primarily (90%) of foliage"

[4]   http://www.scoop.co.nz/stories/PA1501/S00060/1080-suspected-in-disappearance-of-birds.htm and the official DOC site http://www.1080facts.co.nz/the-facts-of-the-missing-rock-wren.html states: *"With no clear picture to why the rock wren are missing, DOC has excluded alpine zones with rock wren populations from future 1080 drops until they know more. They will continue to assess the situation." http://greystar.co.nz/content/more-kea-poisoned-1080-drop* As noted, scientists have yet to study the majority of non-target native species.

[5]   *"This is one of the great difficulties of epidemiology and its role in public health policy, particularly in a culture where an agency producing a contaminant*

is innocent until proven guilty in a court of law" Sean Weaver *A Review of Toxicological Research on Sodium Monofluoroacetate (1080) and its Policy Implications* Victoria University of Wellington Research Report Number 18 April 2003

6   Animal Health Board's original goal was achieved before AHB as an organisation was to due to expire in 2013. Shuffling over from AHB is Jeff Grant and William McCook and from NAIT Ted Coats joins the directors. Keith Sutton, Lesley Campbell, Michael Spaans and Andrew Coleman are the initial batch. TBFree was beefed up to continue draining money off farmers and the general public while failing miserably to discover a vaccine (or so we are led to believe) or to institute strict stock controls or to support farm margins as possum eradication zones for possible wildlife infections.

7   *The use of 1080 for pest control: A discussion document.* Department of Conservation and Animal Health Board Green, Wren 2004

8   Pietak, Alexis Mari *A Critical Look at Aerial-Dropped, Posion-Laced Food in New Zealand's Forest Ecosystems* 2010

Mana Party policy: *Ban the use of 1080 and invest in alternative methods (and employment opportunities) to control pest and rodents.* http://www.landcareresearch.co.nz/__data/assets/pdf_file/0006/75498/kararehe-kino-issue-24.pdf Cultural Control of Possums Kevin Prime (Ngatihine)

9   Sweetapple, Peter and Nugent, Graham *Ship rat demography and diet following possum control in a mixed podocarp-hardwood forest New Zealand Journal of Ecology* 2007 From Abstract: "Mean ship rat abundance indices increased nearly fivefold after possum control and remained high for up to 6 years after the 1994 poisoning....These results are consistent with the hypothesis that increased rat abundance following possum control is a consequence of greater availability of, or reduced competition for, seeds and fruit."

10   http://www.australiazoo.com.au/our-animals/mammals/possums-and-gliders/common-brushtail-possum/ and http://www.teara.govt.nz/en/possums/page-4

11   *Straight Furrow* December 8, 2009

12   First published *NZ Outdoor*, original typed version handed to UCLA. And the *Hauraki Herald* of June 11, 1994 published a letter from Bill Axbey covering the mulit-million dollar 1080 poison business that keeps a tight rein on the money continuing to oppose even a $5.00 bounty to hunters and trappers. He can find "no advocate of its biodegradability prepared to drink water that has poison added".

13   May 16 *Hauraki Herald (HH)*

14   Temple, Philip *Kea the feisty parrot* published October-December 1994 *New Zealand Geographic* notes "this is one of the worst cases of avicide in history. That the kea survived this massive slaughter, and the continuing pressures on its environment, seems little short of a miracle."

15   *Hauraki Herald* July 18, 2008

16 Weaver, Sean *Policy Implications of 1080 Toxicology in New Zealand, Journal of Rural and Remote Environmental Health 2003* and *A Review of Toxicological Research on Sodium Monofluoroacetate (1080) and its Policy Implications* in *NZ Journal of Rural and Remote Environmental Health* (2003) Sean Weaver Environmental Studies, School of Earth Sciences, Victoria University of Wellington Research Report Number 18 April 2003

17 *ibid.*

18 Notman, Peter *A Review of invertebrate poisoning by compound 1080 for the DSIR 1989* New Zealand Entomologist Vol.12 "High concentrations of 1080 can persist in arthropods for 4 days after they consume 1080 baits."

Booth and Wickstrom *The Toxicity of sodium monofluoroacetate (1080) to Huberia striata a NZ native ant* in *The New Zealand Journal cf Ecology* 23, 161-165, 1999

19 A Chris Ogilvy (*HH* March 19, 2010) emphasizes the temporary damage caused by 1080 is "well worth the huge relief caused by the reduction of pests." A writer with the same name bounces up in the *NZ Listener* (June 25 2011) "I don't like 1080. But I dislike possums, rats anc stoats even more. Until we have something better, bring on the 1080."

20 Spurr, Eric *A Theoretical Assessment of the Ability of Bird Species to recover from an imposed Reduction in Numbers, with particular reference to 1080 poisoning* 1979 references kiwi and falcon

21 *NZ Herald* 12 November 1996

22 In 2013 a government tender was advertised involving collaboration with Waikato Regional Council to provide a *National Monitoring Programme to Determine Effects of Agrichemicals Used in Aquatic Pest Plant Control.* Agrichemical companies, not ratepayers, should be required to do their own research before any approval is granted. This practice merely exposes how government plays its role as a pawn in the hands of the industrial chemical multinationals.

23 Letter of 1 June, 2013 from Barry Brickell, Driving Creek Wildlife Sanctuary Trust Inc. wanting a "proper scientific approach concerning the evaluation of 1080 poison for both manual and aerial distribution." He emphasizes a need for a detailed assessment of "all detectable fauna" that must be carried out "independently" both before and after the experiment.

24 http://anpsa.org.au/APOL7/sep97-4.html "A good example cf the adaption of mammals to a plant toxin by developing an efficient chemical detoxication method in the liver is the interaction of some Western Australian animals with many fluoroacetate-containing plants (*Gastrolobium* species) in the south-western part of the state. Brush-tailed possums, bush rats and western grey kangaroos from this area are capable of safely eating these plants which are rapidly fatal for livestock, red kangaroos, eastern grey kangaroos and for brush-tailed possums and bush rats from eastern Australia. *Gastrolobium grandiflorum* and *Acacia georginae*, which grow in Queensland, also contain this toxin which is the toxic component of 1080 poison." http://www.anbg.gov.au/cpbr/publications/bayer-publications/71.Aust.Syst.Bot.15_619-739.pdf   "As

Gastrolobium evolved the ability to synthesise monofluoroacetic acid, native herbivores apparently co-evolved a tolerance to this toxin. This tolerance is most pronounced in species native to Western Australia, but its extent depends very much on diet (Twigg and King 1991). For example, the emu (Dromaius novohollandiea) had the highest tolerance of any birds tested (Twigg and King 1991), as it is a seed-eater, although the seeds of Gastrolobium are known to have particularly high fluoroacetate levels. Likewise, seed weevils also have a high tolerance for the same reasons (Twigg and King 1991)

25 "The inability to prevent the imposition of unwanted pesticides may affect mental if not physical health, certification for organic growers, and the ability of tangata whenua to exercise kaitiakitanga…" Helen Hughes, Parliamentary Commissioner for the Environment *Summary of Findings, Possum Management in NZ* (1994)

26 Local scientist Quinn Whiting-O'Keefe says "the question is: how long is the stuff around, in what concentrations and what it takes to break down the monofluroacetate? … it is quite a bit. It is pretty stable so that effectively the only protection the environment has is to dilute the concentration … As long as it is around it is one dangerous poison. Ultimately it will break down to something, but the fluoride bond is very strong and stable so it is pretty tough to split off the fluoride anion or break one of the C-C bonds … fluorohydrocarbons all tend to behave this way."

27 Wikipedia offers statistics for the town of Oxford AL. For 21,348 people in 2010 there are 50 police officers and their equipment includes a "military surplus armored vehicle, sniper and assault rifles as well as military-style helmets." The native American population was decimated prior to recent occupation however strife continues with regard to sacred burial mounds see NYT story at http://www.nytimes.com/2010/03/14/us/14oxford.html

28 In 2013 Radio New Zealand's *Country Life* farming programme airs an interview with Colin Cox http://podcast.radionz.co.nz/clife/clife-20130531-2125-natures_support_possum_back_belt-048.mp3

29 *Hauraki Herald* May 26, 2006

30 *On This and That, New Zealand Outdoors* 2006

31 *Around the Traps* July 2006

32 *Hauraki Herald* September 8 2006

33 *Hauraki Herald* October 2006

34 *NZ Herald* November 13 2006

35 *Hauraki Herald* September 8 2006

36 *The Bay Beacon* November 2, 2006

37 *The Bay Beacon* August 2006

38 pers.com via email

39 *Hauraki Herald* March 21, 2014

40 *Hauraki Herald* November 10 2006

41   *ibid.*

42   *Hauraki Herald* February 13 2007

43   *Hauraki Herald* December 29 2006

44   *Hauraki Herald* May 22, 2007

45   *Coromandel Town Chronicle (CTC)* May 2007

46   *ibid.*

47   *Hauraki Herald,* June 2007

48   June 5 2007 From UCLA Press Release *Landcare Group Says No to 1080 on Moehau* "The Upper Coromandel Landcare Association, a broad-based community group in the Moehau area, notified the Department of Conservation today of their strong opposition to DOC's planned application of 1080 toxin on the sacred mountain at the top of the Coromandel Peninsula."

49   UCLA's spokesperson met with newly appointed Director General of DOC, Al Morrison who had been a Radio NZ reporter. (He subsequently left DOC and moved to the State Services sector in 2013.) As one former colleague of Al Morrison states in a *NZ Listener* article from December 16, 2006, "Al is extraordinarily gifted at explaining, at making issues accessible." The *NZ Listener* article goes on "Journalists, amazed to think that Al Morrison had gone to the dark side, nevertheless thought he must be the department's new spin-doctor." Fast forward to 2013 to see how little regard people have for the so-called Department of Conservation. Check the following website to see an ex-DOC employee analyzing the new commercialization of conservation— http://www.docwatchnz.com/

50   *Hauraki Herald* June 8 2007

51   January 13, 2010 meeting of the Regional Pest Management Advisory Subcommittee

52   *Moehau Messenger* June 21, 2007

53   *Regional Pest Management Strategy Discussion Document 2006*

54   Sweetapple, P and Nugent G *Shiprat demography and diet following possum control in a mixed podocarp-hardwook forest* in *New Zealand Journal of Ecology* 2007

55   *Review of Thames Monitoring for Biophysical Benefits from Annual Pest Control* by Reece Hill and Bruce Willoughby of Ecometrics, 7 March 2011

56   *Peninsula Post* December 10 2009

57   *Regional Pest Management Strategy Discussion Document 2006*

58   *Hauraki Herald* June 22 2007

59   *Coastal News* June 28

60   *Waikato Times* June 13 2007

61   *ibid.*

62   *Coromandel Town Chronicle (CTC)* July

63   "Jacinta Ruru, advancing a somewhat idiosyncratic 'Maori viewpoint'… Wilderness, to her, is entirely a colonial construct with 'little place in the twenty-first century', and designated wilderness areas are merely 'walled gardens' from which Maori have been denied harvest of indigenous fauna and flora. These effete preserves, she maintains, are incompatible with the Treaty." *Wild Heart The Possibility of Wilderness in Aotearoa New Zealand* edited by Mick Abbott and Richard Reeve.

64   *Straight Furrow* July 10 2007

65   *Moehau Messenger* July 19, 2007

66   *Hauraki Herald* August 8 2007

67   *ibid.*

68   *Alternatives to brodifacoum and 1080 for possum and rodent control — how and why?* June 2010 *Journal of Zoology*

69   *Hauraki Herald* August 10

70   *ibid.*

71   *Bay Beacon* August 2

72   DOC's own report in the September issue of *Panui*

73   *ibid.*

74   *Hauraki Herald* September 7

75   November *Coromandel Town Chronicle*

76   *E Karangahia,The Crier* February 2008

77   *NZ Herald* Feb 28, 2008

78   *ibid.*

79   *Hauraki Herald* July 4 2008

80   *Hauraki Herald* July 15

81   *Hauraki Herald* July 18

82   *Peninsula Post* July 31 2008

83   *Hauraki Herald* April 4 2008

84   *Hauraki Herald* May 16 2008

85   *Hauraki Herald* May 27 2008

86   9 June 2008 *Council Plans To Charge Those Who Don't Agree To Aerial 1080* Upper Coromandel Landcare Association (UCLA) has lodged a strong objection with EW's finance committee, which received a staff recommendation in favour of the new levies at a meeting Hamilton. "EW staff say choosing pure drinking water and a toxin-free food supply is like sending the kids to private school. They say it's a privilege for which they should collect what amounts to user-pays. We say pure food and water are basic human rights that EW has no business whatsoever charging for."

87   Robbie Graham's attempt to use cyanide brought opposition from the authorities, backed by the Ombudsman.

⁸⁸ *NZ Farmers Weekly* November 24 2008

⁸⁹ *Hauraki Herald* April 11 2008

⁹⁰ *Kararehe Kino Vertebrate Pest Research Newsletter,* December 2008

⁹¹ *Rural News* August 21, 2007 The paper referenced is by Potter, Stringer, Wakelin, Barrett, and Hedderley DOC Series 230 (2006)

⁹² Conservation Advisory Science Notes No 108 *Evaluating the Potential Hazard of Aerial 1080 Poison Operations to Short-Tailed Bat Populations,* 1994 by B.D. Lloyd states "there is a possibility of secondary poisoning caused by bats consuming arthropods that have fed on 1080 baits."

⁹³ *Persistence of Residual Dipahcinone Concentrations in Pig Tissues Following Sub-lethal Exposure* 2006 Penny Fisher Landcare Research

⁹⁴ *Waikato Times* September 19, 2009

⁹⁵ *Hauraki Herald* November 17 2009

⁹⁶ *Informer* November 24 2009

⁹⁷ http://www.doc.govt.nz/ngawhenuarahui

⁹⁸ Wren Green *Toxins and Pest Control Feathers to Fur* conference 2007

⁹⁹ "Secondary poisoning has been well documented for predators feeding on the carcasses of other pests that have been poisoned as primary targets in New Zealand pest control operations using brocifacoum and monosodium fluoroacetate (1080) (Alterio 1996, Alterio et al. 1997, Alterio and Moller 2000, Department of Conservation 2006)" This quote is from *Pest Eradication Technology—the critical partner to pest exclusion technology: the Maungatautari experience* Cam Speedy, Tim Day, John Innes

¹⁰⁰ *Coast and Country* January 7 2010

¹⁰¹ *Hauraki Herald* February 5 2010

¹⁰² To read the full article in *NZ Farmers Weekly* January 18 2010 see *The Killing Nation New Zealand's State-Sponsored Addiction to Poison 1080* 2017

¹⁰³ *New Zealand Farmers Weekly* February 22 2010

¹⁰⁴ *Peninsula Post* February 26 2010

¹⁰⁵ *NZ Listener* March 6 2010

¹⁰⁶ McBreen, Kim Suzanne *Kamahi decline in Tongariro National Park: a thesis presented for the degree of Doctor of philosophy in Ecology at Massey University* 1999

¹⁰⁷ P.J. Bellingham, S.K. Wiser, G.M.J. Hall, J.C. Alley, Rob B. Allen, and P.A. Suisted *Impacts of possum browsing on the long-term maintenance of forest biodiversity Science for Conservation* The following is taken from Project Crimson's September 2005 *True Colours* newsletter. Dr Bellingham, forest ecologist at Landcare Research, Lincoln, Canterbury, agrees possums are predators browsing local Westland kotukutuku to possible extinction and probably hastening the demise of aging rata trees, but he is clear that "there is much we still do not know about Westland's rain forests, the

effects of possums, and the long term prospects for southern rata." The article is entitled *Natural causes likely for plight of southern rata*

"Amongst Dr Bellingham's favourite research interests are the effects of natural disturbances on forests, including hurricanes, landslides and floods. He has worked in the Kokatahi Valley in Westland for the past decade. The demise of vast areas of major canopy trees like southern rata and kamahi through New Zealand rain forests began decades ago and continues to this day. The process, known as "dieback", has affected several hundred hectares, especially in valleys in the steep ranges of Westland. Many believe possums cause dieback because they browse rata and kamahi. However, dieback can occur in forests where there are no possums. It now appears natural factors: the regeneration of rata, natural disturbance, and changes in soil fertility, all contribute as the main causes of dieback. Trapping and poisoning of possums has been conducted for the last four decades to arrest dieback in several Westland valleys, yet it continues. Southern rata's tiny wind-dispersed seeds seldom colonise litter on the forest floor. Instead they colonise bare surfaces such as landslides and floodplains. Mass regeneration of rata can occur when many bare surfaces arise, especially after earthquakes. Between these events, high rainfall causes landslides that provide more sites for rata to colonise. Thus, most valleys contain rata stands of many ages, from seedlings to dying trees. Even in the Kokatahi Valley in central Westland, where dieback is conspicuous, 30 years of forest measurement show some rata regeneration that offsets death of canopy trees elsewhere. Older rata stands are more prone to dieback. A likely reason for this is that the soils on which young stands, up to 100 years old grow, have the most available nutrients. The very high rainfall, up to 11 m per year, causes rapid depletion of soil nutrients so their capacity to maintain tall forests declines with time. Low nutrient supply to tree crowns results in their becoming sparse and prone to damage by wind, fungi and other agents, including possums. Comparing several Westland valleys, dieback occurs independently of when possums colonised and irrespective of whether or not there has been possum control. Dieback is scarcely apparent in stable, very infertile granite areas but is pronounced in unstable, more fertile schist valleys."

[108] *Hauraki Herald* March 19, 2010

[109] The consents were issued with no public notification. The report (EW Document #1699809) by Sheryl Roa, a Senior Resource Officer at EW outlines the assumptions upon which the decisions were made to grant the consents and what conditions would be applied to the consents.

[110] *Straight Furrow* March 23 2010

[111] *Hauraki Herald* June 25 2010

[112] The Robinson Report *Hamilton News* August 2010

[113] *Hauraki Herald* August 17 2010

[114] *Peninsula Post* August 12 2010

[115] *Peninsula Post* September 23 2010

[116] *The Informer* October 2010 Stephanie McKee pens an excellent article, *The Mad Hatter's Ten-Eight-Tea Party?* recounting the government poison business, Animal Control Products (ACP) "has stockpiled 4 years worth of 1080 "beyond commercial requirements". (This has been estimated to amount to more than 10,000kg of pure 1080.)… It has stated that should the government take any action to restrict 1080 use, thereby making these stocks "valueless", it will assert its right to seek compensation…sufficient to allow the Company's position to be restored." (Source: http://www.comu.govt.nz/pdfs/ACP-SCI-2009-10.pdf). http://www.radionz.co.nz/national/programmes/countrylife Currently, ACP through Pestoff Products based in Wanganui, exports container loads of poisons to many overseas nations including Iran, Pakistan, Turkey and Kyrgyzstan. www.pestoff.co.nz/

[117] The request to the Select Committee was to investigate the misuse of 1080 on the Coromandel

[118] *Tabled report by Theodora Ward*: Beef, Mutton and Wool producer, Coromandel Peninsula includes the following points: "l Totally Oppose the use of 1080. I have had firsthand experience of the horrendous type of death it inflicts upon its victims both in target and non-target species. I have experienced the direct result to my livestock and farming operation from errors made in application. Future generations may have to pay the cost of the effects of its widespread use at present. Indeed perhaps the widespread use of any residual poisons."

Tabled: letter from Arthur Attfield spokesperson East Coromandel Landcare Association titled *From Hell to Heaven?* "Last year the Thames Coromandel District Council voted unanimously to advocate the banning of 1080 poison. The United Future Party has made it a nationwide political platform at the next general election, and the Maori Party has also voiced its concern. …The Parliamentary Select Committee has invited our combined conservation groups on the Coromandel to put forward our concerns regarding 1080 and other toxins…The stopping of the actual 1080-drop by our organization was a final message to seriously listen to the people."

Tabled documents: A Review of Toxicological Research on Sodium Monofluoroacetate (1080) and its Policy Implications Sean Weaver Environmental Studies, School of Earth Sciences, Victoria University of Wellington Research Report Number 18 April 2003. UCLA requested additional comments from Weaver referencing toxin 1080. Weaver noted "Key points: a) biodegradation is relatively slow in colder conditions (such as winter time when this toxin is used, b) evidence that this toxin could be disrupting hormone systems in non-target animals at sub-lethal doses and therefore need for further research to clarify this point, c) research claiming to demonstrate no harm in terms of disruption to hormone systems have flawed design and incapable of actually testing hormone disruption. Weaver states on P51 of his research: *Policy Implications of 1080 Toxicology in New Zealand 2003 in Journal of Rural and Remote Environmental Health* "According to an editorial in *Lancet* in 1992 relatively few studies have shown clear associations between environmental pollutants and actual increase in death rates "(*Lancet* 1992) The footnote reads: "This is one of the great difficulties of epidemiology and its role in public health policy, particularly in a culture where an agency producing a contaminant is innocent until proven guilty in a court of law."

Tabled *NZ Statement on 1080 – December 2010* by Pesticide Action Network, Aotearoa. Excerpts include "The main issue with the use of 1080 is not human health effects, although there have been poisonings, but effects on wildlife, farm animals, and companion animals. Many New Zealanders are very deeply concerned about the effects of aerial dispersal of 1080 on animals and the ecosystem, and are strongly opposed to it (ERMA 2007)… New Zealand uses between 2,500 and 4,000 kg/year of 1080.

Tabled position paper from Soil & Health Association of New Zealand (Est. 1941) Publishers of *ORGANIC NZ* includes the following comments:

The Soil & Health position is best encapsulated in the media release of 11 February 2010 http://www.organicnz.org/soil-and-health-press/1208/new-pro-1080-alliance-lacks-sustainability-vision/ Soil & Health believes its position to be a progressive approach that seeks a compromise and ideally consensus in finding solutions to the problems that drive the widespread use of 1080. Soil & Health's solutions allow for significant employment and new enterprise, with benefits especially for rural communities and the environment.

[119] This information comes from the July 1 2010 DOC response to the petition presented by Mr P. Findlay on behalf of the Thames Landcare Group and 3,107 others.

[120] *ibid.*

[121] *Hamilton News* the Robinson Report: *Playing Politics With Poison Policy*

[122] *Straight Furrow* May 29 2012

[123] A letter written by Catchment Committee representative, Reihana Robinson, sent to Coromandel secondary and total-immersion schools in April 2016 documents this on-going struggle.

[124] *Peninsula Post* 21 June 2012 and read for reference: http://flyingdoctor. co.nz/images/custom/possum_pies.pdf

[125] *Hauraki Herald* April 26, 2013

[126] Coromandel Catchment Committee agenda May 20, P 80

[127] *Hamilton News* April 26 2013

[128] The report referred to in Graeme and Julie Sturgeon's letter is Mike Meads *Effect of sodium monofluoroacetate (1080) on non-target invertebrates of Whitecliffs Conservation Area, Taranaki.* June 1994

[129] *Hauraki Herald* May 8 2013

[130] Notman, Peter *A review of invertebrate poisoning by compound 1080* DSIR Ecology Division, Private Bag, Lower Hutt, New Zealand *Abstract*: Compound 1080 is widely used in New Zealand for the control of wild animals. The tendency of 1080 to poison non-target birds and mammals is recognised, but its effects on invertebrates have gone mostly unnoticed. At least 9 invertebrate orders are prone to 1080 poisoning. Invertebrates have been observed eating baits, and their habitats are contaminated by

residues leaching from baits, and from animal by-products and carcasses. Poisoned insects provide a means of secondary poisoning for insectivores. Therefore, 1080 should not be used where susceptible invertebrate species or rare insectivores are found.

[131] Hutcheson, John *Impact of 1080 on weta populations prepared for DOC* June 1989.

[132] Beasley, Fisher, O'Connor, Eason, *The NZ Medical Journal Journal of the New Zealand Medical Association* 4 September 2009 *Sodium fluoroacetate (1080): assessment of occupational exposures and selection of a provisional biological exposure index (BEI)*"Our initial findings indicated there remained a need for further improvements in exposure reduction and ongoing monitoring. The derived BEI should be regarded as provisional and subject to ongoing review in the light of further information, particularly any monitoring results relatable to demonstrable adverse health effects in humans from chronic, low level exposures."

[133] *Coromandel Town Chronicle* June 2013

[134] Further excerpts from *Matariki over Moehau* by Wendy Pond written in 2013: "There were no sightings of Departmental staff collecting carcasses as a precautionary measure. On 8 June a phone call to Department of Conservation at the Kaueranga Information Centre confirmed no DOC officers were on duty to monitor the area of the drop (DOC staff to Naomi Pond) A pair of falcons under daily observation in the Te Mata valley had disappeared on Sunday 9 June and were not again seen thereafter. Falcons are rare on the Coromandel peninsula. They were first observed in the Te Mata valley around November 2012. DOC office Hauraki confirmed that the presence of falcons had been reported some time before the Moehau and Papakai drops (Melissa King to Wendy Pond, 14 June 2013)… Weather patterns for the period of the drop were: 4 & 5 June heavy rain and flooding. 6 June Moehau drop, weather fine. Pellets dropped into wet forest. Rain at 5 pm and again during the night from 2 am. 7 June Papakai drop after weather cleared. Rest of day fine. 8 June Papakai drop. Morning fine. Showers in the afternoon. 9 June (Sunday) heavy rain until 3 pm. Pellets observed in the Papakai block on 9 June were disintegrating…In the latitude of Moehau, the constellation Matariki (Pleiades, Seven Sisters) rose on 10 June, signalling the renewal of health and growth. Moehau is covered in trap lines. It is an avoidable harm for DOC to broadcast 1080 poison over a terrain where targeted trapping is advocated by the community. It is a contradiction for DOC to drop 1080 poison into the Moehau range on the grounds that the terrain is inaccessible to trapping, and at the same time send out staff to clear carcasses from waterways. What happens to poisoned carcasses in headwaters and ravines that are "inaccessible"? It seems they are left for predation, allowing secondary poisoning of eels, moreporks, falcons and hawks and many species not targeted. Over Moehau the rising of Matariki signals a season of agony and unreckoned consequences.

[135] *Bay Beacon* November 2006

[136] Ngati Huarere whanau

137 Monin, Paul *This is My Place, Hauraki Contested 1769-1875* P 210 Bridget Williams Books 2001

138 *Peninsula Post* 20 March 2014

139 Hugh Robertson provides in his 2004 DOC report: *Research and monitoring plan for the kiwi sanctuaries*—Sufficient nests need to be monitored in each kiwi sanctuary to ensure that at least 20 chicks, preferably more, are radio-tagged each year—The sample of radio-tagged chicks should be spread geographically through the kiwi sanctuaries, with no undue bias towards nests near or away from the forest edge or other natural entry points for predators. Different habitats in the sanctuaries should be fairly represented—The sample of chicks should be spread chronologically throughout the whole hatching season, with no undue bias towards early-, mid- or late-hatching chicks. From known hatching chronology and estimates of the number of chicks that should hatch in a season in each kiwi sanctuary, the monthly number of nests in which chicks are to be radio-tagged should be decided in advance to ensure that samples are stratified according to season—Where one chick in a nest with two chicks is to be radio-tagged, a coin should be tossed to decide which is to be radio-tagged—Although it is ideal to check to see if chicks are alive each week, so causes of deaths can be more accurately determined, excessive disturbance and handling of chicks should be avoided as this may affect their growth rate, behaviour and vulnerability to predators. In some sites, where radio tracking is difficult, fortnightly checks to see if a chick is dead or alive are probably more realistic without greatly increased staffing. Monthly checks of each chick are an absolute minimum, otherwise valuable data on the causes of death are lost, and too many chicks disappear or lose their transmitters between checks. ...and for sub-adult kiwi. Acquisition of radio-telemetry data on the survival and dispersal of subadult kiwi is a very high priority in all kiwi sanctuaries.

2 April, 2014 from a letter sent to DOC Hauraki, Nicki Douglas Waikato Partnership Director DOC, Jeannie Hogarth for Director Conservation Services Northern North Island and copied to Wendy Sporle employed by Kiwisforkiwi: It would appear that intensive monitoring is no longer carried out so who knows how many kiwi are on Moehau? Who is monitoring the seven kiwi currently residing on Motutapu? From various DOC reports we note kiwi adults are strongly territorial, occupy territories ranging from 2–3ha to 100ha, in the absence of predation life expectancy is between 25 and 50 years, and that adults are monogamous, forming persistent pair bonds, although occasional divorces do occur. The Whenuakite Kiwi group supposedly achieved a percentage increase of 169% males, 92% females from 2001 to 2005 due to a track network for traps and bait stations however after multiple 1080 drops kiwi hunters came up empty handed. It appears obvious that kiwi at the 1080 soused Whenuakite zone are missing in action. Why is this not a concern to kiwi carers? According to Arthur Hinds report to the May 20 Coromandel Catchment committee 'birds were "meant to be moved in 2015 but this was put back a year.' But again in 2016 kiwi are not found for relocation purposes. After many days of hunting just two are taken.

140 Kelsey, Jane *Reclaiming the Future New Zealand Economy and the Global Economy* 1999

141 (http://www.huffingtonpost.com/maggie-sergio/the-farallon-islands-usfw_b_5267529.html)

The Killing Nation: New Zealand's State-Sponsored Addiction to Poison 1080—by Reihana Robinson—Companion volume to *Rural Revolt: In Defence of Coromandel's Wild Kingdom*

The Killing Nation explodes the carefully cultivated myth of New Zealand as the "Clean and Green" paradise of the South Pacific. While the government and tourism industry promote images of exotic native bush, rare avian species, clean running streams, and untainted farms, Robinson lays bare New Zealand's "Dirty Little Environmental Secret" – the wholesale poisoning of the landscape with one of the world's deadliest poisons to combat pest species, all in the name of "conservation". New Zealand stands alone in the world for its widespread and growing use of the supertoxin "1080", spread by helicopter over hundreds of thousands of hectares of conservation land, rolling hills, and even into waterways and drinking water catchments. The toxin, made in batches at a small factory in backwoods Alabama USA and shipped to far-off Kiwiland, deals a grisly death to all oxygen-breathing species – among them countless birds, deer, mice, frogs, eels, and invertebrates of all description. While failing to achieve proven conservation gains, New Zealand's poison-industrial complex taints more and more of the country's pristine natural wealth with each passing year. Robinson recounts the surprising history of her country's unusual and failing attempt to poison its way to a clean environment, and with classic investigative reporting and research, exposes the conflicts and professional intrigue that keep the poison flowing. Robinson chronicles the fightback by environmentalists, animal welfare advocates, and growing numbers in the scientific community against the increasing use of the poison in what has become an unhealthy growth industry protected by the New Zealand government. Her expose is a must-read for every student of environmental science – and an important introduction to "the real New Zealand" for tourists and international travelers expecting just the opposite.